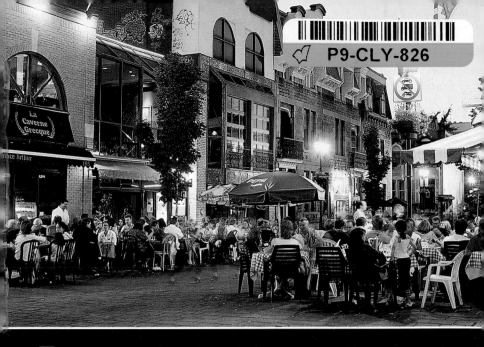

Frommer's®
Montréal & Québec City

My Montréal & Québec City

by Herbert Bailey Livesey

ON MY FIRST VISIT TO QUÉBEC, HALF A LIFETIME AGO, I TOOK FULL advantage of the local sidewalk cafes. Nowhere else can a visitor more readily absorb the distinctive customs and rhythms of another culture. It was in just such a cafe, in Québec City, looking out over the silvered expanse of the St. Lawrence River and up to the peaked copper roofs of the Château Frontenac, that I began to understand what this singular province was all about. The couple at the next table was in deep conversation. She spoke only French, he only English, and yet they understood each other perfectly.

That's the key to Québec's self-labeled "distinct society." French and British traditions exist side by side, peppered with an internationalism that reflects Canada's liberal immigration policies. Old Francophones still play petanque in the parks on warm days, and in winter their grandchildren bobsled down the run from the capital's fortress to its grand château, the Frontenac. Unilingual Anglophones take high tea in Montréal's grand hotels of the privileged, while their progeny speak Franglish in *boîtes de nuit,* where the singers sound like Piaf and Azvanor. The two cities compete in mounting shoulder-to-shoulder festivals that celebrate everything from jazz to winter to comedy to film.

The photographs on the following pages are just a taste of the many reasons to put Montréal and Québec City on your list of must-see destinations.

MONTMORENCY FALLS (left) are higher than Niagara—as anyone is sure to be told, several times, upon visiting. Back in the 18th century, British and French forces lobbed cannonballs at each other from entrenchments on both banks. These days, fireworks, sometimes seen above the falls, are strictly for fun, and launched during annual festivals.

In this view from the east end of the **MONTREAL'S OLD PORT (above),** the silver-domed 1847 Bonsecours building is in the foreground, with Colonial-era Vieux Montréal surrounding it, and modern-day office towers rising behind. In summer, the rehabilitated park in front hosts concerts, rollerbladers, cyclists, sunbathers, and others who enjoy *le pic-nic.*

The high altar of the **BASILIQUE NOTRE-DAME (left),** easily the most beautifully embellished of Montréal's hundreds of churches, is richly carved linden wood, as is most of the interior. The bell in the tower weighs 12 tons, and the floor rumbles when it rings. Orchestras perform here, drawn by the magnificent acoustics. The church's Protestant Irish-American architect, James O'Donnell, was so stirred by what he had wrought that he converted to Catholicism.

Pedestrian-only **RUE DU TRESOR (above)** in Québec City is an obligatory stop on every stroll through the old Upper Town. Artists line both sides of the narrow lane, their watercolors, prints, and drawings on display. There's no pressure to buy. Subject matter is mostly various vistas and details of their city, but some artists set up easels beside nearby outdoor cafes and offer to do portraits.

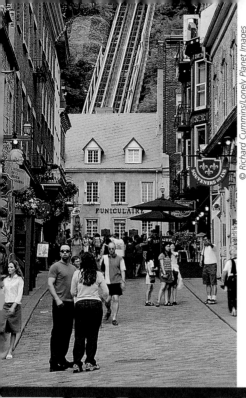

The historic district of Québec City is the only walled city north of Mexico. It's divided into two parts: Basse-Ville, the older part down by the river where the first European settlers built and farmed, and Haute-Ville, atop the steep-sided cliff to which the French citizens withdrew for greater safety from invaders. This **FUNICULAIRE (left)** connects the two, affording spectacular views and escape from the Breakneck Stairs, the other pedestrian route down the hill.

SUGARING-OFF (below) season is February through March, when sap is drawn from the vast stands of sugar maples with which the province is blessed. At first, the sap was merely processed, transformed into syrup and candies, and sent off to eager buyers. Then some canny Québecer decided to offer meals in his *cabane à sucre*—sugar shack. That evolved into an industry, and some sugar shacks stay open all year, providing gargantuan farm meals, live folkloric entertainment, simple lodgings, and even sleigh rides.

Boosters call Montréal the "City of Festivals," and justifiably so. Apart from a few bereft weeks here and there in the coldest months, it takes specific intent and careful planning to avoid celebratory events of one kind or another. Festivals throughout the year highlight comedy, film, cuisine, theater, cycling, motor racing, and fireworks. The greatest explosion of energy and talent, however, is during the annual **JAZZ FESTIVAL (above),** with hundreds of performances in scores of venues, many of them free.

Montréal's **HÔTEL DE VILLE (right)** stands at the top of the Place Jacques-Cartier, which was the open-air market square of 19th-century Montréal. The extravagantly detailed French Second Empire style of the building is seen to best effect at night, and a dozen other impressive structures are similarly illuminated, constituting a rewarding—and safe—after-dark walking tour.

© Cosmo Condina/Alamy

Few municipal symbols are as power-
fully evocative as Québec's **CHATEAU
FRONTENAC (above)**. In style, it is a Loire
castle on steroids, one of a chain
strung along the route of the Trans-
Canada railway to encourage tourism
at the start of the last century.

The long staircase leading down from
the elevated La Citadelle to the
promenade known as Terrace Dufferin
is transformed into a **BOBSLED RUN
(right)** during Québec City's annual
winter carnival. No special skills or
particular athleticism is required for
the short but thrilling run, unless you
count climbing up to the starting point.

© Stephen Saks/Lonely Planet Images

Opposite page: © Walter Bibikow/Getty Images

Routinely designated the premier ski resort east of the Mississippi, **TREMBLANT** marches up the slopes of its namesake mountain. Active all year, Tremblant also offers water-sports on the town-mile lake at its base. Lodgings, dining, and nightlife range from economical to deluxe, and while kids are catered to, there are plenty of times and places for parents to get away for a few hours.

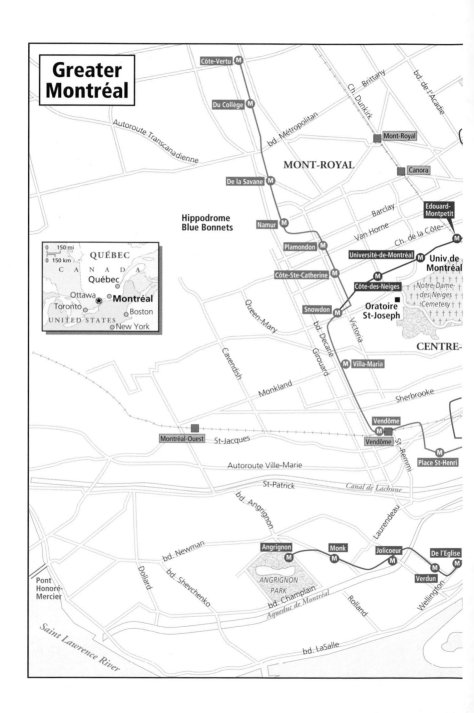

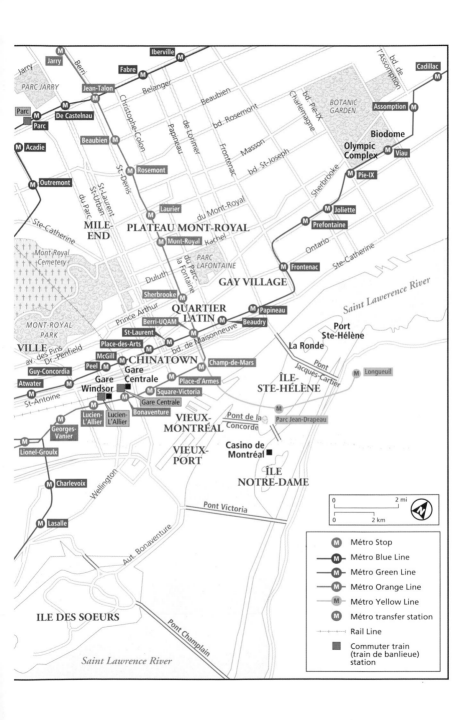

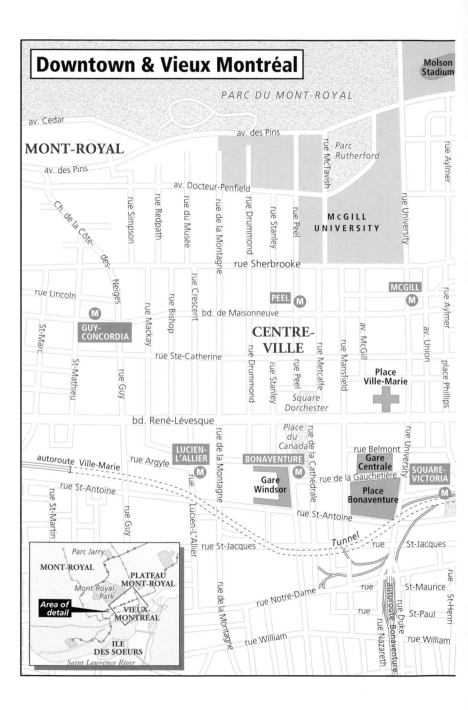

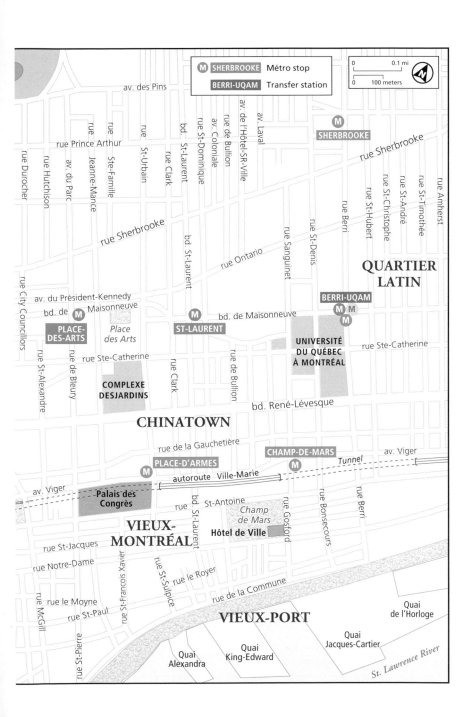

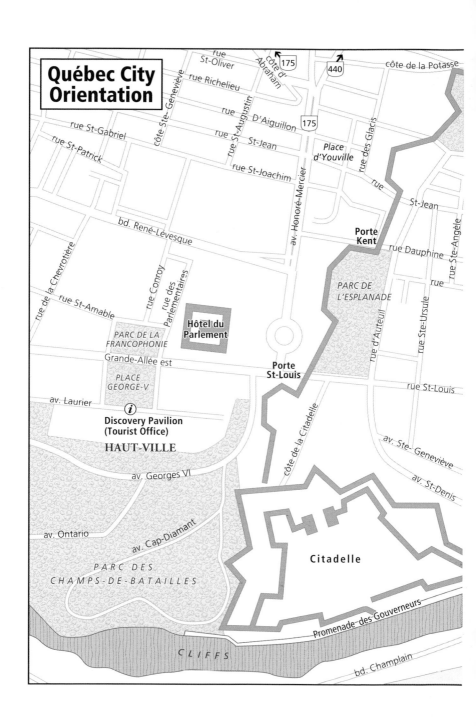

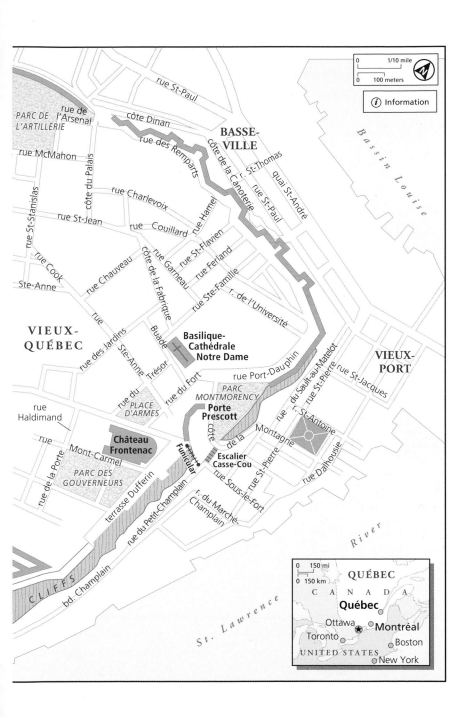

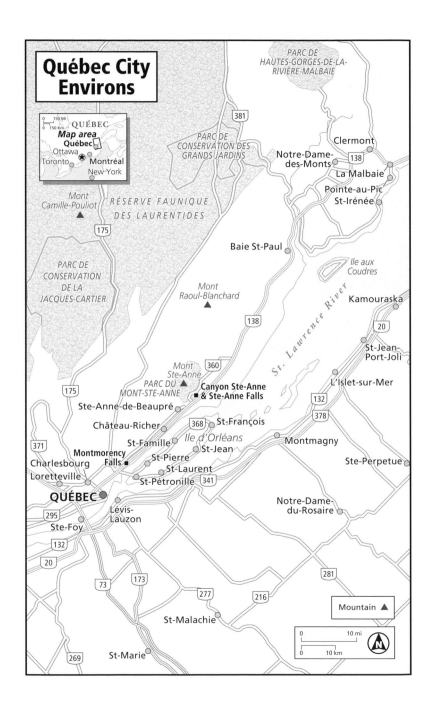

Frommer's®

Montréal & Québec City

2006

by Herbert Bailey Livesey

Here's what the critics say about Frommer's:

"Amazingly easy to use. Very portable, very complete."
—*Booklist*

"Detailed, accurate, and easy-to-read information for all price ranges."
—*Glamour Magazine*

"Hotel information is close to encyclopedic."
—*Des Moines Sunday Register*

"Frommer's Guides have a way of giving you a real feel for a place."
—*Knight Ridder Newspapers*

WILEY

Wiley Publishing, Inc.

About the Author

Herbert Bailey Livesey has written about food and travel for over 30 years. Among the many magazines that have published his articles are *Travel + Leisure, Food & Wine, Playboy, New York,* and *Yankee.* He is the author of a dozen books, including six travel guides, and contributes to several others, including *Frommer's New England, Frommer's Canada,* and *Frommer's Europe.*

Published by:

Wiley Publishing, Inc.

111 River St.
Hoboken, NJ 07030-5774

ISBN-13: 978-0-7645-9547-9
ISBN-10: 0-7645-9547-4

Editor: Cate Latting
Production Editor: Bethany J. André
Cartographer: Anton Crane
Photo Editor: Richard Fox
Production by Wiley Indianapolis Composition Services

Front cover photo: Cyclist passes building exterior with stone cladding facade
Back cover photo: Interior of Notre Dame Cathedral

For information on our other products and services or to obtain technical support, please contact our Customer Care Department within the U.S. at 800/762-2974, outside the U.S. at 317/572-3993 or fax 317/572-4002.

Wiley also publishes its books in a variety of electronic formats. Some content that appears in print may not be available in electronic formats.

Manufactured in the United States of America

5   4   3   2   1

Contents

Appendix: Montréal & Québec City in Depth   288

Index   295

List of Maps

An Invitation to the Reader

In researching this book, we discovered many wonderful places—hotels, restaurants, shops, and more. We're sure you'll find others. Please tell us about them, so we can share the information with your fellow travelers in upcoming editions. If you were disappointed with a recommendation, we'd love to know that, too. Please write to:

Frommer's Montréal & Québec City 2006
Wiley Publishing, Inc. • 111 River St. • Hoboken, NJ 07030-5774

An Additional Note

Please be advised that travel information is subject to change at any time—and this is especially true of prices. We therefore suggest that you write or call ahead for confirmation when making your travel plans. The authors, editors, and publisher cannot be held responsible for the experiences of readers while traveling. Your safety is important to us, however, so we encourage you to stay alert and be aware of your surroundings. Keep a close eye on cameras, purses, and wallets, all favorite targets of thieves and pickpockets.

Other Great Guides for Your Trip:

Frommer's Canada
Montréal & Québec City For Dummies

Frommer's Star Ratings, Icons & Abbreviations

Every hotel, restaurant, and attraction listing in this guide has been ranked for quality, value, service, amenities, and special features using a **star-rating system.** In country, state, and regional guides, we also rate towns and regions to help you narrow down your choices and budget your time accordingly. Hotels and restaurants are rated on a scale of zero (recommended) to three stars (exceptional). Attractions, shopping, nightlife, towns, and regions are rated according to the following scale: zero stars (recommended), one star (highly recommended), two stars (very highly recommended), and three stars (must-see).

In addition to the star-rating system, we also use **seven feature icons** that point you to the great deals, in-the-know advice, and unique experiences that separate travelers from tourists. Throughout the book, look for:

Finds	Special finds—those places only insiders know about
Fun Fact	Fun facts—details that make travelers more informed and their trips more fun
Kids	Best bets for kids and advice for the whole family
Moments	Special moments—those experiences that memories are made of
Overrated	Places or experiences not worth your time or money
Tips	Insider tips—great ways to save time and money
Value	Great values—where to get the best deals

The following **abbreviations** are used for credit cards:

AE	American Express	DISC	Discover	V	Visa
DC	Diners Club	MC	MasterCard		

Frommers.com

Now that you have the guidebook to a great trip, visit our website at **www.frommers.com** for travel information on more than 3,000 destinations. With features updated regularly, we give you instant access to the most current trip-planning information available. At Frommers.com, you'll also find the best prices on airfares, accommodations, and car rentals—and you can even book travel online through our travel booking partners. At Frommers.com, you'll also find the following:

- Online updates to our most popular guidebooks
- Vacation sweepstakes and contest giveaways
- Newsletter highlighting the hottest travel trends
- Online travel message boards with featured travel discussions

What's New in Montréal & Québec City

Montréal continues its recovery from the economic malaise of the 1990s. Optimism and prosperity have returned, and, with them, an era of (mostly) good feeling likely to last well into the future. The Canadian dollar strengthened significantly against its U.S. counterpart (but not enough to diminish Québec's desirability as a tourist destination), unemployment is at its lowest rate in many years, and a billion-dollar construction boom continues.

In January 2002, the 28 towns and cities that occupied the Island of Montréal were merged into a metropolis of 1.8 million inhabitants, making it the second-largest city in Canada after Toronto. The merger decision was made by fiat, not referendum, and, inevitably, a movement to reverse the action boiled up. When a Liberal Party government took provincial office a year later, it promised to let vote on whether to let the changes stand. In 2004, as promised, 15 of the 28 municipalities voted to *de*-merge. There were similar results in other metropolitan areas in the province. A visible victim of these back-and-forth events appears to be Montréal's streets, once pristine and now undeniably messy.

A corruption scandal involving kickbacks and money laundering has shattered confidence in the federal Liberal Party. The resulting furor led to an investigative commission, and, by only a single vote, the Liberals won a vote of confidence in the House of Commons in May 2005. Until then, separatist sentiments had been muffled, and talk of seceding from the rest of Canada occupied less public and private discussion. The cultural divide between the Francophone majority and Anglophone and Allophone minorities hadn't melted away, but it had mellowed. The scandal brought that progress toward harmony to a screeching halt, leaving the near political future impossible to predict.

PLANNING YOUR TRIP   Even in the face of a slide against several of the world's major currencies, the U.S. dollar continues to be relatively strong against the Canadian version, making Québec an increasingly rare travel bargain for American travelers.

While Montréal is a fairly easy city to get around by private car, it also has an excellent subway system, the Métro, which reaches every attraction and neighborhood of interest to visitors. Note that the name of the stop formerly known as Île Ste-Hélène is now **Parc Jean-Drapeau.**

WHERE TO STAY   A seemingly irrational exuberance caused a surge in hotel construction in recent years, notably in the historic riverside district known as Vieux-Montréal (Old Montréal). An unprecedented taste for boutique hotels got underway in 2001 with the 48-room **Hôtel Place d'Armes,** 701 Côte de la Place d'Armes (© **514/842-1887**). Another half-dozen followed, all housed in rehabilitated structures dating from the 19th and early 20th century. The impulse continues, with the 2004 opening of the ultrachic **W Montréal,** 901 rue Square Victoria (© **514/395-3100).** Dazzling design, a stylish restaurant, and four bars are trumped by superb service in observance of the house motto, "Whatever, whenever." Outside Vieux-Montréal, but within a block of some of St-Laurent's hottest resto-clubs, is the even newer **Hôtel Godin,** 10 rue Sherbrooke (© **514/843-6000).** It melds an old structure with a new section devoted to the virtues of minimalism. A two-level lounge and 200-seat dining room were under construction at press time, but the bedrooms were complete to the last sybaritic detail. Most of the boutique hotels also opened restaurants of note, including the new **Aix Cuisine du Terroir,** in the Hôtel Place d'Armes, and **Otto,** in the W Montréal. See chapters 5 and 6 for more details on the hotels and their restaurants.

In Québec City, the **Auberge Saint-Antoine,** 10 rue St-Antoine (© **888/692-2211),** has undergone a transformation so profound that it will be all but unidentifiable to guests who last saw it 5 years ago. While excavating the parking lot behind the original inn, thousands of artifacts from 400 years of European settlement were unearthed, many of them now on display in public and private spaces throughout what is now the most luxurious hotel in the Lower Town. A full-service restaurant, **Panache,** has been opened in the brick-and-timber former lobby. Also in the Lower Town, **Le Port-Royal,** 1144 rue Saint-Pierre (© **418/692-2777),** accepted its first guests in spring 2005. An all-suite property (albeit employing the "studio suite" rubric for some spaces), each unit can accommodate up to four people in considerable style. In the Upper Town, a block from the Château Frontenac, a 19th-century row house has been converted into a Euro-style boutique hotel with 28 units,

the **Hôtel Sainte-Anne,** 32 rue Sainte-Anne (© **418/694-1455).**

WHERE TO DINE With more than 5,000 restaurants, Montréal has little practical need for more. Obviously, practicality has nothing to do with the boom in exciting new eateries, formal and casual, elegant and ethnic, costly and modest. Quebecers were a little slow to embrace the food revolution that swept North America in the '80s and '90s, but that hesitancy has been cast aside. Widespread experimentation and prodigious use of regional products have brought about many species of fusion cookery. While French menus and techniques continue to dominate, with Italianate kitchens close behind, it is increasingly difficult to label precisely the food offered at these new breeds of dining places.

Glamour is often a major component, with dishy waitresses and hunky waiters bringing excellent food to clients as stylish and good-looking as they. Velvet ropes are almost as common at these restaurants as at fashionable late-hours clubs. A leading example of this ongoing resto-as-club trend is hot **Cavalli,** 2040 rue Peel (© **514/843-5100).** No gatekeepers are seen at **Le Club Chasse et Peche,** 423 rue St-Claude (© **861-1112),** in part because of the somewhat obscure Vieux-Montréal address, and because the name, "Hunting and Fishing Club" doesn't exactly suggest fine dining. It received enthusiastic reviews after its early 2005 opening, but needs to work a little harder to earn them. **Brunoise,** 3807 rue St-Andre (© **514/523-3885),** tones down the glamour aspect but has ratcheted its food to even higher levels. A trendsetter of another sort is **BU,** 5245 bd. St-Laurent (© **514/276-0249).** An award-winning designer bar-resto, its long wine card eschews the same old bottlings in favor of discoveries from lesser-known regions, the wines complemented by antipasti-style eats. **Les Chevres,** 1201 rue Van

Home (© 514/270-1119), makes the clearest challenge in years to the perennially top-rated **Toqué!**, 900 place Jean-Paul-Piopelle (© 514-499-2084), and it does it with a menu composed primarily of exquisitely prepared and presented vegetables. (There are two or three meat or fish dishes on the nightly card.)

Culinary changes are less numerous in smaller Québec City, but what has seemed a somewhat static dining scene is being shaken up by young chefs and restaurateurs. They are setting up shop well away from the heavily touristed districts of the old city. One of the hottest newcomers was **Yuzu**, 438 rue de L'Eglise (© 418/521-7253), but the chef who made it sparkle with audacity moved to Montréal. It was followed in the same downtown St-Roch neighborhood by seriously hip **Utopie**, 226 rue St-Joseph (© 418/523-7878), which has solidified its early promise. **Laurie Raphaël**, 117 rue Dalhousie (© 418/692-4555), which shares the gastronomic throne with **Initiale**, 54 rue St-Pierre (© 418/694-1818), is all but unrecognizable since it completely refurbished its rooms last year. Its food—remarkably, given its long preeminence—seems to have been upgraded as well. Initiale has kept up.

Smoking was banned in restaurants, bars, and most other public places in the province as of January 2006.

SIGHTSEEING After paying out in excess of C$85 million over 5 years, the **Lachine Canal** has reopened, a major recreational resource for boaters, kayakers, cyclists, and rollerbladers. A canal around the once-impassable Lachine rapids had been a dream of the earliest settlers, but several attempts failed before eventual completion in 1825. Manufacturing and workers' housing occupied the banks, making the canal one of Montréal's major industrial centers. Completion of the St. Lawrence Seaway in 1959 rendered the Lachine Canal irrelevant,

and it was closed. Active once again as a 15km (9-mile) linear park with bike paths, picnic areas, new condos, and ample dock space, the canal connects a new marina at the foot of rue Peel with the popular Atwater Market. Guided Parks Canada cruises with historical commentary are available from mid-May to mid-October, as are rentals of electric boats, kayaks, and pedal boats.

AFTER DARK Montréal's racy nightlife reputation dates from the 1920s Great Experiment south of its border. Hearty partyers still pour into the city for the season of summer festivals that celebrate jazz, comedy, fast cars, and ethnic cultures.

Although some of Montréal's newest music bars, dance clubs, and otherwise unclassifiable retreats are too hot not to cool down (and a couple mentioned here last year have already disappeared), an incendiary list of possibilities along St-Laurent includes the relentlessly scruffy good-time rock bars **Le Bifteck,** 3702 bd. St-Laurent (© 514/844-6211), and **Barfly,** 4062a bd. St-Laurent (© 514/993-5154), while the similarly grungy **Casa del Popolo,** 4873 bd. St-Laurent (© 514/284-3804), has live music of every conceivable genre and even runs its own minifestival in June. At the other end of the scale, the self-consciously designed **Mile End Bar,** 5322 bd. St-Laurent (© 514/279-0200), has a compact tasting menu and a DJ Thursday through Saturday nights.

Downtown, the former Biddle's has been redecorated and renamed, but the **Maison de Jazz,** 2060 rue Alymer (© 514/842-8656), stills serves up racks of ribs and live mainstream jazz nightly. In the manufacturing and loft district immediately west of Vieux-Montréal, **Cluny ArtBar,** 257 rue Prince (© 514/866-1213), attracts an arty/boho crowd that attends exhibitions and performances in the vast adjoining gallery.

1

The Best of Montréal & Québec City

The duality of Canadian life has been called the "Twin Solitudes." One Canada, English and Calvinist in origin, is said to be staid, smug, and work-obsessed. The other, French and Catholic but highly secular, is thought of as more creative, lighthearted, and inclined to see pleasure as the end purpose of labor. Or so go the stereotypes.

These two peoples live side by side throughout Québec and in the nine provinces of English Canada, but the blending occurs in particularly intense fashion in Québec province's largest city, Montréal. French speakers, known as Francophones, constitute about 70% of the city's population, while most of the remaining population speaks English—Anglophones. (The growing number of residents who have another primary tongue, and speak neither English nor French, are called Allophones.) Although both groups are decidedly North American, they are no more alike than Margaret Thatcher and Charles de Gaulle.

Montréal is a modern city in every regard. Its downtown bristles with skyscrapers, but many of them are playful, almost perky, with unexpected shapes and bright, uncorporate colors. The city above ground is mirrored by another below, an underground labyrinth of shops, restaurants, movie theaters, and offices where an entire winter can be avoided in coatless comfort.

To the west and north of downtown are Anglo commercial and residential neighborhoods, centered around Westmount. To the east and north are Francophone *quartiers,* notably Plateau Mont-Royal and Outremont. In between are the many dialects and skin tones of the immigrant rainbow.

Over the past decade, a bleak mood prevailed in Québec, driven by lingering recession and uncertainty over the future. After all, it still remained possible that Québec would choose to fling itself into independence from the rest of Canada. Lately, though, passions have cooled, and now, something else is going on.

Ripples of optimism have become waves, spreading through the province and its largest city. The Canadian dollar has strengthened against its U.S. counterpart. Unemployment in Québec, long in double digits, shrank to under 6%, the lowest percentage in more than 2 decades, and below that of archrival Toronto. In another (perhaps connected) trend, crime in Montréal (already one of the safest cities in North America) has hit a 20-year low. Favorable currency exchange and the presence of skilled workers have made the city a favored site for Hollywood film and TV production. The rash of FOR RENT and FOR SALE signs that disfigured the city in the 1990s has evaporated, replaced by a welcome shortage of store and office space and a billion-dollar building boom that's filling up vacant lots all over downtown. The beloved old hockey arena was converted to a dining and entertainment center called Forum Pepsi, and La

Ronde, a popular amusement park that was experiencing a sharp decline that threatened to end in bankruptcy, was saved by its sale to the Six Flags empire.

To be sure, not every project has enjoyed smooth sailing. A plan to build a downtown baseball stadium collapsed soon after it was proposed, as did a plan for a new theme park. But those stumbles won't matter to American visitors, for whom Montréal already might seem an urban near-paradise. The subway system, called the Métro, is modern and swift. Streets are safe. Montréal's best restaurants are the equals of their south-of-the-border compatriots in every way, yet they are as much as 20% to 30% cheaper. And the government gives visitors back most of the taxes it collects from them.

Québec City is less sophisticated, more conservative, and more French. With its impressive location above the St. Lawrence River and its virtually unblemished Old Town of 18th- and 19th-century houses, it even looks French. Probably 95% of its residents speak French, and far fewer are bilingual, as most Montrealers are. (In the province as a whole, about 81% of citizens are Francophones.) With that homogeneity and the city's status as the supposed capital of a future independent nation, citizens seem to suffer less angst over what might happen down the road. They are also aware that a critical part of their economy is based on tourism, and they are far less likely to vent the open hostility that American visitors occasionally experience in English Canada.

1 Frommer's Favorite Montréal & Québec City Experiences

MONTREAL

- **Exploring Vieux-Montréal.** The old quarter has an overwhelmingly European flavor. Wander place Jacques-Cartier, the most engaging of the district's squares; explore museums and the stunning architecture of the churches; and stroll along the revitalized waterfront. See chapter 7, "Exploring Montréal," and the walking tour of Vieux-Montréal in chapter 8.
- **Feasting on Table d'Hôte Specials.** Indulge in three or four courses for a fixed price that is only slightly more than the cost of an a la carte main course alone. Most full-service restaurants offer the table d'hôte, if only at midday. See chapter 6, "Where to Dine in Montréal."
- **Listening to Jazz.** Downtown, Old Town, the Latin Quarter, all over, this is a favorite pastime of locals and visitors alike, especially in late June and early July during the renowned Montréal Jazz Festival. See p. 22.
- **Savoring French and International Cuisine.** Experience all of French cuisine's permutations—traditional, haute, bistro, original Quebecois—but sample as well the city's Fusion and Asian hybrids and the legion of ethnic restaurants representing dozens of foreign cuisines, notably Italian, Mexican, Thai, Chinese, Greek, Polish, and Indian. See chapter 6, "Where to Dine in Montréal."
- **Shopping.** Browse the shops of world-class domestic designers, from the up-and-coming to the well established; search for Inuit (Eskimo) sculptures of the highest order (with prices to match); and take in the scores of eclectic antiques shops along rue Notre-Dame between rue Guy and rue Atwater. See chapter 9, "Montréal Shopping."

QUEBEC CITY

- **Admiring the Skyline from the Lévis Ferry.** The ferry provides quite a view for very little money, and passengers can stay onboard and come right back without disembarking. See p. 246.
- **Discovering the Blossoming Lower Town.** All but abandoned to shipping

and grimy industry, the old riverside neighborhood is reborn, with antiques shops, bistros, and boutique hotels filling its rehabilitated 18th- and 19th-century buildings. See chapter 15, "Exploring Québec City," and the walking tour of the Lower Town in chapter 16, "Québec City Strolls."

- **Lingering at an Outdoor Cafe.** Tables are set out at place d'Armes, in the Quartier du Petit-Champlain, and along the Grande-Allée—a quality-of-life invention the French and their Quebecois brethren have perfected. See chapter 14, "Where to Dine in Québec City."

- **Relaxing in Battlefields Park (Parc des Champs-de-Bataille).** This park is beautifully situated, overlooking the St. Lawrence River, and is particularly lively on weekends, when families and lovers come here to picnic and play. See p. 241.

- **Strolling and Lounging on the Terrasse Dufferin.** Captivating Québec City is at its best here, with the copper-spired Château Frontenac rearing up behind, the Lower Town below, and ferries, freighters, and pleasure craft moving on the broad, silvered river. See chapter 15 for more on Terrasse Dufferin.

2 Best Hotel Bets

MONTREAL

- **Best Historic Hotel:** No contest. The **Ritz-Carlton Montréal,** 1228 rue Sherbrooke ouest (© **800/ 363-0366** or 514/842-4212), has been around since 1913, giving it a half-century lead on the closest competition. See p. 75.

- **Best for Business Travelers:** A closer call, with several worthy candidates, but **Fairmont The Queen Elizabeth,** 900 bd. René-Lévesque ouest (© **800/ 441-1414** or 514/861-3511), gets the nod for its central location atop the railroad station, concierge floors, fully equipped health club, and excellent bus connections to the airport. See p. 71.

- **Best New Luxury Hotel Downtown:** The nearby Omni, Ritz, and Vogue are challenged by the first Canadian branch of a pervasive chain, the **Sofitel,** 1155 rue Sherbrooke ouest (© **877/285-9001** or 514/285-9000), which matches its rivals in every detail. See p. 76.

- **Best for a Romantic Getaway:** With ancient cut-stone walls, swags of velvet and brocade, and tilting floors that Benjamin Franklin once trod upon, as well as a baronial dining room and a breakfast nook under a peaked glass roof, **La Maison Pierre du Calvet,** 405 rue Bonsecours (© **866/544-1725** or 514/282-1725), provokes memories of lovers' hotels by the Seine. See p. 81.

- **Best Old Boutique Hotel:** Not really *that* old, **Hôtel Le Germain,** 2050 rue Mansfield (© **877/333- 2050** or 514/849-2050), brought a needed jolt of panache to the too-often-stodgy corps of downtown business hotels, and helped inspire a boom in small, stylish hotels in Vieux-Montréal. See p. 75.

- **Best New Boutique Hotels (Posh Category):** In Old Montréal, the **Hôtel Le St-James,** 355 rue St-Jacques (© **866/841-3111** or 514/ 841-3111), raises the bar to an almost impossibly high level, with a superbly Sybaritic spa and gorgeous grand hall, but the **Hôtel Nelligan,** 106 rue St-Paul ouest (© **877/788- 2040** or 514/788-2040), counters with a great full-service restaurant and rooftop terrace. See p. 78 for

Hôtel Le St-James and p. 80 for Hôtel Nelligan.

- **Best New Boutique Hotels (Minimalist Category):** Also in Old Montréal, **Hôtel St-Paul,** 355 rue McGill (℃ **866/380-2202** or 514/380-2222), softens its austere lines with fur throws, while the eagerly anticipated **Hôtel Gault,** at 449 rue Ste-Hélène (℃ **866/904-1616** or 514/904-1616), leaves its raw concrete walls uncovered and uses furniture that was startlingly modern in the 1950s. See p. 81 for Hôtel St-Paul and p. 78 for Hôtel Gault.
- **Best Lobby for Pretending That You're Rich:** A tie—the woody, hushed **Ritz-Carlton Montréal** (see "Best Historic Hotel," above) exudes old money, while the new **Hôtel Le St-James** (see "Best New Boutique Hotels [Posh Category]," above) caters to the cellphone and international bespoke tailored set. See p. 75 for the Ritz-Carlton Montréal and p. 80 for Hôtel Le St-James.
- **Best for Families:** The **Delta Montréal,** 475 av. du President-Kennedy (℃ **877/286-1986** or 514/286-1986), keeps the kids blissfully waterlogged with *two* pools—one inside, one outside. The young ones can also be placed under watchful eyes in the play center, giving their parents a break. See p. 77.
- **Best Moderately Priced Hotel:** While it can't measure up to the dash of the many nearby boutique hotels of Old Montréal, most expected services are at hand and the cheapest rooms dip into the budget category (as low as C$96/US$77 for suites) at the **SpringHill Suites,** 445 rue St-Jean-Baptiste (℃ **866/875-4333** or 514/875-4333). See p. 82.
- **Best B&B:** Located in a 1723 house in Vieux-Montréal, **Auberge Les**

Passants du Sans Soucy, 171 rue St-Paul ouest (℃ **514/842-2634**), is more upscale and stylish than most of its peers, and it's located near the top restaurants and clubs in the old town. See p. 83.

- **Best Service:** It's tough to choose among the troops at the **Hôtel Le St-James** (see "Best New Boutique Hotels [Posh Category]," above), the **Ritz-Carlton Montréal** (see "Best Historic Hotel," above), and the **Hôtel Inter-Continental Montréal,** 360 rue St-Antoine ouest (℃ **800/361-3600** or 514/987-9900). All three teams display an almost equal amount of grace and care when it comes to tending to their guests. See p. 80, p. 75, and p. 80 for each hotel, respectively.
- **Best Location:** Airport buses leave regularly from the front door of **Fairmont The Queen Elizabeth** (see "Best for Business Travelers," above). The main railroad station is just a couple of levels down in the hotel elevator, and most of the major corporate buildings are accessible through the corridors of the underground city. See p. 71.
- **Best Hotel Health Club:** **Hôtel Omni Mont-Royal,** 1050 rue Sherbrooke ouest (℃ **514/284-1110**), lays on aerobics classes with instructors, free weights *and* weight machines, and Exercycles, as well as saunas, a steam room, whirlpools, and massages to recover from the workout. See p. 76. **Fairmont The Queen Elizabeth** (see "Best Location," above), is a close second. See p. 71.
- **Best Views:** With 32 stories, the **Hôtel Omni Mont-Royal** (see "Best Health Club," above) has the loftiest rooms, with some of the most panoramic views, in town. See p. 76.

QUEBEC CITY

- **Best Historic Hotel: Fairmont Le Château Frontenac,** 1 rue des Carrières (© **800/828-7447** or 418/692-3861), is more than a century old. It was one of the first hotels built to serve railroad passengers and to encourage tourism at a time when most people stayed close to home— and it still rewards a visit. See p. 217.
- **Best for Business Travelers:** A tie. Both the **Hilton Québec,** 1100 bd. René-Lévesque est (© **800/447-2411** or 418/647-6508), and the **Delta Québec,** 690 bd. René-Lévesque est (© **888/884-7777** in Canada, 800/333-3333 from elsewhere, or 418/647-1717), have as central locations as can be found, with good fitness centers and executive floors with concierges and business services. See p. 222 for the Hilton Québec and p. 223 for the Delta Québec.
- **Best for a Romantic Getaway:** It's hard to beat curling up with a glass of wine beside the fire in one of the cozy alcoves of the **Auberge Saint-Antoine,** 8 rue St-Antoine (© **888/692-2211** or 418/692-2211). See p. 224.
- **Best Boutique Hotel:** The **Auberge Saint-Antoine** (above) moves into first place with its grand new wing and archaeological displays from lobby to bedside. Still, the sleek **Dominion 1912,** 126 rue Saint-Pierre (© **888/833-5253** or 418/692-2224), remains a personal favorite, infusing a pre–World War I building with cunning modernist flavor, continuing a trend in designer hotels and inns in the Basse-Ville. See p. 225.

The Best of Montréal & Québec City Online

There's lots of information on Montréal and Québec City on the Internet. Here are a few of our favorite planning and general information sites:

- **Bonjour Québec** (www.tourisme.gouv.qc.ca), the official site of the government of the Province of Québec, endeavors to be a comprehensive information bank about all things Québec, and nearly succeeds. You'll find information on upcoming events and ongoing attractions, and you can search for hotels and reserve online.
- **Bonjour à la Montréal** (www.tourisme-montreal.org), another official tourism site, constitutes a first source that hits the highlights rather than delving in depth. Check the "traveler" box for a directory of attractions, guided tours, entertainment, accommodations, and restaurants. Be sure to scope the "Sweet Deals" on lodging and activities from October to May.
- **Hour** (www.hour.ca) is a Montréal culture magazine that highlights local happenings. Read entertainingly grumpy and often profane takes on current events from several columnists, as well as regularly updated restaurant and film reviews.
- **Québec** (www.quebecregion.com) is sponsored by the Greater Québec Area Tourism and Convention Bureau and is full of information about Québec City's accommodations, attractions, sports, shopping, dining, history, and culture.

- **Best Location:** Where else? For tourists, nothing can beat **Fairmont Le Château Frontenac** (see "Best Historic Hotel," above) for proximity to all the sights. In fact, the château *is* one of the sights. See p. 217.
- **Best Health Club and Pool:** At the **Delta Québec** (see "Best for Business Travelers," above), weights, Exercycles, and a workout room with instructors, as well as a whirlpool and sauna, will help you ease out the kinks. Slip into the heated pool inside and swim out to the open air. See p. 223.

3 Best Dining Bets

For a discussion of dining in Québec, see "Cuisine Haute, Cuisine Bas: Smoked Meat, Fiddleheads & Caribou," in the appendix.

MONTREAL

- **Best Spot for a Business Lunch:** **Otto,** in the new W Hôtel, 901 Square Victoria, at rue St-Antoine (✆ 514/395-3183), won't disappoint, especially the young, hip international execs who feel both the restaurant and the hotel speak to their needs and desires. See p. 93.
- **Best Spot for a Celebration:** No need to rake in stacks of chips at the gambling tables in the casino to join the festive crowd at **Nuances,** 1 av. du Casino (✆ 514/392-2708), the gracious multistarred *temple de cuisine* on the top floor of the casino. You'll get superb service, astonishing food, and spectacular views of the skyline to boot. See p. 105.
- **Best Wine List:** An award-winning designer bar, **BU,** 5245 bd. St-Laurent, at avenue Fairmont (✆ 514/276-0249), serves food, but wine wags the dog. The long card lists dozens of bottlings simply not seen anywhere else, and the manager has an encyclopedic knowledge of his cellar. See p. 106.
- **Best Decor:** With its exposed brick-and-stone walls, ceiling-high shelves of wine behind the handsomely turned-out center bar, and candle flames flickering in the breezes through the big open windows along the front and side, **Modavie,** 1 rue St-Paul ouest in Vieux-Montréal (✆ 514/287-9582), pleases the eye at every turn. See p. 98.
- **Best Value:** At lunch, the all-you-can-eat Indian buffet at **Le Taj,** 2077 rue Stanley, near rue Sherbrooke (✆ 514/845-9015), is a wonder. At dinner, even the *expensive* four-course table d'hôte at **Le Bourlingueur,** 363 St-François-Xavier, at rue St-Paul (✆ 514/845-3646), comes in under C$17 (US$14). See p. 92 for Le Taj and p. 99 for Le Bourlingueur.
- **Best for Kids:** On the assumption that a kid who doesn't like pizza is as rare as fish feathers, get over to **Pizzédélic,** on The Main at 3509 bd. St-Laurent, near rue Sherbrooke (✆ 514/282-6784). They have all manner of toppings, from the utterly conventional to just short of odd, and pastas too—all to be eaten while looking out at the street, or while enjoying the open terrace in the back. See p. 109.
- **Best Italian Cuisine:** Super-chic **Buona Notte,** 3518 bd. St-Laurent, near rue Sherbrooke (✆ 514/848-0644), may look as if it's more concerned with being a place to be seen than with what it sends out of the kitchen, but the pastas, focaccias, and risottos rival the occasional celebrity sightings. See p. 101.
- **Best Thai Cuisine:** **Chao Phraya,** 50 av. Laurier ouest, near boulevard

St-Laurent (℃ **514/272-5339**), purveys examples of a most complex Asian cooking style at good value in a sophisticated setting that eschews snarling gold temple dogs. See p. 106.

- **Best Seafood:** Few Montréal restos focus on fish, although most make a requisite bow to the sea. At **Maestro S.V.P.** (p.103), 3615 bd. St-Laurent, near rue Prince Arthur (℃ **514/842-6447**), land-based dishes are in the minority and the raw bar rules, producing a memorable *plateau de fruits de mer.* Another candidate is **Café Ferreira** (p. 88), 1446 rue Peel (near bd. Maissonnueve) ℃ **514/848-0988**), which does extremely well by its repertoire of marine-focused Portuguese cuisine.

- **Best Guilty Treats:** *Poutine* is a plate of french fries drenched with gravy with cheese curds, a bedrock Québec comfort food. At **Au Pied de Cochon** (p. 102), 536 rue Duluth, near rue St-Hubert (℃ **514/281- 1116**), the dish is elevated to mid-haute levels with the addition of foie gras.

- **Best Pizza:** The name says it all: **Pizzédélic** (see "Best for Kids," above), where they do anything from same-old, same-old tomato and cheese to cutting-edge designer concoctions with unlikely toppings like snails. See p. 109.

- **Best Late-Night Dining:** Plateau Mont-Royal's most Parisian bistro, **L'Express,** 3927 rue St-Denis, at Rue Roy (℃ **514/845-5333**), doesn't need a sign out front, because it stays full nightly until 3am (Sun only until 2am). Simple but toothsome recipes prepared with the freshest ingredients keep the night owls coming. See p. 102.

- **Best Outdoor Dining:** Serious food isn't the lure at **Le Jardin Nelson,** 407 place Jacques-Cartier (℃ **514/ 861-5731**). Music—classical or jazz—is what draws the crowds, who partake of sweet or savory crepes or very good pizzas under the crabapple tree in the garden. See p. 173.

- **Best People-Watching:** Any of a dozen cafes along St-Denis will fit this bill, especially on weekends, when the Plateau Mont-Royal boulevard comes alive. But **Café Cherrier,** 3635 rue St-Denis, at rue Cherrier (℃ **514/843-4308**), might be the most fun, if you can find a seat on the wraparound terrace. See p. 108.

- **Best Steaks: Moishes** (p. 101) at 3961 bd. St-Laurent, near rue Prince Arthur (℃ **514/845-3509**), has had decades to perfect its charbroiling techniques and uses only real prime beef. It's a pleasure to pull up a chair in the recently redecorated premises. Check your cholesterol concerns at the door and pay up your credit cards.

- **Best Brunch:** Crepes with multitudes of fillings make for Frenchified brunches at **Le Jardin Nelson** (see "Best Outdoor Dining," above), which are served in the garden, inside, or on the terrace facing place Jacques-Cartier. See p. 173.

- **Best Smoked Meat:** It'll only throw another log on the local battle for the title of "best smoked meat," which has blazed for at least a century, but **Chez Schwartz Charcuterie Hébraïque de Montréal** on The Main at 3895 bd. St-Laurent, north of rue Prince-Arthur (℃ **514/842-4813**), serves up the definitive version of this untransplantable deli treat. See p. 103.

- **Best Sandwiches:** Open only from early morning to midafternoon, **Titanic,** 45 rue St-Pierre, near rue Le Moyne (℃ **514/849-0894**), puts tasty, unusual ingredients between split halves of freshly baked baguettes with uncommon artistry. See p. 99. For burgers, it's impossible to argue with the local conviction that the biggest, juiciest ones are assembled at **La Paryse** (p. 107), 302 rue Ontario, at rue Sanguinet (© **514/842-2040**).

- **Best Bagels:** Montréal's bagels are clearly superior to versions produced south of the border, and **St-Viateur Bagel & Café,** at 1127 av. Mont-Royal est, near rue La Roche (© **514/528-6361**), is the place to assess that claim. See p. 110.
- **Best New Restaurant:** Hotel restaurants are getting a good name with the ongoing appearances of such exciting rooms as **Otto** (p. 93), in the W Hôtel, 901 Square Victoria (© **514/395-3183**). Both guests and waitstaff are uncommonly attractive, and the progressive Italian menu is deeply satisfying.
- **Best Restaurant, Period:** Ever-questing Normand Laprise and partner Christine Lamarche keep **Toqué!,** 900 place Jean-Paul Riopelle, near rue St-Antoine (© **514/499-2084**), in a league of its own. It's postmodern, it's post-nouvelle, it's dazzling! Nipping at their heels, though, is **Les Chevres,** 1201 rue Van Horne, at avenue Bloomfield (© **514/270-1119**), where vegetables and a very few meats and fishes are elevated to haute status. See p. 93 for Toqué! and p. 105 for Les Chevres.

QUEBEC CITY

- **Best Spot for a Romantic Dinner:** Stars above, tables illuminated by the flicker of candlelight, unobtrusive service, and even the name, **Le Saint-Amour,** 48 rue Ste-Ursule (© **418/694-0667**), bespeak romance. See p. 229.
- **Best View:** Revolving rooftop restaurants rarely dish out food as elevated as their lofty venues. **L'Astral** (p. 271) in the Loews Le Concorde hotel, 1225 cours du Généralde Montcalm (© **418/647-2222**), is an exception.

The food here is above average and the cost is entirely reasonable.

- **Best Bistro:** In a city that specializes in the informal bistro tradition, **L'Echaudé,** 73 rue Sault-au-Matelot, near rue St-Paul (© **418/692-1299**), is a star. Classic dishes are all in place, from *confit de canard* to steak frites. The dining terrace is on a pedestrian-only street. See p. 233.
- **Best New Restaurant:** Amid the cluster of innovative new restaurants that have blessed the city in the past couple of years, **Utopie** (p. 235), 226 rue St-Joseph, near rue Caron (© **418/523-7878**), is a standout, the one most likely to equal the current champs (see below).
- **Best Restaurant: Laurie Raphaël,** 117 rue Dalhousie (© **418/692-4555**), has been the sole occupier of the apex of the local pyramid, and just completed a total physical overhaul. See p. 232. However, **Initiale** (p. 232), 54 rue St-Pierre, at Côte de la Montagne (© **418/694-1818**), can no longer be denied equal status. Visitors can have the best meals of their lives at these stellar restaurants.
- **Best Rockin' Hot Spot with Good Food:** You don't have to be young, gorgeous, and hip to get into the **Voodoo Grill,** 575 Grande-Allée est (© **418/647-2000**), but there seems to be a lot of self-selection going on. As part of a complex that includes two bars and the Maurice disco, the noise level is brutal and the pace frantic, making the surprisingly good food all the more remarkable. See p. 232.
- **Best Seafood:** The owner of **Le Marie-Clarisse,** 12 rue du Petit-Champlain (© **418/692-0857**), selects all the just-off-the-boat seafood served at his comfortable bistro at the bottom of Breakneck Stairs. There's a fireplace inside and a terrace outside. See p. 234.

- **Best Sugar Pie:** Québec's favorite dessert reaches its apogee at **Aux Anciens Canadiens** (p. 228), 34 rue St-Louis (© **418/692-1627**). Think smooth maple sugar with a crust, at the ideal end of a traditional meal.

- **Best People-Watching:** The few outdoor tables at **Le Marie-Clarisse** (see "Best Seafood," above)—perched above the main pedestrian intersection of Quartier du Petit-Champlain—

monopolize an unsurpassed observation point. See p. 234.

- **Best Place to Take a Teenager:** Pizza-sized crepes packed with meats, eggs, peppers, cheese, or, for dessert, jams or fruit are made before your eyes at **Le Casse-Crêpe Breton** (p. 229), 1136 rue St-Jean (© **418/692-0438**), and it's open just about anytime your teenager gets hungry.

Planning Your Trip to Montréal & Québec City

Montréal and Québec City have a stronger foreign flavor than other cities in Canada, and the first language of most residents is French. But once you decide to go, pulling together information on ways to get there, border formalities, exchanging money, climate, lodging possibilities, and related details is almost as easy as getting from Illinois to Florida. The information below and in the "Fast Facts" sections in chapters 4 and 12 should help speed the process along.

1 Visitor Information

Québec tourism authorities produce detailed and highly useful publications, and they're easy to obtain by mail, by phone, or in person. To contact **Tourisme Québec,** write C.P. 979, Montréal, Québec H3C 2W3; call ℂ **877/266-5687;** or visit their website at **www.bonjourquebec. com.**

The Québec government maintains a number of offices in the United States and abroad, which provide specific tourism information about the province:

In the U.S.: Délégation du Québec, 1 Rockefeller Plaza, 26th Floor, New York, NY 10020 (ℂ **212/397-0200**).

Délégation du Québec, 444 N. Michigan Ave., Suite 1900, Chicago, IL 60611 (ℂ **312/645-0392**).

Délégation du Québec, 10940 Wilshire Blvd., Suite 720, Los Angeles, CA 90024 (ℂ **310/824-4173**).

In the U.K.: Délégation du Québec, 59 Pall Mall, London SW1Y 5JH, England (ℂ **071/930-8314**).

High Commission of Canada, Canada House, Cockspur Street, Trafalgar Square, London SW1Y 5BJ, England (ℂ **071/ 258-6600**).

Besides these offices outside Québec, the province has a large office in Montréal (see contact information above), and there is a convenient regional office in Québec City as well. See "Visitor Information," in chapters 4 and 12, for more details on the regional offices.

2 Entry Requirements & Customs

ENTRY REQUIREMENTS

For information on how to get a passport, see "Obtaining a Passport," at the end of this section—the websites listed provide downloadable passport applications as well as the current fees for processing passport applications. For an up-to-date country-by-country listing of passport requirements around the world, go to the "Foreign Entry Requirement" Web page of the U.S. State Department at **http:// travel.state.gov.**

U.S. citizens or permanent residents of the United States require neither passports

---

Tips   **Passport Savvy**

Allow plenty of time before your trip to apply for a passport; processing normally takes 3 weeks but can take longer during busy periods (especially spring). And keep in mind that if you need a passport in a hurry, you'll pay a higher processing fee. When traveling, safeguard your passport in an inconspicuous, inaccessible place like a money belt, and keep a copy of the critical pages with your passport number in a separate place. If you lose your passport, visit the nearest consulate of your native country as soon as possible for a replacement.

---

nor visas but will need some proof of citizenship, such as a birth certificate, plus a photo ID, to enter Canada and to reenter the United States. A passport is the logical and preferred document, even though it isn't specifically required. (At least not yet. There has been talk of requiring passports in both directions.) Permanent U.S. residents who are not citizens must have their alien registration cards (Green Cards) with them. If you plan to drive into Canada, be sure to have your car's registration handy as well.

An important point for teenage travelers: All persons under 19 require a letter from a parent or guardian granting them permission to travel to Canada. The letter must state the traveler's name and the duration of the trip. It is also essential that teenagers carry a photo ID. Otherwise, the letter from Mom and Dad is useless at the border.

An important point for parents: If you are divorced, separated, or traveling without your spouse and are bringing your children to Canada, bring a document, preferably notarized, certifying the permission of the other spouse or proof of legal custody.

Citizens of Australia, New Zealand, the United Kingdom, and Ireland need only carry a valid passport. Citizens of many other countries must have visas, applied for well in advance at their nearest Canadian embassy or consulate. Questions can be addressed to the **Canadian Immigration Division,** place du

Portage, 140 Promenade du Portage, Phase 4, Hull, Québec K1A 1L1 (© **819/ 994-2424;** www.cic.gc.ca).

OBTAINING A PASSPORT

For Residents of the United States Whether you're applying in person or by mail, you can download passport applications from the U.S. State Department website at **http://travel.state.gov.** For general information, call the **National Passport Agency** (© **202/647-0518**). To find your regional passport office, either check the U.S. State Department website or call the **National Passport Information Center** (© **900/225-5674**); the fee is 55¢ per minute for automated information and $1.50 per minute for operator-assisted calls. Designated post offices also accept applications.

For Residents of the United Kingdom To pick up an application for a standard 10-year passport (5-year passport for children under 16), visit your nearest passport office, major post office, or travel agency, or contact the **United Kingdom Passport Service** at © **0870/521-0410** or search its website at www.ukpa.gov.uk.

For Residents of Ireland You can apply for a 10-year passport at the **Passport Office,** Setanta Centre, Molesworth Street, Dublin 2 (© **01/671-1633;** www. irlgov.ie/iveagh). Those under age 18 and over 65 must apply for a 12€ 3-year passport. You can also apply at 1A South Mall, Cork (© **021/272-525**), or at most main post offices.

For Residents of Australia You can pick up an application from your local post office or any branch of Passports Australia, but you must schedule an interview at the passport office to present your application materials. Call the **Australian Passport Information Service** at (C) **131-232,** or visit the government website at www.passports.gov.au.

For Residents of New Zealand Pick up a passport application at any New Zealand Passports Office or download it from their website. Contact the **Passports Office** at (C) **0800/225-050** in New Zealand or 04/474-8100, or log on to www.passports.govt.nz.

CUSTOMS
WHAT YOU CAN BRING INTO CANADA

Regulations are flexible in most respects, but visitors can expect at least a probing question or two at the border or airport. Normal baggage and personal possessions should be no problem, but tobacco and alcoholic beverages face limitations. Individuals 18 years or over are only allowed to bring in 50 cigars, 200 cigarettes, and 400 grams of loose tobacco. In addition, an imperial quart (just over a liter) of wine or liquor may be brought in, or a curiously generous case (24 cans or bottles) of beer, assuming the bearer is at or over the minimum drinking age in Québec, which is 18.

Pets with proper vaccination records may be admitted, but inquire in advance about necessary procedures at one of the Délégation du Québec offices listed above and see "Pets" in "Fast Facts: Montréal," in chapter 4. Talk to U.S. Customs (see below) about bringing pets back home.

There are strict regulations regarding the import of plants, food products, and firearms. Hunters with valid licenses can bring in some gear, but handguns and fully automatic firearms are prohibited. Fishing tackle poses no problem as long as the proper nonresident license is obtained before a lure is cast. Licenses are available at the Hôtel de Ville (City Hall).

For more detailed information concerning Customs regulations, write to the **Canada Customs Office,** 400 place d'Youville, 2nd Floor, Montréal, PQ H2Y 2C2 ((C) **514/283-2949** or 514/283-2959), or check out the Customs website at www.ccra-adrc.gc.ca.

A car that is driven into Canada can stay for up to a year, but it must leave with the owner or a duty will be levied. The possession or use of a radar detector is prohibited, whether or not it is connected. Police officers can confiscate it and fine the owner C$500 to C$1,000 (US$400–US$800).

WHAT YOU CAN TAKE HOME FROM CANADA

Returning **U.S. citizens** who have been away for at least 48 hours are allowed to bring back, once every 30 days, $800 worth of merchandise duty-free. You'll be charged a flat rate of 4% duty on the next $1,000 worth of purchases. Be sure to have your receipts handy. On mailed gifts, the duty-free limit is $200. With some exceptions, you cannot bring fresh fruits and vegetables into the United States. For specifics on what you can bring back, download the invaluable free pamphlet *Know Before You Go* online at **www.customs.gov.** (Click on "Travel," and then click on "Know Before You Go Online Brochure.") Or contact the **U.S. Customs Service,** 1300 Pennsylvania Ave. NW, Washington, DC 20229 ((C) **877/287-8867**).

U.K. citizens returning from **a non-E.U. country** have a customs allowance of: 200 cigarettes or 50 cigars or 250 grams of smoking tobacco; 2 liters of still table wine; 1 liter of spirits or strong liqueurs (over 22% volume); 2 liters of fortified wine, sparkling wine, or other liqueurs; 60cc (ml) of perfume; 250cc (ml) of toilet water; and £145 worth of all other goods, including gifts and souvenirs. People under 17 cannot have the tobacco or alcohol allowance. For more information, contact HM Customs & Excise at © **0845/010-9000** (from outside the U.K., 020/8929-0152), or consult their website at www.hmce.gov.uk.

The duty-free allowance in **Australia** is A$400 or, for those under 18, A$200. Citizens can bring in 250 cigarettes or 250 grams of loose tobacco, and 1,125 milliliters of alcohol. If you're returning with valuables you already own, such as foreign-made cameras, you should file form B263. A helpful brochure available from Australian consulates or Customs offices is *Know Before You Go.* For more information, call the **Australian Customs Service** at © **1300/363-263,** or log on to www.customs.gov.au.

The duty-free allowance for **New Zealand** is NZ$700. Citizens over 17 can bring in 200 cigarettes, 50 cigars, or 250 grams of tobacco (or a mixture of all three if their combined weight doesn't exceed 250g); plus 4.5 liters of wine and beer, or 1.125 liters of liquor. New Zealand currency does not carry import or export restrictions. Fill out a certificate of export, listing the valuables you are taking out of the country; that way, you can bring them back without paying duty. Most questions are answered in a free pamphlet available at New Zealand consulates and Customs offices: *New Zealand Customs Guide for Travellers, Notice no. 4.* For more information, contact **New Zealand Customs,** The Customhouse, 17–21 Whitmore St., Box 2218, Wellington (© **04/473-6099** or 0800/428-786; www.customs.govt.nz).

3 Money

CURRENCY

Canadian money comes in graduated denominations of dollars and cents. Although the Canadian dollar has been gathering strength of late, the exchange rate is still fairly good for Americans, because the Canadian dollar is worth about 80¢ in U.S. currency, give or take a couple of points' daily variation. This is the exchange rate used to convert prices in this book. Put another way, one U.S. dollar buys about $1.25 in Canadian money. This means that U.S. dollars gain more spending power the moment they are changed for local currency (a return, for example, of approximately C$500 Canadian for every US$400). And because prices are roughly on par with those in the U.S., the difference is real, not imaginary. Prices in this book, unless otherwise indicated, are given in both Canadian and U.S. dollars.

Visitors can bring in or take out any amount of money they wish, but if U.S. citizens import or export sums of US$5,000 or more, a report of the transaction must be filed with U.S. Customs.

Aside from the $2 coin, Canadian coins are similar to their American counterparts: 1¢, 5¢, 10¢, 25¢. Bills—$2, $5, $10, $20, $50, $100—are all the same size but have different colors, depending on the denomination. The gold-colored $1 coin (called a "loonie" by Canadians because of the depiction of a loon on one side) has replaced the $1 bill. A $2 coin, with a bronze center surrounded by a nickel disk, has replaced the old $2 bill. (The $2 coin is sometimes called a "twonie," a reference to the next-smaller coin.) French speakers sometimes refer to a dollar as a "piastre."

Many stores accept U.S. dollars, often posting a sign to that effect and giving the percentage "exchange" rate they offer. Usually, that amount is less than what banks offer, but sometimes it is more favorable because many establishments are eager to attract U.S. tourist dollars. As a rule, though, it's more advantageous to change money and traveler's checks at a

The Canadian Dollar, the U.S. Dollar & the British Pound

The prices quoted in this guide are in Canadian dollars, with the U.S. equivalent in parentheses. The exchange rate we've used is $1.25 Canadian to $1 American. The conversion rate for the British pound is $2.20 Canadian. For the most up-to-date exchange rates, visit **www.oanda.com/convert/classic**.

Here's a quick table of equivalents:

C$	US$	UK£
1.00	0.80	0.45
5.00	4.00	2.25
10.00	8.00	4.50
20.00	16.00	9.00
50.00	40.00	22.50
80.00	64.00	36.00
100.00	80.00	45.00

bank, and better still to obtain cash at ATMs or use credit cards (see below).

It's a good idea to exchange at least some money—just enough to cover airport incidentals and transportation to your hotel—before you leave home so that you can avoid lines at airport ATMs. You can exchange money at your local American Express or Thomas Cook office or at some banks. If you're far away from a bank with currency-exchange services, American Express offers traveler's checks and foreign currency at www.americanexpress.com or © **800/807-6233,** though this carries a $15 order fee and additional shipping costs. An excellent source of international financial information and of foreign currency and traveler's checks is www.oanda.com. They send various amounts of either or both to your home with two-day shipping, charged against your credit card.

ATMs

The easiest and best way to get cash away from home is from an ATM. As ubiquitous in Québec and the rest of Canada as in the United States, ATMs are found in most of the same places, outside or inside

bank branches, but also increasingly at other locations, including the province's new casinos. Look for signs reading GUICHET AUTOMATIQUE or SERVICES ATUOMATISES.

The **Cirrus** (www.mastercard.com) and **PLUS** (www.visa.com) networks span the globe; look at the back of your bank card to see which network you're on, and then call or check online for ATM locations at your destination. Be sure you know your personal identification number (PIN) before you leave home, and also find out your daily withdrawal limit before you depart. Also keep in mind that many banks impose a fee every time a card is used at a different bank's ATM, and that fee can be higher for international transactions (up to $5 or more) than for domestic ones (where they're rarely more than $1.50). On top of this, the bank from which you withdraw cash may charge its own fee. For international withdrawal fees, ask your bank.

You can also get cash advances on your credit card at an ATM. Keep in mind that credit card companies try to protect themselves from theft by limiting the funds someone can withdraw outside their home country, so call your credit card company before you leave home to let it know that you'll be using your card in a different place.

TRAVELER'S CHECKS

Traveler's checks are fast becoming an anachronism from the days before the ATM made cash accessible at any time. The prepaid checks used to be the only sound alternative to traveling with dangerously large amounts of cash. While as reliable as currency, they could be replaced if lost or stolen, unlike cash.

These days, traveler's checks are less necessary because most cities have 24-hour ATMs that allow withdrawal of small amounts of cash as needed. However, keep in mind that you will likely be charged an ATM withdrawal fee if the bank is not your own, so if you're withdrawing money every day, you might be better off with traveler's checks—provided that you don't mind showing identification every time you want to cash one.

You can get traveler's checks at almost any bank. **American Express** offers denominations of $20, $50, $100, $500, and (for cardholders only) $1,000. You'll pay a service charge ranging from 1% to 4%. You can also get American Express traveler's checks over the phone by calling Ⓒ **800/221-7282;** Amex gold and platinum cardholders who use this number are exempt from the 1% fee. AAA members can obtain checks without a fee at most AAA offices.

Visa offers traveler's checks at banks nationwide, as well as at other locations.

The service charge ranges between 1.5% and 2%; checks come in denominations of $20, $50, $100, $500, and $1,000. Call Ⓒ **800/227-6811** for information. **MasterCard** also offers traveler's checks. Call Ⓒ **800/223-9920** for a location near you.

Foreign currency traveler's checks may be useful for some visitors. They're accepted at locations such as stores and bed-and-breakfasts where U.S. dollar checks may not be, and they minimize the amount of math you have to do at your destination. **American Express** offers checks in Australian dollars, Canadian dollars, British pounds, euros, and Japanese yen. **Visa** checks come in Australian, Canadian, British, and euro versions; **MasterCard** offers those four plus yen and South African rands.

If you choose to carry traveler's checks, be sure to keep a record of their serial numbers separate from your checks in the event that they are stolen or lost. You'll get a refund faster if you know the numbers.

CREDIT CARDS

Credit cards are accepted as widely in Québec as in the United States. Visa and MasterCard dominate the market, followed by the American Express card, Diners Club, and its Canadian cousin, enRoute. The Discover and Carte Blanche cards fall well behind the others in usage. Charge slips are written up in Canadian dollars, and card companies convert the amount to U.S. dollars when they credit the transaction to your account.

Credit cards are a safe way to carry money. They provide a convenient record of all your expenses, and they generally

---

Tips **Small Change**

When you change money, ask for some small bills or loose change. Petty cash will come in handy for tipping and public transportation. Consider keeping the change separate from your larger bills so that it's readily accessible and you'll be less of a target for theft.

Tips   **Dear Visa: I'm Off to Québec!**

Some credit card companies recommend that you notify them of any impending trip abroad so that they don't become suspicious when the card is used numerous times in a foreign destination and block your charges. Even if you don't call your credit card company in advance, you can call the card's toll-free emergency number if a charge is refused—a good reason to carry the phone number with you. But perhaps the most important lesson here is to carry more than one card with you on your trip; a card might not work for any number of reasons, so having a backup is the smart way to go.

---

offer good exchange rates. You can also withdraw cash advances from your credit cards at banks or ATMs, provided you know your PIN. If you've forgotten yours, or didn't even know you had one, call the number on the back of your credit card and ask the bank to send it to you. It usually takes 5 to 7 business days, though some banks will provide the number over the phone if you tell them your mother's maiden name or some other personal information.

Your credit card company will likely charge a commission (1% or 2%) on every foreign purchase you make, but for most purchases, you'll still get the best deal with credit cards when you factor in things like ATM fees and higher traveler's check exchange rates.

4 When to Go

High season is late May through early September, when hotels are most likely to be full and charge their highest rates. Even then, though, weekends are cheaper and package plans reduce the bite, so advance planning has its rewards. The period from Christmas to New Year's is also busy (and more expensive), as are the days given to winter festivals in both Montréal and Québec City. The least appealing months are March and April, when few events are scheduled and winter sports start to be iffy, and the increasingly colder months of October and November have all but empty calendars.

CLIMATE

Temperatures are usually a few degrees lower in Québec City than in Montréal. Spring, short but sweet, arrives around the middle of May. Summer (mid-June through mid-Sept) tends to be humid in Montréal, Québec City, and other communities along the St. Lawrence River, and drier at the inland resorts of the Laurentides and the Cantons-de-l'Est. Intense but usually brief heat waves mark July and early August, but temperatures rarely remain oppressive in the evening.

Autumn (Sept–Oct) is as short and changeable as spring, with warm days and cool or chilly nights. Canadian maples blaze with color for weeks. Winter brings dependable snows for skiing in the Laurentides, the Cantons-de-l'Est, and Charlevoix. After a sleigh ride or a ski run in Parc Mont-Royal, Montréal's underground city is a climate-controlled blessing. Mid-February is the time for Québec City's robust Carnaval d'Hiver (Winter Carnival). Snow and slush are more or less constantly present from November to March.

Montréal's Average Monthly Temperatures (°F/°C)

	Jan	Feb	Mar	Apr	May	June	July	Aug	Sept	Oct	Nov	Dec
High(°F)	22	24	34	50	65	74	78	77	67	55	40	27
(°C)	–6	–4	1	10	18	23	26	25	19	13	4	–3
Low (°F)	8	10	21	35	47	57	62	60	52	41	29	14
(°C)	–13	–12	–6	2	8	14	17	16	11	5	–2	–10

Québec City's Average Monthly Temperatures (°F/°C)

	Jan	Feb	Mar	Apr	May	June	July	Aug	Sept	Oct	Nov	Dec
High(°F)	19	21	32	45	60	70	77	74	65	51	39	23
(°C)	–7	–6	0	7	16	21	24	23	18	11	4	–5
Low (°F)	3	8	19	35	43	53	58	56	48	37	28	12
(°C)	–16	–13	–7	2	6	12	14	13	9	3	–2	–11

HOLIDAYS

In Québec province, the important public holidays are New Year's Day (Jan 1); Good Friday and Easter Monday (late Mar or Apr); Victoria Day (May 24 or nearest Mon); St-Jean-Baptiste Day, Québec's "national" day (June 24); Canada Day (July 1); Labour Day (first Mon in Sept); Canadian Thanksgiving Day (second Mon in Oct); Remembrance Day (Nov 11); and Christmas (Dec 25 and 26).

MONTREAL & QUEBEC CITY CALENDAR OF EVENTS

From June to September, only a serious misadventure in planning might allow visitors to miss a celebration of some sort in Montréal and Québec City. If something's not going on in one city, it's bound to be happening in the other, and it's easy to get from one to the other.

January

La Fête des Neiges (Snow Festival), Montréal. Montréal's answer to Québec City's Winter Carnival features outdoor events such as harness racing, barrel jumping, racing beds on ice, canoe races, snowshoeing, skating, and cross-country skiing. The less athletically inclined can cheer from the sidelines and then inspect the snow and ice sculptures. The event, held during the first 2 weeks of February, takes place mostly on Ile Ste-Hélène, in the Port and Vieux-Montréal, and in Parc Maisonneuve. Call ℂ 514/872-4537 or visit www.fetedesneiges.com for details. The festival is held the last week in January and the first in February.

February

Carnaval de Québec (formerly Carnaval d'Hiver), Québec City. Usually Québec is courtly and dignified, but all that is cast aside when the symbolic snowman called Bonhomme (Good Fellow) comes onto the scene to preside over these 15 days of merriment in early February every year. During the event, more than a million revelers descend upon the city, eddying around the monumental ice palace and ice sculptures and attending a full schedule of concerts, dances, and parades. The mood is heightened by the availability of plastic trumpets and canes filled with a concoction called "Caribou," the principal ingredients of which are cheap liquor and sweet red wine. Perhaps its abundant availability explains the eagerness with which certain Quebecois participate in the canoe race across the treacherous ice floes of the St. Lawrence.

Much of the Carnival is held in front of the Parliament Building—just outside the walls to the Old City—in early February. Hotel reservations must be made far in advance. Scheduled events are free. Call ℂ **866/422-7628** or visit www.carnaval.qc.ca for details. Dates in 2006 are January 27 through February 12.

Montréal Highlights Festival (Montréal en Lumière), Montréal. Filling a hole in the yearly schedule, the self-dubbed City of Festivals has created this "High Lights" celebration. Over 500,000 participants take in a somewhat disparate collection of creative and performing events, including nearly 200 culinary competitions and wine tastings, special museum exhibitions and multimedia light shows, and classical and pop concerts by international musical greats. Much of the activity centers on the Place d'Arts complex, but there are other venues throughout the city. Call ℂ **888/477-9955** or see www.montrealhighlights.com for more information. Dates in 2006 are February 16 to February 26.

May/June

Montréal Museums Day, Montréal. On this day museums are free for all visitors, and free shuttle buses carry visitors to most of them. Call the tourism office (ℂ **877/266-5687**) for details. Last Sunday in May.

Montréal Bike Fest, Montréal. Early in June, more than 45,000 enthusiasts converge on Montréal to participate in a variety of cycling competitions, including a nocturnal bike ride, a 26km (16-mile) outing for up to 10,000 children, and the grueling Tour de l'Île, a daylong 66km (41-mile) race around the rim of the island before more than 120,000 spectators. The Tour de l'Île, which began in 1984, attracts 30,000 participants, almost as

many of them women as men. Call ℂ **800/567-8356** or see www.velo.qc.ca for details. First week in June.

Festival Mondial de la Bière, Montréal. Yes, brew fans, this 5-day festival in Windsor Station is devoted to your favorite beverage. From world brands to boutique microbreweries, more than 70 companies showcase more than 250 brands of their pride and joys, employing workshops, cooking demos, musical performances, and, of course, pub food and tastings, tastings, tastings of the featured hoppy tipple. For info and tickets, call ℂ **514/722-9640** or check www.festivalmondialbiere.qc.ca. Early June.

Saint-Ambroise Montréal Fringe Festival, Montréal. In performance spaces clustered along or near boulevard St-Laurent, about 70 theater groups perform in highly esoteric productions that often defy classification. As in all such endeavors, satisfaction cannot be guaranteed, but then, tickets are only C$10 (US$8) and you may find a gem. Call ℂ **514/849-3378** or check www.montrealfringe.ca. Ten days starting in mid-June.

Grand Prix du Canada. The only Formula 1 race in Canada roars around the Île Notre-Dame, where the Casino de Montréal is located. The annual event began in 1967 and was permanently moved to the Circuit Gilles-Villeneuve in 1982. There were 317,000 ticket buyers in 2004 and they spent $75 million on lodging, food, shopping, and entertainment over the long weekend. Much of the partying takes place on downtown rue Crescent. For information, log on to www.grandprix.ca. Three days in June.

Jean-Baptiste Day. Honoring Saint John the Baptist, the patron saint of French Canadians, this *fête nationale* is marked by more festivities and far more enthusiasm throughout Québec province than Canada Day on July 1. It's Québec's "national" holiday. In the past, its hallmark parade had been marred by considerable drunkenness and vandalism in both Montréal and Québec City. In a successful effort to control such problems in Montréal, the parade is now held along the streets of Vieux-Montréal on the night of June 23, the day before the actual holiday. Call ℂ **418/849-2560** or log on to www.cfn.org for details. June 24.

Le Mondial SAQ (International Fireworks Competition), Montréal. The open-air theater in La Ronde amusement park on Île Ste-Hélène is the best place to view this fireworks extravaganza, although fireworks can be enjoyed from almost any point overlooking the river. Tickets to the show also provide entrance to the amusement park. Kids, needless to say, love the whole explosive business. The 30-minute shows, with music, are staged by companies from several countries. Because parking is limited, it's best to use the Métro. Call ℂ **514/790-1245** or visit www.lemondialsaq.com/en for details. Wednesdays and Saturdays in late June, Sundays in July.

July

Festival International de Jazz de Montréal. Montréal has a long tradition in jazz, and this enormously successful festival has been celebrating America's art form since 1979. Pat Metheny, Bill Frisell, Dave Holland, and Sonny Rollins have been among the many acts in recent years, but it costs money to hear stars of such magnitude. Fortunately, hundreds of other concerts are free, and are often presented on the streets and plazas of the city. You can see (and hear) events along rue Ste-Catherine and rue Jeanne-Mance. For information and tickets, call ℂ **800/361-4595** or 514/790-1245 or visit www.montreal jazzfest.com. Late June to mid-July. Call or visit the site for exact dates.

Festival d'Eté (Summer Festival), Québec City. The largest cultural event in the French-speaking world, or so its managers say, this festival has attracted artists from Africa, Asia, Europe, and North America since it began in 1967. There are more than 500 events showcasing theater, music, and dance, with nearly 500 performers from 22 countries. Over one million people come to watch and listen. Jazz and folk combos perform free in an open-air theater next to City Hall; visiting dance and folklore troupes put on shows; and concerts, theatrical productions, and related events fill the days and evenings. Call ℂ **888/992-5200** or 418/529-5200 for details or check www.infofestival.com. Ten days in mid-July.

Festival International Nuits d'Afrique, Montréal. This World Beat musical event showcases nearly 300 musicians from the Caribbean, the Americas, and Africa. Performances take place in Club Soda, Club Balattou, and Place Berri. Call ℂ **514/790-1245** or check out www.festivalnuitsdafrique.com for details. Ten days in mid-July.

Festival Juste pour Rire (Just for Laughs Festival), Montréal. This celebration strives to do for humor what the more famous jazz festival has done for that musical form. Comics perform in many venues, some free, some not. Both Francophone and Anglophone comics, jugglers, and other acts from many countries participate. Over 2,000 performances are made, mostly along rue St-Denis and elsewhere in the Latin Quarter. Call ℂ **888/244-3155** or 514/790-4242 for details or check www.hahaha.com. Ten days in mid-July.

Les Grands Feux Loto-Québec, Québec City. The capital has its own fireworks festival, overlapping the one in Montréal, and using the highly scenic Montmorency Falls as its setting. Five pyrotechnical teams are invited from as many different countries in this international competition. Their explosive displays are coordinated with appropriate music, as in Montréal. Call © **888/934-3473** or 418/523-3389 or check www.quebecfireworks.com. Wednesdays and Saturdays from late July to mid-August.

August

Festival des Films du Monde (World Film Festival), Montréal. This festival has been an international film event since 1976. Some 500 indoor and outdoor screenings take place over 12 days, including 200 feature films from more than 70 countries, drawing the usual throngs of directors, stars, and wannabes. It isn't as gaudy or as media-heavy as Cannes, but it's taken almost as seriously. Various movie theaters play host. Call © **514/848-3883** or check www.ffm-montreal.org for details. Late August to early September.

September

Fall Foliage. The maple trees blaze with color and a walk in the parks and squares of Montréal and Québec City is a refreshing tonic. It's a perfect time for a drive in the Laurentides or Cantons-de-L'Est (near Montréal) and Île d'Orléans or up into Charlevoix from Québec City. Mid- to late September.

October

Festival du Nouveau Cinéma, Montréal. Screenings of new and experimental films ignite controversy, and forums are held on the latest trends in film and video. Events take place at halls and cinemas throughout the city. Call © **514/847-1242** or check www.nouveaucinema.ca for details. Ten days in mid-October.

November

Festival d'Automne. A relatively new event, the short Autumn Festival is essentially an expanded Halloween celebration. Concerts feature various musical forms, and there are magic and ice shows as well as sound-and-light presentations. Check out www.infofestival.com/faq. October 30 through November 1.

December/January

Christmas/New Year's, Québec City. Celebrating the holidays a la Française is a particular treat in Québec City, with its streets banked with snow and almost every ancient building sporting wreaths and decorated fir trees.

5 Travel Insurance

Check your existing insurance policies and credit card coverage before you buy travel insurance. You may already be covered for canceled tickets, lost luggage, or medical expenses. The cost of travel insurance varies widely, depending on the cost and length of your trip, your age, your health, and the type of trip you're taking, but expect to pay between 5% and 8% of the vacation itself.

TRIP-CANCELLATION INSURANCE Trip-cancellation insurance helps you get your money back if you have to back out of a trip, if you have to go home early, or if your travel supplier goes bankrupt. Allowed reasons for cancellation can range from sickness to natural disasters to the State Department declaring your destination unsafe for travel. (Insurers usually won't cover vague fears, though, as many travelers discovered who tried to cancel their trips in Oct 2001 because they were wary of flying.) Trip-cancellation insurance is a good buy if you're getting tickets well in advance—who knows what the state of the world, or of your airline, will be in 9 months? Insurance policy details vary, so read the fine print—and especially make sure that your airline or cruise line is on the list of carriers covered in case of bankruptcy. A good resource is **"Travel Guard Alerts,"** a list of companies considered high-risk by Travel Guard International (see website below). Protect yourself further by paying for the insurance with a credit card—by law, consumers can get their money back on goods and services not received if they report the loss within 60 days after the charge is listed on their credit card statement.

Note: Many tour operators, particularly those offering trips to remote or high-risk areas, include insurance in the cost of the trip or can arrange insurance policies through a partnering provider, a convenient and often cost-effective way for the traveler to obtain insurance. Make sure the tour company is a reputable one, however: Some experts suggest you avoid buying insurance from the tour or cruise company you're traveling with, saying it's better to buy from a "third party" insurer than to put all your money in one place.

For more information, contact one of the following recommended insurers: **Access America** (© 866/807-3982; www.accessamerica.com); **Travel Guard International** (© 800/826-4919; www.travel guard.com); **Travel Insured International** (© 800/243-3174; www.travel insured.com); and **Travelex Insurance Services** (© 888/457-4602; www.travelex-insurance.com).

MEDICAL INSURANCE For travel overseas, most health plans (including Medicare and Medicaid) do not provide coverage, and the ones that do often require you to pay for services upfront and reimburse you only after you return home. Medical treatment in Canada isn't free for foreigners, and hospitals make you pay your bills at the time of service. They'll send you a refund after you've returned home and filed the necessary paperwork. In a worst-case scenario, there's the high cost of emergency evacuation. If you require additional medical insurance, try **MEDEX Assistance** (© 410/453-6300;** www.medexassist.com) or **Travel Assistance International** (© 800/821-2828;** www.travelassistance.com; for general information on services, call the company's Worldwide Assistance Services, Inc., at © **800/777-8710**).

LOST-LUGGAGE INSURANCE On domestic flights, checked baggage is covered up to $2,500 per ticketed passenger. On international flights (including U.S. portions of international trips), baggage is limited to approximately $9.07 per pound, up to approximately $635 per checked bag. If you plan to check items more valuable than the standard liability, see if your valuables are covered by your homeowner's policy, get baggage insurance as part of your comprehensive travel-insurance package, or buy Travel Guard's "BagTrak" product. Don't buy insurance at the airport, as it's invariably overpriced. Be sure to take any valuables or irreplaceable items with you in your carry-on luggage, as many valuables (including books, money, and electronics) aren't covered by airline policies.

If your luggage is lost, immediately file a lost-luggage claim at the airport, detailing the luggage contents. For most airlines, you must report delayed, damaged, or lost baggage within 4 hours of arrival. The airlines are required to deliver luggage, once found, directly to your house or destination free of charge.

6 Health & Safety

STAYING HEALTHY

Not a single case of SARS has been reported in Québec, and the Toronto area in neighboring Ontario has been declared free of the disease by the World Health Organization.

GENERAL AVAILABILITY OF HEALTH CARE

Canada has a state-run health system. It is suffering a number of problems, including a nurse shortage, overcrowded emergency rooms, and budgetary difficulties. With ever-longer waits even for essential treatments, many Quebecois now cross the border to enter U.S. hospitals. That said, Québec hospitals are modern and decently equipped, and staffs are well trained.

WHAT TO DO IF YOU GET SICK AWAY FROM HOME

No shots are required upon entering Québec. Familiar over-the-counter medicines are widely available. If there is a possibility you will run out of prescribed medicines during your visit, take along a prescription from your doctor. Prescription drugs are usually cheaper in Canada than in the U.S.

In many cases, your existing health plan will provide the coverage you need. But double-check; you may want to buy **travel medical insurance** instead. (See the section on insurance, above.) Bring your insurance ID card with you when you travel.

If you suffer from a chronic illness, consult your doctor before your departure. For conditions like epilepsy, diabetes, or heart problems, wear a **MedicAlert Identification Tag** (© **800/825-3785;** www.medic alert.org), which will immediately alert doctors to your condition and give them access to your records through MedicAlert's 24-hour hot line.

Pack **prescription medications** in your carry-on luggage, and carry prescription medications in their original containers, with pharmacy labels—otherwise they may not make it through airport security. Also bring along copies of your prescriptions in case you lose your pills or run out. Don't forget an extra pair of contact lenses or prescription glasses. Carry the generic name of prescription medicines, in case a local pharmacist is unfamiliar with the brand name.

7 Specialized Travel Resources

TRAVELERS WITH DISABILITIES

Most disabilities shouldn't stop anyone from traveling. There are more options and resources out there than ever before.

Québec regulations regarding accessibility for wheelchairs are similar to those in the United States, including curb cuts, entrance ramps, designated parking spaces, and specially equipped bathrooms. However, access to the restaurants and inns housed in 18th- and 19th-century buildings, especially in Québec City, is often difficult or impossible.

Advice for travelers with physical limitations is provided in a brochure, *Accessible Québec*. It lists hundreds of accessible

hotels, restaurants, theaters, and museums. The price is C$15 (US$12) from Kéroul, 4545 av. Pierre de Coubertin, P.O. Box 1000, Station M, Montréal, Québec H1V 3R2 (© **514/252-3104;** www.keroul.qc.ca). When calling to make an airline reservation or talking with a travel agent, inquire where a wheelchair will be stowed on the plane or train, or confirm that a Seeing Eye dog or hearing dog may accompany you. Remember that special meals can be preordered when making airline reservations.

Many travel agencies offer customized tours and itineraries for travelers with disabilities. **Flying Wheels**

Travel (© 507/451-5005; www.flying
wheelstravel.com) offers escorted tours
and cruises that emphasize sports and
private tours in minivans with lifts.
Access-Able Travel Source (© 303/232-
2979; www.access-able.com) offers extensive access information and advice for traveling around the world with disabilities.
Accessible Journeys (© 800/846-4537 or
610/521-0339; www.disabilitytravel.com)
caters specifically to slow walkers and
wheelchair travelers and their families and
friends.

Avis Rent a Car has an "Avis Access"
program that offers such services as a dedicated 24-hour toll-free number (© 888/
879-4273) for customers with special
travel needs; special car features such as
swivel seats, spinner knobs, and hand
controls; and accessible bus service.

Organizations that offer assistance to
travelers with disabilities include **Moss-
Rehab** (www.mossresourcenet.org), which
provides a library of accessible-travel
resources online; **SATH (Society for
Accessible Travel & Hospitality;** © 212/
447-7284; www.sath.org; annual membership fees: $45 adults, $30 seniors and
students), which offers a wealth of travel
resources for all types of disabilities and
informed recommendations on destinations, access guides, travel agents, tour
operators, vehicle rentals, and companion
services; and the **American Foundation
for the Blind (AFB;** © 800/232-5463;
www.afb.org), a referral resource for travelers who are blind or visually impaired
that includes information on traveling
with Seeing Eye dogs.

For more information specifically targeted to travelers with disabilities, the community website **iCan** (www.icanonline.
net/channels/travel/index.cfm) has destination guides and several regular columns
on accessible travel. Also check out the
quarterly magazine **Emerging Horizons**
($14.95 per year, $19.95 outside the
U.S.; www.emerginghorizons.com), and

Open World magazine, published by
SATH (see above; subscription: $13 per
year, $21 outside the U.S.).

GAY & LESBIAN TRAVELERS

In Montréal, gay and lesbian travelers
head straight to the Gay Village, lying
primarily along rue Ste-Catherine est
between rue St-Hubert and rue Papineau,
where there are numerous meeting spots,
shops, bars, and clubs. **Gay Line** (© 514/
866-5090 or 888/505-1010 outside the
514 area code; www.gayline.qc.ca) describes
current events and activities in English,
daily from 7 to 10pm. Try to visit Montréal during the annual Diver/Cité, the
Gay & Lesbian Pride Festival; it takes
place in late July to early August, with a
parade, concerts, parties, and art shows
(© 514/285-4011; www.diverscite.org).
During the second week of October in
Montréal, the **Black & Blue Festival** is 7
days of gay benefit parties at various locations throughout the city (© 514/875-
7026; www.bbcm.org). Two additional
websites that may prove useful are www.
gaywired.com and www.fugues.com. The
latter is a leisure guide to gay life in Montréal and other Québec cities; you can
find the printed version in bars and hotels
in and around the Village. Additional
information is available at **The Village
Tourist Information Centre** at 576 rue
Ste-Catherine est opposite the Berri-
UQAM Métro station (© 514/522-
1885; www.infovillagegai.com).

The gay community in Québec City is
relatively small, centered in the Upper
Town just outside the city walls, near
Porte Saint-Jean. At the end of August, a
5-day gay festival, **Fête Arc-en-Ciel,** is
held in the city. Call © 418/264-3365
for information.

The following travel guides are available
at most travel bookstores and gay and lesbian bookstores, or order them from **Gio-
vanni's Room** bookstore, 1145 Pine St.,
Philadelphia, PA 19107 (© 215/923-
2960; www.giovannisroom.com): *Out*

and About (© **800/929-2268** or 415/644-8044; www.outandabout.com), which offers guidebooks and a newsletter 10 times a year packed with solid information on the global gay and lesbian scene; *Spartacus International Gay Guide* and *Odysseus,* annual English-language guidebooks focused on gay men; the *Damron* guides, with separate, annual books for gay men and lesbians; and *Gay Travel A to Z: The World of Gay & Lesbian Travel Options at Your Fingertips,* by Marianne Ferrari (Ferrari Publications; Box 35575, Phoenix, AZ 85069), a gay and lesbian guidebook series.

SENIOR TRAVEL

Mention the fact that you're a senior citizen when you make your travel reservations. Although all of the major U.S. airlines except America West have cancelled their senior discount and coupon book programs, many hotels still offer discounts for seniors. In most cities, people over the age of 60 qualify for reduced admission to theaters, museums, and other attractions, as well as discounted fares on public transportation.

Members of **AARP** (formerly known as the American Association of Retired Persons), 601 E St. NW, Washington, DC 20049 (© **888/687-2277;** www.aarp.org), get discounts on hotels, airfares, and car rentals. AARP offers members a wide range of benefits, including *AARP: The Magazine* and a monthly newsletter. Anyone over 50 can join. Many reliable agencies and organizations target the 50-plus market. **Elderhostel** (© **877/426-8056;** www.elderhostel.org) arranges study programs for those ages 55 and over (and a spouse or companion of any age) in the U.S. and in more than 80 countries around the world. Most courses last 5 to 7 days in the U.S. (2–4 weeks abroad), and many include airfare, accommodations in university dormitories or modest inns, meals, and tuition. **ElderTreks** (© **800/741-7956;**

www.eldertreks.com) offers small-group tours to off-the-beaten-path or adventure-travel locations, restricted to travelers 50 and older.

Recommended publications offering travel resources and discounts for seniors include the quarterly magazine *Travel 50 & Beyond* (www.travel50andbeyond.com); *Travel Unlimited: Uncommon Adventures for the Mature Traveler* (Avalon); *101 Tips for Mature Travelers,* available from Grand Circle Travel (© **800/221-2610** or 617/350-7500; www.gct.com); and *Unbelievably Good Deals and Great Adventures That You Absolutely Can't Get Unless You're Over 50* (McGraw-Hill), by Joann Rattner Heilman.

FAMILY TRAVEL

If you have enough trouble getting your kids out of the house in the morning, dragging them thousands of miles away may seem like an insurmountable challenge. But family travel can be immensely rewarding, giving you new ways of seeing the world through smaller pairs of eyes.

Montréal and Québec City offer an abundance of family-oriented activities, many of them outdoors, even in winter. Dog sledding, watersports, river cruises, and frequent festivals and fireworks displays are among the family-friendly attractions. The walls and fortifications of Québec City are fodder for imagining the days of knights and princesses, and both cities have horse-drawn sightseeing carriages, a surefire hit with most youngsters. Many museums make special efforts to address children's interests and enthusiasms. For more details, see the "Especially for Kids" sections in chapters 7 and 15. For family-friendly lodgings in Montréal, see p. 77; for family-friendly lodgings in Québec City, see p. 220. For family-friendly restaurants in Montréal, see p. 92.

Familyhostel (© **800/733-9753;** www.learn.unh.edu/familyhostel) takes the whole family, including kids ages 8 to 15, on moderately priced domestic and international learning vacations. Lectures, fields trips, and sightseeing are guided by a team of academics.

Recommended family travel Internet sites include **Family Travel Forum** (www.familytravelforum.com), a comprehensive site that offers customized trip planning; **Family Travel Network** (www.familytravelnetwork.com), an award-winning site that offers travel features, deals, and tips; **Traveling Internationally with Your Kids** (www.travelwithyourkids.com), a comprehensive site offering sound advice for long-distance and international travel with children; and **Family Travel Files** (www.thefamilytravelfiles.com), which offers an online magazine and a directory of off-the-beaten-path tours and tour operators for families.

WOMEN TRAVELERS

Montréal and Québec City are among the safest cities in North America, so only the basic urban cautions about dark streets and care in giving out hotel room numbers need be observed.

Check out the award-winning website **Journeywoman** (www.journeywoman.com), a "real life" women's travel information network where you can sign up for a free e-mail newsletter and get advice on everything from etiquette and dress to safety; or the travel guide *Safety and Security for Women Who Travel,* by Sheila Swan and Peter Laufer (Travelers' Tales, Inc.), offering common-sense tips on safe travel.

STUDENT TRAVELERS

Many of the tips that apply to single travelers (see the next section) apply to students (who may or may not be traveling solo). Always carry a university or similar ID card to obtain the many available discounts, especially at museums, theaters, and other attractions. Both Montréal and Québec City have their designated Latin

Quarters, centrally located university areas filled with students.

To save money on lodging, consider the YMCA or the YWCA in Montréal and hostels in Québec City. For information about hostels in Québec and the rest of Canada, contact **Hostelling International,** 400–205 Catherine St., Ottawa, ON K2P 1C3 9 (© **613/237-7884;** www.hihostels.ca).

If you're planning to travel outside the U.S., you'd be wise to arm yourself with an **International Student Identity Card (ISIC),** which offers substantial savings on rail passes, plane tickets, and entrance fees. It also provides you with basic health and life insurance and a 24-hour help line. The card is available for $22 from **STA Travel** (© **800/781-4040** in North America; www.sta.com or www.statravel.com), the biggest student travel agency in the world. If you're no longer a student but are still under 26, you can get an **International Youth Travel Card (IYTC)** for the same price from the same people, which entitles you to some discounts (but not on museum admissions). (*Note:* In 2002, STA Travel bought competitors **Council Travel** and **USIT Campus** after they went bankrupt. It's still operating some offices under the Council name, but it's owned by STA.) **Travel CUTS** (© **800/667-2887** or 416/614-2887; www.travelcuts.com) offers similar services for both Canadians and U.S. residents. Irish students may prefer to turn to **USIT** (© **01/602-1600;** www.usitnow.ie), an Ireland-based specialist in student, youth, and independent travel.

SINGLE TRAVELERS

Two problems crop up most often for solo travelers: added costs and feelings of isolation, especially on Friday and Saturday nights, when everyone else seems to be out and about in numbers divisible by two. Check the sections in this book on popular local bars (see chapters 10 and 18) for possibilities for meeting locals and engaging in some lively conversation. Jazz and folk music spots, especially those that charge no cover—and most in Montréal and Québec City do not—are also fertile ground for meeting and chatting with Quebecois.

Bed-and-breakfast inns are often a good choice for meeting people, and both Montréal and Québec City have them. Guests come together over breakfast and might end up going out to explore or dine together. Prices are often (but not always) lower than those at hotels, many of which charge the same rate for a room whether it's occupied by one or two people. Guided walking tours are another excellent way to explore the city and enjoy a couple of hours of social interaction at the same time.

Many people prefer traveling alone, and for independent travelers, solo journeys offer infinite opportunities to make friends and meet locals. Unfortunately, if you like resorts, tours, or cruises, you're likely to get hit with a "single supplement" to the base price. Single travelers can avoid these supplements, of course, by agreeing to room with other single travelers on the trip. An even better idea is to find a compatible roommate before you go from one of the many roommate locator agencies.

Travel Buddies Singles Travel Club (© 800/998-9099; www.travelbuddies worldwide.com), based in Canada, runs small, intimate, single-friendly group trips and will match you with a roommate free of charge. **TravelChums** (© 212/787-2621; www.travelchums.com) is an Internet-only travel-companion matching service with elements of an online personals-type site, hosted by the respected New York–based Shaw Guides travel service. **The Single Gourmet Club** (www.singlegourmet.com/chapters.html) is an international social, dining, and travel club for singles of all ages, with offices in 21 cities in the U.S. and Canada. Annual membership fees vary from city to city.

For more information, check out Eleanor Berman's *Traveling Solo: Advice and Ideas for More Than 250 Great Vacations* (Globe Pequot), a guide with advice on traveling alone, whether on your own or on a group tour.

8 Planning Your Trip Online

SURFING FOR AIRFARES

The "big three" online travel agencies, **Expedia.com, Travelocity,** and **Orbitz,** sell most of the air tickets bought on the Internet. (Canadian travelers should try expedia.ca and travelocity.ca; U.K. residents can go to expedia.co.uk and opodo.co.uk.) Each has different business deals with the airlines and may offer different fares on the same flights, so it's wise to shop around. Expedia and Travelocity will also send you **e-mail notification** when a cheap fare becomes available to your favorite destination. Of the smaller travel-agency websites, **SideStep** (www.sidestep.com) is a browser add-on that purports to "search 140 sites at once," but in reality only beats competitors' fares as often as other sites do.

Also remember to check **airline websites,** especially those for low-fare carriers such as Southwest, JetBlue, AirTran, WestJet, or Ryanair, whose fares are often misreported or simply missing from travel-agency websites. Even with major airlines, you can often shave a few bucks from a fare by booking directly through the airline and avoiding a travel agency's transaction fee. But you'll get these discounts only by **booking online:** Most airlines now offer online-only fares that even their phone agents know nothing about. For the websites of airlines that fly to and from your destination, go to "Getting There," p. 34.

Frommers.com: The Complete Travel Resource

For an excellent travel-planning resource, we highly recommend **Frommers.com** (www.frommers.com), voted Best Travel Site by *PC Magazine*. We're a little biased, of course, but we guarantee that you'll find the travel tips, reviews, monthly vacation giveaways, bookstore, and online-booking capabilities thoroughly indispensable. Among the special features are our popular **Destinations** section, where you'll get expert travel tips, hotel and dining recommendations, and advice on the sights to see for more than 3,500 destinations around the globe; the **Frommers.com Newsletter,** with the latest deals, travel trends, and money-saving secrets; our **Community** area featuring **Message Boards,** where Frommer's readers post queries and share advice (sometimes even our authors show up to answer questions); and our **Photo Center,** where you can post and share vacation tips. When your research is done, the **Online Reservations System** (www.frommers.com/book_a_trip) takes you to Frommer's preferred online partners for booking your vacation at affordable prices.

Great **last-minute deals** are available through free weekly e-mail services provided directly by the airlines. Most of these are announced on Tuesday or Wednesday and must be purchased online. Most are only valid for travel that weekend, but some (such as Southwest's) can be booked weeks or months in advance. Sign up for weekly e-mail alerts at airline websites, or check megasites that compile comprehensive lists of last-minute specials, such as **Smarter Travel** (smartertravel.com). For last-minute trips, **site59.com** and **lastminutetravel.com** in the U.S. and **lastminute.com** in Europe often have better air-and-hotel package deals than the major-label sites. A website listing numerous bargain sites and airlines around the world is **www.itravelnet.com**.

If you're willing to give up some control over your flight details, use what is called an **"opaque" fare service** like **Priceline** (www.priceline.com; www.priceline.co.uk for Europeans) or its smaller competitor **Hotwire** (www.hotwire.com). Both offer rock-bottom prices in

exchange for travel on a "mystery airline" at a mysterious time of day, often with a mysterious change of planes en route. The mystery airlines are all major, well-known carriers—and the possibility of being sent from Philadelphia to Chicago via Tampa is remote; the airlines' routing computers have gotten a lot better than they used to be. But your chances of getting a 6am or 11pm flight are pretty high. Hotwire tells you flight prices before you buy; Priceline usually has better deals than Hotwire, but you have to play their "name our price" game. If you're new at this, the helpful folks at **BiddingFor-Travel** (www.biddingfortravel.com) do a good job of demystifying Priceline's prices and strategies. Priceline and Hotwire are great for flights within North America and between the U.S. and Europe. But for flights to other parts of the world, consolidators will almost always beat their fares. *Note:* In 2004 Priceline added non-opaque service to its roster. You now have the option to pick exact flights, times, and airlines from a list of offers—or opt to bid on opaque fares as before.

SURFING FOR HOTELS

Canada has a good online B&B network at www.bbcanada.com. Of the "big three" sites, **Expedia.com** offers a long list of special deals and "virtual tours" or photos of available rooms so you can see what you're paying for (a feature that helps counter the claims that the best rooms are often held back from bargain booking websites). **Travelocity** posts unvarnished customer reviews and ranks its properties according to the AAA rating system. Also reliable are **Hotels.com** and **Quikbook.com**. An excellent free program, **TravelAxe** (www.travelaxe.net), can help you search multiple hotel sites at once, even ones you may never have heard of—and conveniently lists the total price of the room, including the taxes and service charges. Another booking site, **Travelweb** (www.travelweb.com), is partly owned by the hotels it represents (including the Hilton, Hyatt, and Starwood chains) and is therefore plugged directly into the hotels' reservations systems—unlike independent online agencies, which have to fax or e-mail reservation requests to the hotel, a good portion of which get misplaced in the shuffle. More than once, travelers have arrived at the hotel, only to be told that they have no reservation. To be fair, many of the major sites are undergoing improvements in service and ease of use, and Expedia will soon be able to plug directly into the reservations systems of many hotel chains—none of which can

be bad news for consumers. In the meantime, it's a good idea to **get a confirmation number** and **make a printout** of any online booking transaction.

In the opaque website category, **Priceline** and **Hotwire** are even better for hotels than for airfares; with both, you're allowed to pick the neighborhood and quality level of your hotel before offering up your money. Priceline's hotel product even covers Europe and Asia, though it's much better at getting five-star lodging for three-star prices than at finding anything at the bottom of the scale. On the downside, many hotels stick Priceline guests in their least desirable rooms. Be sure to go to the BiddingforTravel website (see above) before bidding on a hotel room on Priceline; it features a fairly up-to-date list of hotels that Priceline uses in major cities. For both Priceline and Hotwire, you pay upfront, and the fee is nonrefundable. *Note:* Some hotels do not provide loyalty program credits or points or other frequent-stay amenities when you book a room through opaque online services.

SURFING FOR RENTAL CARS

For booking rental cars online, the best deals are usually found at rental-car company websites, although all the major online travel agencies also offer rental-car reservations services. Priceline and Hotwire work well for rental cars, too; the only "mystery" is which major rental company you get, and for most travelers the difference between Hertz, Avis, and Budget is negligible.

9 The 21st-Century Traveler

INTERNET ACCESS AWAY FROM HOME

Travelers have any number of ways to check their e-mail and access the Internet on the road. Of course, using your own laptop—or even a PDA (personal digital assistant) or an electronic organizer with a modem—gives you the most flexibility. But if you don't have a computer, you can still access your e-mail and even your office computer from cybercafes.

WITHOUT YOUR OWN COMPUTER

It's hard nowadays to find a city that *doesn't* have a few cybercafes. Although there's no definitive directory for cyber-cafes—these are independent businesses, after all—two places to start looking are at **www.cybercaptive.com** and **www. netcafeguide.com.**

Aside from formal cybercafes, most **public libraries** across the world offer Internet access free or for a small charge. **Hotels** that cater to business travelers usually have **in-room dataports** and **business centers,** and high-speed Inter-net access and wireless hot spots are increasingly available. Also, most **youth hostels** nowadays have at least one com-puter where you can access the Internet. Some of Québec's post offices have com-puters for customer use.

Most major airports now have **Inter-net kiosks** scattered among their gates. These kiosks, which you'll also see in shopping malls, hotel lobbies, and tourist information offices around the world, give you basic Web access for a per-minute fee that's usually higher than cybercafe prices. The kiosks' clunkiness and high price means they should be avoided whenever possible.

To retrieve your e-mail, ask your **Inter-net service provider (ISP)** if it has a Web-based interface tied to your existing e-mail account. If your ISP doesn't have such an interface, you can use the free **mail2web** service (www.mail2web.com) to view and reply to your home e-mail. For more flexibility, you may want to open a free, Web-based e-mail account with **Yahoo! Mail** (mail.yahoo.com). (Microsoft's Hotmail is another popular option, but Hotmail has severe spam problems.) Your home ISP may be able to forward your e-mail to the Web-based account automatically.

If you need to access files on your office computer, look into a service called **GoToMyPC** (www.gotomypc.com). The service provides a Web-based interface for you to access and manipulate a distant PC from anywhere—even a cybercafe—provided your "target" PC is on and has an always-on connection to the Internet (such as with Road Runner cable). The service offers top-quality security, but if you're worried about hackers, use your own laptop rather than a cybercafe to access the GoToMyPC system.

WITH YOUR OWN COMPUTER

Wi-Fi (wireless fidelity) is the buzzword in computer access, and more and more hotels, cafes, and retailers are signing on as wireless "hot spots" where you can get high-speed connection without cable wires, networking hardware, or a phone line (see below). You can get a Wi-Fi con-nection in one of several ways. Many lap-tops sold in the past year have built-in Wi-Fi capability (an 802.11b wireless Ethernet connection). Mac owners have their own networking technology, Apple AirPort. For those with older computers, an 802.11b/**Wi-Fi card** (around $50) can be plugged into your laptop. You sign up for wireless access service much as you do cellphone service, through a plan offered by one of several commercial companies that have made wireless service available in airports, hotel lobbies, and coffee shops, primarily in the U.S. (followed by the U.K. and Japan). **T-Mobile Hotspot** (www.t-mobile.com/hotspot) serves up wireless connections at more than 1,000 Starbucks coffee shops nationwide. **Boingo** (www.boingo.com) and **Wayport** (www. wayport.com) have set up networks in air-ports and high-class hotel lobbies. IPass providers (see below) also give you access to a few hundred wireless hotel lobby setups. Best of all, you don't need to be staying at the Four Seasons to use the hotel's network; just set yourself up on a nice couch in the lobby. The companies' pricing policies can be byzantine, with a variety of monthly, per-connection, and per-minute plans, but in general you pay around $30 a month for limited access—and as more and more companies jump on the wireless bandwagon, prices are likely to get even more competitive.

There are also places that provide **free wireless networks** in cities around the world. To locate these free hot spots, go to **www.personaltelco.net/index.cgi/ WirelessCommunities**.

If Wi-Fi is not available at your destination, most business-class hotels throughout the world offer dataports for laptop modems, and a few thousand hotels in the U.S. and Europe now offer free high-speed Internet access using an Ethernet network cable. You can bring your own cables, but most hotels rent them for around $10. **Call your hotel in advance** to see what your options are.

In addition, major Internet service providers have **local access numbers** around the world, allowing you to go online by simply placing a local call. Check your ISP's website or call its toll-free number and ask how you can use your current account away from home, and how much it will cost.

If you're traveling outside the reach of your ISP, the **iPass** network has dial-up numbers in most of the world's countries. You'll have to sign up with an iPass provider, who will then tell you how to set up your computer for your destination(s). For a list of iPass providers, go to www. ipass.com and click on "Individuals Buy Now." One solid provider is **i2roam** (www.i2roam.com; **©** **866/811-6209** or 920/235-0475). Wherever you go, bring a **connection kit** of the right power (110–120 volts AC [60 cycles] in Canada) and phone adapters, a spare phone cord, and a spare Ethernet network cable.

USING A CELLPHONE IN CANADA

Keep it simple: Sign up for a wireless system that covers both the U.S. and Canada. Verizon is one. Otherwise, it gets complicated, to wit:

If your cellphone is on a GSM system, and you have a world-capable phone such as many (but not all) Sony Ericsson, Motorola, or Samsung models, you can make and receive calls across civilized areas on much of the globe, from Andorra

Online Traveler's Toolbox

Veteran travelers usually carry some essential items to make their trips easier. Following is a selection of online tools to bookmark and use:

- **Visa ATM Locator** (www.visa.com), for locations of PLUS ATMs worldwide, or **MasterCard ATM Locator** (www.mastercard.com), for locations of Cirrus ATMs worldwide.
- **Foreign Languages for Travelers** (www.travlang.com). Learn basic terms in more than 70 languages and click on any underlined phrase to hear what it sounds like.
- **Intellicast** (www.intellicast.com) and **Weather.com** (www.weather.com). These give weather forecasts for all 50 states and for cities around the world.
- **Mapquest** (www.mapquest.com). This best of the mapping sites lets you choose a specific address or destination, and in seconds, it will return a map and detailed directions.

to Uganda. Just call your wireless operator and ask for "international roaming" to be activated on your account. Unfortunately, per-minute charges can be high.

World-phone owners can bring down their per-minute charges with a bit of trickery. Call up your cellular operator and say you'll be going abroad for several months and want to "unlock" your phone to use it with a local provider. Usually, they'll oblige. Then, in your destination country, pick up a cheap, prepaid phone chip at a mobile phone store and slip it into your phone. (Show your phone to the salesperson, as not all phones work on all networks.) You'll get a local phone number in your destination country—and much, much lower calling rates.

Otherwise, **renting** a phone is a good idea. While you can rent a phone from any number of overseas sites, including kiosks at airports and at car-rental agencies, we suggest renting the phone before you leave home. That way you can give loved ones your new number, make sure the phone works, and take the phone wherever you go—especially helpful when you rent overseas, where phone-rental agencies bill in local currency and may not let you take the phone to another country.

Phone rental isn't cheap. You'll usually pay $40 to $50 per week, plus airtime fees of at least a dollar a minute. Shop around.

Two good wireless rental companies are **InTouch USA** (© 800/872-7626; www.intouchglobal.com) and **RoadPost** (www.roadpost.com; © 888/290-1606 or 905/272-5665). Give them your itinerary, and they'll tell you what wireless products you need. InTouch will also, for free, advise you on whether your existing phone will work overseas; simply call © 703/222-7161 between 9am and 4pm EST, or go to http://intouchglobal.com/travel.htm.

For trips of more than a few weeks spent in one country, **buying a phone** becomes economically attractive, as many nations have cheap, no-questions-asked prepaid phone systems. Stop by a local cellphone shop and get the cheapest package; you'll probably pay less than $100 for a phone and a starter calling card. Local calls may be as low as 10¢ per minute, and in many countries incoming calls are free.

10 Getting There

Served by highways, transcontinental trains and buses, and an international airport, Montréal and Québec City are easily accessible from any part of the United States and Europe.

BY PLANE

TO MONTREAL Pierre-Elliot-Trudeau Airport accepts most of the world's major airlines, nearly 50 in all. (Mirabel Airport, farther from the city, accepts only airfreight and some charter flights.) Most visitors fly into **Trudeau** from other parts of North America on **Air Canada** (© 888/247-2262; www.aircanada.ca), **American** (© 800/433-7300; www.aa.com), **Continental** (© 800/231-0856; www.continental.com), **Delta** (© 800/361-1970; www.delta.com), or **US Airways** (© 800/432-9768; www.usairways.com). In the United States, Air Canada flies out of New York (Newark and LaGuardia), Miami, Tampa, Chicago, Los Angeles, and San Francisco. Air Canada has launched a small low-cost airline, **Jazz** (© 888/247-2262; www.flyjazz.ca), which connects Montréal and Québec City with Hartford, Connecticut; White Plains, New York; LaGuardia, New York City; and Newark, New Jersey.

Other carriers that serve Montréal include **Air France** (© 800/667-2746; www.airfrance.com) and **British Airways** (© 800/247-9297; www.britishairways.com). Regional airlines, such as Air

Atlantic, American Eagle, and Inter-Canadian, also fly into the city.

For details on getting from the airport to downtown and the city center, see p. 57.

TO QUEBEC CITY Québec City is served from the United States by a number of major airlines, notably Air Canada, but most air traffic comes by way of Montréal (see above) or Toronto. **Continental** flies into Québec City from international destinations outside the U.S. (ⓒ **800/525-0280;** www.continental. com). **Air Canada** (ⓒ **888/247-2262;** www.aircanada.ca) and **Tango** (ⓒ **800/ 315-1390;** www.aircanada.ca), a new, low-fare subsidiary of Air Canada, are good choices for flying from Montréal to Québec City and vice versa.

GETTING THROUGH THE AIRPORT

With the federalization of airport security, security procedures at U.S. airports are more stable and consistent than ever. Generally, you'll be fine if you arrive at the airport **1 hour** before a domestic flight and **2 hours** before an international flight; if you show up late, tell an airline employee and she'll probably whisk you to the front of the line.

Bring a **current, government-issued photo ID** such as a driver's license or passport. Keep your ID at the ready to show at check-in, the security checkpoint, and sometimes even the gate. (Children under 18 do not need government-issued photo IDs for domestic flights, but they do for international flights to most countries.)

In 2003, the TSA phased out **gate check-in** at all U.S. airports. And **e-tickets** have made paper tickets nearly obsolete. Passengers with e-tickets can beat the ticket-counter lines by using airport **electronic kiosks** or even **online check-in** from your home computer. Online check-in involves logging on to your airline's website, accessing your reservation,

and printing out your boarding pass—and the airline may even offer you bonus miles to do so! If you're using a kiosk at the airport, bring the credit card you used to book the ticket or your frequent-flier card. Print out your boarding pass from the kiosk and simply proceed to the security checkpoint with your pass and a photo ID. If you're checking bags or looking to snag an exit-row seat, you will be able to do so using most airline kiosks. Even the smaller airlines are employing the kiosk system, but always call your airline to make sure these alternatives are available. **Curbside check-in** is also a good way to avoid lines, although a few airlines still ban curbside check-in; call before you go.

Security checkpoint lines are getting shorter than they were during 2001 and 2002, but some doozies remain. If you have trouble standing for long periods of time, tell an airline employee; the airline will provide a wheelchair. Speed up security by **not wearing metal objects** such as big belt buckles. If you've got metallic body parts, a note from your doctor can prevent a long chat with the security screeners. Keep in mind that only **ticketed passengers** are allowed past security, except for folks escorting passengers with disabilities or children.

Federalization has stabilized **what you can carry on** and **what you can't.** The general rule is that sharp things are out, nail clippers are okay, and food and beverages must be passed through the X-ray machine—but that security screeners can't make you drink from your coffee cup. Bring food in your carry-on rather than checking it, as explosive-detection machines used on checked luggage have been known to mistake food (especially chocolate, for some reason) for bombs. Travelers in the U.S. are allowed one carry-on bag, plus a "personal item" such as a purse, briefcase, or laptop bag. Carry-on hoarders can stuff all sorts of things

Travel in the Age of Bankruptcy

Several major U.S. airlines are struggling to avoid bankruptcy, due in large part to competition with younger discount lines. To protect yourself, **buy tickets with a credit card,** as the Fair Credit Billing Act guarantees that you can get your money back from the credit card company if a travel supplier goes under (and if you request the refund within 60 days of the bankruptcy). **Travel insurance** can also help, but make sure it covers against "carrier default" for your specific travel provider. And be aware that if a U.S. airline goes bust mid-trip, a 2001 federal law requires other carriers to take you to your destination (albeit on a space-available basis) for a fee of no more than $25, provided you rebook within 60 days of the cancellation.

into a laptop bag; as long as it has a laptop in it, it's still considered a personal item. The Transportation Security Administration (TSA) has issued a list of restricted items; check its website (www.tsa.gov/public/index.jsp) for details.

Airport screeners may decide that your checked luggage needs to be searched by hand. You can now purchase luggage locks that allow screeners to open and relock a checked bag if hand-searching is necessary. Look for Travel Sentry certified locks at luggage or travel shops and Brookstone stores (you can buy them online at www.brookstone.com). These locks, approved by the TSA, can be opened by luggage inspectors with a special code or key. For more information on the locks, visit www.travelsentry.org. If you use something other than TSA-approved locks, your lock will be cut off your suitcase if a TSA agent needs to hand-search your luggage.

FLYING FOR LESS: TIPS FOR GETTING THE BEST AIRFARE

Passengers sharing the same airplane cabin rarely pay the same fare. Travelers who need to purchase tickets at the last minute, change their itinerary at a moment's notice, or fly one-way often get stuck paying the premium rate. Here are some ways to keep your airfare costs down.

- Passengers who can book their ticket **long in advance** or who **fly midweek** or **at less-trafficked hours** will pay a fraction of the full fare. If your schedule is flexible, say so, and ask if you can secure a cheaper fare by changing your flight plans.

- You can also save on airfares by keeping an eye out in local newspapers for **promotional specials** or **fare wars,** when airlines lower prices on their most popular routes. You rarely see fare wars offered for peak travel times, but if you can travel in the off-months, you may snag a bargain.

- Search **the Internet** for cheap fares (see "Planning Your Trip Online," earlier in this chapter).

- Try to book a ticket **in its country of origin.** For instance, if you're planning a one-way flight from Johannesburg to Bombay, a South Africa–based travel agent will probably have the lowest fares. For multi-leg trips, book in the country of the first leg; for example, book New York–London–Amsterdam–Rome–New York in the U.S.

- Join **frequent-flier clubs.** Accrue enough miles, and you'll be rewarded with free flights and elite status. It's free, and you'll get the best choice of seats, faster response to phone inquiries, and prompter service if your luggage is stolen, if your flight is canceled or delayed, or if you want to change your seat. You don't need to fly to build frequent-flier miles—**frequent-flier credit cards** can provide thousands of miles for doing your everyday shopping.

LONG-HAUL FLIGHTS: HOW TO STAY COMFORTABLE

Long flights can be trying; stuffy air and cramped seats can make you feel as if you're being sent parcel post in a small box. But with a little advance planning, you can make an otherwise unpleasant experience almost bearable.

- Your choice of airline and airplane will definitely affect your legroom. Find out which ones are most accommodating at www.seatguru.com, a site with extensive details about almost every seat on six major U.S. airlines. For international airlines, research firm Skytrax has posted a list of average seat pitches at www.air linequality.com.
- Emergency exit seats and bulkhead seats typically have the most legroom. Emergency exit seats are usually held back to be assigned the day of a flight (to ensure that the seat is filled by someone able-bodied). It's worth getting to the ticket counter early to snag one of these spots for a long flight. Keep in mind that bulkheads are where airlines often put baby bassinets, so you may be sitting next to an infant.
- To have two seats for yourself, try for an aisle seat in a center section toward the back of coach. If you're traveling with a companion, book an aisle and a window seat. Middle seats are usually booked last, so chances are good you'll end up with three seats to yourselves. And in the event that a third passenger is assigned the middle seat, he or she will probably be more than happy to trade for a window or an aisle.

- Ask about entertainment options. Many airlines offer seatback video systems where you get to choose your movies or play video games—but only on some of their planes. (Boeing 777s are your best bet.)
- To sleep, avoid the last row of any section or a row in front of an emergency exit, as these seats are the least likely to recline. Avoid seats near highly trafficked toilet areas. You also may want to reserve a window seat so that you can rest your head and avoid being bumped in the aisle.
- Get up, walk around, and stretch every 60 to 90 minutes to keep your blood flowing. This helps avoid deep vein thrombosis, or "economy-class syndrome," a rare but sometimes deadly condition that can be caused by sitting in cramped conditions for too long.
- Drink water before, during, and after your flight to combat the lack of humidity in airplane cabins—which can be drier than the Sahara. Bring a bottle of water onboard. Avoid alcohol, which will dehydrate you.

BY TRAIN

For **VIA Rail** information, call ✆ **888/ VIA-RAIL** (842-7245) or log on to www. viarail.ca.

TO MONTREAL   Montréal is a major terminus on Canada's **VIA Rail** network, with its station, **Gare Centrale,** at 935 rue de la Gauchetière ouest (✆ **514/989-2626**). The city is served by comfortable VIA Rail trains—some equipped with dining cars, sleeping cars, and cellphones—from other cities in Canada. There is scheduled service to Québec City, and to and from Ottawa, Toronto, Winnipeg, and points west. At this writing, **Amtrak** (✆ **800/USA-RAIL [872-7245];** www.amtrak.com) has one train a day to Montréal from Washington and New York that makes intermediate stops.

Called the *Adirondack,* it is a no-frills, coach-only affair, and very slow, but its scenic route passes along the eastern shore of the Hudson River and west of Lake Champlain. The *Adirondack* takes about 10½ hours from New York if all goes well, but delays aren't unusual.

Passengers from Chicago can get to Montréal most directly by taking Amtrak to Toronto, then switching to VIA Rail.

Fairmont The Queen Elizabeth (Le Reine Elizabeth) hotel is located directly above the train station in Montréal, and less expensive lodging is only a short cab or Métro ride away. Seniors 62 and older are eligible for a 15% discount on some Amtrak trains on the U.S. segment of the trip. VIA Rail has a 10% senior discount. Don't forget to bring along proof of citizenship (a passport or birth certificate) to use when crossing the border.

TO QUEBEC CITY Québec City's train station, the **Gare du Palais,** is in the Lower Town at 450 rue de la Gare-du-Palais (© **418/692-3940**). At least four trains run between Montréal and Québec City daily between 7am and 11pm, and they have snack and beverage services. Travel time between the two cities is about 3 hours. One-way fares vary substantially, with many kinds of discounts for seniors and students, and different fares for different days of departure, but round-trip prices generally run from about C$87 (US$70) for supersaver economy class to around C$175 (US$140) for first class, which provides meal service and more legroom.

BY BUS

TO MONTREAL Montréal's main bus terminal is the **Terminus Voyageur,** 505 bd. de Maisonneuve est (© **514/842-2281**). The Voyageur company operates buses between here and all parts of Québec, with frequent runs through the Cantons-de-l'Est to Sherbrooke, to the various villages in the Laurentians, and to

Québec City. Morning, noon, early afternoon, and midnight buses cover the distance between Toronto and Montréal in less than 7 hours. From Boston or New York, there is daily bus service to Montréal on **Greyhound** (© **800/229-9424** or 514/843-8495; www.greyhound.com) and between New York and Montréal on **Adirondack Trailways** (© **800/858-8555**). The trip from Boston takes about 8 hours; from New York City, it takes 9 hours. Both companies have departures from New York City five times daily.

TO QUEBEC CITY From New York or Boston, take **Greyhound** (© **800/229-9424**) to Montréal and change for the bus to Québec City, a 3-hour ride away. The bus traffic between Québec City and Montréal is frequent, with express buses from **Orléans Express** (© **514/842-2281** in Montréal, or **418/524-4692** in Québec City) running almost every hour on the hour from 7am to 1am. The bus line also links Québec City to the rest of Québec province, with connections to the rest of Canada. Ask about excursion tickets and discounts for seniors and children.

BY CAR

Highway distances and speed limits are given in kilometers (km) in Canada. The speed limit on the autoroutes (limited-access highways) is 100kmph (62 mph), although enforcement is lax. In the unlikely event you are stopped, there is a stiff penalty for not wearing seatbelts. And if you possess a radar detector, it can be confiscated, even if it isn't connected. Passengers must buckle up in the backseat as well as in the driver's and passenger's seats up front.

Members of the **American Automobile Association (AAA)** should bring along their membership cards. The 24-hour hot line for emergency service provided by the **Canadian Automobile Association (CAA),** which is affiliated with AAA, is © **514/861-7575** in

Montréal and ✆ **418/624-0708** in Québec City. Headquarters for CAA-Québec is 444 rue Bouvier, Québec City, PQ G2J 1E3.

For information on road conditions in and around Québec City from November through mid-April, there is a 24-hour hot line (✆ **418/643-6830**). For the same information in Montréal, call ✆ **514/284-2363**; outside Montréal, call ✆ **514/636-3248**.

TO MONTREAL Interstate 87 runs due north from New York City to link up with Canada's Autoroute 15 at the border, and the entire 644km (400-mile) journey is on expressways. Likewise, from Boston, I-93 north joins I-89 just south of Concord, New Hampshire. At White River Junction there is a choice between continuing on I-89 to Lake Champlain, crossing the lake by roads and bridges to join I-87 and Canada Autoroute 15 north, or picking up I-91 at White River Junction to go due north toward Sherbrooke, Québec. At the border, I-91 becomes Canada Route 55 and joins Canada Route 10 west through Estrie to Montréal. The Trans-Canada Highway, which connects both ends of the country, runs right through Montréal. From Boston to Montréal is about 515km (320 miles); from Toronto, 540km (335 miles); from Ottawa, 190km (118 miles). Once you're in Montréal, Québec City is an easy 3-hour drive.

TO QUEBEC CITY Québec City is slightly more than 805km (500 miles) from New York, and less than 644km (400 miles) from Boston. Coming from New York and points farther south, pick up Interstate 91 at New Haven, and follow it right up to the Canadian border. From Boston, take I-93 out of the city and link up with I-91 at St. Johnsbury, Vermont. After crossing the border, I-91 becomes Québec Autoroute 55, to Sherbrooke and Drummondville. From Sherbrooke, there is a choice. To make the trip quickly, take Autoroute 55 to Autoroute 20. But Route 116, which heads northeast from Richmond, midway between Sherbrooke and Drummondville, is more scenic, if a bit slower.

On the approach to the city, follow signs for Pont Pierre-Laporte. After crossing the bridge, turn right onto boulevard Wilfrid-Laurier (Rte. 175), which later changes names and becomes the Grande-Allée. Past the Old City walls it becomes rue St-Louis, which leads straight to the Château Frontenac. For the most scenic entrance into the city, take an immediate exit onto boulevard Champlain after crossing the bridge, and turn left at the entrance to Parc des Champs-de-Bataille (Battlefields Park), up a steep hill to follow chemin Grande-Allée to the Musée du Québec. Drive halfway around the circle in front of the museum, and then take avenue Montcalm-Wolfe to the Grande-Allée and turn right.

FROM MONTREAL TO QUEBEC CITY (& VICE VERSA) When you're driving to Québec City from Montréal (a car can be rented in the train station), Autoroute 40, which runs along the north shore of the St. Lawrence, is faster than Autoroute 20, on the south shore. The trip takes less than 3 hours without stops.

11 Packages for the Independent Traveler

Before you start your search for the lowest airfare, you may want to consider booking your flight as part of a travel package. Package tours are not the same thing as escorted tours. Package tours are simply a way to buy the airfare, accommodations, and other elements of your trip (such as car rentals, airport transfers, and sometimes even activities) at the same time and often at discounted prices, amounting to one-stop shopping. Packages are sold in bulk to tour operators—who resell them to the public at a cost that usually undercuts standard rates.

Air Canada (☎ **800/247-2262;** www.aircanada.ca) assembles custom packages that include round-trip air, lodging, sightseeing, and some meals in Québec City, Montréal, and Laurentian resorts.

Yankee Holidays (☎ **800/225-2550;** www.yankee-holidays.com) has packages of 2 to 5 nights in Montréal, Mont-Tremblant, and Québec City. Dinners at prominent restaurants are often included, as is VIP admission to the Montréal Casino, plus bus tours and harbor cruises. Airfare is optional.

One good source of package deals is the airlines themselves. Most major airlines offer air/land packages, including **American Airlines Vacations** (☎ 800/321-2121; www.aavacations.com), **Delta Vacations** (☎ 800/221-6666; www.deltavacations.com), **Continental Airlines Vacations** (☎ 800/301-3800; www.covacations.com), and **United Vacations** (☎ 888/854-3899; www.unitedvacations.com). Several big **online travel agencies**—Expedia, Travelocity, Orbitz, Site59, and Lastminute.com—also do a brisk business in packages. If you're unsure about the pedigree of a smaller packager, check with the Better Business Bureau in the city where the company is based, or go online to www.bbb.org. If a packager won't tell you where they're based, don't fly with them.

Travel packages are also listed in the travel section of your local Sunday newspaper. Or check ads in the national travel magazines such as *Arthur Frommer's Budget Travel Magazine, Travel & Leisure, National Geographic Traveler,* and *Condé Nast Traveler.*

Package tours can vary by leaps and bounds. Some offer a better class of hotels than others. Some offer the same hotels for lower prices. Some offer flights on scheduled airlines, while others book charters. Some limit your choice of accommodations and travel days. You are often required to make a large payment upfront. On the plus side, packages can save you money, offering group prices but allowing for independent travel. Some even let you add on a few guided excursions or escorted day trips (also at prices lower than if you booked them yourself) without booking an entirely escorted tour.

Before you invest in a package tour, get some answers. Ask about the **accommodations choices** and prices for each. Then look up the hotels' reviews in a Frommer's guide and check their rates online for your specific dates of travel. You'll also want to find out what **type of room** you get. If you need a certain type of room, ask for it; don't take whatever is thrown your way. Request a nonsmoking room, a quiet room, a room with a view, or whatever you fancy.

Finally, look for **hidden expenses.** Ask whether airport departure fees and taxes, for example, are included in the total cost.

12 Escorted General-Interest Tours

Escorted tours are structured group tours with leaders. The price usually includes everything from airfare to hotels, meals, tours, admission costs, and local transportation.

Tauck Tours (☎ **800/468-2825** or 203/226-6911; www.tauck.com) has a 7-day, 6-night tour that includes Vermont, New Hampshire, Montréal, and Québec

City. It's offered spring through October, and it provides the opportunity to view the fall foliage in both countries. For different perspectives, the company has cruises to Kingston (Ontario), Ottawa, Toronto, Montréal, and Québec City, as well as a week's combined rail, boat, and coach tour from Montréal around the Gaspé Peninsula to Charlevoix and Québec City.

Many people derive a certain ease and security from escorted trips. Escorted tours—whether by bus, motorcoach, train, or boat—let travelers sit back and enjoy their trip without having to spend lots of time behind the wheel or worrying about details. You know your costs upfront, and there are few surprises. Escorted tours can take you to the maximum number of sights in the minimum amount of time with the least amount of hassle—you don't have to sweat over the plotting and planning of a vacation schedule. Escorted tours are particularly convenient for people with limited mobility. They can also be a great way to make new friends.

On the downside, an escorted tour often requires a big deposit upfront, and lodging and dining choices are predetermined. You'll get little opportunity for serendipitous interactions with locals. The tours can be jampacked with activities, leaving little room for individual sightseeing, whim, or adventure—plus they also often focus only on the heavily touristed sites, so you miss out on the lesser-known gems.

Before you invest in an escorted tour, ask about the **cancellation policy:** Is a deposit required? Can they cancel the trip if they don't get enough people? Do you get a refund if they cancel? If *you* cancel? How late can you cancel if you are unable to go? When do you pay in full? *Note:* If you choose an escorted tour, think strongly about purchasing trip-cancellation insurance, especially if the tour operator asks you to pay upfront. See the section "Travel Insurance," p. 23.

You'll also want to get a complete **schedule** of the trip to find out how much sightseeing is planned each day and whether enough time has been allotted for relaxing or wandering solo.

The **size** of the group is also important to know upfront. Generally, the smaller the group, the more flexible the itinerary, and the less time you'll spend waiting for people to get on and off the bus. Find out the **demographics** of the group as well. What is the age range? What is the gender breakdown? Is this mostly a trip for couples or singles?

Discuss what is included in the **price.** You may have to pay for transportation to and from the airport. A box lunch may be included in an excursion, but drinks might cost extra. Tips may not be included. Find out whether you will be charged if you decide to opt out of certain activities or meals.

Before you invest in a package tour, get some answers. Ask about the **accommodations choices** and prices for each. Then look up the hotels' reviews in a Frommer's guide and check their rates online for your specific dates of travel. You'll also want to find out what **type of room** you get. If you need a certain type

Cruising to Montréal & Québec City

Cruises from New York and New England through the Maritime Provinces and down the St. Lawrence to Québec City and Montréal are increasingly popular, especially from June through the foliage season. Among the lines offering these cruises, which are usually 6 to 12 days long, are **Clipper** (© 800/325-0010; www.clippercruise.com), **Crystal Cruises** (© 866/446-6625; www.crystalcruises.com), **Holland America** (© 877/724-5425; www.hollandamerica.com), **Norwegian** (© 800/327-7030; www.ncl.com), **Princess** (© 800/774-6237; www.princess.com), **Seabourn** (© 800/929-9391; www.seabourn.com), and **Silversea** (© 888/313-8883; www.silversea.com).

of room, ask for it; don't take whatever is thrown your way. Request a nonsmoking room, a quiet room, a room with a view, or whatever you fancy.

Finally, if you plan to travel alone, you'll need to know if a **single supplement** will be charged and if the company can match you up with a roommate.

13 Tips on Accommodations

SAVING ON YOUR HOTEL ROOM

The **rack rate** is the maximum rate that a hotel charges for a room. Hardly anybody pays this price, however. To lower the cost of your room:

- **Ask about special rates or other discounts.** Always ask whether a room less expensive than the first one quoted is available, or whether any special rates apply to you. You may qualify for corporate, student, military, senior, or other discounts. Mention membership in AAA, AARP, frequent-flier programs, or trade unions, which may entitle you to special deals as well. Find out the hotel policy on children—do kids stay free in the room or is there a special rate?

- **Dial direct.** When booking a room in a chain hotel, you'll often get a better deal by calling the individual hotel's reservation desk than by calling the chain's 800 (or 888) reservation number. The 800 operators are rarely in the hotel in which you're interested or even in the same city, and they have little authority to negotiate. The hotel's reservation desk, on the other hand, uses a "yield management" chart, which gives the agent a clear idea of how much wiggle room he or she has in adjusting rates according to dates, seasons, events, and demand.

- **Book online.** Many hotels offer Internet-only discounts, or supply rooms to Priceline, Hotwire, or Expedia at rates much lower than the ones you can get through the hotel itself.

- **Remember the law of supply and demand.** Resort hotels are most crowded and therefore most expensive on weekends, so discounts are usually available for midweek stays. Business hotels in downtown locations are busiest during the week, so you can expect big discounts over the weekend. Many hotels have high-season and low-season prices, and booking the day after "high season" ends can mean big discounts.

- **Look into group or long-stay discounts.** If you come as part of a large group, you should be able to negotiate a bargain rate, since the hotel can then guarantee occupancy in a number of rooms. Likewise, if you're planning a long stay (at least 5 days), you might qualify for a discount. As a general rule, expect 1 night free after a 7-night stay.

- **Avoid excess charges and hidden costs.** When you book a room, ask whether the hotel charges for parking. Use your own cellphone, pay phones, or prepaid phone cards instead of dialing direct from hotel phones, which usually have exorbitant rates. And don't be tempted by the room's minibar offerings: Most hotels charge through the nose for water, soda, and snacks. Finally, ask about local taxes and service charges, which can increase the cost of a room by 15% or more. If a hotel insists upon tacking on a surprise "energy surcharge" that wasn't mentioned at check-in or a "resort fee" for amenities you didn't use, you can often make a case for getting it removed.

14 Recommended Reading

Writing from the perspective of a minority within a minority, the late Jewish Anglophone Mordecai Richler inveighed against the excesses of Québec's separatists and language zealots in a barrage of books and critical essays in newspapers and magazines. His outrage and mordant wit can be sampled in *Oh Canada! Oh Québec!* (Knopf, 1992) and *Home Sweet Home: My Canadian Album* (Knopf, 1984; paperback, Penguin, 1985). An amusing, less caustic look at the Anglophone-Francophone conflict is provided by *The Anglo Guide to Survival in Québec* (Eden Press, 1983). A serious, relatively balanced view—with a slight lean to the French-Canadian side of the issue—is given by Brian Young and John A. Dickinson in *A Short History of Québec: A Socio-Economic Perspective* (Copp Clark Pitman Ltd., 1988). One of the authors taught at McGill University, the other at the Université de Montréal. *Sacré Blue* (Macfarlane Walter & Ross, 2002, in paperback) carries the subtitle "An Unsentimental Journey Through Québec." Written by Montréal journalist Taras Grescoe, it presents his affectionate but balanced assessment of his adopted province.

3

Suggested Montréal & Québec City Itineraries

While Québec is vast, larger than Texas, most of its people live in the 121km (75-mile) band immediately adjacent to the northern borders of the states of New York and New England. Its major cities and towns, including Montréal and the capital of Québec City, as well as most of its developed resort and scenic areas, lie within easy reach. For that reason, many visitors, especially those who live in the northeastern U.S., choose to drive their own cars.

While portions of the following itineraries are more readily accomplished with a car, there are intercity buses and shuttle services to reach major destinations in the outer districts. Public transportation in the cities is good to excellent, so there is little need for a personal vehicle while enjoying their attractions. Further, if you plan to combine visits to both Montréal and Québec City, train service between them is frequent, fairly priced, and of high quality. With a few adjustments, then, an entire Québec vacation can be completed without a personal or rental car. That's often desirable, especially when weather is variable, or when winter carnivals or skiing are prime reasons for going.

On the assumption that most visitors plan to visit either Montréal or Québec City but not both, the two itineraries focus on each of those cities and their environs.

1 The Best of Montréal in 1 Day

This itinerary outlines a carefully paced exploration of this cosmopolitan city with ample time for shopping, random exploring, or simply lingering in sidewalk cafes. While it assumes that yours will be a warm-weather visit, there are periodic suggestions for the winter months. Even if you're staying only 1 night, do book a room in one of the new boutique hotels in Vieux-Montréal, the old quarter beside the port on the Saint Lawrence River. Visitors find themselves drawn again and again to the plazas and narrow cobblestone streets of this 18th- and 19th-century neighborhood, so you might as well be based there. *Start: Vieux-Montréal.*

❶ Place d'Armes ⟡⟡⟡

Begin the day in the heart of **Vieux-Montréal** ⟡⟡⟡, at the place where the French settlers fought a bloody but decisive battle with the Iroquois in 1653. At the southeast corner of the plaza is the oldest building in the city, the **Séminaire de St-Sulpice** (p. 134), erected by Sulpician priests who arrived in 1657. Next to it is the **Basilique Notre-Dame** ⟡⟡⟡ (p. 116), an 1824 church with a stunning interior of intricately gilded rare woods. Its acoustics are so clear that Pavarotti has sung there several times. If it's still early, pick up "Walking Tour 1" in chapter 8, which will take you past every historic structure in Vieux-Montréal.

❷ Pointe-à-Callière ✿✿✿

From the Basilique Notre-Dame, walk down the slope to the riverside edge of the district and **Pointe-à-Callière,** the Museum of Archaeology and History. After viewing the multimedia show above the ruins of the ancient city, descend below the streets to discover remnants of Amerindian camps and early French settlements unearthed and displayed where they were found. See p. 117.

> **3 OLIVE & GOURMANDO**
> A couple of cobblestone blocks away is Olive & Gourmando. It started out as a bakery, added prepared foods, and evolved into a full-service cafe. Fresh baguettes march out the door throughout the morning, but you can still put together an appetizing picnic lunch to carry to the nearby park of the Vieux-Port. 351 rue St-Paul ouest. ✆ 514/350-1083. See p. 111.

❹ Downtown

After lunch, take the Métro to the Peel station and walk to the **Musée McCord d'Histoire Canadienne,** opposite the campus of English-language McGill University. The somewhat eccentric collections are the gifts of 19th-century benefactors, a kind of cataloged provisional attic, including objects gathered from Québec's native peoples. See p. 113.

From the McCord, turn west up Sherbrooke to:

❺ Musée des Beaux-Arts ✿✿✿

This is the city's most important fine-arts museum. The original building opened in 1912, and was augmented by the addition of a modern annex across the street in 1991. The ever-expanding permanent collection includes painting and sculpture from the Middle Ages to the 20th century, supplemented by displays from Oceania and Africa. An excellent art and gift shop is attached. See p. 112.

❻ Rue Crescent ✿✿

By now, you deserve a stroll and a sit-down, a little shopping and people-watching. Walk south on rue Crescent. At first, it's lined with boutiques both hip and chic; soon it merges into downtown's primary nightlife district. By 5pm on a Thursday, at least when it's warm enough not to see your breath, the pedestrian traffic thickens and grows ever more intriguing.

> **7 SIR WINSTON CHURCHILL PUB**
> Grab a sidewalk seat at the Sir Winston Churchill Pub. It's been an epicenter of the rue Crescent singles scene for ages, filled with 20- and 30-somethings seeking companionship for the coming weekend. The hamburgers look better than they are, so nurse a pint or two of cold beer instead, while taking in the passing parade. 1459 rue Crescent near rue Ste-Catherine. ✆ 514/288-0623. See p. 172.

When it's time for dinner, there are several worthy restaurants on this and adjacent streets suggested in chapter 6.

2 The Best of Montréal in 2 Days

With the absolute essentials of historic Old Montréal and downtown Anglophone cultural institutions under your belt, prepare to take a journey deep into French Montréal. When the Olympics were awarded to Montréal for 1976, it was the plan of the municipal authorities to erect some of the principal venues in the eastern, overwhelmingly

Suggested Montréal Itineraries

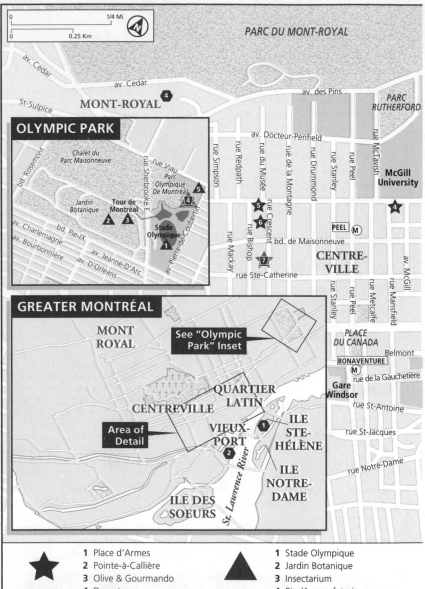

DAY 1

1 Place d'Armes
2 Pointe-à-Callière
3 Olive & Gourmando
4 Downtown
5 Musée des Beaux Arts
6 Rue Crescent
7 Sir Winston Churchill Pub

DAY 2

1 Stade Olympique
2 Jardin Botanique
3 Insectarium
4 Biodôme cafeteria
5 Biodôme de Montréal
6 St-Denis & St-Laurent
7 Fonduementale

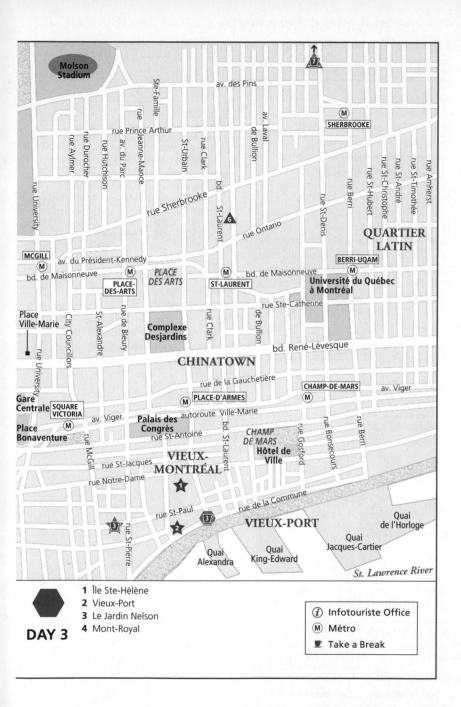

Molson Stadium

av. des Pins

Ste-Famille

rue Prince Arthur

rue Aylmer
rue Durocher
rue Hutchison
av. du Parc
rue Jeanne-Mance
St-Urbain
rue Clark
av. de Bullion
av. Laval

SHERBROOKE (M)

rue St-Christophe
rue St-André
rue St-Timothée
rue Amherst

rue Sherbrooke

bd. St-Laurent
St-Laurent 6

rue Ontario

rue St-Denis
rue Berri
rue St-Hubert

QUARTIER LATIN

MCGILL (M)

av. du Président-Kennedy

bd. de Maisonneuve

(M) PLACE-DES-ARTS

PLACE DES ARTS

(M) ST-LAURENT

bd. de Maisonneuve

BERRI-UQAM

Université du Québec à Montréal

rue Ste-Catherine

Place Ville-Marie

City Councillors
St-Alexandre
rue de Bleury

Complexe Desjardins

rue Clark
de Bullion

bd. René-Lévesque

rue University

CHINATOWN

rue de la Gauchetière

CHAMP-DE-MARS

av. Viger

Gare Centrale

SQUARE VICTORIA (M)

av. Viger

PLACE-D'ARMES (M)

(M)

Place Bonaventure

Palais des Congrès

rue McGill

rue St-Antoine

autoroute Ville-Marie

bd. St-Laurent

CHAMP DE MARS

rue Gosford
rue Bonsecours
rue Berri

rue St-Jacques

rue Notre-Dame

VIEUX-MONTRÉAL
1

Hôtel de Ville

rue St-Pierre

rue St-Paul

3

2

3

rue de la Commune

VIEUX-PORT

Quai de l'Horloge

Quai Alexandra

Quai King-Edward

Quai Jacques-Cartier

St. Lawrence River

DAY 3

1 Île Ste-Hélène
2 Vieux-Port
3 Le Jardin Nelson
4 Mont-Royal

ⓘ Infotouriste Office
Ⓜ Métro
♨ Take a Break

Francophone precincts of the city. **Start:** *Take the Métro to the Viau station (it's at some distance, and a taxi would be very expensive).*

---

❶ Stade Olympique

The controversial Olympic Stadium was long scorned as the "Big Owe" due to cost overruns that provoked elevated taxes. Its fabric roof was meant to be retractable, but never did work to anyone's satisfaction. Nevertheless, it was the home of baseball's National League Expos until the team moved to Washington, D.C., in 2005. It now houses a natatorium with six pools open to the public and has an inclined tower over 180m high (600 ft.) with a funicular that scoots to the observation level at the top in seconds. The vista afforded reaches as far as 56km (35 miles) over the city and the mountains beyond. See p. 119.

A shuttle van can carry you from the Stade Olympique to the Jardin Botanique (Botanical Garden).

❷ Jardin Botanique ✶✶✶

The garden boasts 74 hectares (185 acres) of plants and flowers in 31 specialized sections, including those sponsored by China and Japan. Ten greenhouses assure there are things to see all year, although from May to September is best. A small train makes regular runs through the gardens. Plan to spend at least an hour or two. See p. 119.

❸ Insectarium ✶

Kids love the collection of more than 3,000 mounted and live bugs, beetles, spiders, and other sinister critters gathered in the two-story building on the grounds of the Jardin Botanique. Adults are more likely to enjoy the summer displays of gorgeous specimens in the adjacent Butterfly House. During November and December, there are "Insect Tastings," which are exactly that.

Take the shuttle back to the Olympic Stadium and walk to the adjacent Biodôme.

☕ BIODÔME

You might want to eat before you take on the Biodôme (see below), which can easily occupy another hour or so, especially if you have youngsters in tow. The in-house cafeteria and casual restaurant won't soon win any gastronomic awards, but it's at least serviceable, and there's also an adjoining game room for kids, called Naturalia. 4777 av. Pierre-de-Coubertin (next to Olympic Stadium). ℭ 514/868-3000. See p. ###.

❺ Biodôme de Montréal ✶✶✶

Originally a velodrome built for the 1976 Olympics, this unique facility's four fascinating sections replicate four ecosystems, complete with 4,000 trees and plants, more than 6,000 animals, and four distinctive climates, from tropical to polar. See p. 118.

Take the Métro to Square Victoria or Place d'Armes.

❻ St-Denis & St-Laurent ✶✶

After all this, it might well be midafternoon, time to get back to your hotel for a recuperative lie-down.

When rested, take the path of generations of immigrants from your base in Vieux-Montréal—walk due north on boulevard St-Laurent (French for Saint Lawrence). St-Laurent passes through the expanding **Quartier Chinois (Chinatown),** past the western edge of the **Gay Village** and the bohemian **Quartier Latin (Latin Quarter),** and into the lower precincts of the Plateau Mont-Royal. Turn right along the pedestrian rue Prince Arthur, and reach rue St-Denis. Turn north (left). There are no must-see monuments or sights along this route, so surrender to the color and vitality of the heart of French Montréal.

"Walking Tour 3" in chapter 8 (p. 144) provides guidance to some notable shops and cafes along the way.

> **7 FONDUEMENTALE**
>
> If it's time for dinner, chapter 6 recommends at least a dozen likely restaurants along this route. But if it's still early or you'd prefer to eat lightly, it's hard to beat the longtime favorite, Fonduementale. Fondues and the related Swiss specialty raclette come in many guises, from snacks to full meals. There are a terrace in front and a garden in back. 4325 rue St-Denis. 🕐 **514/499-1446.** See p. 144.

You're in the right neighborhood if you want to follow dinner with a bit of bar- or club-hopping. The Main, as boulevard St-Laurent is known, is lined with amiable and/or hard-driving places to bend an elbow and attend to music, from around avenue du Mont-Royal south to rue Sherbrooke.

3 The Best of Montréal in 3 Days

Following these suggestions, you have now visited the primary must-see sights. On this third day, it's time to slack off a bit, combining a morning of re-created history with idylls in the park and a ride on the St. Lawrence—tranquil or thrilling, your choice. *Start: Take the Métro to the Parc Jean-Drapeau stop. Follow the signs to the Vieux Fort and Musée David M. Stewart, about a 15-minute walk.*

❶ Île Ste-Hélène 🛪

The island in the middle of the St. Lawrence was doubled in size with landfill for the 1967 Expo World's Fair to allow for the construction of national pavilions. A facility that dated from long before that event was the moated fortress ordered built by the Duke of Wellington and completed in 1824. It is now the **Musée David M. Stewart** 🛪, the original low stone barracks of the fort now housing a museum of military history from then until when the British left in 1840. There are parades and simulated military ceremonies from late June to late August. While the island is pleasant for strolling, with its views of the downtown skyline, there's no compelling reason to stay much longer. See p. 123.

Take the Métro to place d'Armes and walk down to the Vieux-Port.

❷ Vieux-Port 🛪🛪

A grey, ragged industrial/commercial harbor less than 20 years ago, the Old

Port at the edge of Vieux-Montréal was transformed into a broad linear park with frequent live concerts, abundant recreational activities, and several attractions of note. Principal among these is **Le Centre des Sciences** (p. 116), King Edward Pier, which contains a popular IMAX cinema in addition to room after room of computer-driven interactive displays sure to enthrall your inner geek. At the east end of the park, near the old clock tower, is the departure point for **Saute Moutons** (🕐 **514/284-9607**). The company entices adventurous spirits with special flat-bottomed boats that travel upriver in wet and wild challenges to the roiling Lachine Rapids. As well, there are several companies that provide more sedate river cruises. And that's not all: Several agencies in or bordering the park rent bicycles and in-line skates by the hour or day. See p. 118.

③ LE JARDIN NELSON
As you will already have noticed, Vieux-Montréal harbors a considerable number of eating places catering to most tastes and wallets. One of the most visible and popular is Le Jardin Nelson. Head for the garden in back if the weather is right, for on many days there are live musical performances at lunch hour. The menu has something for everyone, from soups, sandwiches, and pizzas to a delectable roster of stuffed main-course and dessert crepes. 407 place Jacques-Cartier. ⓒ 514/861-5731. See p. 173.

④ Mont-Royal 𝒜𝒜

Montrealers choose to think of the hill that rises behind the spires of downtown office towers as "The Mountain" that gave the city its name, "Mont-Real." The rounded crest of the hill was made into a public park according to plans by Frederick Law Olmsted, the designer of New York's Central Park. It draws throngs of citizens to its nearly 200 hectares (500 acres) of rolling lawns and meadows throughout the year. Join them with a hike up from the Peel Métro station (if you're in reasonably good shape) or take a taxi up to Lac des Castors (Beaver Lake).

In winter, horse-drawn calèches switch wheels for runners to tour the snow-covered top. A slope above the lake allows for some gentle skiing. If you've rented bikes or skates, you'll find miles of paved trails to work out the kinks. However athletic or sedentary your appreciation of the terrain, by all means make your way to the southern edge of the mountain as dusk approaches. (Head in the general direction of the giant illuminated steel cross, erected in homage to a wooden one placed there by the founders of the city in 1642.) A building called Chalet Lookout backs a plaza that overlooks the city and the river—an unforgettable panorama. Take in the view; it's a fine way to end your stay in the Queen City of Québec.

4 The Best of Québec City in 1 Day

The capital of this singular province bears scant resemblance to Montréal. The oldest walled city north of Mexico sustains the look of a European provincial city while overlooking the expanse of the powerful St. Lawrence. Entrancing in both winter and summer, it lays out a yearlong banquet of festivals and celebrations. To take greatest advantage of all that the city has to offer, book a hotel or B&B within the walls of the Haute-Ville (Upper Town) or in the revitalized Basse-Ville (Lower Town). *Start: Château Frontenac.*

❶ Terrasse Dufferin 𝒜𝒜𝒜

First thing after unpacking and a rest, get to the **Château Frontenac** 𝒜 (p. 217)—its peaked copper roofs can be seen from everywhere. In front of the hotel is a long promenade, the Terrasse Dufferin, which affords panoramic views of the **Basse-Ville (Lower Town)** 𝒜𝒜𝒜 (p. 211) and the wide, wide river. In good weather, street performers entertain passersby, with musical saws, pan flutes, conga drums, and partially filled water glasses among their instruments.

❷ Funicular 𝒜

Take the funicular down from the north end of the Terrasse Dufferin. Traveling at a steep angle, it's enclosed in glass to take advantage of the views. (An alternative descent is via the Escalier Casse-Cou, which translates as "Breakneck Stairs" for reasons that are immediately apparent.) Both funicular and stairs wind up at rue du Petit-Champlain, down to the right, a street of shops and cafes populated largely by tourists. Save that for later. See p. 211.

Continue straight ahead down rue Sous-le-Fort, and make the first left turn.

❸ Place Royale 🏵🏵🏵

This enclosed, tilted square was the site of the first European colony in Canada and is surrounded by 17th- and 18th-century houses. The church on one side is the Eglise Notre-Dame-des-Victoires, built in 1688. Walk straight ahead past the Centre d'Interprétation de Place-Royale, on the left. At the end of the block, turn around to view a *trompe l'oeil* mural depicting citizens of the early city. See p. 240.

Continue in the same direction, making the first right turn (Rue de la Barricade) down toward the river. Turn left on rue Dalhousie and follow for a couple of blocks until you get to:

❹ Musée de la Civilisation 🏵🏵🏵

This ambitious young museum, filled with fascinating exhibits, can easily fill 2 or 3 hours. At the least, take in the permanent exhibit, *Memoires,* but there are other reasons to linger, many involving interactive displays. See p. 237.

Leaving, turn left, then left again, and right on rue du Sainte-au-Matelot.

> ### ☕ A BOUNTY OF BISTROS
> Starting at the corner of rue St-Paul and rue Sault-du-Matelot is a continuous strand of bistros and casual eating places bending around to the left on rue St-Paul. Almost any of them will do for a snack or a meal, but the clearest choices are 5A **L'Echaudé** 🏵, 73 rue Sault-du-Matelot (📞 **418/692-1299**), and 5B **L'Ardoise**, 71 rue St-Paul (📞 **418/694-0213**). Both offer excellent value for classic French dishes, and both have sidewalk tables in summer. The first has an edge in quality and wine list; the second is known for its mussel choices and is preferable for families.

After eating continue along St-Paul.

❻ Rue St-Paul 🏵

In the past decade or so, St-Paul has become the prime street for antiques and collectibles browsing. Turn right at rue St-Thomas and (carefully) cross busy rue St-André. Over to the left is the Marché du Vieux-Port (Old Port Market). Produce and other products of the farming island of Orleans, seen downriver beyond the market, are sold here. See p. 262.

❼ Centre d'Interpretation du Vieux-Port 🏵

To the right (South) of the market is the Old Port Interpretation Center. Run by the national park service; its displays and exhibits show the Port of Québec as it was in the mid–19th century, with costumed docents telling the story. Waterborne tours of the harbor are available at modest prices. See p. 244.

Retrace your steps along rue Dalhousie, the Château Frontenac looming up to your right. Soon you'll see the dock for the ferry to Lévis, on the opposite shore. While it's intended for commuters, it makes an inexpensive, diverting crossing in a round-trip of under an hour. See p. 246.

Upon return, the funicular is only a short walk away. After this day, you'll want to take it, not the stairs, back to the Upper Town. Alternatively, you might want to stop in for dinner at one of the bistros you've passed along the way.

5 The Best of Québec City in 2 Days

During the repeated conflicts with the British during the 18th century, the residents of New France moved to the top of the cliffs of Cap Diamant that rise behind the Basse-Ville, which is down at river level. Over the years, they threw up fortifications with battlements and artillery emplacements that eventually encircled the city as it

Suggested Québec City Itineraries

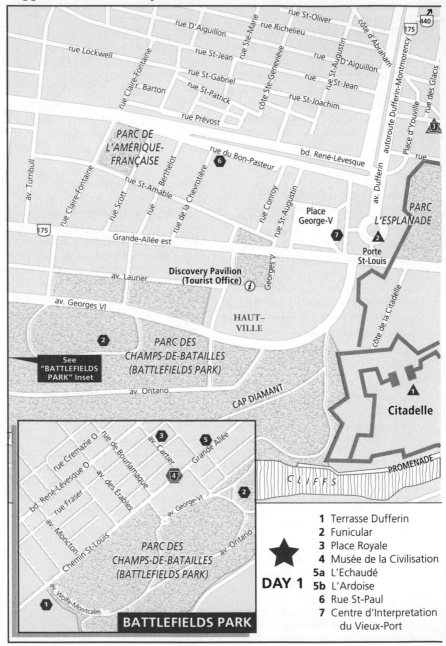

rue St-Oliver
rue D'Aiguillon
rue Richelieu
côte d'Abraham
rue Lockwell
rue St-Jean
rue Ste-Marie
rue St-Augustin
rue D'Aiguillon
rue St-Gabriel
r. Barton
rue Claire-Fontaine
rue St-Patrick
côte Ste-Geneviève
rue St-Jean
rue St-Joachim
rue Prévost

PARC DE L'AMÉRIQUE-FRANÇAISE

rue du Bon-Pasteur
bd. René-Lévesque
rue St-Amable
rue Berthelot
rue de la Chevrotière
rue Conroy
rue St-Augustin
autoroute Dufferin-Montmorency
Place d'Youville
rue des Glacis
rue
av. Turnbull
rue Claire-Fontaine
rue Scott
rue
Grande-Allée est

Place George-V

PARC L'ESPLANADE

av. Dufferin
Porte St-Louis

Georges V

Discovery Pavilion (Tourist Office)
av. Laurier
av. Georges VI

HAUT–VILLE

côte de la Citadelle

See "BATTLEFIELDS PARK" Inset

PARC DES CHAMPS-DE-BATAILLES (BATTLEFIELDS PARK)

av. Ontario
CAP DIAMANT

Citadelle

PROMENADE
CLIFFS

rue Cremazie O
rue de Bourlamaque
av. Cartier
Grande Allée
René-Lévesque O
rue Fraser
av. des Érables
av. Moncton
Chemin St-Louis
av. George-VI
av. Ontario
av. Wolfe-Montcalm

PARC DES CHAMPS-DE-BATAILLES (BATTLEFIELDS PARK)

BATTLEFIELDS PARK

DAY 1

1 Terrasse Dufferin
2 Funicular
3 Place Royale
4 Musée de la Civilisation
5a L'Echaudé
5b L'Ardoise
6 Rue St-Paul
7 Centre d'Interpretation du Vieux-Port

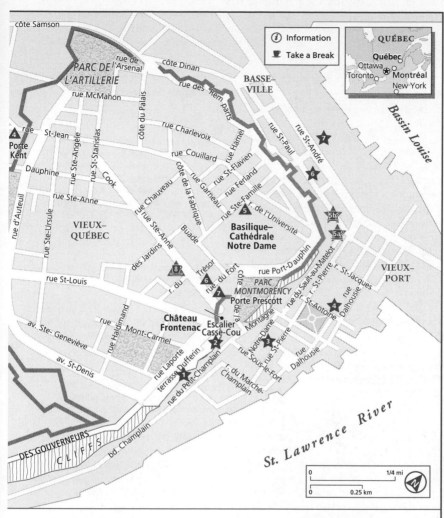

Château
Frontenac

Escalier
Cassè-Cou

Porte Prescott

PARC
MONTMORÉNCY

Basilique–
Cathédrale
Notre Dame

VIEUX–
QUÉBEC

BASSE–
VILLE

VIEUX–
PORT

PARC DE
L'ARTILLERIE

Porte
Kent

DES GOUVERNEURS CLYFFS

St. Lawrence River

Bassin Louise

QUÉBEC

Québec
Ottawa
Toronto   Montréal
New York

ⓘ Information
🍴 Take a Break

côte Samson
rue de l'Arsenal
côte Dinan
rue McMahon
rue des Remparts
rue Charlevoix
rue du Palais
côte du Palais
rue Couillard
rue Hamel
rue St-Paul
rue St-André
rue St-Jean
St-Jean
Dauphine
rue Ste-Angèle
rue St-Stanislas
Cook
rue Ste-Anne
côte de la Fabrique
rue Chauveau
rue Ste-Anne
Buade
rue Garneau
rue St-Flavien
rue Ferland
rue Ste-Famille
r. de l'Université
rue d'Auteuil
rue Ste-Ursule
des Jardins
rue St-Louis
Trésor
r. du
rue du Fort
côte de la Montagne
rue Port-Dauphin
rue du Sault-au-Matelot
r. St-Pierre
r. St-Jacques
r. St-Antoine
rue Dalhousie
av. Ste- Geneviève
rue Haldimand
rue Mont-Carmel
av. St-Denis
rue Laporte
terrasse Dufferin
rue du Petit-Champlain
rue Notre-Dame
rue Sous-le-Fort
r. du Marché-Champlain
rue St-Pierre
rue Dalhousie
bd. Champlain

0   1/4 mi
0   0.25 km

53

existed at that time. Most of them remain, albeit restored repeatedly over the years. Along with the narrow streets, leafy plazas, and leaning houses that compose the old town, they are the reason to spend the day within the walls. **Start:** *Return to the Terrasse Dufferin to begin the day. Take your camera.*

❶ La Citadelle 𝒢𝒢

Today, walk in the opposite direction on the Terrasse, south onto the staircase that goes up to what's called the Promenade des Gouverneurs. Spread below is an extension of the views seen from the Terrasse, and to the right is the La Citadelle, a partially star-shaped fortress built in anticipation of an American invasion that never happened. Walk around the rim. The fortress has a low profile, dug into the land rather than rising above it. At the far end is a courtyard where a ceremonial Changing of the Guard occurs at 10am every day in summer. It can be viewed from above, saving the admission fee and avoiding the rather boring guided tour. See p. 240.

Walk down the hill to avenue St-Denis, continuing as it drops down to the corner of rue St-Louis, the main road into the old town.

❷ Porte St-Louis to Parc de l'Artillerie

The main gate in the city walls is over to the left. Near it is a gathering place for some of the city's horse-drawn carriages. If you're in the mood and the fare doesn't seem too expensive, take a ride. Otherwise, cross over to the long greensward known as the Parc l'Esplanade and continue along rue Ste-Ursule down a steep hill to the other main gate, Porte St-Jean (a 20th-century re-creation). Next to it is the entrance to the **Parc de l'Artillerie** (p. 244), recently reconstituted as a national park. On view are an officers' mess and their quarters, and an old iron foundry, shown by costumed guides.

Return to rue St-Jean and walk west, through the gate. This is **place d'You-ville,** a well-used space with hotels, a concert hall, vending stalls, and an open-air venue for the concerts of the city's many festivals.

Bear right around the plaza.

❸ IL TEATRO

A good bet for lunch, especially if you can snare a table out under the umbrellas on the sidewalk, is Il Teatro. It's part of the hotel-theater complex Le Capitole. Pasta is a specialty, as with duck ravioli and sausage and mushrooms with linguini in an earthy demi-glace. 972 rue St-Jean. ✆ **418/694-9966.**

After lunch, walk back through the gate and down bustling rue St-Jean.

❹ Rue St-Jean

One of the liveliest of Haute-Ville streets, rue St-Jean is lined with a great variety of shops, cafes, pubs, clubs, and restaurants. A stroll down its length can easily occupy an hour or two.

At the end, bear right up the Côte de la Fabrique, passing the Hôtel de Ville (City Hall) on the right. Bear around the small plaza at the top and turn right.

❺ Basilique Notre-Dame 𝒢

What with bombardments, fires, and repeated rebuilding, this representative of the oldest Christian parish north of Mexico is nothing if not perseverant. Parts of it, including the bell tower, survive from the 1647 structure, but most of what remains is from a 1771 reconstruction. Summers, it's the site of a 30-minute sound-and-light show. See p. 248.

When leaving the church, walk along rue Baude.

❻ Rue du Trésor

This narrow pedestrian alley cuts up through the block to the Place d'Armes. It's lined with the etchings, drawings, and watercolors of artists seeking tourist dollars. Nearly all the renderings are of Québec City scenes, and while they won't soon join the collections of major museums, they are competently done and make worthwhile souvenirs. See p. 265.

Turn left at the top of the alley.

❼ Musée du Fort

This daylong walk through history may have whet your curiosity about the history of the city. While it is a commercial enterprise, the **Musée du Fort** stages a multimedia show that outlines the battles and evolutionary changes of the capital using a 37 sq. m (400sq. ft.) scale model of the city with film, light, and rousing music to tell the story. See p. 244

> **🍵 AUBERGE DU TRESOR**
> If it's too early for dinner, see if you can cadge an outdoor table at the red-roofed Auberge du Trésor, half a block from the Musée du Fort. Though meals are served, stick to coffee or a pint and save the calories for one of the superior restos described in chapter 14. 20 rue Ste-Anne. ✆ 418/694-1876.

6 The Best of Québec City in 3 Days

While the romance of the capital is largely contained within the Lower and Upper Towns, there is much to experience outside the walls. And though the suggested itineraries for the first 2 days can easily be extended over 3 days, especially if children and those of limited mobility are involved, do try to make time for at least one or two of the following attractions. *Start: Take a taxi ride to the Musée des Beaux-Arts (although it isn't too long a hike, about 30 min., for those so inclined).*

❶ Musée des Beaux-Arts du Québec 🏵🏵

Standing at the southwestern end of the Parc des Champs de Bataille (aka Plains of Abraham), the capital's most important art museum focuses on the works of Québec-born painters and sculptors. Jean-Paul Riopelle, one of the best-known Abstract-Expressionists, has his own permanent exhibition. Other galleries feature works of provincial artists from the earliest days of the colony to the present. The original 1933 museum is now connected to an adjacent structure by a glass-roofed pavilion that houses the reception area, museum shop, and cafe. Note the presence of the last, for you might wish to return for lunch at one of the better eateries in the area. See p. 241.

Walk to the adjoining building.

❷ Parc des Champs-de-Bataille 🏵🏵

Attached to the museum is a former prison that serves as an interpretation centre for the **Parc des Champs-de-Bataille (Battlefields Park)**, the 107-hectare (267-acre) parkland that is the city's playground. Tours through what were once corridors and cells of the prison incorporate sound-and-film dramatizations of Québec's history. Van and walking tours of the park are available. Along the route are Martello Towers, cycling and rollerblading paths, picnic grounds, and live theatrical and musical venues. See p. 241.

❸ Avenue Cartier

Opposite the museum, avenue Cartier is a street of intriguing shops and restaurants. Foodies will want to check out **Les Halles du Petit-Cartier,** 1191 av. Cartier, near rue Fraser. The indoor mall has shops purveying fish, meats, cheeses, produce, pâtés, and deli treats. It's open 7 days a week. Down the street is one of the largest **SAQ** outlets in the city, selling a wide selection of wines and spirits. See p. 266.

⁴ʳ GRAFFITI

You could put together an entirely satisfying *pique-nique* at Les Halles, but if you'd prefer a sit-down lunch, a solid candidate is Graffiti. It's an ebullient neighborhood establishment, a mostly Italian trattoria with more than sufficient pastas on the card, but with forays into less expected areas, such as roasted pike with leeks and toasted almonds. 1191 av. Cartier. ⓒ 418/529-4949.

⑤ Grande-Allée

Walk back toward Haute-Ville along the Grande-Allée. It's a lot easier this way, as it's mostly downhill. In about 3 blocks, the shoulder-to-shoulder rows of cafes and clubs begin, with one of the largest on the right, **Maurice** (p. 270). You might want to keep it in mind for this evening; it's a one-stop dining and entertainment emporium, with terrace bars, a good restaurant, **Voodoo Grill** 𝔉 (p. 232), and a disco.

Turn left onto rue de la Chevrotière,

⑥ edifice Marie-Guyart

Near the end of the second block, at no. 1037, just before boulevard René-Lévesque, find the entrance of this anonymous-looking office building. Look for signs and elevators directing to the *Observatoire de la Capitale*, on the 31st floor. Sky-high views of Québec City are always rewarding, and this is the highest overlook in the city. See p. 242.

Leave the building onto René-Lévesque. Bear right at the next angled corner and walk around to the front entrance of the Second Empire château commanding the space above a wide lawn.

⑦ Hôtel du Parlement

This august structure houses the legislative body that Quebecers proudly proclaim their "National Assembly." The building can be toured independently or by a free 30-minute guided tour. Among the best tours are the Assembly Chamber and the Room of the Old Legislative Council. Exiting, the Porte St-Louis is over to your left, the way back to your hotel. See p. 245.

4

Getting to Know Montréal

For a city of nearly two million inhabitants, getting to know and getting around Montréal is remarkably easy. Montréal-Trudeau Airport is only 23km (14 miles) away, and once you're in town, the Métro (subway) system is fast and efficient. Walking, of course, is the best way to enjoy and appreciate this vigorous, multidimensional city, neighborhood by neighborhood.

1 Orientation

ARRIVING

BY PLANE The **Aéroport International Pierre-Elliot-Trudeau de Montréal** (© **800/465-1213** or 514/394-7377; www.admtl.com), known less cumbersomely as Montréal-Trudeau Airport, is 23km (14 miles) southwest of downtown, and accepts nearly all commercial flights. A phased C$700-million expansion program is nearing completion. The ride into town takes less than 30 minutes if traffic isn't tangled, and a taxi trip costs C$31 (US$25) plus tip. Montréal's **Aéroport Mirabel,** 55km (34 miles) northwest of the city, used to accept international carriers from outside North America, but now receives only freight and charter flights.

Montréal-Trudeau is served by **L'Aérobus** (© **514/931-9002**), which shuttles between the airport and the company's downtown terminal at 777 rue de la Gauchetiére ouest, near Fairmont The Queen Elizabeth (Fairmont Le Reine Elizabeth) hotel. One-way fares are C$13 (US$10) adults, C$12 (US$9.20) seniors, C$9.25 (US$7.40) children. Free minibuses take passengers from the terminal to 60 major hotels. Schedules change frequently, but buses usually operate daily every 20 to 30 minutes from Trudeau between 4:45am and 11:45pm.

BY TRAIN Montréal has one intercity rail terminus, **Gare Centrale (Central Station),** situated directly beneath Fairmont The Queen Elizabeth hotel at the corner of boulevard René-Lévesque and rue Mansfield. Gare Centrale (© **514/989-2626**) is part of the underground city and is connected to the Métro (Bonaventure Station).

BY BUS The bus station, called **Station Centrale d'Autobus** (© **514/842-2281**), has a bar, a cafeteria, and a travel agency. There is a rental-car desk and an information booth. Beneath the terminal is the Berri-UQAM Métro station, the junction of several important Métro lines and a good starting point for trips to most quarters of the city. (UQAM—pronounced "*oo*-kahm"—stands for Université de Québec à Montréal.) Alternatively, taxis usually line up outside the terminal building.

BY CAR For driving directions to Montréal, see "Getting There," in chapter 2.

VISITOR INFORMATION

The main information center for visitors in Montréal is the large and efficiently organized **Infotouriste Centre,** at 1001 rue du Square-Dorchester (© **877/266-5687** from

---

Impressions

You cannot fancy you are in America; everything about it conveys the idea of a substantial, handsomely built European town, with modern improvements of half English, half French architecture.

—Lt. Col. B. W. A. Sleigh, *Pine Forests and Hacmatack Clearings,* 1853

---

anywhere in Canada and the U.S., or 514/873-2015; www.bonjourquebec.com), between rue Peel and rue Metcalfe in the downtown hotel and business district. To get there, take the Métro to the Peel stop. The office is open daily from late June to early September from 8:30am to 7:30pm, and early September through May from 9am to 5pm (closed Christmas, New Year's Day, and Easter Sunday). Employed by the Québec Ministry of Tourism, the bilingual staff workers are quite knowledgeable, and the center is a useful information resource for dining, accommodations, and attractions throughout the province and in Montréal itself. In addition to the large number of brochures and publications on hand, there are counters for tour companies, hotel reservations, currency exchange, and car rental. There is an Internet terminal for use with cash or credit cards. You'll find a cafeteria and restrooms downstairs.

The city has its own convenient Montréal-specific **information bureau** in Vieux-Montréal (Old Montréal) at 174 rue Notre-Dame (corner of place Jacques-Cartier), near the monument to Lord Nelson (© **514/871-1595**). It's open daily early June through early October from 9am to 7pm; mid-October through June from 9am to 5pm.

CITY LAYOUT

For a map of Greater Montréal, please see the color insert at the front of this guide.

For the duration of your visit, it makes sense to accept local directional conventions, strange as they may seem. The city borders the **St. Lawrence River.** As far as its citizens are concerned, that's south, looking toward the United States, although the river in fact runs almost north and south at that point, not east and west. For that reason, it has been observed that Montréal is the only city in the world where the sun rises in the south. Don't fight it: Face the river. That's south. Turn around. That's north. When examining a map of the city, note that such prominent thoroughfares as rue Ste-Catherine and boulevard René-Lévesque are said to run "east" and "west," with the dividing line being boulevard St-Laurent, which runs "north" and "south." To ease the confusion, the directions given throughout the Montréal section conform to local directional tradition. However, the maps in this book have the true compass on them.

MAIN ARTERIES & STREETS   In **downtown Montréal,** the principal streets running east–west include boulevard René-Lévesque, rue Ste-Catherine (*rue* is the French word for "street"), boulevard de Maisonneuve, and rue Sherbrooke; the north–south arteries include rue Crescent, rue McGill, rue St-Denis, and boulevard St-Laurent, which serves as the line of demarcation between east and west Montréal (most of the downtown area of interest to tourists and businesspeople lies to the west). In **Plateau Mont-Royal,** northeast of the downtown area, major streets are avenue du Mont-Royal and avenue Laurier. In **Vieux-Montréal,** rue St-Jacques, rue Notre-Dame, and rue St-Paul are the major streets, along with rue de la Commune, which hugs the park that borders the Flueve Saint-Laurent (St. Lawrence River).

Neighborhood street plans are found inside the free tourist guide supplied by **Tourisme Montréal** (② **514/844-5400;** www.tourisme-montreal.org) and distributed at the information bureau described in "Visitor Information," above. The Infotouriste Centre (described at the beginning of this chapter) provides a free large foldout city map.

FINDING AN ADDRESS   Boulevard St-Laurent is the dividing point between east and west (*est* and *ouest*) in Montréal. There's no equivalent division for north and south (*nord* and *sud*)—the numbers start at the river and climb from there, just as the topography does. When you're driving along boulevard St-Laurent and passing no. 500, that's Vieux-Montréal, near rue Notre-Dame; no. 1100 is near boulevard René-Lévesque; no. 1500 is near boulevard de Maisonneuve; and no. 3400 is near rue Sherbrooke. Even numbers are on the west side of north–south streets and the south side of east–west streets; odd numbers are on the east and north sides, respectively.

In earlier days, Montréal was split geographically along ethnic lines: Those who spoke English lived predominantly west of boulevard St-Laurent, and French speakers were concentrated to the east. Things still do sound more French as you walk east: Street names and Métro station names change from Peel and Atwater to St-Laurent and Beaudry. While boulevard St-Laurent is the east–west dividing line for the city's street-numbering system, the "ethnic split" comes farther west, roughly at rue de Bleury/avenue de Parc.

THE NEIGHBORHOODS IN BRIEF

Centre Ville/Downtown This area contains the most striking elements of the dramatic Montréal skyline and includes the main railroad station, as well as most of the city's large luxury and first-class hotels, principal museums, corporate headquarters, and department stores. The district is loosely bounded by rue Sherbrooke to the north, boulevard René-Lévesque to the south, boulevard St-Laurent to the east, and rue Drummond to the west. Downtown Montréal incorporates the neighborhood formerly known as "The Golden Square Mile," an Anglophone district once characterized by dozens of mansions erected by the wealthy Scottish and English merchants and industrialists who dominated the city's politics and social life well into the 20th century. Many of those stately homes were torn down when skyscrapers began to rise here after World War II, but some remain, often converted to institutional use. At

the northern edge of the downtown area is the urban campus of prestigious McGill University, which retains its Anglophone identity.

The Underground City During Montréal's long winters and humid summers, life slows on the streets of downtown as people escape down escalators and stairways into *la ville souterraine,* which amounts to a parallel subterranean universe. Down there, in a controlled climate that's eternally spring, it's possible to arrive at the railroad station, check into a hotel, go out for lunch at any of 350 fast-food counters and full-service restaurants, see a movie, attend a concert, conduct business, shop in hundreds of stores, and even take a swim—all without unfurling an umbrella or donning an overcoat.

This underground "city" evolved when major building developments in the downtown area such as Place Ville-Marie, Place Bonaventure, Complexe Desjardins, Palais des Congrès, and

Place des Arts put their below-street-level areas to profitable use, leasing space for shops and other enterprises. Over time, in fits and starts and with no master plan in place, these spaces became connected with Métro stations and with each other. It became possible to ride long distances and walk the shorter ones, through mazes of corridors, tunnels, and plazas. There are now more than 1,700 shops, 40 banks, 200 restaurants, 10 Métro stations, and about 30 cinemas down there.

Admittedly, the term "underground city" is not entirely accurate, because some parts—such as Place Bonaventure and Complexe Desjardins—define their own spaces, which may have nothing to do with "ground level." In Place Bonaventure, passengers may leave the Métro and then wander around on the same level only to find themselves, at one point, peering out a window several floors above the street.

The city beneath the city has obvious advantages, including the elimination of traffic accidents and avoidance of the need to deal with winter slush or summer rain. Natural light is let in wherever possible, which drastically reduces the feeling of claustrophobia that some malls evoke. However, the underground city covers a vast area, without the convenience of a logical street grid, and can be confusing at times. There are plenty of signs, but it's wise to make careful note of landmarks at key corners along your route in order to get back to your starting point. Expect to get lost anyway—but, being that you're in an underground maze, that's part of the fun.

Rue Crescent One of Montréal's major dining and nightlife districts lies in the western shadow of the massed phalanxes of downtown skyscrapers. It holds hundreds of restaurants, bars, and clubs of all styles between Sherbrooke and René-Lévesque, centering on rue Crescent and spilling over onto neighboring streets. From east to west, the Anglophone origins of the quarter are evident in the surviving street names: Stanley, Drummond, Crescent, Bishop, and MacKay. The party atmosphere that pervades after dark never quite fades, and it builds to crescendos as weekends approach, especially in warm weather, when the quarter's largely 20- and 30-something denizens spill out into sidewalk cafes and onto balconies in even greater numbers than during the winter months.

Vieux-Montréal The city was born here in 1642, down by the river at Pointe-à-Callière, and today, especially in summer, activity centers around place Jacques-Cartier, where cafe tables line narrow terraces and sun worshipers, flower sellers, itinerant artists, street performers, and strolling locals and tourists congregate. The area is larger than it might seem at first, bounded on the north by rue St-Antoine, once the "Wall Street" of Montréal and still home to some banks, and on the south by the Vieux-Port (Old Port), a linear park bordering rue de la Commune that gives access to the river and provides welcome breathing room for cyclists, in-line skaters, and picnickers. To the east, Vieux-Montréal is bordered by rue Berri, and to the west by rue McGill. Several small but intriguing museums are housed in historic buildings, and the architectural heritage of the district has been substantially preserved. The restored 18th- and 19th-century structures have been adapted for use as shops, boutique hotels, studios, galleries, cafes, bars, offices, and apartments. Take a walk through the district in the evening, when many of the finer buildings are illuminated.

Quartier International When the cross-town highway, Rte. 720, was constructed some years ago, it left behind a desolate swath of derelict buildings, parking lots, and empty spaces. That eyesore is slowly being addressed with new parks, office buildings, and a recently expanded Palais des Congrès (Convention Center). A small plaza, opposite the west end of the Convention Center, is named for Jean-Paul-Piopelle, a prominent Québec artist of the latter half of the 20th century. One of his sculptures stands there. By some definitions, the Quartier incorporates the World Trade Center Montréal, a complex of brokerage houses, law firms, and import-export companies. The new W Hotel is at the corner of St-Antoine and rue McGill. Between the Place d'Arts and Vieux Montréal, the Quartier is bounded, more or less, by rue St-Antoine on the south, avenue Viger on the north, rue St-Urbain on the east, and rue University on the west.

St-Denis Rue St-Denis, from rue Ste-Catherine est to avenue du Mont-Royal, is the thumping central artery of Francophone Montréal, running from the Latin Quarter downtown and continuing north into the Plateau Mont-Royal district. Thick with cafes, bistros, offbeat shops, and lively nightspots, it is to Montréal what boulevard St-Germain is to Paris, and indeed, once you're here, it isn't difficult to imagine that you've been transported to the Left Bank. At the southern end of St-Denis, near the concrete campus of the Université du Québec à Montréal (UQAM), the avenue is decidedly student-oriented, with indie rock cranked up in the inexpensive bars and clubs, and kids in jeans and leather swapping philosophical insights and telephone numbers. It is rife with the visual messiness that characterizes student/bohemian quarters. Farther north,

above Sherbrooke, a raffish quality persists along the facing rows of three- and four-story Victorian row houses, but the average age of residents and visitors nudges past 30. Prices are higher, too, and some of the city's better restaurants are located here. This is a district for taking the pulse of Francophone life, not for absorbing art and culture of the refined sort, for there are no museums or important galleries on St-Denis, nor is most of the architecture notable. But, then, that relieves visitors of the chore of obligatory sightseeing and allows them to take in the passing scene—just as the locals do—over bowls of café au lait at any of the numerous terraces that line the avenue.

Plateau Mont-Royal Northeast of the downtown area, this may be the part of the city where Montrealers feel most at home—away from the chattering pace of downtown and the crowds of heavily touristed Vieux-Montréal. Bounded roughly by boulevard St-Joseph to the north, rue Sherbrooke to the south, avenue Papineau to the east, and rue St-Urbain to the west, this area has a vibrant ethnicity that fluctuates with each new surge in immigration. Rue St-Denis (see above) runs the length of the district, but boulevard St-Laurent, running parallel to rue St-Denis, has a more polyglot flavor. Known to all as "The Main," it was the boulevard first encountered by foreigners tumbling off ships at the waterfront. They simply shouldered their belongings and walked north on St-Laurent, peeling off into adjoining streets when they heard familiar tongues, saw people who looked like them, or smelled the drifting aromas of food they once cooked in the old country. New arrivals still come here to start their lives in Montréal, and in the usual pattern, most work hard, save their money, and move to the suburbs.

But some stay on. Without its people and their diverse interests, St-Laurent would be another urban eyesore. But ground-floor windows here are filled with glistening golden chickens, collages of shoes and pastries and aluminum cookware, curtains of sausages, and the daringly far-fetched garments of those designers on the forward edge of Montréal's active fashion industry. Many warehouses and former tenements have been converted to house this panoply of shops, bars, and high- and low-cost eateries, and their often-garish signs draw eyes away from the still-dilapidated upper stories above. (See chapter 8 for a detailed walking tour of this fascinating neighborhood.)

Mile End Adjoining Plateau Mont-Royal at its upper west corner, this blossoming neighborhood is contained by rue St-Laurent on the east, avenue Du Parc on the west, rue Bernard in the north, and avenue Laurier on the south. Although it is outside the usual tourist orbit, it has a growing number of retail attractions, including stores selling designer clothing, furniture, household goods, and secondhand books and music. There has been a surge in worthwhile restaurants in recent years, too, several of which are reviewed in chapter 6. The remnants of what some still call Greektown are found along avenue du Parc, largely in the form of social clubs and taverns.

Parc du Mont-Royal Not many cities have a mountain at their core. Okay, reality insists that it's just a tall hill, not a true mountain. Still, Montréal is named for it—the "Royal Mountain"—and it's a soothing urban pleasure to drive, walk, or take a horse-drawn calèche to the top for a view of the city, the island, and the St. Lawrence River, especially at dusk. The famous American landscape architect Frederick Law Olmsted, who created

Manhattan's Central Park and Brooklyn's Prospect Park, among others, designed Parc du Mont-Royal, which opened in 1876. On its far slope are two cemeteries—one used to be Anglophone and Protestant, the other Francophone and Catholic—reminders of the linguistic and cultural division that persists in the city. With its skating ponds and trails for hiking, running, and cross-country skiing, the park is well used by Montrealers, who refer to it simply and affectionately as "The Mountain."

Chinatown Just north of Vieux-Montréal, south of boulevard René-Lévesque, and centered on the intersection of rue Clark and rue de la Gauchetière (pedestrianized at this point), Montréal's pocket Chinatown is mostly restaurants and a tiny park, with the occasional grocery, laundry, church, and small business. For the benefit of outsiders, most signs are in French or English as well as Chinese. Community spirit is strong—it has had to be to resist the bulldozers of commercial proponents of redevelopment—and Chinatown's inhabitants remain faithful to their traditions despite the encroaching modernism all around them. Concerned investors from Hong Kong, wary of their uncertain future as part of mainland China, have poured money into the neighborhood, producing signs that the neighborhood's shrinkage has been halted, and even reversed. Signaling that optimism, there are new gates to the area on boulevard St-Laurent, guarded by white stone lions.

The Village The city's gay and lesbian enclave, one of North America's largest, runs east along rue Ste-Catherine from rue St-Hubert to rue Papineau. A compact but vibrant district, it's filled with clothing stores, antiques shops, bars, dance clubs, and cafes, and houses the

Gay and Lesbian Community Centre, at 1301 rue Ste-Catherine est. A rainbow, symbolic of the gay community, marks the Beaudry Métro station, in the heart of the neighborhood. Two major annual celebrations are the Diver/Cité (the gay pride festival) in August and the Black & Blue Party in October.

Ile Ste-Hélène & Ile Notre-Dame St. Helen's Island in the St. Lawrence River was altered extensively to become the site of Expo '67, Montréal's very successful world's fair. In the 4 years before the Expo opened, construction crews reshaped the island and doubled its surface area with landfill, then went on to create beside it an island that hadn't existed before, Île Notre-Dame. Much of the earth needed to do this was dredged up from the bottom of the St. Lawrence River, and 15 million tons of rock from the excavations for the Métro and the Décarie Expressway were carried in by truck. The city built bridges and 83 pavilions. When Expo closed, the city government preserved the site and a few of the exhibition buildings. Parts were used for the 1976 Olympics, and today Île Ste-Hélène is home to Montréal's popular casino and an amusement park, La Ronde.

2 Getting Around

BY METRO

For speed and economy, nothing beats Montréal's Métro system for getting around. The stations are marked by blue-and-white signs that show a circle enclosing a down-pointing arrow. Clean, relatively quiet trains whisk passengers through an expanding network of underground tunnels, with 65 stations at present and more scheduled to open. Fares are by the ride, not by distance. **Single rides** cost C$2.50 (US$2), a **strip of six tickets** is C$11 (US$9), and a **weekly pass,** good for unlimited rides, is C$18 (US$15). Buy tickets at the booth in any station, or from a convenience store. Slip your ticket into the slot in the turnstile to enter the system. Take a transfer *(correspondence)* from the machine just inside the turnstiles of every station, which allows transfers from a train to a bus at any other Métro station for no additional fare. Remember to take the transfer ticket at the station where you first enter the system. When starting a trip by bus and intending to continue on the Métro, ask the bus driver for a transfer. Connections from one Métro line to another can be made at the Berri-de Montigny, Jean-Talon, Lionel-Groulx, and Snowdon stations. The orange, green, and yellow Métro lines run from about 5:30am to 12:30am (until 11:30pm on Sat), and the blue line runs from 5:30am to 11:10pm.

A caveat: Convenient as the Métro is, there can be substantial distances between stations, and accessibility is sometimes difficult for people with mobility problems. For example, to get from the lobby of the centrally located Queen Elizabeth to the platform of the Bonaventure station directly beneath the hotel takes the equivalent of 3 city blocks and the use of four escalators.

BY BUS

Buses cost the same as Métro trains, and Métro tickets are good on buses, too. Exact change is required to pay bus fares in cash. Although they run throughout the city (and give riders the decided advantage of traveling aboveground), buses don't run as frequently or as swiftly as the Métro. If you start a trip on the bus and want to transfer to the Métro, ask the bus driver for a transfer ticket.

BY TAXI

There are plenty of taxis run by several different companies. Cabs come in a variety of colors and styles, so their principal distinguishing feature is the plastic sign on the roof. At night, the sign is illuminated when the cab is available. Fares aren't too expensive, with an initial charge of C$2.75 (US$2.20) at the flag drop, C$1.30 (US$1) per kilometer (⅗ mile), and C50¢ (US40¢) per minute of waiting. A short ride from one point to another downtown usually costs about C$6 (US$4.80). Tip about 10% to 15%. Members of hotel and restaurant staffs can call cabs, many of which are dispatched by radio. They line up outside most large hotels or can be hailed on the street.

Montréal taxi drivers range in temperament from sullen cranks to the unstoppably loquacious. Some know their city well, others have sketchy knowledge and poor language skills, so it's a good idea to have your destination written down—with cross street—to show your driver.

Cyclists should know that several taxi companies participate in the "Taxi+Bike" program. Call one of them, specify that you have a bicycle to transport, and a cab with a specially designed rack arrives. Up to three bikes can be carried at a fee of C$3 (US$2.40) for each. For information call (C **514/521-8356** or go to www.velo.qc.ca.

BY CAR

Montréal is an easy city to navigate by car. Visitors arriving by plane or train, however, will probably want to rely on public transportation and cabs rather than rent a car. A rental car can come in handy, though, for trips outside of town or if you plan to drive to Québec City.

RENTALS   Terms, cars, and prices for rentals are similar to those in the United States. All the larger U.S. companies operate in Canada. Basic rates are about the same from company to company, although a little comparison shopping can unearth modest savings. A charge is usually levied when you return a car in a city other than the one in which it was rented.

All of the companies listed here also have counters at Trudeau Airport. Major car-rental companies include **Avis,** 1225 rue Metcalfe ((C 800/321-3652 or 514/866-7906); **Budget,** Gare Centrale ((C 800/268-8900 or 514/938-1000); **Hertz,** 1073 rue Drummond ((C 800/263-0678 or 514/938-1717); **National,** 1200 rue Stanley ((C 800/387-4747 or 514/878-2771); and **Thrifty,** 1076 rue de la Montagne ((C 800/367-2277 or 514/845-5954).

GASOLINE   Gasoline and diesel fuel are sold by the liter, at prices somewhat higher than those in the United States. In Québec, it costs about C$35 (US$28) to fill the tank of a small car with the lowest grade of unleaded gasoline. To convert the approximate cost of Canadian gas to familiar U.S. standards, multiply the cost per liter in Canadian dollars by four. Then convert the price to U.S. dollars.

PARKING   It can be difficult to park for free on the heavily trafficked streets of downtown Montréal, but there are plenty of metered spaces, with varying hourly rates. (Look around before walking off without paying. Meters are set well back from the curb so they won't be buried by plowed snow in winter.)

If there are no parking meters in sight, you're not off the hook. The city has started to install new black metal columns about six feet tall with a white "P" in a blue circle. Press the "English" button, enter the letter from the space where you are parked, then pay with cash or a credit card, following instructions on the screen.

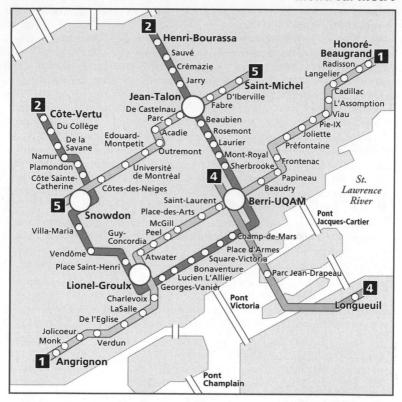

Montréal Métro

In addition, check for signs noting restrictions, usually showing a red circle with a diagonal slash. The words LIVRAISON SEULEMENT, for example, mean "delivery only." Most downtown shopping complexes have underground parking lots, as do the big downtown hotels. Some of the hotels don't charge extra to take cars in and out of their garages during the day, which can save money for those who plan to do a lot of sight-seeing by car.

DRIVING RULES The limited-access expressways in Québec are called *autoroutes,* and distances and speed limits are given in kilometers (km) and kilometers per hour (kmph). Some highway signs are in French only, although Montréal's autoroutes and bridges often bear dual-language signs. Seat-belt use is required by law while driving or riding in a car in Québec. One of the functions of traffic signals often confuses newcomers: Should you wish to make a turn and you know that the street runs in the correct direction, you may be surprised to see a green arrow pointing straight ahead instead of a green light permitting the turn. Wait a few seconds, for the arrow is just to give pedestrians time to cross the intersecting street, and it soon turns from arrow to regular green light, when you can proceed.

Turning right on a red light is still prohibited on the island of Montréal, except where specifically allowed by an additional green arrow. Outside the island of Montréal, it is now legal to turn right after stopping at red lights, but the change has caused authorities to put up numerous signs prohibiting that move at what they believe to be dangerous intersections.

Note: Too many Québec drivers take perverse pride in their reputation as dangerously fast at the wheel and are prone to such maneuvers as making sudden U-turns and cutting across two lanes to snare a parking space. Growing indignation with such practices, with newspapers decrying excess speed and the accidents that result from it, doesn't seem to have curbed the behavior. Be aware.

FAST FACTS: Montréal

American Express Offices of the American Express Travel Service are located at 1141 bd. de Maisonneuve ouest near rue Stanley (✆ 514/284-3300), and in La Baie (The Bay) department store, 585 rue Ste-Catherine ouest (✆ 514/281-4777). For lost or stolen cards, call ✆ 800/434-2941.

Babysitters Nearly all large hotels offer babysitting services *(garderie des enfants)*. In the smaller hotels and guesthouses, managers often know of sitters they believe to be reliable. Give as much notice as possible, and make certain about rates and extra charges, such as carfare, before making a commitment.

Business Hours Most **stores** are open from 9 or 10am to 6pm Monday through Wednesday, 9am to 9pm on Thursday and Friday, and 9am to 5pm on Saturday. Many stores are now also open on Sunday from noon to 5pm. **Banks** are usually open Monday through Friday from 8 or 9am to 4pm.

Currency Exchange There are currency-exchange offices (sometimes called *bureaux de change*) near most locations where they're likely to be needed: at the airports, in the train station, in and near Infotouriste on Dorchester Square, and near Notre-Dame Basilica at 86 rue Notre-Dame. The **Bank of America Canada**, 1230 rue Peel, also offers foreign-exchange services Monday through Friday 8:30am to 5:30pm and Saturday 9am to 5pm.

Doctors & Dentists The front desks at hotels can contact a doctor quickly. If it's not an emergency, call your country's consulate and ask for a recommendation (see "Embassies & Consulates," below). Consulates don't guarantee or certify local doctors, but they maintain lists of physicians with good reputations. Even if the consulate is closed, a duty officer should be available to help. For dental information, call the hot line at ✆ 514/288-8888 or the 24-hour dental clinic at ✆ 514/342-4444. In a medical emergency, dial ✆ 911.

Drugstores Open 24 hours a day, 365 days a year, the branch of **Pharmaprix** at 5122 Côte-des-Neiges, at chemin Queen Mary (✆ 514/738-8464), has a fairly convenient location.

Electricity Like the United States, Canada uses 110–120 volts AC (60 cycles) compared to 220–240 volts AC (50 cycles) in most of Europe, Australia, and New Zealand. If your small appliances use 220–240 volts, you'll need a 110-volt transformer and a plug adapter with two flat parallel pins to operate them here.

Embassies & Consulates All embassies are in Ottawa, the national capital. In Montréal, the American consulate general is located at 1155 rue St-Alexandre (✆ 514/398-9695). The United Kingdom has a consulate general at 1000 rue de la Gauchetière ouest, Suite 4200 (© **514/866-5863**). Other English-speaking countries (Australia and New Zealand) have their embassies or consulates in Ottawa.

Emergencies Dial © **911** for the police, firefighters, or an ambulance.

Hospitals Hospitals with emergency rooms are Hôpital Général de Montréal, 1650 rue Cedar (© **514/937-6011**), and Hôpital Royal Victoria, 687 av. des Pins ouest (© **514/842-1231**). Hôpital de Montréal pour Enfants (© **514/934-4400**) is a children's hospital with a poison center. Other prominent hospitals are Hôtel-Dieu, 209 av. des Pins ouest (© **514/843-2611**), and Hôpital Notre-Dame, 1560 rue Sherbrooke est (© **514/281-6000**).

Internet Access The **CyberGround NetCafé**, 3672 bd. St-Laurent (© **514/842-1726**), has 16 computers with big 21-inch monitors for e-mailing, word processing, or just surfing. Time at the keyboard costs C$3.50 (US$2.80) per half-hour, plus tax. Hours are Monday through Friday from 10am to 11pm; Saturday and Sunday from 11am to 11pm. Another possibility is **Club Internaute Montréal Café**, 5825 rue Sherbrooke (© **514/256-3336**). They charge C$5 (US$4.15) for 30 minutes, C$8 (US$6.40) for an hour. Sandwiches and light meals are available. Large hotels have business centers with computers for guests' use, as do many of the smaller boutique hotels in Vieux-Montréal.

Liquor Laws All hard liquor and spirits in Québec are sold through official government stores operated by the Québec Société des Alcools (look for maroon signs with the acronym SAQ). Wine and beer can be bought in grocery stores and convenience stores, called *dépanneurs.* The legal drinking age in the province is 18. Liquor is sold every day of the week in SAQ stores.

Mail All mail posted in Canada must bear Canadian stamps. That might seem painfully obvious, but apparently large numbers of visitors use stamps from their home countries, especially the United States. To receive mail in Montréal, have it addressed to you, c/o Poste Restante, Station "A," 1025 rue St-Jacques ouest, Montréal, PQ H3C 1G0, Canada. It can be claimed at the main post office (see below). Take along valid identification, preferably with a photo. Within Canada, letters cost C49¢ (US39¢), letters to the United States are C80¢ (US64¢), and they're C$1.40 (US$1.12) anywhere else. Postal cards cost the same as a first-class letter. These prices are increased by the astonishing imposition of a *sales tax,* another C8¢ (US7¢) for a first-class stamp!

Newspapers & Magazines Montréal's primary English-language newspaper is the *Montréal Gazette.* (To familiarize yourself with events in the city and province before your arrival, log on to the paper's website, **www.montreal gazette.com.**) Most large newsstands and those in the larger hotels also carry the *Wall Street Journal,* the *New York Times, USA Today,* and the *International Herald Tribune.* These papers are available at several branches of the **Maison de la Presse Internationale,** two of which are at 550 and 728 rue Ste-Catherine ouest. In Plateau Mont-Royal, a similar operation called **Multimags,** at 3550 av. St-Laurent, sells hundreds of foreign newspapers and magazines. For information about current happenings in Montréal, pick up the Friday or Saturday edition of the *Gazette,* or the free bimonthly booklet called *Montréal Scope,* available in some shops and many hotel lobbies.

Pets Dogs and cats can be taken into Québec, but the Canadian Customs authorities at the frontier will want to see a rabies vaccination certificate less than 3 years old signed by a licensed veterinarian. If a pet is less than 3 months old and obviously healthy, the certificate isn't likely to be required. Check with U.S. Customs about bringing your pet back into the United States. Most hotels in Montréal either do not accept pets or will require that they be kept in cages, so inquire about their policy before booking a room.

Police Dial © 911 for the police. There are three types of officers in Québec: municipal police in Montréal, Québec City, and other towns; Sûreté de Québec officers, comparable to state police or the highway patrol in the United States; and RCMP (Royal Canadian Mounted Police), who are similar to the FBI and handle cases involving infraction of federal laws. RCMP officers speak English and French. Other officers are not required to know English, though many do.

Post Office The main post office, at 1250 rue University, near Ste-Catherine (© 514/395-4909), is open Monday through Friday 8am to 6pm. A convenient post office in Vieux-Montréal is at 155 rue St-Jacques (at rue St-François-Xavier). See "Mail," above, for information on having mail sent to you in Montréal.

Safety Montréal is a far safer city than its U.S. counterparts of similar size, but common sense insists that visitors stay alert to their surroundings and observe the usual urban precautions. It's probably best to stay out of the larger parks at night, for example. There are reports of escalating road-rage incidents, so expressions of impatience and anger with the actions of other drivers can be unwise.

Taxes Most goods and services in Canada are taxed 7% by the federal government. On top of that, the province of Québec has an additional 8% tax on goods and services, including those provided by hotels. In Québec, the federal tax appears on the bill as the TPS, and the provincial tax is known as the TVQ. Nonresident tourists can receive a rebate on both the federal and the provincial tax on items they have purchased but not used in Québec, as well as on lodging. To take advantage of this refund, request the booklet called *Tax Refund for Visitors to Canada* at duty-free shops, hotels, and tourist offices. It contains the necessary forms. Complete and submit them, with the *original* receipts, within a year of the purchase. Each receipt for goods eligible for refunds must show a minimum purchase amount, before taxes, of C$50. If you leave Canada by plane, train, bus, ferry, or boat, you'll have to attach your original boarding pass or travel ticket to the application. Tax rates rise and new procedures are always being phased in, so contact the Canadian consulate or Québec tourism office for up-to-the-minute information about taxes and rebates.

Telephones The telephone system, operated by Bell Canada, closely resembles the American model. All operators (dial © 00 to get one) speak French and English, and respond in the appropriate language as soon as callers speak to them. Pay phones in Québec require C25¢ (US20¢) for a 3-minute local call. Directory information calls (dial © 411) are free of charge. Both local and long-distance calls usually cost more from hotels—sometimes a lot more, so check.

Directories *(annuaires des téléphones)* come in White Pages (residential) and Yellow Pages (commercial). The area code for Montréal Island is **514**, but surrounding areas now use the **450** code.

Time Montréal, Québec City, and the Laurentians are all in the eastern time zone. Daylight saving time is observed as in the U.S., moving clocks ahead an hour in the spring and back an hour in the fall.

Tipping Practices are similar to those in the United States: 15% to 20% of restaurant bills, 10% to 15% for taxi drivers, C$1 (US80¢) per bag for porters, C$1 (US80¢) per night for the hotel room attendant. Hairdressers and barbers expect 10% to 15%. Hotel doormen should be tipped for calling a taxi or other services.

Transit Information Call **STCUM** (© **514/288-6287**) for information about the Métro and city buses. For airport transportation, call **L'Aérobus** (© **514/931-9002**).

Useful Telephone Numbers For **Alcoholics Anonymous,** call © 514/376-9230; for the **Institute for the Blind,** call © 514/934-4622; for transport for persons with disabilities, call © 514/280-5341; for the **Poison Centre,** call © 800/463-5060; for 24-hour pharmacies, call © 514/738-8464; for the **Sexual Assault Center,** call © 514/934-4504; for **Canadian Customs,** call © 514/283-9000; for **U.S. Customs,** call © 514/636-3875.

5

Where to Stay in Montréal

Montréal hoteliers go the extra mile to make guests feel welcome, at least in part because there are proportionally more hotel rooms here than in other North American cities of similar size, still more are constructed every year, and all these hotels are hoping to have their rooms (there are more than 25,000 in the city) filled throughout the year. With that competition and the continued favorable exchange rate of the U.S. dollar in relation to its Canadian counterpart, this is the place to step up in class.

Accommodations options range from soaring glass skyscraper lodgings to grand boulevard hotels to converted row houses. Stylish inns and boutique hotels appear in ever-increasing numbers, especially in Vieux-Montréal, and several of them are recommended in this chapter. Except in bed-and-breakfasts, visitors can almost always count on discounts and package deals, especially on weekends, when the hotels' business clients have packed their bags and gone home.

Though they don't usually offer discounts, B&Bs boast cozier settings than many hotels, often (but not always) at lower prices than comparable hotels. Plus, B&Bs give visitors the opportunity to get to know a Montréaler or two. By the nature of the trade, bed-and-breakfast owners are among the most outgoing and knowledgeable guides one might want. For information about downtown B&Bs, contact **Bed & Breakfast Downtown Network,** 3458 av. Laval (at rue Sherbrooke), Montréal, PQ H2X 3C8 (© **800/267-5180** or 514/289-9749; www.bbmontreal.qc.ca).

As a referral agency for homeowners who have one or more rooms available for guests, this company represents about 30 properties with 46 guest rooms. Doubles are typically C$60 to C$90 (US$48–US$72), but can go as high as C$225 (US$180). Rooms with private bathrooms are more expensive than those that share facilities. Accommodations and the rules of individual homeowners vary significantly, so it's wise to ask all pertinent questions up front, such as if children are welcome or if all guests share bathrooms. Deposits are usually required, with the balance payable upon arrival. American Express, Visa, and MasterCard are accepted.

Québec's tourist authorities have drawn up a six-level rating system (zero to five stars) for all establishments offering six or more rooms to travelers. No star is assigned to hotels or inns meeting only basic minimum standards, and five stars are reserved for establishments that are deemed exceptional in terms of facilities and services. An ocher-and-brown shield bearing the assigned rating is found near the entrance to most hotels and inns. Most of the recommendations listed below are in the three- or four-star categories. The stars that you will see in the reviews in this chapter are based on Frommer's star system, which assigns between zero and three stars. The Québec system of rating is based necessarily on quantitative measures, while the Frommer's star ratings are more subjective, taking into account such considerations as price-to-value ratios, quality of service, location, helpfulness of staff,

Best Hotel Bets

For a roundup of my favorite Montréal hotels, see chapter 1.

and the presence of such facilities as spas and fitness centers.

Three useful websites for exploring lodging possibilities and making reservations online are www.tourisme-montreal.org, www.canadianhotelguide.com, and www.bookyourcanadianhotels.com. There is also a **free hotel reservation hot line,** *①* **800/665-1528** or 514/287-9049.

Note: Nearly all hotel staff members, from front-desk personnel to porters, are reassuringly bilingual.

See "Tips on Accommodations," on p. 42, for more ideas on scoring the lodging of your dreams.

RATES   The rates quoted in the listings in this chapter are "rack rates"—the maximum rates that a hotel charges for rooms. The lowest room rate is for off-season months, the highest for summer and major festivals. These rates are used to divide the hotels into four price categories, ranging from "Very Expensive" to "Inexpensive," for easy reference. But rack rates are only guidelines, and most people end up paying less, often *much* less. See "Saving on Your Hotel Room," on p. 42, for information on how to save.

You'll find the highest hotel rates during Montréal's busiest times, from May through October, reaching a peak in July and August. High rates also pop up during the frequent summer festivals, during annual holiday periods (Canadian or American), and when Montréal and Québec City hold their winter carnivals in February (p. 19). At those times, reserve well in advance, especially if you're looking for special rates or packages. Most other times, expect to find plenty of available rooms.

CATEGORIES   For convenience, the recommendations below have been categorized first by neighborhood, then by price. At most hotels and inns, the price differential from low to high season is rarely more than 15% or 20%, so in the listings below, the lowest price is usually for a January stay, the highest for a room in the peak summer months. All rooms have private bathrooms unless otherwise noted. The more luxurious hotels, it should be noted, have stopped providing coffeemakers in their rooms, so check if this feature is important to you.

TAXES   The provincial government imposes an 8% tax on accommodations (TVQ) in addition to the 7% federal goods and services tax (TPS). Foreign visitors can get most of the hotel tax back, assuming they save their receipts and file the necessary refund form. Unless specifically noted, prices given here do *not* include taxes—federal or provincial.

1 Centre Ville/Downtown

VERY EXPENSIVE

Fairmont The Queen Elizabeth (Le Reine Elizabeth) 𝒜𝒜   Montréal's largest hotel has lent its august presence to the city since 1958. Its 21 floors sit atop VIA Rail's Gare Centrale (the main train station), with the Métro and popular areas like Place Ville-Marie and Place Bonaventure all accessible through underground arcades. This desirable location makes "the Queenie" a frequent choice for heads of state and touring celebrities, even though other hotels in town offer higher standards of personalized pampering. February of 2004 marked the 35th anniversary of John Lennon and

Where to Stay in Downtown Montréal

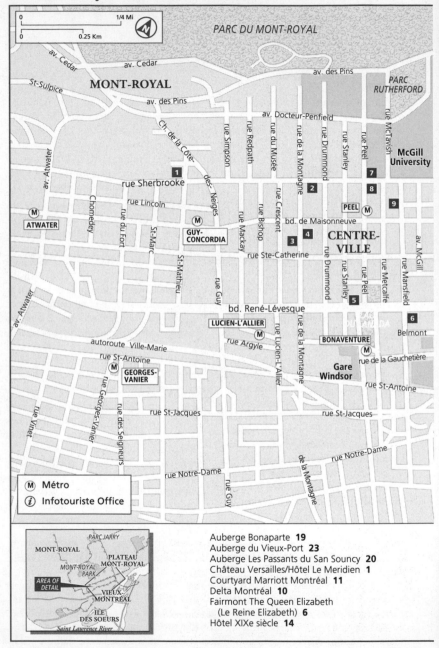

Auberge Bonaparte **19**
Auberge du Vieux-Port **23**
Auberge Les Passants du San Souncy **20**
Château Versailles/Hôtel Le Meridien **1**
Courtyard Marriott Montréal **11**
Delta Montréal **10**
Fairmont The Queen Elizabeth
  (Le Reine Elizabeth) **6**
Hôtel XIXe siècle **14**

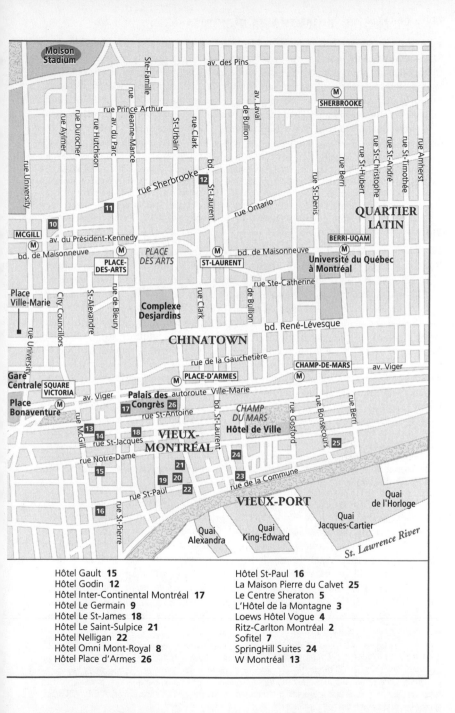

Hôtel Gault **15**
Hôtel Godin **12**
Hôtel Inter-Continental Montréal **17**
Hôtel Le Germain **9**
Hôtel Le St-James **18**
Hôtel Le Saint-Sulpice **21**
Hôtel Nelligan **22**
Hôtel Omni Mont-Royal **8**
Hôtel Place d'Armes **26**

Hôtel St-Paul **16**
La Maison Pierre du Calvet **25**
Le Centre Sheraton **5**
L'Hôtel de la Montagne **3**
Loews Hôtel Vogue **4**
Ritz-Carlton Montréal **2**
Sofitel **7**
SpringHill Suites **24**
W Montréal **13**

Yoko Ono's weeklong "Bed-In for Peace" (in suite 1742, if you're a fan). The Fairmont Gold 18th and 19th floors have a private concierge and reception and a lounge serving complimentary breakfasts and cocktail-hour canapés to go with the honor bar. Less exalted rooms on floors 4 through 17 are entirely satisfactory, with most of the expected comforts and gadgets in price ranges to satisfy most budgets. High-speed Internet access is available in 800 rooms and there are two wireless hot spots in the hotel. Rooms range from smallish to large (ask when reserving) and are furnished traditionally.

900 bd. René-Lévesque ouest (at rue Mansfield), Montréal, PQ H3B 4A5. ℂ 800/441-1414 or 514/861-3511. Fax 514/954-2258. www.fairmont.com. 1,039 units. C$189–C$399 (US$151–US$319) double; from C$399 (US$319) suite. Children 18 and under stay free in parent's room. Various discounts (including weekend discounts) and excursion packages available. AE, DC, MC, V. Valet parking C$22 (US$18). Métro: Bonaventure. Pets accepted. **Amenities:** 3 restaurants (French/International); 3 bars; heated indoor pool; exceptional health club and spa w/Jacuzzi, steam room, and instructors; concierge; large business center; shopping arcade; salon; 24-hr. room service; in-room massage; babysitting; laundry service; same-day dry cleaning; executive floors. *In room:* A/C, TV w/pay movies, dataport, minibar, coffeemaker, hair dryer, iron.

Le Centre Sheraton 𝒜   Ever bustling, this sterling representative of the familiar brand goes about its business with efficiency and surety of purpose. That figures, since earnest people in suits make up most of the clientele. They gravitate toward the separate Towers section, which offers guests complimentary breakfast and a private lounge with expansive views and free evening hors d'oeuvres. Rising a few steps off Dorchester Square, a couple blocks from Gare Centrale (the main train station), and within a short walk of the high-stepping rue Crescent dining and nightlife district, the hotel has as good a downtown location as might be asked. Most of the rooms have minibars, and all have robes and the upgraded beds and bedding the chain has installed in recent years. At least half are nonsmoking as well. If driving, note that the main entrance is off René-Lévesque, on rue Drummond.

1201 bd. René-Lévesque ouest (between rue Drummond and rue Stanley), Montréal, PQ H3B 2L7. ℂ 514/878-2000. Fax 514/878-3958. www.sheraton.com/lecentre. 825 units. C$233–C$570 (US$186–US$456) double; club floor additional. Children under 17 stay free in parent's room. Packages available. AE, DC, DISC, MC, V. Valet parking C$24 (US$19), self-parking C$18 (US$14). Pets accepted, but must be caged when owner is out. Métro: Bonaventure or Peel. **Amenities:** Restaurant (International); 2 bars; indoor pool; health club and spa; concierge (in Towers); business center; shopping arcade; 24-hr. room service; babysitting; laundry service; same-day dry cleaning; executive floors. *In room:* A/C, TV w/pay movies, coffeemaker, hair dryer, iron.

Loews Hôtel Vogue 𝒜𝒜   The Vogue created quite a stir when it opened in 1990. The hotel, whose interior was done over in spring 2001, instantly joined the Ritz-Carlton at the top tier of the local luxury-hotel pantheon. While it is no longer the hip retreat it once was, confidence and capability resonates from every member of its staff, and luxury permeates the hotel from the lobby to the well-appointed guest rooms. Feather pillows and duvets dress the oversize beds, and marble bathrooms are fitted with Jacuzzis—double-sized in suites—and separate shower stalls. Extra room amenities include TVs in the bathroom, lighted makeup mirrors, high-speed Internet connection, and robes. The lobby bar has piano music on the weekends and opens an outdoor terrace in the summer.

1425 rue de la Montagne (between bd. de Maisonneuve and rue Ste-Catherine), Montréal, PQ H3G 1Z3. ℂ 800/465-6654 or 514/285-5555. Fax 514/849-8903. www.loewshotels.com/vogue. 142 units. C$264–C$299 (US$211–US$239) double. Children under 16 stay free in parent's room. Lower weekend rates. AE, DC, DISC, MC, V. Valet parking C$25 (US$20). Métro: Peel. **Amenities:** Restaurant (International); bar; small exercise room; concierge; modest business center; 24-hr. room service; babysitting; laundry service; same-day dry cleaning. *In room:* A/C, TV/VCR w/pay movies, fax, dataport, minibar, hair dryer, safe.

The Ritz-Carlton Montréal 🍷🍷 In 1912, the Ritz-Carlton opened its doors to the carriage trade, and that clientele has remained faithful. Over the years, however, their Pierce-Arrows gave way to Rolls-Royces and Mercedes, and a few of these are always parked in readiness near the front door. A much-needed $10-million renovation restored the gloss and excellence of service that this hotel had long possessed. Rooms are large and traditional, most with tinkly glass chandeliers; some have marble fireplaces. Bathrooms are equipped with robes and speakers carrying TV sound. High-speed Internet connections are provided in every room. An umbrella is stashed in the closet in case of rain. The Café de Paris is favored for its high tea, weekend brunches, and weekday power breakfasts, but serves all meals on the terrace in summer, next to the famous duck pond. There's piano music in the Ritz Bar and Le Grand Prix, with dancing nightly in the latter.

1228 rue Sherbrooke ouest (at rue Drummond), Montréal, PQ H3G 1H6. 🕐 800/363-0366 or 514/842-4212. Fax 514/842-3383. www.ritzcarlton.com/hotels/montreal. 230 units. C$169–C$325 (US$135–US$260) double; from C$195 (US$156) suite. Children under 14 stay free in parent's room. Packages available. AE, DC, MC, V. Valet or self-parking C$25 (US$20), with in/out privileges. Métro: Peel. Pets accepted (deposit required). **Amenities:** 2 restaurants (French, International); bar; adequate fitness room; concierge; business center; 24-hr. room service; in-room massage; babysitting; laundry service; same-day dry cleaning; executive floors. In room: A/C, TV w/pay movies, fax on request, dataport, minibar, hair dryer, iron, safe.

EXPENSIVE

Hôtel Godin 🍷🍷 We'll probably add another star when they complete their ambitious plans. In the meantime, the very new Godin projects the sort of voluptuous minimalism that characterizes forward-edge design in Montréal. The owners also launched a group of hot resto-lounges including Buonanotte and Globe, both of which are a couple of blocks away. The dazzling two-level lounge wasn't finished at this writing, but is certain to be a magnet for the city's restless night people, as will the 200-seat restaurant and terrace. The sizable bedrooms have high-speed Internet access, widescreen LCD televisions that also serve as computers, and beds and bedding you'll not want to leave. A complimentary newspaper is at the door each morning.

10 rue Sherbrooke ouest (at bd. St-Laurent), Montréal, PQ H2X 4C9. 🕐 866/744-6346 or 514/843-6000. Fax 514/843-6810. www.hotelgodin.com. 136 units. C$195–C$300 (US$156–US$240). Rates include breakfast. AE, DC, MC, V. Valet parking C$20 (US$16). Children 12 and under stay free in parent's room. Packages available. Métro: St-Laurent. Pets accepted for C$50 (US$40) per night. **Amenities:** Restaurant (Eclectic); bar; 24-hour fitness center; concierge; 24-hour room service; laundry service; same-day dry cleaning. In room: A/C, TV, wireless Internet access, minibar, hair dryer, safe.

Hôtel Le Germain 🍷🍷🍷 This undertaking by the owner of equally desirable boutique hotels in Québec City and Toronto brought a big shot of panache to the downtown lodging scene, foretelling the explosion of similar hostelries in Vieux-Montréal. It features a magical mix of Asian minimalism combined with all the Western comforts that international executives might anticipate—and a few they might not. You'll discover three polished apples sitting in designated depressions on the shelves opposite the elevators—help yourself. In the capacious rooms, check out the vase containing an orchid, the CD player, the big wicker chairs with fat cushions, and the beds with down comforters and pillows that are so comfortable they can cure insomnia. Self-serve breakfasts, with perfect croissants, excellent café au lait fabricated by a magical machine, and choices of newspapers in French and English are set out on the mezzanine. A little too sophisticated for families, this gem of a hotel would be ideal for any other travelers.

2050 rue Mansfield (west end of av. du President-Kennedy), Montréal, PQ H3A 1Y9. ℭ 877/333-2050 or 514/849-2050. Fax 514/849-1437. www.hotelboutique.com. 101 units. C$210–C$450 (US$168–US$360). Rates include breakfast. AE, DC, MC, V. Valet parking C$18 (US$14). Métro: Peel. Pets accepted. **Amenities:** Restaurant (Eclectic); bar; exercise room; limited room service; babysitting; laundry service; same-day dry cleaning. *In room:* A/C, TV, dataport, minibar, coffeemaker, hair dryer, iron.

Hôtel Omni Mont-Royal ℛℛ   This Omni outpost is a worthy competitor to the nearby Ritz-Carlton, especially because of an all-floors multimillion-dollar renovation by the most recent owners. The coolly austere lobby, lined with marble, is softened by banks of plants and flowers. Rooms are large, with new-looking furnishings, and are offered in escalating categories of relative luxury, from standard to premium. Robes, CD players, and high-speed Internet access are available in each room (coffeemakers are only available on request). There are 12 nonsmoking floors, an unusually large number. Buffet breakfasts and lunches are served in the lobby bar, which features piano music in the evenings. The hotel's health club is the best in town, offering everything from aerobics classes to massages. This is a great place for businesspeople, honeymooners, and well-to-do families.

1050 rue Sherbrooke ouest (at rue Peel), Montréal, PQ H3A 2R6. ℭ 514/284-1110. Fax 514/845-3025. www.omni hotels.com. 299 units. C$161–C$295 (US$129–US$236) double. Children under 14 stay free in parent's room. Weekend rates and special packages available. AE, DC, MC, V. Valet parking C$24 (US$19); self-parking C$18 (US$14). Métro: Peel. **Amenities:** 2 restaurants (Chinese, International); bar; heated outdoor pool; impressive health club and spa featuring aerobics classes; children's programs; concierge; complete business center; shopping arcade; 24-hr. room service; in-room massage; babysitting; laundry service; same-day dry cleaning; executive floors. *In room:* A/C, TV/VCR w/pay movies, fax, dataport, minibar, hair dryer, iron, safe.

Sofitel ℛℛ   Creating a stir as the first downtown luxury hotel in many years, this representative of the French chain turned a bland 1970s office tower into a destination instantly coveted by visiting celebrities and the power elite. From the moment of arrival, guests are impressed by both the light-filled stone-and-wood lobby and the universally warm welcome of the staff. Off to the right is the ambitious Renoir restaurant and lounge. Also on the right is a custom-designed Aubusson carpet that celebrates Montréal's annual jazz festival, winter sports, the Grand Prix, and the Cirque du Soleil. Standard rooms (called "Superior") make full use of current technology, with speakerphones, CD players, TV sound in the bathrooms, and high-speed Internet access through the TV, with wireless keyboards. Beds have duvets and goose-down mattress covers. Chairs are a bit too over-designed for comfort. The fitness center is open 24 hours.

1155 rue Sherbrooke ouest (at Peel), Montréal, PQ H3A 2N3. ℭ 877/285-9001 or 514/285-9000. Fax 514/289-1155. www.sofitel.com or www.accorhotels.com. 258 units. C$199–C$465 (US$159–US$372) double; from C$469 (US$375) suite. Packages available. AE, DC, DISC, MC, V. Valet parking C$24 (US$19). Métro: Peel. Pets accepted. **Amenities:** Restaurant (French Contemporary); bar; complete health club w/sauna; concierge; business center; 24-hr. room service; massage; babysitting; laundry service; same-day dry cleaning. *In room:* A/C, TV w/pay movies, dataport, hair dryer, iron.

MODERATE

Château Versailles ℛ   This long-popular facility underwent a remarkable transformation from a popular but dowdy inn to a full member of the growing local ranks of snappy boutique hotels. It began as a European-style pension in 1958, expanding into adjacent pre–World War I town houses. The spacious rooms have enjoyed the full decorator treatment, with rich colors, fine modern furnishings with faint Deco tinges, and some Second Empire touches. Some have fireplaces. Only one deficiency remains:

the lack of an elevator to deal with the three floors. Price and location (near Sherbrooke shopping and the Museum of Fine Arts) are competitive, so reserve well in advance.

A modern tower across the street that used to be part of the property is now **Le Meridien Versailles** (1808 rue Sherbrooke ouest; © **888/933-8111** or 514/933-8111). It has 106 units, a fitness center, and a new restaurant, Brontë; rates are C$129 to C$265 (US$103–US$212).

1659 rue Sherbrooke ouest (at rue St-Mathieu), Montréal, PQ H3A 1E3. © **888/933-8111** or 514/933-8111. Fax 514/933-6867. www.versailleshotels.com. 65 units. C$165–C$290 (US$132–US$232) double. Children under 17 stay free in parent's room. Special packages available Nov–May. AE, DC, MC, V. Valet parking C$16 (US$13). Métro: Guy. **Amenities:** Restaurant (Market); bar/lounge; exercise room w/sauna; limited room service; laundry service; same-day dry cleaning. In room: A/C, TV w/pay movies, dataport, minibar, coffeemaker, hair dryer, iron, safe.

Courtyard Marriott Montréal *(Kids)* Formerly La Citadelle, this hotel fulfills the Marriott chain's promise of providing lodging for business travelers at a moderate cost. But with its indoor pool and self-service laundromat, the Courtyard also appeals to families on tight budgets. While the mid-rise slab can hardly be described as grand, necessary renovations have perked it up. Rooms are furnished in accordance with the midlevel standards of the chain; they've added high-speed Internet access. The restaurant sets out a buffet breakfast (not included in the room rate) each morning.

410 rue Sherbrooke ouest (at av. du Parc), Montréal, PQ H3A 1B3. © **800/449-6654** or 514/844-8855. Fax 514/844-0912. www.courtyard.com. 181 units. C$159–C$229 (US$127–US$183). AE, DC, MC, V. Valet parking C$16 (US$13). Métro: Place des Arts. **Amenities:** Restaurant (Italian); bar; heated indoor pool; compact health club w/sauna and steam room; concierge; limited room service; coin-op washers and dryers; same-day laundry; dry cleaning. In room: A/C, TV w/pay movies, dataport, coffeemaker, hair dryer, iron.

Delta Montréal *(R) (Kids)* This carefully maintained hotel is owned by the reliable Canadian hotel chain (there's another one in town, the Delta Centre-Ville at 777 rue University; © 514/879-1370). It targets the business traveler, but its supervised children's crafts and games center, two squash courts, electronic-games room, indoor pool, and in-room Nintendo make it clear that families are welcome, too. Rooms in the 23-story tower have angular dimensions, getting away from the boxiness that defines

---

(Kids) Family-Friendly Hotels

Courtyard Marriott Montréal (above)   Parents will appreciate the self-service laundry, kids will love the indoor pool, and the whole family will enjoy the choices at the buffet breakfast.

Delta Montréal (above)   The Children's Creative Center for supervised play and crafts making is a big draw for small kids, and kids of all ages will enjoy the indoor swimming pool and electronic-games room.

Hyatt Regency Montréal   The glass-enclosed elevators scooting up and down the heart of this complex are fun for kids, as are the indoor pool and the easily accessible subterranean levels of the underground city. Children stay free with a parent. 1255 rue Jeanne-Mance, Montréal, PQ H5B 1E5; © **800/361-8234** or 514/982-1234. C$139 to C$275 (US$111–US$220).

many contemporary hotels. Most rooms have small balconies. A new wave of renovations was completed in 2005, upgrading every bedroom, public areas, the bar, and the restaurant, Aroma. High-speed Internet access is now available in all rooms. Delta's executive floors, called Signature Club, have private lounges with concierge; complimentary breakfasts and cocktail hour hors d'oeuvres are served.

475 av. du President-Kennedy (at rue City Councillors), Montréal, PQ H3A 1J7. ℂ **877/286-1986** or 514/286-1986. Fax 514/284-4306. www.deltamontreal.com. 453 units. C$176–C$233 (US$141–US$186) double; from C$350 (US$280) suite. Children under 19 stay free in parent's room. Weekend packages available. AE, DC, DISC, MC, V. Valet parking C$18 (US$14). Métro: Place des Arts or McGill. **Amenities:** 2 restaurants (International, Bistro); bar; 2 pools (outdoor pool open July–Aug; indoor lap pool open year-round); superior health club and spa w/aerobics instruction and 2 squash courts; game room; concierge; courtesy car; expansive business center w/translation service; limited room service; laundry service; same-day dry cleaning; executive floors. *In room:* A/C, TV w/pay movies, dataport, coffeemaker, hair dryer, iron.

L'Hôtel de la Montagne ⏣ Two white lion sculptures stand sentinel at the front door, and the doorman has been known to wear a pith helmet. The fauna fixation continues in a crowded lobby that incorporates a pair of 1.8m (6-ft.) carved elephants, two gold-colored crocodile sculptures, and a nude female figure with stained-glass butterfly wings sitting atop a splashing fountain. Clearly we are not in Kansas. A French-style brasserie is the main restaurant. Light meals are available beside the pool on the roof, 20 stories up, with dancing under the stars. Off the lobby, a cabaret lounge featuring a piano player and jazz duos (Thurs–Sat) leads into Thursday's, a bar/restaurant with a spangly disco and a terrace opening onto lively rue Crescent. After all that, the relatively serene bedrooms seem downright bland. Given all these inducements, a stay here is a genuine bargain, especially in contrast to the expensive Hôtel Vogue across the street.

1430 rue de la Montagne (north of rue Ste-Catherine), Montréal, PQ H3G 1Z5. ℂ **800/361-6262** or 514/288-5656. Fax 514/288-9658. www.hoteldelamontagne.com. 136 units. C$185–C$210 (US$148–US$168) double. Children under 16 stay free in parent's room. Packages available. AE, MC, V. Self-parking C$16 (US$13). Métro: Peel. Pets accepted. **Amenities:** 3 restaurants (French); 2 bars; heated outdoor pool; concierge; limited room service; laundry service; same-day dry cleaning. *In room:* A/C, TV/VCR w/pay movies, dataport, minibar, coffeemaker, hair dryer.

2 Vieux-Montréal (Old Montréal)

VERY EXPENSIVE

Hôtel Gault ⏣ This new designer hotel explores the far reaches of minimalism, and guest responses vary from delight to dismay. With raw concrete walls and brushed steel work surfaces, it can seem stark—a recollection of the Brutalist style that was popular 30 years ago. Yet it also seems as new as tomorrow, despite Charles Eames and Pierre Paulin furnishings that harken back to the 1950s. Clearly, everything old is new again. The large bedrooms on the hotel's five floors are loft-style, with curtains instead of walls defining spaces within each room. Select artworks are being added. Other distractions are thoroughly up-to-the-minute, including flat-screen TVs, high-speed Internet access, and DVD and CD players. Tubs aren't available in all rooms, but robes are.

449 rue Ste-Hélène, Montréal, PQ H2Y 2K9. ℂ **866/904-1616** or 514/904-1616. Fax 514/904-1717. www.hotel gault.com. 30 units. C$235–C$749 (US$188–US$599) double. Rates include breakfast. AE, DC, MC, V. Métro: Square Victoria. Pets accepted. **Amenities:** Bar; small exercise room; 24-hr. room service; laundry service; same-day dry cleaning. *In room:* A/C, TV/DVD, dataport, minibar, safe.

Hôtel Le St-James ⏣⏣⏣ This hotel is a triumph of the union of design and preservation that puts the city's old-line luxury hotels in the shade. Montréal's surge of new designer hotels spans the spectrum from superminimalist to gentlemen's club posh. Le St-James sits squarely in the gentlemen's club end of the range. It began life as a merchant's bank in 1870, and the opulence of that station of privilege has been both retained and upgraded. The richly paneled entry hall leads to a grand hall with potted palms, carved urns, bronze chandeliers, a coffered ceiling, Corinthian columns, candelabras, and balconies with gilded metal balustrades. Breakfast, lunch, afternoon tea, and dinner are served there, often accompanied by harp music. Rooms are furnished with entrancing antiques and impeccable reproductions. All have CD players, high-speed Internet access, flat-screen TVs, and phones with video screens that control lights, room temperature, and even the do-not-disturb sign. Pricier rooms—and none are cheap—have DVD players and LCD monitors. The spa, with both a regular massage table and full-body water therapy, has to be seen to be believed. The Rolling Stones have stayed here. Obviously they have excellent taste in lodging—perhaps the two-bedroom Presidential suite at C$3,500 (US$2,800) a night?

355 rue St-Jacques, Montréal, PQ H2Y 1N9. (©) 866/841-3111 or 514/841-3111. Fax 514/841-1232. www.hotellest james.com. 61 units. C$400–C$475 (US$320–US$380) double; from C$675 (US$540) suite. AE, DC, MC, V. Valet parking C$24 (US$19). Métro: Square Victoria. **Amenities:** Restaurant (International); bar; small but complete health club and spa; concierge; business center; 24-hr. room service; babysitting; laundry service; same-day dry cleaning. *In room:* A/C, TV w/pay movies, dataport, minibar, hair dryer, iron, safe.

W Montréal ❋❋❋ The stakes have been raised. The high standards set in recent years by several Old Montréal boutique hotels were exceeded as soon as this exemplar of the growing W chain opened in late 2004. "Whatever, whenever" is the shorthand motto of the staff, meaning that they endeavor to satisfy swiftly any guest request, however unusual. Said employees, male and female, are young and distractingly attractive, and many of the guests fit those parameters as well. If it weren't for the reception and concierge desks at each end, the lobby would suggest an exclusive dance club, what with the blue glow of the wall panels and the 12-foot waterfalls. The hotel restaurant, Otto, drew instant approval from local gourmands, and is filled day and night with a sleek crowd favoring black and Armani. Four bars cater to lovers of the night, from an intimate space featuring martinis to a large lounge with the coolest of DJs. Bedrooms follow through, with goose down comforters and 350-count Egyptian cotton sheets on the beds complemented with imitation mink throws and daily fresh flowers. That plasma TVs, DVD players, and high-speed Internet access are present is only to be expected.

901 rue Square-Victoria, Montréal, PQ H2Z 1R1. (©) 888/625-5144 or 514/395-3100. Fax 514/395-3150. www.w hotels.com/Montreal. 152 units. C$299–C$559 (US$239–US$447) double, C$760 (US$608) suite. AE, DC, MC, V. Valet parking C$24 (US$19). Métro: Square Victoria. **Amenities:** Restaurant (Fusion); 4 bars; fitness room and spa; concierge; business center; 24-hr room service; laundry service; same-day dry cleaning. *In room:* A/C, TV w/ pay movies, dataport, minibar, hair dryer, iron, safe.

EXPENSIVE

Auberge du Vieux-Port ❋❋ Housed in an 1882 building facing the port, this romantic luxury inn has an accomplished cellar restaurant. Polished hardwood floors, exposed brick walls, massive beams, and the original windows define the hideaway bedrooms. Fifteen rooms face the waterfront and 22 have whirlpool tubs. CD players are standard (with a selection of disks available at the main desk), as is high-speed Internet access. All rooms are nonsmoking. The three suitelike "lofts" have kitchenettes. Drinks and sandwiches are served on the rooftop terrace, which has unobstructed views of the Vieux-Port, a particular treat when fireworks are scheduled over the river. Always looking to improve, the management has now converted the cafe adjacent to the lobby into a bar, lounge, and casual restaurant. Meals are prepared by the same kitchen that serves the acclaimed **Les Remparts** (p. 97), one floor below.

97 rue de la Commune est (near rue St-Gabriel), Montréal, PQ H2Y 1J1. © **888/660-7678** or 514/876-0081. Fax 514/876-8923. www.aubergeduvieuxport.com. 27 units. C$175–C$290 (US$140–US$232) double. Rates include full breakfast and afternoon wine and cheese. AE, DC, DISC, MC, V. Valet parking C$18 (US$14). Métro: Champs-de-Mars. Pets in cages accepted. **Amenities:** Restaurant (French Contemporary); concierge; limited room service; in-room massage; babysitting; laundry service; dry cleaning. *In room:* A/C, TV, dataport, kitchenette in suites, minibar, hair dryer, iron, safe.

Hôtel Inter-Continental Montréal 𝕽𝕽𝕽   Only a few minutes' walk from Notre-Dame Basilica and the restaurants and nightspots of Vieux-Montréal, this striking luxury hotel opened in 1991 and was instantly included in the coveted clique of top properties in town. The hotel's tower houses the sleek reception area and guest rooms, while the restored 1888 Nordheimer building contains a bar-bistro. (Take a look at the early-19th-century vaults below.) Guest rooms are quiet, well lit, and decorated with photographs and lithographs by local artists. The turret suites are fun, with their round bedrooms and wraparound windows. All rooms have bathrobes and two or three telephones. The lobby-level piano bar has a light menu and nightly music.

360 rue St-Antoine ouest (at rue de Bleury), Montréal, PQ H2Y 3X4. © **800/361-3600** or 514/987-9900. Fax 514/847-8550. www.montreal.intercontinental.com. 357 units. C$159–C$440 (US$127–US$352) double; from C$550 (US$440) suite. Packages available. AE, DC, DISC, MC, V. Valet parking C$23 (US$18). Métro: Square Victoria. **Amenities:** 2 restaurants (International); 2 bars; small enclosed rooftop lap pool; health club w/sauna and steam rooms; concierge; substantial business center; salon; 24-hr. room service; massage; laundry service; same-day dry cleaning; executive floors. *In room:* A/C, TV w/pay movies, dataport, minibar, coffeemaker, hair dryer, iron, safe.

Hôtel Le Saint-Sulpice 𝕽𝕽   One of the wave of high-style boutique hotels that has washed across Vieux-Montréal, Le Saint-Sulpice impresses with an all-suites configuration, an ambitious restaurant, and courtly service. The hotel is a member of the international Concorde chain, and it easily meets the demanding standards of the chain. The suites come with a panoply of conveniences and gadgets, including TVs both in sitting areas and in bedrooms, PlayStations, and high-speed Internet access. Most have gas or electric fireplaces as well as minikitchens with microwave ovens, stoves, and fridges. Guests who wish to cook their own meals can order groceries through the concierge. Many suites have balconies.

414 rue St-Sulpice (behind the Notre-Dame Basilica), Montréal, PQ H2Y 2V5. © **877/785-7423** or 514/288-1000. Fax 514/288-0077. www.lesaintsulpice.com. 108 units. C$169–C$519 (US$135–C$415) suite. Rates include breakfast. AE, DC, MC, V. Valet parking C$25 (US$20). Métro: Place d'Armes. **Amenities:** Restaurant (Contemporary); bar; compact health club and spa; concierge; business center; 24-hr. room service; babysitting; laundry service; same-day laundry; dry cleaning. *In room:* A/C, TV w/pay movies, dataport, minibar, hair dryer, iron, safe.

Hôtel Nelligan 𝕽𝕽𝕽   Occupying two adjoining 1850 buildings, the Nelligan got itself up and running in 2002. It's named for a Canadian poet whose lines are excerpted on the walls of its rooms and suites. The staff performs its duties admirably, and the building has beautiful spaces, from the sun-splashed atrium and Verses restaurant (p. 97) on the ground floor to the rooftop terrace, where drinks and light meals are served in good weather. (Get a room on the fifth floor and be steps away from both the terrace and the fitness center.) Brick, wood, and leather compose much of the decor in the public spaces, while bedrooms are luxurious retreats you'll want to hide in for hours at a time. Puffy goose-down duvets and heaps of pillows are inviting, and the CD player and high-speed Internet connection are additional draws. DVD players are available on request. Suites have whirlpool tubs. There's a computer for guest use behind the front desk. Claiming an enveloping lobby chair facing the open front to the street, with a book and a cold drink at hand, is one definition of utter contentment.

106 rue St-Paul ouest (1 block west of St-Laurent), Montréal, PQ H2Y 1Z3. (C) **877/788-2040** or 514/788-2040. Fax 514/788-2041. www.hotelnelligan.com. 63 units. C$210–C$240 (US$168–US$192) double; from C$280 (US$224) suite. Rates include breakfast and afternoon wine and cheese. AE, DC, MC, V. Valet parking C$24 (US$19). Métro: Square Victoria. **Amenities:** Restaurant (French Contemporary); bar; exercise room; concierge; business center; limited room service; massage; laundry service; same-day dry cleaning. *In room:* A/C, TV/DVD/CD w/pay movies, dataport, minibar, hair dryer, safe.

Hôtel Place d'Armes 𝕽𝕽   This highly desirable property is housed in a cunningly converted office building dating from the late 19th century. The elaborate architectural details of that era are in abundant evidence, especially in the ground-floor lobby, with its high ceilings and richly carved capitals and moldings. An afternoon wine-and-cheese party is held around the lobby fireplace and bar in back. Goodies in the simply decorated modern rooms include robes, down comforters, high-speed Internet access, and CD players (a collection of discs is available at the front desk). Few desires are not catered to—there's even a rooftop sun deck. The chef at Les Remparts (p. 97) has taken the helm at the hotel's acclaimed new restaurant, **Aix Cuisine du Terroir** (p. 94). A free morning shuttle service takes guests to several downtown business locations.

701 Côte de la Place d'Armes, Montréal, PQ H2Y 2X6. (C) **888/450-1887** or 514/842-1887. Fax 514/842-6469. www.hotelplacedarmes.com. 48 units. C$190–C$270 (US$152–US$216) double; from C$280 (US$224) suite. Rates include breakfast and afternoon cocktail. AE, DC, DISC, MC, V. Valet parking C$18 (US$14). Métro: Place d'Armes. **Amenities:** Restaurant (French Contemporary); bar; small but efficient rooftop exercise room; concierge; secretarial services; limited room service; in-room massage; babysitting; laundry service; same-day dry cleaning. *In room:* A/C, TV, dataport, minibar, hair dryer, iron, safe.

Hôtel St-Paul 𝕽𝕽   Joining the laudable Vieux-Montréal ranks of worthwhile old buildings converted to hotels and other contemporary uses, the St-Paul was an instant frontrunner. The exterior is a product of the Beaux Arts school, but minimalism prevails inside, with simple lines, muted tones, and materials that don't deny their identity—leather, wool, rosewood, bronze, as well as fur throws here and there. Most of the guests are as trim and understated as the surroundings. An alabaster fireplace anchors one end of the long lobby and a bar is situated at the other end, next to the hotel's popular restaurant, **Cube** (p. 96). Rooms verge on design-run-amok. Marble sinks are square, as are the lampshades, the wastebaskets, and the plastic cube covering the toiletries. That doesn't affect comfort or convenience, as extras include robes, CD players, fax machines, and high-speed Internet access. Mobile phones and laptops are available upon request.

355 rue McGill (at rue St-Paul), Montréal, PQ H2Y 2E8. (C) **866/380-2202** or 514/380-2222. Fax 514/380-2200. www.hotelstpaul.com. 120 units. C$205–C$325 (US$164–US$260) double; from C$365 (US$292) suite. Rates include breakfast. AE, DC, MC, V. Métro: Square Victoria. **Amenities:** Restaurant (Eclectic); bar; exercise room; modest 24-hour fitness room; concierge; 24-hr. business center; 24-hr. room service; laundry service; same-day dry cleaning. *In room:* A/C, TV w/pay movies, fax, dataport, minibar, coffeemaker, hair dryer, iron.

La Maison Pierre du Calvet 𝕽   When Ben Franklin was in Montréal in 1775 during his attempt to enlist Canada in the revolt against the British, this house was already 50 years old. After a stint as a theme restaurant, the same owners converted it into an atmospheric inn that attempts to transport guests to an elegant Breton manor in France. The beamed public rooms are luxuriously furnished with original antiques, not reproductions, including antique carpets on the ancient stone floors, leather sofas, gilt-framed portraits, a marquetry-topped reception desk, and ship models. A voluptuously furnished dining room, called **Les Filles du Roy,** suggests a 19th-century ducal hunting lodge. Bedrooms are no less opulent, some with fireplaces and heavily carved four-poster canopied beds. TV sets would only spoil the ambience. A 50% room deposit is required.

405 rue Bonsecours (at rue St-Paul), Montréal, PQ H27 3C3. ℂ 866/544-1725 or 514/282-1725. Fax 514/282-0456. www.pierreducalvet.ca. 9 units. C$235–C$295 (US$188–US$236). Rates include full breakfast. AE, MC, V. Self-parking C$10 (US$8). Métro: Place d'Armes or Champ-de-Mars. **Amenities:** Restaurant (French); laundry service; dry cleaning. *In room:* A/C, dataport, hair dryer, iron on request.

MODERATE

Auberge Bonaparte ℛ   The restaurant of the same name on the ground floor has long been one of Vieux-Montréal's favorites. Romantic and faded in a Left Bank of Paris way, the restaurant experienced massive renovations in 1999. While they were at it, the owners transformed the overhead floors into this fashionable urban inn, which continues the restaurant's romantic style. Even the smallest rooms are surprisingly spacious, and they have a variety of combinations of furniture—queen, king, and/or double beds—that are useful for families. Of the eight units on each floor, four have whirlpool tubs with separate showers. Spring for the handsome suite on the top floor and get superb views of Notre-Dame, cloistered gardens, and cobblestone streets.

447 rue St-François-Xavier (north of rue St-Paul), Montréal, PQ H2Y 2T1. ℂ 514/844-1448. Fax 514/844-0272. www.bonaparte.com. 31 units. C$135–C$185 (US$108–US$148) double; C$300 (US$240) suite. Rates include full breakfast. AE, DC, MC, V. Parking C$13 (US$10). Métro: Place d'Armes or Square Victoria. **Amenities:** Restaurant (French); access to nearby health club; concierge; 24-hr. room service; in-room massage; babysitting; laundry service; same-day dry cleaning. *In room:* A/C, TV/VCR, dataport, hair dryer, iron.

Hôtel XIXe Siècle   This tidy little hotel is worth seeking out for its central location and quiet demeanor. The building began life in 1870 as a bank in the Second Empire style, and the interior reflects these stately origins, with 4.5m (15-ft.) ceilings and a lobby that looks like a Victorian library. Three vaults remain from the building's original use as a bank, and one of them has been converted to a small bedroom. The other units are quite spacious, most with one queen- or king-size bed, and about half the bathrooms have whirlpool tubs. Work desks and voice mail are provided.

262 rue St-Jacques (at rue St-Jean), Montréal, PQ H2Y 1N1. ℂ 877/553-0019 or 514/985-0019. Fax 514/985-0059. www.hotelxixsiecle.com. 59 units. C$150–C$240 (US$120–US$192) double; from C$240 (US$192) suite. AE, DC, MC, V. Métro: Square Victoria. **Amenities:** Bar; small exercise room; laundry service; same-day dry cleaning. *In room:* A/C, TV, dataport, hair dryer.

SpringHill Suites   While it can't compete in style with Vieux-Montréal's dashing boutique hotels, this representative of one of Marriott's various subcategories compensates with gentler prices and a quiet location on an inconspicuous side street in the middle of the quarter. To justify the "suites" designation, some of the smaller units have tortured floor plans bristling with alcoves and partitions, making the trip from door to bathroom an obstacle course. That aside, they have kitchenettes with fridges, microwaves, and sinks. High-speed Internet access is provided. The hotel is connected to a bar/restaurant next door. A newspaper is delivered each morning.

445 rue St-Jean-Baptiste (between rue Notre-Dame and rue St-Paul), Montréal, PQ H2Y 2Z7. ℂ 866/875-4333 or 514/875-4333. Fax 514/875-4331. www.springhillsuites.com. 124 units. C$115–C$375 (US$92–US$300) suite. Rates

include breakfast. AE, DC, MC, V. Métro: Square Victoria. **Amenities:** Exercise room w/small pool; business center; limited room service; coin-operated laundry; same-day dry cleaning. *In room:* A/C, TV, dataport, unstocked fridge, hair dryer, iron.

INEXPENSIVE

Auberge Les Passants du Sans Soucy *(Value)*   This cheery bed-and-breakfast in Vieux-Montréal is a 1723 fur warehouse craftily converted into an inn by the bilingual owners. (Its seemingly misspelled name is a play on the name of one of them, Daniel Soucy. *Sans souci* means "without care.") Exposed brick, beams, and a marble floor form the entry space, which serves as the reception area as well as an art gallery, and leads to a breakfast nook with a skylight. Each of the rooms upstairs has mortared stone walls, a buffed wood floor, a clock radio, fresh flowers, lace curtains, and a wrought-iron or brass bed. All rooms now have jet tubs, and electric fireplaces have been added, as well. Free wi-fi access is available. The substantial breakfasts include chocolate croissants and café au lait.

171 rue St-Paul ouest, Montréal, PQ H2Y 1Z5. (✆ **514/842-2634.** Fax 514/842-2912. www.lesanssoucy.com. 9 units. C$125–C$175 (US$100–US$140) double; C$205 (US$164) suite. Rates include full breakfast. AE, DC, MC, V. Self-parking C$13 (US$10). Métro: Place d'Armes. *In room:* A/C, TV, hair dryer, iron.

6

Where to Dine in Montréal

With more than 5,000 dining spots, Montréal is filled to the brim with choices. Less than a generation ago, most restaurants here served only French cuisine. A few *temples de cuisine* delivered haute standards of gastronomy, numerous accomplished bistros served up humbler ingredients in less grand settings, and folksy places featured the hearty fare of the colonial era, which employed the ingredients available in New France—game, maple syrup, and root vegetables. Everything else was considered "ethnic." Yes, some places offered Asian and Mediterranean cooking, but they weren't nearly as popular as they were in other North American cities. Québec was French, and that was that.

While waves of ethnic food crazes washed over Los Angeles, Chicago, Toronto, and New York in the 1980s, introducing people to Cajun, Tex-Mex, Southwestern, and such Fusion cuisines as Franco-Asian, Pacific Rim, and Cal-Ital, the diners of Montréal were resolute. They stuck to their French culinary traditions.

Over the past decade, however, this attitude changed dramatically. The recession of the 1990s put many restaurateurs out of business and forced others to reexamine and streamline their operations. Immigration continued to increase, and along with it, more and more foreign cooking styles were introduced. Montrealers began sampling the exotic edibles emerging from the new storefront eateries all around them—Thai, Moroccan, Vietnamese, Portuguese, Turkish, Mexican, Indian, Creole, Szechuan, and Japanese.

Innovation and intermingling of styles, ingredients, and techniques were inevitable. The city, long one of the world's elite gastronomic centers, is now as cosmopolitan in its tastes and offerings as any city on the continent. True, some of the silliness that has attended culinary innovation elsewhere has afflicted chefs here too. Plates arrive with towering, overwrought presentations that might well incorporate spiky snow pea fans amid ponds of raspberry-beet coulis beneath wild rice and minced portobello mushrooms from which minigroves of rosemary and thyme sprout. But for most chefs, novelty is still secondary to the freshness and appropriateness of ingredients.

Deciding where to dine among the many tempting choices can be bewildering. The establishments recommended in this chapter should help you get started, and not only because they include some of the most popular and honored restaurants in town. Getting to any of them involves passing many other worthy possibilities, for numbers of good restaurants often cluster together in certain neighborhoods or along particular streets, such as Laurier, St-Denis, or St-Laurent. Nearly all restaurants have menus posted outside, prompting the local tradition of stopping every few yards for a little salivation-inducing reading and comparison shopping before deciding on a place for dinner.

It's a good idea, and an expected courtesy, to make a reservation if you wish to dine at one of the city's top restaurants. Unlike in larger American and European cities, however, a few hours or a day in advance is usually sufficient at most restaurants. A hotel concierge can make the reservation, even though nearly all restaurant hosts will switch immediately into English when they sense that a caller doesn't speak French. Dress codes are all but nonexistent, except in a handful of luxury restaurants, but adults who show up in T-shirts and jeans should feel uncomfortably out of place at the better establishments. Montrealers are a fashionable lot, and manage to look smart even in casual clothes.

Few people want to dine in five-fork restaurants all the time. Many of this city's moderately priced bistros, cafes, and ethnic joints offer outstanding food, congenial surroundings, and amiable service at reasonable prices. And, speaking of value, the city's table d'hôte (fixed-price) meals are eye-openers. Entire two- to four-course meals, often with a beverage, can be had for little more than the price of an a la carte main course alone. Even the best restaurants offer them, so tables d'hôte present the chance to sample some excellent restaurants without breaking the bank. Having your main meal at lunch instead of dinner keeps costs down, too, and is the most economical way to sample the top establishments, at least those that are open for lunch. The delectable bottom line of dining in Montréal is that a meal here can be the equal in every dimension to the best offered anywhere in the world.

Alcohol-based beverages are heavily taxed, imported varieties even more so than domestic versions. To save a little, buy Canadian. That's not difficult when it comes to beer, for there are many breweries, micro to national, that produce highly palatable products. The sign BIÈRES EN FÛT tells you that a bar has brews on draft. Wine is another matter. Wine is not produced in significant quantities in Canada due to a climate inhospitable to the essential grapes. Given the high cost of Californian and European pressings, though, you might want to try bottles from the Cantons-de-l'Est (east of Montréal), from British Columbia, and from the Niagara Frontier. The vineyards near the famous falls actually take advantage of the frigid winters, allowing grapes to freeze in order to make the sweet dessert "ice wines." If you usually drink more than one glass of wine with dinner, the half- or quarter-liter of house wine offered at many restaurants is a better deal than ordering by the glass.

Québec cheeses deserve attention, and many can only be sampled in Canada because they are often unpasteurized in the French manner, and cannot be sold in the United States. Quebecois themselves have come to a new appreciation of this native product, in part due to past interruptions in importation of European varieties. Of the more than 70 Québec cheeses available, often served as a separate course in better restaurants, you might look for Mimolette Jeune (firm, fragrant, orange in color), Valbert St-Isidor (similar to Swiss in texture, but more assertive nose), St-Basil de Port Neuf (buttery), Cru des Erables (soft, ripe, made of raw milk), Oka (semisoft, pleasantly smelly, made of cow's milk in a monastery), Le Migneron (semisoft, from goat's milk), and Le Chèvre Noire (a sharp goat variety covered in black wax).

When "cuisine" is the last thing on your mind and you want a quick meal that will do minimal damage to your credit card balance, Montréal doesn't disappoint. Numerous places serve sandwiches and snacks for only a few dollars. Many of them go by the generic name casse-croûte—which means, literally, "break crust." They couldn't be simpler:

often just a few stools at a counter, with a limited number of menu items that might include soup and *chien chaud* (hot dog) augmented by such homey Quebecois favorites as *tourtière* (beans and pork baked in maple syrup and served as a pie) and *poutine* (french fries doused with gravy and cheese curds). In addition, a number of mostly ethnic eateries serve two-course lunch specials for under C$9 (US$7.20). Look, in particular, to Thai, Chinese, and Indian restaurants for all-you-can-eat lunch buffets at that price.

For a more extended discussion of Québec dining, see "Cuisine Haute, Cuisine Bas: Smoked Meat, Fiddleheads & Caribou," in the appendix at the end of this guide.

An insider website of irreverent reviews and observations about the local dining scene is www.montrealfood.com.

PRICES   The restaurants recommended below have been categorized by neighborhood and then by the cost of an average dinner for one person. Prices listed for main courses in these entries are for dinner unless otherwise indicated (luncheon prices are usually lower). Prices *do not*

include wine, tip, or the 7% federal tax and 8% provincial tax that are added to the restaurant bill. Food purchased in a market or grocery store is not taxed.

PARKING   Because parking space is at a premium in most restaurant districts in Montréal, take the Métro or a taxi to the restaurant (most are within 1 or 2 blocks of a Métro station). Alternatively, when making a reservation, ask if valet parking is available.

SMOKING   The Quebecois are no longer the heaviest smokers in Canada, that distinction having shifted to Nova Scotia's puffers. And even in still-addicted Montréal, smoking in bars and restaurants was supposed to cease altogether by January 2006. Many places started observing the rule months before the deadline.

TIPPING   Montrealers consider 15% of the check (before taxes) to be a fair tip, increased only for exceptional food and service. The easiest way to calculate the amount is to add together the federal and provincial taxes, separately listed on the check. They total 15%.

1 Restaurants by Cuisine

The prices within each review refer to the cost in U.S. dollars of individual main courses, using the following categories: Very Expensive, main courses at dinner average more than $30; Expensive, $21 to $30; Moderate, $10 to $20; and Inexpensive, $10 and under.

BREAKFAST/BRUNCH

Café Cherrier ✹ (Plateau Mont-Royal, $, p. 108)
Claude Postel (Place d'Armes, $, p. 109)
Eggspectation (Downtown, $, p. 109)

DELI

Ben's (Downtown, $, p. 108)
Chez Schwartz Charcuterie Hébraïque de Montréal ✹ (Plateau Mont-Royal, $, p. 103)

FRENCH BISTRO

Boris Bistro ✹ (Vieux-Montréal, $$, p. 97)
Chez Lévêsque (Mile End & Outer Districts, $$, p. 107)
Holder (Vieux-Montréal, $$, p. 98)
La Gargote (Vieux-Montréal, $$, p. 98)
Le Bourlingueur (Vieux-Montréal, $, p. 99)

Leméac (Mile End & Outer Districts, $$, p. 107)

L'Express (Plateau Mont-Royal, $$, p. 102)

FRENCH CONTEMPORARY

Aix Cuisine du Terroir 🍴 (Vieux-Montréal, $$$, p. 94)

Café Méliès (Plateau Mont-Royal, $$, p. 102)

Chez l'Epicier 🍴 (Vieux-Montréal, $$$, p. 94)

Europea 🍴🍴 (Downtown, $$$, p. 89)

Julien (Downtown, $$$, p. 89)

Les Chevres 🍴🍴🍴 (Mile End & Outer Districts, $$$$, p. 105)

Les Remparts 🍴🍴 (Vieux-Montréal, $$$, p. 97)

Nuances 🍴🍴 (Mile End & Outer Districts, $$$$, p. 105)

Rosalie 🍴 (Downtown, $$$, p. 92)

Toqué! 🍴🍴🍴 (Vieux-Montréal), $$$$, p. 93)

Verses 🍴 (Vieux-Montréal, $$$, p. 97)

FRENCH TRADITIONAL

Chez Queux 🍴 (Vieux-Montréal, $$$, p. 96)

FUSION

Area 🍴 (Mile End & Outer Districts, $$$, p. 106)

Brunoise 🍴🍴 (Plateau Mont-Royal, $$$$, p. 100)

Cube 🍴 (Vieux-Montréal, $$$, p. 96)

La Chronique 🍴🍴 (Mile End & Outer Districts, $$$$, p. 104)

Le Blanc 🍴 (Plateau Mont-Royal, $$$, p. 101)

Le Club Chasse et Peche (Vieux-Montréal, $$$, p. 96)

Renoir (Downtown, $$$, p. 89)

Savannah 🍴🍴 (Plateau Mont-Royal, $$, p. 103)

ICE CREAM

Bilboquet 🍴 (Mile End & Outer Districts, $, p 108)

INDIAN

Gandhi 🍴 (Vieux-Montréal, $, p. 99)

Le Taj (Downtown, $$, p. 92)

ITALIAN

BU (Mile End & Outer Districts, $$, p. 106)

ITALIAN CONTEMPORARY

Buona Notte 🍴 (Plateau Mont-Royal, $$$, p. 101)

Cavalli 🍴🍴 (Downtown, $$$$, p. 88)

Globe 🍴 (Plateau Mont-Royal, $$$$, p. 100)

Otto 🍴 (Vieux-Montréal, $$$$, p. 93)

LIGHT FARE

Café Cherrier 🍴 (Plateau Mont-Royal, $, p. 108)

Claude Postel (Place d'Armes, $, p. 109)

Eggspectation (Downtown, $, p. 109)

La Brioche Lyonnaise (Quartier Latin, $, p. 109)

Santropol (Plateau Mont-Royal, $, p. 109)

St-Viateur Bagel & Café 🍴 (Plateau Mont-Royal, $, p. 110)

Titanic (Vieux-Montréal, $, p. 99)

Wilensky Light Lunch (Mile End & Outer Districts, $, p. 110)

MEDITERRANEAN

Modavie 🍴 (Vieux-Montréal, $$, p. 98)

PIZZA

Pizzédélic (Plateau Mont-Royal, $, p. 109)

POLISH

Stash (Vieux-Montréal, $, p. 99)

PORTUGUESE

Café Ferreira 🍴 (Downtown, $$$, p. 88)

QUEBECOIS

Au Pied de Cochon 🍴🍴 (Plateau Mont-Royal, $$, p. 102)

SANDWICHES
La Paryse (Mile End & Outer Districts, $, p. 107)

SEAFOOD
Maestro S.V.P. (Plateau Mont-Royal, $$, p. 103)

STEAKHOUSE
Moishes ℛ (Plateau Mont-Royal, $$$$, p. 101)

THAI
Chao Phraya (Mile End & Outer Districts, $$, p. 106)

VEGETARIAN
Le Commensal (Downtown, $, p. 93)
Santropol (Plateau Mont-Royal, $, p. 109)

VIETNAMESE
Ru de Nam (Mile End & Outer Districts, $, p. 107)

2 Centre Ville/Downtown

VERY EXPENSIVE

Cavalli ℛℛ   ITALIAN CONTEMPORARY   Repeating the formula that brought them success, the owners of the hot Med Grill filled this glamorous space with striking young women in snug black dresses and hunky young men with spiky hair and requisite 4-day beards. It's like joining the after-party of a Hollywood premiere. Being seen and making connections is top priority, but the food is noteworthy, too. Most dishes stick to four or five main ingredients, the better to appreciate the impeccably fresh components. The appetizer of pickled boned skate with roasted portobellini, anchovy, roasted tomatoes, and green-olive sauce is exemplary, as are the wild shrimp tempura with jalapeño mayo and the whitefish carpaccio with tamari vinaigrette. Tempting as it is to simply make a meal of antipasti, that would be to ignore such eminently worthwhile main events as the rack of venison with roasted garlic crust, chestnuts, and grape-caper-olive salsa. Lighter appetites have eight pastas to choose among. Prices are high, assuring a somewhat more prosperous crowd than usually found at similar St-Laurent emporia. The glowing pink bar is a heavy scene later in the evening; Thursday is the big night.

2040 rue Peel (north of rue Ste-Catherine). © 514/843-5100. Reservations recommended. Main courses C$30–C$40 (US$24–US$32). AE, MC, V. Mon–Fri 11:30am–3pm and 5:30–10:30pm; Sat–Sun 5:30–10:30pm (bar open later). Métro: Peel.

EXPENSIVE

Café Ferreira ℛ   PORTUGUESE   *Cataplana* is the name of both a venerated Portuguese recipe and the hinged copper clamshell-style pot in which it is cooked. Ingredients vary depending on the cook, but at this extremely popular downtown spot, that means a fragrant stew of mussels, clams, potatoes, chouriço sausage, and chunks of cod and salmon. The decor won a prize back in 1997; it looks a little dated now, but most of the regulars probably don't notice. Mostly middleaged and dressed in business wear, they fill every seat at lunchtime, but go home at night, which is when to visit if you prefer a bit of tranquility with your caldo verde soup, grilled sardines, or the classic clams and pork, also cooked in a *cataplana*. While the kitchen observes tradition much of the time, it isn't hidebound. In one case, it pairs barely seared tuna with tuna tartare and anoints them with Asian essences; in another, grilled squid with black bean salsa. Many dishes are priced according to the daily market.

1446 rue Peel (near bd. de Maisonneuve). © 514/848-0988. Reservations recommended. Main courses C$27–C$89 (US$22–US$71); table d'hôte lunch C$17–C$32 (US$14–US$26). AE, MC, V. Mon–Fri 11:30am–3pm and 5:30–11pm; Sat 5:30–11:30pm. Métro: Peel.

Europea 👁👁 FRENCH CONTEMPORARY When viewed from the outside, Europea may not appear to be an obvious spot for a meal. Its neighbor, Rosalie (see below), might well seem more appealing. Europea looks like any of a multitude of low-brow cellar eateries found throughout the city. Even once inside, the low ceiling, bare wood floors, and brick walls fail to impress. Then comes the food. The *amuse* (preappetizer) is in a three-segment dish with different tasty nibbles in each. That's followed by an unannounced "teaser," a demitasse of lobster bisque with a shot of truffle oil. A salad follows, perhaps slivers of duck confit arranged with greens and nubbins of goat cheese. The parade of complimentary little bites continues even after the appetizer, possibly a spoonful of venison tartare spiked with fennel threads. Gaps in the procession are short, leading to the main event, maybe the *coquelet* (cockerel) in three sections with garlic mashed potatoes or the filet mignon with cèpes. There are two rooms, one with a bar, and an open kitchen in between. They don't court the family trade—no kiddie menu here—and the average age of diners tends toward the far side of 40. Service is watchful and efficient.

1227 rue de la Montagne (south of rue Ste-Catherine). ℂ 514/398-9229. Reservations strongly recommended. Main courses C$30–C$43 (US$24–US$34); table d'hôte lunch C$21–C$39 (US$17–US$31). AE, DC, MC, V. Mon–Fri noon–2pm and 6–10pm; Sat–Sun 6–10pm. Métro: Peel.

Julien FRENCH CONTEMPORARY A quiet downtown block in the financial district has been home to this relaxed bistro for over 15 years, hosting businesspeople at lunch and just after work and mostly tourists from nearby hotels in the evening. Much of the year diners have the option of tables in the heated patio/garden. They aren't looking for pyrotechnics. The chef isn't interested in being edgy, although he does start out with a trendy *amuse* of marinated salt cod in a porcelain Chinese spoon. Beef cheeks are on almost as many menus as foie gras, and here their silken flesh is set out with carmelized onions atop squash purée. Fresh salmon tartare is joined in a disk with a smoked version of the same fish, belted with a wide ribbon of cucumber. Tuna, duck confit, and lobster salad are entirely satisfactory, brought by an efficient staff working under the steady hand of the witty maitre d'. The cheese selection is good, as is the tiramisu.

1191 av. Union (south of Square Phillips). ℂ 514/871-1581. Reservations suggested. Main courses C$16–C$34 (US$13–US$27); table d'hôte C$16–C$34 (US$13–US$27). AE, DC, DISC, MC, V. Mon–Fri 11:30am–2:30pm and 5:30–10pm; Sun 5:30–10pm. Métro: McGill.

Renoir FUSION Lodged in the instantly popular new Sofitel, this ambitious restaurant likes to think of its food as "inspired." Make that "cautiously creative"— not ostentatious enough to halt conversation in midsentence, but worth an approving comment *en passant* about the sushi-like *amuse-bouche,* perhaps, or the squid stuffed with oxtail and foie gras. Plates are beautifully presented, with the main event, perhaps rib-eye or salmon or crab cake, supported by baby vegetables—haricot verts, teardrop turnips, whole red and yellow peppers no bigger than a thumb. The kitchen's taste for citrus flavors, mainly lemon and orange, appears in several dishes. Lunch is the busiest time, while dinner is quieter, populated mostly by hotel guests (yes, that was Halle Berry at the next table). A large terrace thrusts out toward busy Sherbrooke; in summer, jazz trios entertain diners and passersby. Inside, a pianist plays Thursday through Saturday evenings.

1155 rue Sherbrooke ouest (in the Sofitel Hotel, at rue Stanley). ℂ 514/285-9000. Reservations suggested. Main courses C$18–C$34 (US$14–US$27); table d'hôte lunch C$25 (US$20), dinner C$40 (US$32). AE, DC, DISC, MC, V. Daily 6–10am (until 11am Sat–Sun), 11:30am–2:30pm, and 6–10:30pm. Métro: Peel.

Where to Dine in Downtown Montréal

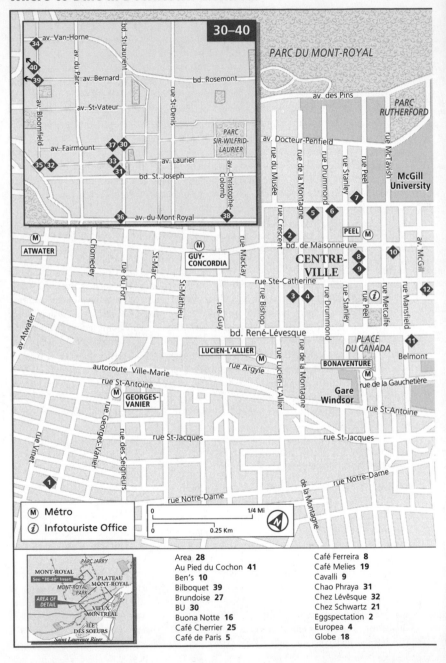

Area 28
Au Pied du Cochon 41
Ben's 10
Bilboquet 39
Brundoise 27
BU 30
Buona Notte 16
Café Cherrier 25
Café de Paris 5

Café Ferreira 8
Café Melies 19
Cavalli 9
Chao Phraya 31
Chez Lévêsque 32
Chez Schwartz 21
Eggspectation 2
Europea 4
Globe 18

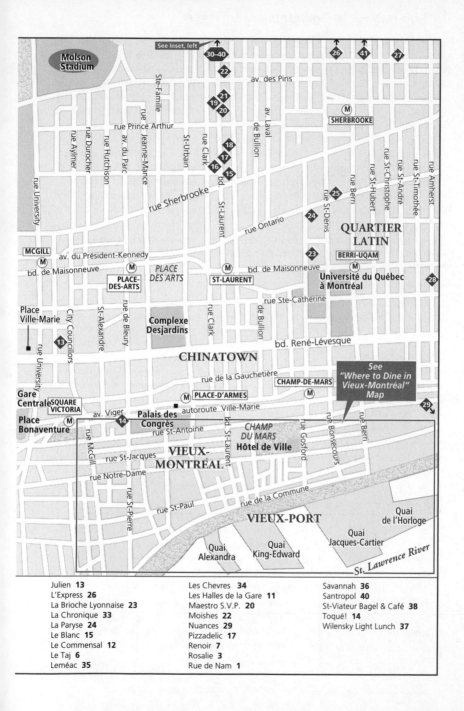

See Inset, left

Molson Stadium

av. des Pins

rue Prince Arthur

rue Sherbrooke

rue Ontario

QUARTIER
LATIN

rue Ste-Famille
rue Ste-Urbain
rue Clark
bd. St-Laurent
rue Aylmer
rue Durocher
rue Jeanne-Mance
rue Hutchison
av. du Parc
rue University
av. Laval
rue de Bullion
rue Berri
rue St-Denis
rue St-Hubert
rue St-Christophe
rue St-André
rue St-Timothée
rue Amherst

M SHERBROOKE

MCGILL
M
av. du Président-Kennedy
bd. de Maisonneuve

PLACE
DES ARTS

M PLACE-DES-ARTS

M ST-LAURENT

bd. de Maisonneuve

BERRI-UQAM

Université du Québec
à Montréal

M

rue Ste-Catherine

Place
Ville-Marie

City Councillors
St-Alexandre
rue de Bleury
rue Clark
rue de Bullion
rue University

Complexe
Desjardins

bd. René-Lévesque

CHINATOWN

rue de la Gauchetière

See
"Where to Dine in
Vieux-Montréal"
Map

CHAMP-DE-MARS

Gare
Centrale SQUARE
VICTORIA
M

M PLACE-D'ARMES

Place
Bonaventure
M

av. Viger
Palais des
Congrès

autoroute Ville-Marie

bd. St-Laurent
rue Gosford
rue Bonsecours
rue Berri

CHAMP
DU MARS
Hôtel de Ville

rue McGill
rue St-Jacques
rue Notre-Dame
rue St-Pierre
rue St-Paul

rue St-Antoine

VIEUX-
MONTRÉAL

rue de la Commune

VIEUX-PORT

Quai
de l'Horloge

Quai
Jacques-Cartier

Quai
Alexandra

Quai
King-Edward

St. Lawrence River

Julien **13**	Les Chevres **34**	Savannah **36**
L'Express **26**	Les Halles de la Gare **11**	Santropol **40**
La Brioche Lyonnaise **23**	Maestro S.V.P. **20**	St-Viateur Bagel & Café **38**
La Chronique **33**	Moishes **22**	Toqué! **14**
La Paryse **24**	Nuances **29**	Wilensky Light Lunch **37**
Le Blanc **15**	Pizzadelic **17**	
Le Commensal **12**	Renoir **7**	
Le Taj **6**	Rosalie **3**	
Leméac **35**	Rue de Nam **1**	

Rosalie ℛ FRENCH CONTEMPORARY   Big, boisterous, congenial—this eat-ing-and-meeting spot in the midst of the rue Crescent hubbub is all of that. The owner, David McMillan (who is also boisterous and congenial), also is involved with the similar Globe on St-Laurent and the Time Supper Club, among other trendy enterprises. He seems to have discovered a bottomless source of great-looking young men and women to compose the staffs. They are very friendly, and good enough at their tasks. They attend to throngs of people who look like they spend most of their evenings in places like this, including the beefy guys who sometimes frequent the long marble bar looking like candidates for *The Sopranos: North*. Out front is an active ter-race; inside, patrons draw leather-sling chairs up to the ranks of bare tables. Food is of the updated bistro style, including such dishes as an appetizer of thinly sliced roast rabbit with leek rémoulade and a hanger steak with carmelized onions. None of the food is too complicated, and most of it is tasty. After 8pm, the lights go down and the decibel level shoots up.

1232 rue de la Montagne (south of rue Ste-Catherine). ✆ 514/392-1970. Reservations advised. Main courses lunch C$16–C$24 (US$13–US$19), dinner C$17–C$29 (US$14–US$23). AE, DC, MC, V. Mon–Fri 11am–midnight; Sat–Sun 5pm–midnight. Métro: Peel.

MODERATE

Le Taj *Value* INDIAN   They've modified the decor, eliminated the gift shop at the front, and painted and carpeted. But this remains one of the tastiest bargains down-town. The price of the lunch buffet has barely changed in 20 years, and the five-course dinner costs less than C$24 (US$19). The kitchen specializes in the mughlai cuisine of the subcontinent. Seasonings tend more toward the tangy than the incendiary, but say you want your food spicy and you'll get it. (And watch out for the innocent-looking green coriander sauce.) Whatever the level of heat, dishes are perfumed with turmeric, saffron, ginger, cumin, mango powder, and *garam masala* (a spice combination that usually includes cloves, cardamom, and cinnamon). For a real treat, order the mari-nated lamb chops roasted in the tandoor; they arrive at the table sizzling and nested on braised vegetables. Vegetarians have ample choices, the chickpea-based *channa masala* among the most complex. Main courses are huge, arriving in a boggling array of bowls,

---

⟨Kids⟩ Family-Friendly Restaurants

Bilboquet (p. 108)   They have sandwiches and other light snacks, but the attraction (and justification for the long ride from downtown) is the ice cream. It's made right there, and while youngsters may prefer plain vanilla, their adult companions find themselves immobilized with choice over con-coctions that incorporate such ingredients as passion fruit and maple taffy.

Magnan   Known especially for its supercheap all-you-can-eat lobster and beef extravaganzas, the menu also has lots of sandwiches and other simple foods that kids like. Parents don't have to worry about inevitable messes, especially since they'll be making big ones themselves. 2602 rue St-Patrick, Pointe St-Charles. ✆ 514/935-9647.

Pizzédélic (p. 109)   Pizza never fails to please the younger set, and these places cater to any taste, with toppings that stretch the imagination.

saucers, cups, and dishes, all accompanied by naan (the pillowy flat bread) and basmati rice. Evenings are quiet, and lunchtimes are busy but not hectic.

2077 rue Stanley (near rue Sherbrooke). 🕿 **514/845-9015.** Main courses C$10–C$14 (US$8–US$11); lunch buffet C$10 (US$8); table d'hôte dinner C$23 (US$19). AE, DC, MC, V. Mon–Fri 11:30am–2:30pm and 5–10:30pm; Sat 5–11pm; Sun 5–10:30pm. Métro: Peel.

INEXPENSIVE

Le Commensal VEGETARIAN *(Value*   Le Commensal serves vegetarian fare buffet-style. Most of the dishes are so artfully conceived, with close attention paid to aroma, color, and texture, that even avowed meat eaters don't feel deprived. The only likely complaint is that dishes that are supposed to be hot are too often lukewarm. There are more than 100 items, from appetizers to desserts. Patrons circle the table helping themselves, and then pay the cashier by weight—C$1.69 (US$1.35) per 100 grams for the main buffet, C$1.85 (US$1.50) for desserts. The second-floor location affords a view, which compensates for the utilitarian decor. There is no tipping. Beer and wine are available.

Le Commensal has been expanding, with nine branches scattered around the greater Montréal area and in Toronto. Another convenient in-town location is at 1720 rue St-Denis (Sherbrooke; 🕿 **514/845-2627**).

1204 av. McGill College (at rue Ste-Catherine). 🕿 **514/871-1480.** Reservations not accepted. Most meals under C$12 (US$9.60). AE, MC, V. Daily 11am–10:30pm (until 11pm Fri–Sat). Métro: McGill or Bonaventure.

3 Vieux-Montréal (Old Montréal)

VERY EXPENSIVE

Otto 🛪 ITALIAN CONTEMPORARY   The new upscale hotels opened in the city over the past several years have made a point of creating desirable in-house restaurants, many of them recommended in these pages. This one, in the glossy new W Hotel, hit the ground running. It's a proper reflection of the stylish thrust of the building surrounding it, in design, clientele, and character of cuisine. The waitstaff is unrelentingly gorgeous, and serves patrons as lean, well-coifed, and stylishly attired as they. (Wear black. Armani is good.) Decor, admittedly rather overwrought, incorporates an undulating biomorphic ceiling, and red, black, and grey-striped wallpaper. The largely Italian repertoire is given fresh interpretation, from antipasti to il dolce. All the current Montréal faves are at hand, each given a special twist. There has to be, and is, a beef tartare, crunchy with green onions, zinged with capers and Japanese mustard, and topped with poached quail eggs. Among the dinner preparations you don't see everywhere else are gnocchi with prawns, sweet peas, corn kernels, and a Champagne clam sauce. Grilled tuna is served with sautéed bok choy and lentils *du puy,* all dressed in a brandy sauce. None of this constitutes a bargain, but the three-course fixed-price lunch menu comes close.

In the W Hôtel, 901 Square Victoria (near rue St-Antoine). 🕿 **514/395-3183.** Reservations recommended. Main courses C$26–C$42 (US$21–US$34); table d'hôte lunch C$24–C$29 (US$19–US$23). Daily 11:30am–2:30pm and 5:30–10:30pm. Métro: Square Victoria.

Toqué! 🛪🛪🛪 FRENCH CONTEMPORARY   Toqué! is a gem that single-handedly raised the gastronomic expectations of the entire city. A meal here is obligatory for anyone who admires superb food, dazzlingly presented. "Post-nouvelle" might be an apt description for the creations of Normand Laprise, for while presentations are eye-opening, the portions are quite sufficient and the singular combinations of ingredients are intensely flavorful. Asian and related Fusion influences are more evident these days, notably with overly pervasive foams, but the chef is still grounded in principles of the French contemporary kitchen. Top-of-the-bin ingredients, some of them rarely seen in combination—for example, Jerusalem artichoke soup with pomegranate reduction and foie gras shavings—ensure that the menu is never set in stone. Consider just one recent dish: roast squab and raspberry vinegar purée, with seasonal root vegetable, girolle mushrooms, and sautéed rapini. Duck, lamb, quail, and venison are unfailingly memorable, while salmon and Arctic char are often the most delectable fishes.

If you choose the tasting menu, the six courses can be accompanied by wines selected to complement each preparation. The restaurant fills up later than most, with prosperous-looking men in suits and women who sparkle at throat and wrist, so while there is no stated dress code, you'll want to look your best. Service is efficient, helpful, and not a bit self-important. Allow 2 hours for dinner. Call at least 3 days ahead for reservations and confirm the night before.

Note: Toqué! has moved from its longtime location on St-Denis in the Plateau Mont-Royal to a site recently designated as the Quartier International, next to Vieux-Montréal and opposite the west end of the new convention center, Palais des Congrès.

900 place Jean-Paul-Riopelle (near rue St-Antoine). (©) **514/499-2084.** Reservations required. Table d'hôte lunch C$38 (US$30); degustation menus C$84 (US$67) or C$94 (US$75); main courses C$28–C$41 (US$22–US$33). AE, MC, V. Tues–Fri 11:30am–2pm and 5:30–10:30pm; Sat 5:30–10:30pm. Closed Dec 24–Jan 6. Métro: Sherbrooke.

EXPENSIVE

Aix Cuisine du Terroir (©) FRENCH CONTEMPORARY   Replacing the less-than-mediocre resto once lodged beneath the Hôtel Place d'Armes, this new addition makes Vieux-Montréal dining even more attractive. It received immediate critical plaudits, if only due to the stark contrast with its predecessor. *Terroir,* to be clear, refers not to unspeakable political acts, but to a gastronomical allegiance to use of the products of the immediate region whenever possible. Contemplate the possibilities with a more generous martini than the highly taxed Canadian norm. An *amuse* of bits of grilled shrimp over seaweed drizzled with sesame oil helps. Among the appetizers might be a foie gras terrine with sun-dried cherries and house-smoked salmon with a buckwheat crepe and salmon roe. After that, perhaps braised wild boar with *choucroute* and stewed baby onions or pan-roasted red snapper with fiddleheads perked with the crunch of sea salt. Restful earth tones and soft lighting keep the mood subdued, especially in the evening.

711 côte de la Place d'Armes (near rue Notre-Dame). (©) **514/904-1201.** Main courses C$27–C$31 (US$22–US$25). AE, DC, MC, V. Mon–Fri 11:30am–2pm and 7–10:30pm; Sat–Sun 6–11pm.

Chez l'Epicier (©) FRENCH CONTEMPORARY   This crisp little eatery opposite the Marché Bonsecours is on the route of the Vieux-Montréal walking tour outlined in chapter 8. And because it's also a delicatessen with an abundance of tempting prepared foods, it's a place to remember for a picnic down the hill in the Vieux-Port. When it started up a few years ago, food here was workman-like, if flavors were too often wan. Over time, the kitchen took a welcome turn to more fashionable, extravagant preparations. Success nurtured ambition, and the chef-proprietor has taken on a new project, a restaurant a few doors away in the old Hotel Rasco. That distraction led to the hiring of a brilliant young chef, David Biron, from Québec City, who has energized the kitchen with his wizardry. Just one example is his amusing dessert, a chocolate "club sandwich," with sliced strawberries standing in for tomato, basil for

Where to Dine in Vieux-Montréal

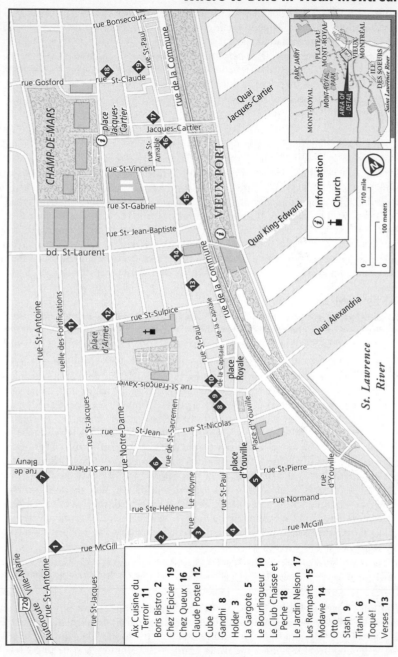

Aix Cuisine du Terroir **11**
Boris Bistro **2**
Chez l'Épicier **19**
Chez Queux **16**
Claude Postel **12**
Cube **4**
Gandhi **8**
Holder **3**
La Gargote **5**
Le Bourlingueur **10**
Le Club Chaisse et Peche **18**
Le Jardin Nelson **17**
Les Remparts **15**
Modavie **14**
Otto **1**
Stash **9**
Titanic **6**
Toqué! **7**
Verses **13**

lettuce, and chocolate for roast beef, with pineapple "fries" on the side. Unfortunately for his current boss, but happily for Montrealers, Biron almost certainly will soon leave to open his own restaurant.

331 rue St-Paul est (at rue St-Claude). ☎ **514/878-2232.** Main courses dinner C$21–C$35 (US$17–US$23); table d'hôte lunch C$15–C$20 (US$12–US$16). AE, DC, DISC, MC, V. Mon–Fri 11:30am–2pm; daily 5:30–10pm. Métro: Champ-de-Mars.

Chez Queux ✱ FRENCH TRADITIONAL   This is a throwback to a time when the only cuisine was French, and that meant chateaubriand for two, showy tableside preparations, and flaming desserts. All the usual suspects, that is, as remembered from birthdays and anniversaries in the '60s. These days, such a menu often results in tired renditions from chefs bored to tears with the weight of tradition. Not so here. A properly romantic mood is nurtured by the baronial setting of a mansion built for a mayor of the city in 1862. Deep paneling contrasts with exposed brick walls, fringed lamp-shades over the tables, wrought-iron chandeliers, weighty velvet drapes, a baby grand, and a two-sided gas fireplace that casts shadows over all. The waiters even wear tuxedos. The food is, no question, decidedly retro, but the execution is superb. Lobster bisque, Dover sole meunière, rack of lamb, sweetbreads with morels, and even crêpes suzette are better than those of a certain age will recall and will be a revelation to those too young to remember the Kennedy administration. A summer dining terrace adds views of the Vieux-Port to the experience. In short, it's a place to fire a new relationship or cement an old one.

158 rue St-Paul est (near place Jacques Cartier). ☎ **514/866-7758.** Reservations suggested. Main courses C$17–C$41 (US$14–US$33); table d'hôte (with wine) C$79 (US$63). AE, DC, DISC, MC, V. Daily 11:30am–3pm and 5–11pm. Métro: Square Victoria.

Cube ✱ FUSION   Its name derives from the shape of the room, which carries through on the rectilinear design that informs the Hôtel St-Paul (p. 81) in which it is housed. It has square bread boxes, inlaid wood squares on the tables, and square wine coolers, salt containers, and butter plates. Happily, the conceit wasn't extended to the soup bowls. None of this should distract from the food, which is some of the best to be enjoyed in Vieux-Montréal. One appetizer on the short menu is a layered cube (of course) of goat cheese, spinach, tomato confit, and yellow sweet pepper. That can be followed by a filet of Chilean sea bass framed with shrimp and clams, dressed with a pistou of basil, garlic, and olive oil, all of it set atop a nest of lemon pasta. A delectable excess is found in the Angus beef topped with oysters, foie gras, and marrow. Now that the white-hot trendiness of its first year has cooled, the rest of us can get a reservation. And, since it's a hotel restaurant, it serves lunch and dinner every day, unlike those delicate little boîtes that can barely bring themselves to open for a couple of hours 5 nights a week.

355 rue McGill (at rue St-Paul). ☎ **514/876-2823.** Reservations recommended. Main courses C$30–C$42 (US$24–US$34); table d'hôte lunch C$23 (US$18). AE, DC, MC, V. Daily 11:30am–2:30pm and 6–11pm. Métro: Square Victoria.

Le Club Chasse et Peche FUSION   It'll be interesting to see how this addition to the Vieux-Montréal scene evolves. The hosannas uttered by local foodies after the December 2004 opening were premature. It still needed work. They say they're getting a sign out front, but since the name translates as "Hunting and Fishing Club," that might not help. The haphazard quality of the interior suggests that no designer had a hand, but its cavern-like character isn't unlikable. The short menu seems simple enough until the waiter comes, kneels beside the table, and describes all 11 items in considerable detail. Happily, the food is pretty good, presented in deep white bowls and on triangular and square plates. Starters include briny oysters with various unusual dressings, including flying fish roe and a zinfandel reduction. "Surf 'n' Turf" turned out to be lobster and rabbit. Time tends to s-t-r-e-t-ch between courses, and the animated patrons at other tables underscore the caution that this isn't a place to go alone. A fairly busy bar has the same menu. This is a work in progress, if you're up for an experiment.

423 rue St-Claude (between rue St-Paul and rue Notre Dame). (*C*) **514/861-1112.** Reservations suggested. Main courses C$22–C$31 (US$18–US$25). AE, MC, V. Tues–Fri 11:30am–2pm and 5–11pm; Sat 5–11pm.

Les Remparts *☞☞* FRENCH CONTEMPORARY   There's no doubt that you're in the basement of the Auberge du Vieux-Port, not when you're seated beneath these heavy beams and copper-painted pipes and vents. A cellar seems an unlikely setting for what is one of Old Montréal's most accomplished kitchens. The chef started here as an assistant and took over a few months later. He works whenever possible with products of the region, redrawing his menu with the seasons to take full advantage of what's available. One of Canada's most desirable fish, Gaspesian char, comes with wild rice and pepper confit. Lunch is a bargain, but the chef's true showmanship blossoms at dinnertime, with sophisticated dishes such as butter-roasted veal chop and rabbit leg confit and saddle stuffed with caramelized hazelnuts in thyme *jus*.

93 rue de la Commune est (near rue St-Gabriel). (*C*) **514/392-1649.** Reservations recommended on weekends. Main courses C$28–C$36 (US$22–US$29); table d'hôte lunch C$14–C$18 (US$11–US$14). Mon–Fri noon–3pm and 6–10:30pm; Sat–Sun 6–11pm. Métro: Place d'Armes.

Verses *☞* FRENCH CONTEMPORARY   The flowering of boutique hotels has given multiple jolts of glamour to Old Montréal, joining daring design with the preservation of historic buildings. An additional benefit has been the creation of hotel restaurants that destroy the image of a threadbare dining room that people conjure up when they hear the words "hotel restaurant." Especially notable are Cube, in the Hôtel St-Paul (p. 81); Les Remparts, in the Auberge du Vieux-Port (p. 79); and this one, Verses, in the Hôtel Nelligan. With its leather lounge chairs, horseshoe bar, and ancient stone and brick walls, it's welcoming and clubby. That ambience contributes to the active bar scene toward week's end, especially when the weather is warm enough to open the doors at the front. Service is adroit and knowledgeable, while thankfully short on pretension, and the pace of a meal is sedate. Lunch can be a burger or seared foie gras with caramelized peaches, while dinner choices have included rack of venison, lobster and scallop risotto, and a 14-ounce New York steak with truffled potatoes. No fancy foams or nasturtiums on these plates.

106 rue St-Paul est (west of bd. St-Laurent). (*C*) **514/842-1887.** Reservations recommended. Main courses lunch C$13–C$34 (US$10–US$27), dinner C$21–C$35 (US$17–US$28). Daily 7am–10:30pm (until 11pm Fri–Sat). Métro: Square Victoria.

MODERATE

Boris Bistro *☞ (Finds)* FRENCH BISTRO   "Boris" is the owner's dog, depicted in the restaurant logo as a canine sophisticate in a turtleneck. Putting aside questions of Gallic relationships with their pets, this hugely popular eatery takes full advantage of the excitement of the western end of Vieux-Montréal, opposite the new Cité Multimédia. Although not much work has gone into the interior (a minimalist environment with a bare concrete floor, beams, and exposed vents), the staff and patrons transform the restaurant into a lighthearted space. The hallmarks here are very reasonable prices and such bistro classics as *blanquette de veau,* bouillabaisse, salmon *tartare,* and mussels du jour. Frites with mayo are a stand-alone appetizer, not as maddeningly tasty as they used to be when deep-fried in duck fat. If it's nice outside, head straight for the court-yard and tables that seat 160 under big square patio umbrellas.

465 av. McGill (near rue des Récollets). ℂ 514/848-9575. Reservations recommended on weekend nights. Main courses C$13–C$19 (US$10–US$15). AE, MC, V. Daily 11:30am–11pm (may close Sun and Mon nights in winter). Closed 3 weeks at Christmas. Métro: Square Victoria.

Holder ⊰ FRENCH BISTRO   Housed in the corner of a squat old office building halfway between Square Victoria and the Old Port, this is a generously proportioned space, more corporate than folksy in tone. That atmosphere is strengthened at lunch, when brokers, lawyers, and execs entertaining clients predominate, most of whom resist the impulse to whip out their cellphones. Evenings, they bring their spouses and girlfriends or boyfriends and mingle with neighborhood residents. It didn't take much imagination to put together the menu, filled out as it is with bistro standards. But just because you've seen these things before—fried calamari, lobster bisque, crab and corn cakes, duck confit, beef tartare—doesn't mean the food isn't satisfying. Dishes are pret-tily composed, often served in deep bowls that the ingredients don't require (a stylis-tic conceit much in vogue). Consider the daily specials, which are often more inventive than the standard menu. One such special was a halibut filet with gently braised celery root and saffron potatoes. If nothing appeals on the specials list, there's always the reliable hanger steak *avec frites.*

407 rue McGill (at rue Le Moyne). ℂ 514/849-0333. Main courses C$15–C$24 (US$12–US$19). AE, DC, MC, V. Mon–Wed 11:30am–11pm; Thurs–Fri 11:30am–midnight; Sat 5:30pm–midnight; Sun 5:30–11pm. Métro: Square Victoria.

La Gargote FRENCH BISTRO   Tourists have discovered this spirited little bistro, which was already packed with locals. (Obviously, they aren't deterred by the name, which is translated as "The Greasy Spoon.") That means the staff is spread thin try-ing to deal with the crush, so swift meals aren't to be expected. The chatty patrons are satisfied by such classics as duck sausage *a l'orange,* and lamb and Merguez sausage couscous, along with less familiar possibilities such as *paupiettes* (rolls) of pheasant with mushrooms and currants. The surroundings are the Vieux-Montréal norm, with stone-and-brick walls and rough-cut rafters overhead. The room is warmed by a fire-place in winter. Meals are also put together for takeout—meant for offices, but useful for a picnic in the nearby waterfront park. Better still is lunch at the tables set out in the plaza May through September.

351 place d'Youville (at rue St-Pierre). ℂ 514/844-1428. Reservations recommended. Main courses and table d'hôte lunch C$15–C$25 (US$12–US$20); table d'hôte dinner C$18–C$23 (US$14–US$18). MC, V. Mon–Fri noon–2pm; Mon–Sat 5:30–10pm. Métro: Square Victoria.

Modavie ⊰ MEDITERRANEAN   A highly visible location no doubt helps keep this wine bar/restaurant filled, but the management leaves little to chance. Arrayed around the handsome center bar are walls of shelves stacked with bottles of wine, sin-gle-malt scotches, and fine cigars. There are free bar snacks during the 4 to 7pm happy hours Monday through Friday. Live jazz is presented at 7pm every night in summer, and Friday and Saturday nights in winter. Candle flames flicker in river breezes that flow in through front and side windows flung wide on summer nights. The food doesn't disappoint, either in preparation or in portion. Lamb is their self-proclaimed specialty; in one version, four double chops are propped over a mixture of sweet peppers, cauliflower, and broccoli rabe. There are specials, too, such as Szechuan pepper-blackened shark with sweet pepper couli.

1 rue St-Paul ouest (corner of rue St-Laurent). © 514/287-9582. Reservations recommended on weekends. Table d'hôte lunch and early-bird dinner (4–6pm) C$16 (US$13); main courses dinner C$15–C$30 (US$12–US$24). Daily 11:30am–3pm and 6–11pm. Métro: Place d'Armes.

INEXPENSIVE

Gandhi ℛ (Value INDIAN   A clear step up in class from those gaudy all-you-can-eat feeding troughs, the interior of this storefront eatery is painted creamy yellow and white, with bare wood floors and white napery. No decorative ethnic excesses are on display here, unless you count a couple of framed embroideries depicting dancers and elephants and the soft sitar music on the stereo. Service is polite but brisk. The cooking is mostly to order and arrives fresh from the pot, pan, or oven. Flavors are delicate and subtle. More authentically assertive seasonings might be wished, but there is no offer to ramp them up according to individual taste. Tandoori duck and lamb and chicken tikka are popular. Vegetarian dishes fill a large section of the card.

230 rue St-Paul ouest (near rue St-François-Xavier). © 514/845-5866. Reservations advised on weekends. Table d'hôte lunch C$14–C$17 (US$11–US$14); main courses dinner C$9.50–C$21 (US$7.60–US$17). AE, MC, V. Mon–Fri 11:30am–2pm; daily 5–10:30pm. Métro: Square Victoria.

Le Bourlingueur (Value FRENCH BISTRO   Although it doesn't look especially promising upon first approach, this is a keeper. The restaurant charges almost unbelievably low prices for several four-course meals daily. The blackboard menu changes depending on what's available at the market that day, making it possible to dine here twice a day for a week without repeating anything, except the uninteresting salad. Roast pork with apples, glazed duck leg, and *choucroute garnie* (sauerkraut with meat) are likely to show up, but the specialty of the house is seafood—watch for the shrimp in Pernod sauce. Well short of chic, the interior doesn't make the most of the stone walls and old beams, but the decor hardly matters at these prices and relative quality. The crowd is diverse, with a wide range of ages, genders, and occupations.

363 rue St-François-Xavier (at rue St-Paul). © 514/845-3646. Reservations recommended on weekends. Main courses and table d'hôte lunch and dinner C$10–C$16 (US$8–US$13). MC, V. Daily 11:30am–9pm. Métro: Place d'Armes.

Stash (Value POLISH   At this site for over a decade, this *restauracja polska* continues to draw throngs of enthusiastic returnees for its abundant offerings and low prices. The interior is composed of brick-and-stone walls, hanging lamps, and wood refractory tables and pews salvaged from an old convent. Roast wild boar has long been featured, along with *bigos,* a cabbage and meat stew, and pirogis, dumplings stuffed with meat and cheese, to be expected in a Polish restaurant. Filling options and sides to these include potato pancakes, borscht with sour cream, and roast duck. A jolly tone prevails, with animated patrons and such menu admonitions as "anything tastes better with wodka, even wodka." An upright piano is played some evenings.

200 rue St-Paul oust (at rue St-François-Xavier). © 514/845-6611. Table d'hôte dinner C$26–C$30 (US$21–US$24); main courses C$12–C$16 (US$9.60–US$13). AE, MC, V. Mon–Fri 11am–10:30pm; Sat–Sun noon–10:30pm. Métro: Place d'Armes.

Titanic LIGHT FARE   Really good sandwiches aren't easy to find, but they come to luscious life here. Freshly baked baguettes are split and filled with such savory combos as coarse country pâté with green peppercorns, or smoked ham and brie, or roast pork with chutney. There's a short cafeteria line of cold dishes, but go for the hot daily specials.

Available extras to go with any of the sandwiches include cornichons (mini gherkin pickles), pickled onions, olive pesto, cukes, and capers. Stop in for a breakfast omelet, a meal-size antipasto plate, or an afternoon snack. No alcoholic beverages, but with good ol' Dad's Root Beer, who needs Chablis? Two ramshackle rooms with overhead pipes contain two counters and a large communal table. Note that the restaurant closes at 4pm. Payment is on the honor system.

45 rue St-Pierre (near rue Le Moyne). ℂ 514/849-0894. Most items under C$12 (US$9.60). MC, V. Mon–Fri 7am–4pm. Métro: Place d'Armes.

4 Plateau Mont-Royal

Most of the restaurants reviewed below can be found on the "Where to Dine in Downtown Montréal" map, on p. 90.

VERY EXPENSIVE

Brunoise 🍷🍷 FUSION   The kitchen half of this two-man partnership takes full advantage of his ingredients. His mussel-and-potato *bourride* (similar to bouillabaisse) gives off a far stronger aroma of saffron than from cooks who simply use it as coloring; vegetables are crunchy, the broth aromatic. Diners are set up with a dashing little *amuse-bouche*—three tiny fiddleheads with shredded celeriac, in one case. After soup or appetizer or both, even the fairly short list of main courses promotes indecision. The choices reveal many influences, as broad as Asian and Mediterranean and as focused as Catalan, seen in quail *escabeche* with lentils, crispy lardoons, and almond cream, and duck breast with Swiss chard, shiitake tatin, and five-spice sauce. In his zeal to innovate, the chef sometimes commits the sin of too many ingredients pushed and pulled into shape for presentation purposes. The square of halibut filet resting on spinach and haricots vert, an artichoke purée to one side, with a tumble of olives and cherry tomatoes over all is an example. But choose the simpler preparations and you can expect sublime satisfaction. Glasses are filled and empty plates are cleared with alacrity by the efficient staff.

3807 rue St-Andre (at rue Roy). ℂ 514/523-3885. Reservations advised. Main courses C$34–C$46 (US$27–US$37). AE, MC, V. Daily 5:30–10:30pm. Closed 3 weeks at Christmas. Métro: Sherbrooke.

Globe 🍷 ITALIAN CONTEMPORARY   Another erotically charged, high-end undertaking from David McMillan (see Rosalie, p. 92), starting with hostesses at the podium who may have just stopped by between runway gigs, continuing with waitresses bringing food that's better than it has to be, and ending with dancing at midnight and a lot of hooking up. In other words, it's not very different from a clutch of similar enterprises at this lively end of The Main north of Sherbrooke—Buona Notte, Med Grill, Le Blanc, Primadonna—just a little pricier. There's a bar down on the left of the row of square mirrored columns where the activity intensifies after 9pm. Meals, if that's why you're here, can begin with selections from an oyster bar listing as many as a dozen varieties, but other appetizers are as appealing. One is a thick disk incorporating layers of warm goat cheese, tomato confit, and potatoes, a scattering of toasted pine nuts over all. After that, robust but uncomplicated helpings of beef, suckling pig, lamb, venison, ribs, and rabbit are the rule, but chicken and salmon are lighter possibilities. A splurge for two is the C$70 (US$56) *plateau de mer*, a wide platter of iced seafood including clams, mussels, crab legs, and other marine critters, depending on availability.

3455 bd. St-Laurent (near rue Sherbrooke). ℂ 514/284-3823. Reservations suggested. Main courses C$27–$C49 (US$22–US$39). AE, DC, MC, V. Daily 6–11pm (until midnight Thurs–Sat). Métro: St-Laurent.

Moishes ✱ STEAKHOUSE   Those who care to spend serious money for a slab of charred beef should take their credit ratings here. The oldest steak-and-seafood house in town is also arguably its finest, and less afflicted with tourists than the popular Gibby's in Vieux-Montréal. It was also dark, musty, and populated with crusty waiters. Recent redecoration changed part of that equation, with four windows installed where there weren't any before. Two out of three isn't bad, and the venerable retainers who bring the food have eased up on the crabbiness. Moishes now gets the trim new breed of up-and-coming executives as well as those of the older generation who didn't know about triglycerides until it was too late. The former are more likely to go for the lighter side of the menu—chicken teriyaki or Arctic char, perhaps—while the latter stick with various cuts of cow in their choice of several sauces. The mixed grill is just the thing for the indecisive, as it includes two lamb chops, a Rumanian sausage, two small filet mignon, and sweetbreads. Dishes of pickles and slaw still come with the bread basket. The wine list is substantial, ranging from a C$40 (US$32) Mouton Cadet to a 1990 Romanée Conti for C$3,600 (US$2,880).

3961 bd. St-Laurent (north of rue Prince Arthur). ✆ 514/845-3509. Reservations suggested. Main courses C$26–C$46 (US$21–US$37). AE, DC, MC, V. Mon–Fri 11:30am–2:30pm and 5:30–11pm. Métro: Sherbrooke.

EXPENSIVE

Buona Notte ✱ ITALIAN CONTEMPORARY   With its high ceiling laced with electric fans and heating ducts, Buona Notte could be in New York's SoHo. A principal component of the decor is the collection of nearly 500 plates painted by celebrity diners, among them George Clooney, Jim Carrey, and Robert De Niro. They are boxed (the plates, that is) and arrayed along the walls. Funk and hip-hop thump over the stereo, and the waitresses look ready to depart on the next fashion shoot. They appear in black (with splashes of carefree gray), as do most of their customers, all with cellphones at the ready. Although the food takes second place to the preening, the dishes are surprisingly worthwhile. Pastas prevail, tumbled with crunchy vegetables or silky walnut sauce or any of 10 or more other combinations. The kitchen exhibits less reliance on meat than the norm. Service is stretched thin at dinner, especially on the weekends, and the noise level cranks up after 7pm. The active bar in back stays open until 3am.

3518 bd. St-Laurent (near rue Sherbrooke). ✆ 514/848-0644. Reservations recommended. Main courses C$11–C$36 (US$8.80–US$29); table d'hôte lunch C$32 (US$26), dinner C$35 (US$28). AE, DC, MC, V. Mon–Sat 11:30am–midnight (until 1am Thurs–Sat); Sun 5pm–midnight (bar until 3am daily). Métro: St-Laurent.

Le Blanc ✱ FUSION   Once a jinxed location that had seen three other restaurants crash in the past decade, this latest manifestation has lasted 6 years, and 80-foot stretch limos regularly pull up to the door. Office workers take advantage of the inexpensive fixed-price lunches, moving aside for a 20- and 30-something crowd in the evening, when jazz combos and singers provide a supper-club atmosphere, with dancing until 3am. The pleasingly Art Deco space has a few romantically secluded booths to one side and the front opens to the street in good weather. Food is of the globe-hopping sort, but none of it is bizarre. One standard menu item is the roasted half-pigeon with wild fruits topped with pan-fried foie gras—tasty. You might make a meal of appetizers— the smoked pepper spring roll with coconut milk sauce and the spicy strawberry and chive bowtie pasta, perhaps. Or, this could be the place to try filet of horse.

3435 bd. St-Laurent (north of rue Sherbrooke). ✆ 514/288-9909. Main courses C$30–C$42 (US$24–US$34); table d'hôte lunch C$15–C$19 (US$12–US$15), dinner C$28–C$41 (US$22–US$33). AE, DC, MC, V. Mon–Fri noon–3pm and 5:30–10:30pm (bar until 3am); Sat–Sun 5:30pm–midnight (bar until 3am). Métro: Sherbrooke.

MODERATE

Au Pied de Cochon 🐷🐷 QUEBECOIS   It might seem like this place is selling Beluga caviar at *hambourgeois* prices, the way it's packed to the walls 6 nights a week. (The crowd starts thinning out after 9pm.) And though it looks like another of the amiable-but-mediocre storefront restos that line most streets in the Plateau, famed chef Normand Laprise of Toqué! (p. 93) reportedly loves the place. Leave cholesterol concerns at the door. As the name—"The Pig's Foot"—suggests, this is all about slabs of beef, pork, lamb, venison, and duck. "The Big Happy Pig's Chop," more than a pound of meat, is emblematic. Meats are roasted to a falling-off-the-bone turn in the brick oven surviving from a previous pizza joint. No subterfuge here: Most dishes have only four or five easily identifiable ingredients, in balanced proportions. They do get clever with one pervasive product: foie gras. It comes in several combinations, including with ground beef, with flan, or stuffed into a ham hock. The version in concert with *poutine* makes one reconsider negative impressions of that classic Quebecoise comfort food. In summer, they offer seafood platters. Sugar pie is the only fitting finisher.

536 rue Duluth est (near rue St-Hubert). © **514/281-1116.** Reservations strongly advised. Main courses C$12–C$33 (US$9.60–US$26). MC, V. Tues–Sun 5pm–midnight. Métro: Sherbrooke.

Café Méliès FRENCH CONTEMPORARY   Located inside the Ex-centris film center, this cafe-lounge has grown into a neighborhood favorite independent of its original function as an appendage to the cinema. Certainly it can be utilized as a quick dinner before the show, but people drop in for light or bountiful breakfasts at week's end, for lunch, for a snack or sandwich, or simply for espresso or a glass of wine to go with a newspaper or a catch-up with friends. Steel, chrome, and glass define the generous space, updating the traditional bistro surroundings of marble-topped tables and eddying streams of cigarette smoke. Most of the familiar staples are here: quiche Lorraine, duck confit with marinated vegetables, hanger steak, bouillabaisse, and the most expensive dish, at C$30 (US$24), grilled veal cutlet with oyster mushrooms and mashed potatoes. The kitchen puts some spins on many of these, but execution can be uneven, nearly always the case with bistros open 12 hours or more a day, so it can be a good idea to go for the less fanciful dishes.

3540 bd. St-Laurent (near av. des Pins). © **514/847-9218.** Reservations rarely necessary. Main courses C$10–C$30 (US$8–US$24). AE, MC, V. Mon–Thurs 11am–11pm; Fri–Sat 8:30–10pm (until 11pm Fri). Métro: Sherbrooke.

L'Express FRENCH BISTRO   No obvious sign announces the presence of this restaurant, only its name discreetly spelled out in white tiles in the sidewalk. There's no need to call attention to itself, since *tout* Montréal knows exactly where it is. While there are no table d'hôte menus, the food is fairly priced for such an eternally busy place and costs the same at midnight as at noon. After a substantial starter like bone marrow with coarse salt or a potted chicken pâté, you may opt for one of the lighter main courses, such as the ravioli *maison,* round pasta pockets filled with a flavorful mixture of beef, pork, and veal. Larger appetites might step up to the full-flavored duck breast with chewy chanterelles in a sauce with the scent of deep woods. Or simply stop by for a *croque monsieur* or a bagel with smoked salmon and cream cheese. This is honest, unpretentious food, thoroughly satisfying, and unlike the flossy new breed of bistro, it's open from breakfast until well after midnight. Although reservations are usually necessary for tables, single diners can often find a seat at the zinc-topped bar, where meals are also served.

3927 rue St-Denis (at rue Roy). © **514/845-5333.** Reservations recommended. Main courses C$12–C$22 (US$9.60–US$18). AE, DC, MC, V. Mon–Fri 8am–3am; Sat 10am–3am; Sun 10am–2am. Métro: Sherbrooke.

Maestro S.V.P. SEAFOOD   You could eat well for a week along the 2 blocks of The Main north of Sherbrooke, and this storefront bistro would surely be one of your stops on that weeklong culinary trek. The name of the place and the musical instruments mounted on the walls have no particular relevance to the menu, unless you count the jazz trio the owner brings in on Sunday evenings at 6:30pm. The decor and music are only a few of the attractions likely to get your attention; others include the several types of oysters always on hand and the all-you-can-eat mussels offered every Monday. Blackboards list the recommended wines of the day, in glasses costing C$6.50 to C$12 (US$5.20–US$9.60). The *dégustation de fruits de mer* (C$62/US$50) is an extravagant medley of clams, oysters, mussels, tiger shrimp, tuna, scallops, *and* king crab. Service is casual but alert, and there is valet parking Thursday through Saturday.

3615 bd. St-Laurent (north of rue Prince Arthur). ℂ **514/842-6447**. Reservations recommended. Main courses C$25–C$55 (US$20–US$44); table d'hôte lunch C$11–C$24 (US$8.80–US$19), dinner C$28 (US$22). AE, DC, MC, V. Mon–Wed 11am–11pm; Thurs–Fri 11am–midnight; Sat 4pm–midnight; Sun 4–11pm. Métro: Sherbrooke.

Savannah 𝕱𝕱 FUSION   The room that houses this restaurant is airy and open, with Art Deco touches, honey-toned woodwork, sliding doors in front, and a large side terrace bordered with greenery. That agreeable but unobtrusive setting allows diners to fully appreciate some of the best food on offer in Montréal these days. This is a kitchen unafraid to play with convention but unwilling to push the limits simply to get attention. While some observers have labeled the results Creole-Cajun inspired (there are some Louisiana touches), much of what appears on the plate is reminiscent of the Carolina Low Country. Creamy hominy, dandelion greens, and oven-roasted tomatoes complement the perky pecan-crusted chicken, which is sautéed just seconds past underdone. Octopus is astonishingly tender after being boiled 3 hours and marinated. Seared crab cakes are combined with mustard sauce, corn relish, and andouille sausage. Jazz trios are on deck at 10pm Friday and Saturday nights. If you only have time for two meals in Montréal, eat one of them here.

4448 bd. St-Laurent (at av. Mont-Royal). ℂ **514/904-0277**. Reservations suggested. Main courses C$18–C$32 (US$14–US$28); table d'hôte lunch C$14–C$22 (US$11–US$18). AE, DC, MC, V. Mon–Fri noon–2:30pm and 5:30pm–midnight; Sat 5:30–11pm; Sun 11am–3pm and 5:30–11pm. Métro: Mont-Royal.

INEXPENSIVE

Chez Schwartz Charcuterie Hébraïque de Montréal 𝕱 DELI   French-first language laws turned this old-line delicatessen into a linguistic mouthful, but it's still known simply as Schwartz's to its many ardent fans. They are convinced it's the only place on the continent to indulge in the guilty treat of *viande fumé*—smoked meat. Housed in a long, narrow storefront, it has a lunch counter and a collection of simple tables and chairs crammed impossibly close to each other. Any empty seat is up for grabs. Few mind the inconvenience or proximity to strangers, for they are soon occupying themselves with plates described either as small (meaning large) or large (meaning humongous), heaped with slices of smoked meat, along with piles of rye bread. Most people also order sides of fries and one or two mammoth garlicky pickles. There is a handful of alternative edibles, but tofu and leafy green vegetables aren't included. Expect a wait. Schwartz's has no liquor license.

3895 bd. St-Laurent (north of rue Prince-Arthur). ℂ **514/842-4813**. Most items under C$12 (US$9.60). No credit cards. Sun–Thurs 9am–12:30am; Fri 9am–1:30am; Sat 9am–2:30am. Métro: St-Laurent.

March of the Tongue Troopers

When the separatist Parti Quebecois took power in the province in 1976, they wasted no time in attempting to make Québec unilingual. They promptly passed Bill 101, which made French the sole official language of the provincial government and sharply restricted the use of other languages in education and commerce. Because about 20% of the population had English as a primary language, one out of five Quebecois felt themselves declared instant second-class citizens. Francophones responded that it was about time *les Anglais,* aka *les autres* (the others), knew what that felt like. They set about enforcing the new law.

The vehicle was *L'Office de la Langue Française.* Its agents fanned out across the province, scouring the landscape for linguistic insults to the state and her people. No offense was too slight for their stern attention. MERRY CHRISTMAS signs were removed from storefronts, and department stores were forced to come up with a new name for Harris Tweed. Any merchant who put up a GOING OUT OF BUSINESS poster faced the possibility of a fine to accompany his already dour situation. By fiat and threat of punishment, hamburgers became *hambourgeois,* a hot dog was rechristened *le chien chaud,* a funeral parlor was transformed into a *salon funéraire,* and Schwartz's Montréal Hebrew Delicatessen became *Chez Schwartz Charcuterie Hébraïque de Montréal.* Particular scrutiny was accorded the Eastern Townships, on the south side of the St. Lawrence River. This area had been settled by United Empire Loyalists, Americans faithful to the British Crown who fled to Canada at the time of the Revolution. The region, known now as Les Cantons de l'Est, had a Tea Table Island and a Molasses Lake, which became *Ile Table à Thé* and *Lac à Mélasse.*

Eventually, it might be assumed, there would be no more Anglophone words to conquer. But bureaucrats will be bureaucrats. Required definitions describe every object in the known world. One is a *petit gâteau de forme rectangulaire, aromatisé au chocolat, dont la texture se situe entre le biscuit sec et le gâteau spongieux.*

Or, in a word, a brownie.

5 Mile End & Outer Districts

VERY EXPENSIVE

La Chronique *&&* FUSION   Montréal's top chefs have been recommending this modest-looking restaurant near Outremont for several years. It was feared that the resulting buzz might spoil the place, but it has only improved, unless you count the hefty increase in prices. You'll discover how remarkable traditional recipes can be in the hands of a master. Presentations are so impeccable you hate to disturb them, and flavors are so eye-rolling you want to scrape up every last smear of food. Even diners who are leery of organ meats will find the veal sweetbreads a silky revelation. The menu includes Mediterranean and Southwestern touches. Originally a more humble bistro, expensive ingredients like foie gras and caviar elevate the place to a grander level. That relates to prices, too, with appetizers costing as much as C$25 (US$20) and one tasting menu reaching C$195 (US$156) per person, with wine. Good as it is, that's much too much, so stick to the available less costly routes. A small but judicious selection of cheeses can precede or replace the tantalizing desserts, which look as if they might take flight. Menus are only in French, but the cordial waiters speak English.

99 rue Laurier ouest (at rue St-Urbain). © 514/271-4770. Reservations required. Main courses C$28–C$36 (US$22–US$29); table d'hôte dinner (Fri–Sat only) C$65 (US$52). AE, DC, MC, V. Tues–Fri 11:30am–2:30pm and 6–10pm; Sat 6–10pm. Closed 1st 2 weeks in July. Métro: Laurier.

Les Chevres 🐐🐐🐐 FRENCH CONTEMPORARY   Since the menu suggests 2½ to 3 hours to give proper attention to the eight-course menu degustation and it takes another hour round-trip from downtown, a dinner at Les Chevres qualifies as a full evening's entertainment. That's not a grim price to pay for a restaurant that has an excellent chance of knocking off the longtime champ, Toqué! So take the time. What makes this experience even more remarkable is that the menu is largely vegetarian. That might seem a deal-breaker for devout flesh-eaters, but they should take the leap. In repeated displays melding audacity and fastidiousness, this kitchen wrests every hint of aroma, taste, contrasting textures, and eye-appeal from its chosen ingredients. One *amuse-bouche* is a cup of creamy vegetable bisque meant to be drunk like a cappuccino. A full course ups the ante with a symphony of beets with crimson bulgar, and disks of white beet showered with minced beet sugar, all floating atop a tablespoon of creamed yellow beet. Then, an eggless flan of cèpes is accompanied with browned gnocchi in an almond mousse dusted with flakes of Perigord truffle. As the meal progresses, it reaches the profoundly savory, then slides toward the sweet in seamless transition. Along the way, the cheese selection is notable. Carnivores take heart—there are usually two or three meat or fish dishes on the card. Wines are impeccably selected to enhance each dish, most in the C$45 to C$75 (US$36–US$60) range.

If these stiff prices are out of reach, even for an "event" meal, the adjoining cafe, **La Chou** (© 514/270-2468), is under the same management and has much lower prices (C$7–C$13/US$5.60–US$10) for food from the same kitchen. It's open Monday through Saturday from 5:30 to 11pm.

1201 rue Van Horne (at av. Bloomfield). © 514/270-1119. Reservations essential. Main courses C$24–C$37 (US$19–US$30); table d'hôte C$48 (US$38); menu degustation C$68 (US$54), with wine C$110 (US$88). Mon–Fri 11:30am–2pm and 6–10pm (until 10:30pm Thurs–Sat).

Nuances 🐐🐐 FRENCH CONTEMPORARY   Unlikely as it may seem, this is haute cuisine in a gambling casino, ensconced atop four floors of blinking lights and the crash of cascading jackpots. This elegant entry in Montréal's gastronomic sweepstakes quickly shouldered its way toward the top, but it seems to have stalled in its upward progress, with fewer flights of fancy in its current offerings. Everything on the plate is identifiable, comforting to diners who prefer not to guess what they're about to fork into their mouths. The original designers didn't stint on the trappings, though, which include mahogany paneling, soaring ceilings, and a lavish deployment of leather and linen. Every member of the staff is qualified to advise on appropriate wines from the extensive cellar. The menu is reworked each season, but one example of a past triumph was the wrapped round stockade of thin asparagus spears topped with greens and surmounted by the meat of a small lobster claw. Among the rhapsody of main courses are likely to be rosy slices of lamb baked in clay, and sushi-quality tuna barely touched by a flame and served with eggplant compote. The *plateau de fromage* has several admirable Québec cheeses. Make it all the way to dessert after all that, and the waiter might suggest a dish of praline mousse and chocolate sherbet. A stiffened dress code keeps out guys in tank tops and shorts—jackets are now required for men, and denim isn't permitted.

1 av. du Casino (in the Casino de Montréal, Ile Ste-Hélène). ℂ **514/392-2708.** Reservations strongly recommended. Jackets for men, no denim. Main courses C$38–C$44 (US$30–US$35); table d'hôte dinner C$60 (US$48), C$85 (US$68), or C$95 (US$76). AE, DC, MC, V. Sun–Thurs 5:30–11pm; Fri–Sat 5:30–11:30pm. Métro: Ile Ste-Hélène.

EXPENSIVE

Area ❦ FUSION   In his showcase at the edge of the Gay Village, chef and co-owner Ian Perreault seems far too young to know as much as he obviously does about the world's cuisines. But he deftly manipulates techniques and ingredients found in a couple dozen countries around the Pacific and Mediterranean rims, in precociously assured concoctions that challenge taste assumptions. In none of this does he neglect such staples of his homeland as duck and venison. The chef-proprietor changes his menu every couple of months, so it isn't possible to describe specific dishes that might be encountered. Be assured that convention will be disregarded, though, with past concoctions like the "brick" of salmon brushed with saffron oil and accompanied by Israeli couscous, and ravioli filled with ricotta and married with duck confit, mushrooms, asparagus, and, oh, yes, white truffle oil. Servings are attractively put together, and, it must be said, often wastefully large. There are two seatings nightly, the times varying according to demand and time of the year.

1429 rue Amherst (north of rue Ste-Catherine). ℂ **514/890-6691.** Reservations recommended. Main courses C$21–C$34 (US$17–US$27); table d'hôte C$40 or C$56 (US$32 or US$45). AE, MC, V. Tues–Fri 11:30am–2pm; daily 6–11pm. Métro: Beaudry.

MODERATE

BU ITALIAN   Not just another award-winning designer bar, this welcome new entry strikes an exquisite balance between wine and food. The eats in question are antipasti, which the manager stoutly contends are far superior to the currently fashionable variations on the tapas tradition ("Everyone has tapas—one bite, gone"). He's right: The bruschetta is a slab of grilled bread rubbed with garlic and drizzled with olive oil, and the Piatto BU is a satisfying assortment of meats, cheese, and grilled vegetables. There are two hot dishes offered nightly, but the purpose of all the food is to complement, not do battle with, the wines. The long card eschews the same old bottlings, and even those who regard themselves as connoisseurs make delightful discoveries, guided by the knowledgeable staff. Consider the soft, flowery Goldmuskateller St-Michael or the aromatic Bricco Manzoni from Piedmont; there are another 20 by the glass. The crowd gets younger as the night rolls on, and because the bar stays open late, off-duty chefs are often in the mix.

5245 bd. St-Laurent (at av. Fairmount). ℂ **514/276-0249.** Reservations recommended. Antipasti C$7–C$16 (US$5.60–US$13). AE, DISC, MC, V. Tues–Fri 11am–2pm; Mon–Sat 5pm–2am. Métro: Laurier.

 Chao Phraya THAI   Contender for the title of best Thai in town, this spot boasts a panache that sets it a few notches above most of its rivals. It brightens its corner on increasingly fashionable Laurier Avenue with white table linens and sprays of orchids on each table. The host helps with suggestions about the most popular items on the menu. Dumplings in peanut sauce are a well-liked appetizer, and a main event of mixed seafood, composed of squid, scallops, shrimp, crab claws, mussels, and chunks of red snapper, is a favorite. The food is tangy at the least, and menu items are given one to three hot pepper symbols grading hotness. Two printed peppers are about right for most people. A cooling cucumber salad helps, and you'll want a side of sticky rice too. Everything comes in attractive bowls and platters. There are several wines by the glass—try the semidry Alsatian wine. The Chao Phraya is a river in Thailand.

50 av. Laurier ouest (1 block west of bd. St-Laurent). ☎ 514/272-5339. Reservations recommended. Main courses C$13–C$18 (US$10–US$14). AE, DC, MC, V. Sun–Wed 5:30–10pm; Thurs–Fri noon–2:30pm; Thurs–Sat 5:30–11pm. Métro: Laurier.

Chez Lévêsque FRENCH BISTRO   In the brasserie tradition, this place opens for breakfast and doesn't shut down until late. Drop by and stay awhile. Have a coffee with croissant, write a poem, peruse *Le Monde,* order a sandwich, or dig through a full four courses. It's a place to hang out. There are the bistro essentials—bouillabaisse (a must), salmon *tartare,* and lamb Provençal—on the menu, but someone in charge apparently thinks Fusion ideas and healthy living are important, too. That conviction shows up in Chilean sea bass laid over a comforter of mixed vegetables, and in the quail infused with a peppery honey-soy marinade and set upon a nest of greens. A ragout of curried pork cubes with mashed potatoes and a mélange of sautéed vegetables was a recent winner. A fireplace blazes much of the year in the upstairs room. In warm weather, the front is opened up.

1030 rue Laurier ouest (near rue Hutchinson, in Outremont). ☎ 514/279-7355. Reservations recommended. Main courses C$15–C$30 (US$12–US$24); table d'hôte lunch C$10–C$14 (US$8–US$11), dinner C$15–C$31 (US$12–US$25). AE, DC, MC, V. Mon–Fri 8am–midnight; Sat–Sun 10:30am–midnight. Métro: Laurier.

Leméac FRENCH BISTRO   Named for the publishing firm that used to occupy the building, this sprightly arrival on the Laurier scene has a long tin-topped bar along one side, well-spaced tables, and, far from least, a crew of cheerful waitresses. While the bistro dishes sound conventional on the page, they are put together in freshly conceived ways. Two examples: The curried mussel soup is capped by a nicely browned pillow of puff pastry, and the salmon *pot-au-feu* is a perfectly cooked filet laid over a healthful selection of small potatoes, carrots, tender Brussels sprouts, and their collective broth. Food is different but not startlingly so, and served in an atmosphere that invites lingering. Weekend brunch is popular, as is the side terrace in warm weather.

1045 rue Laurier (corner of rue Durocher). ☎ 514/270-0999. Reservations advised on weekends. Main courses C$9.75–C$34 (US$7.80–US$27); table d'hôte lunch C$18–C$20 (US$14–US$16). AE, MC, V. Mon–Wed noon–midnight; Thurs–Fri noon–1am; Sat 10:30am–1am; Sun 10:30am–midnight. Métro: Laurier.

INEXPENSIVE

La Paryse *(Value* SANDWICHES   Only slightly larger than your basic hole-in-the-wall, this Latin Quarter standby packs in students, profs, young execs, and middleagers. They come for the burgers, as much the consensus choice for best-in-town as is Schwartz's smoked meat. The featured attractions are loaded up with mustard, grilled mushrooms, pickles, lettuce, onions, mayo, and tomato slices. Unless you possess a really large appetite and a capacious mouth to go with it, you certainly won't need the double burger nor the *frites grosse* (big fries) unless you want to feed your family of four. Wines are available by the glass for C$5.50 (US$4.40). You could have the *végé-*burger, composed of tofu, cukes, and mushrooms, but why? There will be a line, but it moves along fairly quickly.

302 rue Ontario est (at rue Sanguinet). ☎ 514/842-2040. All items under C$10 (US$8). MC, V. Tues–Fri 11am–11pm; Sat noon–10:30pm; Sun noon–10pm. Métro: Berri-UQAM or St-Laurent.

Ru de Nam *(Value* VIETNAMESE   Thai restaurants abound in the city but Vietnamese tastes are more difficult to find. The gracious owner is a lawyer-turned-chef, adept in the techniques of her Southeast Asian homeland. She changes her menu regularly, but frequently available are *gà sà ôt* (chicken with ginger and lemongrass), *cá sâ ôt* (fish with lemongrass and tamarind sauce), and *xôi thit* (pork and sticky rice). In deference to local enthusiasms, she also lists beef tartare, seasoned with lime juice and chiles. There is a daily express lunch that includes soup, main course, tea or coffee, and dessert. No choices, but that too is altered daily and it's a true bargain at C$11 (US$8.80), including taxes. Enter the restaurant through the shop next door, where Asian ceramics and related items are sold. This is a good place to keep in mind when prowling the dozens of antiques shops of rue Notre-Dame.

2501 rue Notre-Dame ouest (near rue Vinet). ✆ 514/989-2002. Reservations suggested. Main courses C$15–C$19 (US$12–US$15); table d'hôte lunch C$11 (US$8.80). AE, MC, V. Tues–Fri noon–2pm and 6:30–10pm; Sat–Sun 6:30–10pm. Métro: Lionel-Groulx.

6 Daylong Munchies & Late-Night Bites

When the yen for coffee and a pastry or a sandwich strikes, you are never far from an outpost of one of the three major cafe chains: **A.L. Van Houtte, Presse Café,** or **Second Cup** (which are usually open 24 hr.). All have reasonable prices for decent food, and many have tables indoors and out for resting tired feet or plotting your next sightseeing moves.

Ben's DELI   This deli-restaurant was founded by Ben and Fanny Kravitz in 1908 and is still in the family. Autographed celebrity photos—including Burl Ives, the Ink Spots, and Ed Sullivan—attest to its heyday. The current owners persist in the claim that this is where Montréal's famous smoked meat originated. Besides the inevitable variations on that much-loved ingredient, the menu meanders through cheese blintzes, potato latkes, corned beef and cabbage, bagels and lox, and much more. They are fully licensed.

990 bd. de Maisonneuve (at rue Metcalfe). ✆ 514/844-1000. Most items under C$12 (US$9.60). MC, V. Sun–Thurs 7:30am–2am; Fri–Sat 7:30am–4am. Métro: Peel.

Bilboquet 𝒢 *Kids* ICE CREAM   Sandwiches are available here, including a good *croque monsieur,* but the reason to seek out this humble spot in Outremont is the splendid ice creams and sorbets. This *artisan glacier* makes its own ice cream, rich with fruits, nuts, and caramel . . . whatever is fresh and available and strikes their fancy. Flavors and pairings that don't show up in many places are offered, including pear, maple taffy, passion fruit, chocolate-orange, and vanilla-raspberry. There's always a line, and there are only a few tables inside and benches outside.

1311 rue Bernard ouest (at av. Outremont). ✆ 514/276-0414. Most items under C$8 (US$6.40). No credit cards. Daily 7am–midnight. Closed Jan–Feb. Métro: Outremont.

Café Cherrier 𝒢 BREAKFAST/BRUNCH/LIGHT FARE   The tables on the terrace that wraps around this corner building are filled whenever there's even a slim possibility that a heavy sweater and a bowl of café au lait will fend off frostbite. In summer, the loyalists get to stay out until way past midnight, and in winter, all the same people squeeze inside. Brunch is popular, even if the food is unexceptional, but consider this place any time a snack or a meal is in order. Portions are ample and inexpensive. An easygoing atmosphere prevails; it's popular with musicians, actors, artists, and journalists, so contrive to look mysterious or celebrated.

3635 rue St-Denis (at rue Cherrier). ✆ 514/843-4308. Main courses C$8–C$17 (US$6.40–US$14); table d'hôte lunch C$14–C$19 (US$11–C$15). AE, MC, V. Mon–Fri 7:30am–10pm; Sat–Sun 8:30am–11pm (to 3am in summer); brunch Sat–Sun 8:30am–3pm. Métro: Sherbrooke.

Claude Postel BREAKFAST/LIGHT FARE   Starting out as a patisserie and choco-
latier, they've added some tables and a short menu of three-course meals under C$12
(US$9.60). Most customers seem to go for other items, though, including salads,
cheeses, pâtés, pastries, and ice cream. Over in the left corner, clerks assemble a variety
of sandwiches to order from an intriguing range of ingredients. Breads are chewy,
crusty, and moist in proper proportion. It's a logical place for a snack or treat in the
midst of a stroll through Vieux-Montréal.

75 rue Notre-Dame ouest (near rue St-Sulpice). © 514/844-8750. Most items under C$12 (US$9.60). MC, V.
Mon–Fri 7am–7pm; Sat–Sun 9am–5pm. Métro: Place d'Armes.

Eggspectation BREAKFAST/BRUNCH/LIGHT FARE   Let the dopey name and
the terribly punny-funny menu deter you and you'll miss a meal that may constitute
one of your best food memories of Montréal, at least if you're of the breakfast-is-best
school of gastronomy. Prices are low and portions are huge, ensuring crowds from early
morning to late afternoon. One reader lauds the thick, creamy slices of French toast
spiked with Grand Marnier and joined with mounds of fresh fruit. Eggs any way are
special, too, even if the dishes are tagged with names like *eggscaliber* and *eggsileration*.
There are 10 variations of eggs Benedict alone. Sandwiches, burgers, and pastas are also
on the menu. In summer, the restaurant stays open into the evening. The ever-expanding chain has additional branches at 198 rue Laurier ouest (© **514/278-6411**), near
rue St-Denis, and at 213 rue St-Jacques in Vieux-Montréal (© **514/282-0119**).

1313 bd. de Maisonneuve ouest (at rue de la Montagne). © 514/842-3447. Most items under C$12 (US$9.60). MC,
V. Mon–Fri 6am–5pm; Sat–Sun 6am–6pm (later in summer). Métro: Guy-Concordia.

La Brioche Lyonnaise LIGHT FARE   There are many delightful patisseries—pastry shops—in this largely French city, and this one, deep in the Quartier Latin, is one
of the most popular. They serve light items—quiches, salads, and sandwiches—but
patrons often settle down for just a sweet cake or a croissant and coffee, perhaps a café
au lait. They stop in after dinner, UQAM classes, or a show at the theater across the
street, or simply for a break in sightseeing. Check out what's available in the display
case—from Marie Claire pastries to mega-meringues—and then find a table in one of
several seating areas. As in most patisseries, there's no pressure to move on soon.

1593 rue St-Denis (near bd. de Maisonneuve). © 514/842-7017. Most items under C$12 (US$9.60). AE, MC, V. Daily
9am–midnight. Métro: Berri-UQAM.

Pizzédélic *(Kids* PIZZA   Pizza here runs the gamut from traditional to as imaginative as anyone might conceive, with toppings from feta cheese to escargots to arti-
chokes to pesto. All toppings are placed on thin, not-quite-crispy crusts. The
difference over ordinary pizzerias is the use of fresh, not canned, ingredients, as in the
antipasto plate of grilled vegetables and calamari strips. Pastas, sandwiches, and meat
dishes are also available. The front opens in warm weather, and there's a terrace in
back. It's a growing chain, with units all over town, but two other conveniently located
Pizzédélics are at 1329 rue Ste-Catherine (© **514/526-6011**) and 370 av. Laurier
ouest (© **514/948-6290**).

3509 bd. St-Laurent (near rue Sherbrooke). © 514/282-6784. Pizzas and pastas C$11–C$16 (US$9–US$13). AE, DC,
MC, V. Daily 11am–midnight. Métro: St-Laurent.

Santropol *(Value* LIGHT FARE/VEGETARIAN   Mostly vegetarian sandwiches, salads, and potpies come in hefty flavorsome proportions at this favorite. The composition of the clientele is alluded to in the sign that reads HEY STUDENTS—BRING OUR

CUTLERY BACK, but families and older folk drop by in substantial numbers, too. They dawdle at tables with chairs that don't even bear a family resemblance amid panels of stamped tin on walls and ceilings and offhanded sculptures beholden to no school. Herbal teas, coffees, and 18 different kinds of milkshakes (almond, maple, and peach-apricot are among the choices) constitute the available nonalcoholic beverages. Occupying a timeworn red-brick house, the restaurant has several dining nooks, along with a tree- and fern-filled courtyard in summer. One percent of the bill is sent to organizations that ease hunger in Québec and developing nations. Takeout is available.

3990 rue St-Urbain (at Rue Duluth). ℂ 514/842-3110. Most items under C$12 (US$9.60). No credit cards; debit cards accepted. Daily 11:30am–midnight (until 1am Fri–Sat). Métro: Mont-Royal; then walk through Jeanne Mance Park.

St-Viateur Bagel & Café ℱ LIGHT FARE   The bagel wars flare as hotly as Montréal's eternal smoked-meat battles once did, but this, an offshoot of a beloved old bakery, is easily among the top contenders. Bagels in these parts are thinner, smaller, and crustier than the bloated, cottony monsters posing as the real thing in most parts of the republic south of the border. These are hand-rolled, twist-flipped into circles, dusted with sesame seeds or whatever, and baked in big wood-fired ovens right on premises. Try them in or take them out. Sandwiches come with soup or salad. Expect a short wait on weekends and not infrequently during the week.

1127 av. Mont-Royal est (between rues Christophe Colomb and La Roche). ℂ 514/528-6361. Most items under C$10 (US$9.60). No credit cards. Daily 6am–midnight. Métro: Mont-Royal.

Wilensky Light Lunch LIGHT FARE   Wilensky's has been a Montréal tradition since 1932, known for its grilled-meat sandwiches, low prices, curt service, and utter lack of decor. Expect to find nine stools at a counter. This is Duddy Kravitz/Mordecai Richler territory, and the ambience is Early Immigrant. The food selections are limited to a few sandwiches—not much more than bologna, salami, and mustard thrown on a bun and squashed on a grill—and hot-dog sandwiches, also squashed. You can wash them down with egg creams or drinks jerked from the rank of syrups—this place has drinks typical of the old-time soda fountain it is. I'm talking tradition here, not cuisine.

34 rue Fairmount ouest (at rue Clark). ℂ 514/271-0247. Most items under C$6 (US$4.80). No credit cards. Mon–Fri 9am–4pm. Closed 2 weeks in July, 2 weeks in Feb. Métro: Laurier; then walk about 12 blocks. Bus: 55 to bd. St-Laurent and av. Fairmount. Walk a block west, and then north if you're coming from the Métro and west if you're coming from the bus.

7 Picnic Fare: Where to Get It, Where to Eat It

When planning a picnic or a meal to eat back in your hotel room, consider a stop at **La Vieille Europe,** 3855 bd. St-Laurent near St-Cuthbert (ℂ 514/842-5773), a compact storehouse of culinary sights and smells. Choose from wheels of pungent cheeses, garlands of sausages, pâtés, cashews, honey, fresh peanut butter, or dried fruits. Coffee beans are roasted in the back, adding to the mixture of maddening aromas. A stroll to the north along St-Laurent reveals other possibilities for mobile edibles.

You'll find similar bounty underground at **Les Halles de la Gare,** an accumulation of food stalls, delis, and cafes beneath Le Reine Elizabeth hotel and adjacent to the main concourse of the railroad station. Among them is an SAQ wine store.

Better still, make the short excursion by Métro (the Lionel-Groulx stop) to **Marché Atwater,** the public market at 3025 St-Ambroise, open 7 days a week. The long shed is bordered by stalls of gleaming produce and flowers, the two-story center section given to wine purveyors, butchers, food counters, bakeries, and cheese stores. The **Boulangerie Première Moison** (© 514/932-0328) fills its space with the tantalizing aromas of baskets of breads and cases of pastries and tables at which to consume its prepared meals and sandwiches. Two of the best cheese purveyors are the **Fromagerie du Deuxième** (© 514/932-5532), whose knowledgeable attendants know every detail of production of the scores of North American and European cheeses on offer, and the **Fromagerie Atwater** (© 514/932-4653), which has about 650 different cheeses, 50 of them from Québec, and also sells pâtés and charcuterie. From either market, it isn't far by taxi to Parc du Mont-Royal, a wonderful place to enjoy a picnic, or by bicycle to a spot along the revamped Lachine Canal.

In Vieux-Montréal, pick up supplies for your picnic at **Olive & Gourmando** (© 514/350-1083) at 351 rue St-Paul ouest and head for the grounds of the Vieux–Port, only steps away. Open Tuesday through Saturday from 8am to 6pm, it started out as a bakery, then added table service and transformed itself into a full-fledged cafe. It still sells near-perfect baguettes, as well as many breads, croissants, and pastries. Put your sandwiches together from the cheeses and sausages in the cold case, or choose from their interesting compositions, including a grilled portobello mushroom with a purée of olives and goat cheese. A lot of the bread is out the door by mid-morning. Right across the street is the **Marché de la Villette,** 324 rue St-Paul ouest (© 514/807-8084), just the place to fill out your picnic list, with sandwiches, miniquiches, sausages, cheeses domestic and imported, freshly baked breads, and pâtés and terrines. They also serve three-course meals at a few tables in front for C$10 to C$13 (US$8–US$10). Open daily.

7

Exploring Montréal

Montréal is a feast of choices, able to satisfy the desires of both physically active and culturally curious visitors. Depending upon what interests you and how much time you have, you can hike up imposing Mont-Royal in the middle of the city, cycle for miles beside the Lachine Canal, take in artworks and ephemera at some 20 museums and as many historic buildings, attend a Canadiens hockey match, party until dawn on rue Crescent and The Main, or soak up the concrete and spiritual results of some 400 years of conquest and immigration. And with riverboat rides, the fascinating Biodôme (which replicates four distinct ecosystems), a sprawling amusement park, the Vieux-Port Science Centre, puppet and magic shows, and unique Cirque du Soleil performances, few cities assure kids of as good a time as this one.

Once you've decided what you want to do, getting from hotel to museum to attraction is pretty easy: The superb Métro system, a fairly logical street grid, wide boulevards, and the vehicle-free underground city all aid in the swift, largely uncomplicated movement of people from place to place.

Montréal's 350th birthday was celebrated in 1992 with the opening or expansion of many of the attractions described in this chapter. Efforts to enhance the cultural offerings have continued since then. If you're not in town on Montréal Museums Day (p. 21), check out the **Montréal Museums Pass,** which allows entry to 30 of the city's museums and attractions, and is available year-round. Good for 3 consecutive days, the pass costs C$39 (US$31) and includes access to public transportation. That's double the price of a couple of years ago, but still a good deal for diligent sightseers, especially since it now includes a 3-day Métro pass. It is sold at all participating museums, at the Infotouriste Centre on Square Dorchester, and at many Montréal hotels. For further information, call © **877/266-5687** from outside Montréal or 514/873-2015 within the metropolitan area.

When planning your visit, you might want to note in the listings below which museums have restaurants so that you can plan a meal in addition to your museum visit. Most museums are closed Mondays.

1 The Top Attractions

DOWNTOWN

Musée des Beaux-Arts ✵✵✵   Montréal's Museum of Fine Arts is the city's most prominent museum, opened in 1912 in Canada's first building designed specifically for the visual arts. The original neoclassical pavilion is on the north side of Sherbrooke. Years ago, museum administrators recognized that the collection, now totaling more than 30,000 works, had outgrown the building. That problem was solved in late 1991 with the completion of the striking new annex, the Jean-Noël Desmarais

Pavilion, directly across the street from the original building. Designed by Montréal architect Moshe Safdie, the new pavilion tripled exhibition space, adding two sub-street-level floors and underground galleries that connect the new building with the old. Throughout the museum, works are nearly always dramatically mounted, carefully lit, and diligently explained in both French and English.

For the best look at the results of the addition, enter the annex, take the elevator to the top, and work your way down. The permanent collection in the annex is largely devoted to international contemporary art and Canadian art created after 1960, and to European painting, sculpture, and decorative art from the Middle Ages to the 19th century. On the upper floors are many of the gems of the collection. On the fourth floor are paintings by 12th- to 19th-century artists, including Hogarth, Tintoretto, Reynolds, Brueghel, El Greco, Ribera, and portraitist George Romney. On the third floor are works—representative, if not world-class—by more recent artists, including Renoir, Monet, Picasso, Matisse, Cézanne, Léger, and Rodin. The principal temporary exhibitions are also mounted on this floor. On the subterranean floors are works by 20th-century modernists, primarily those who rose to prominence after World War II, including the Abstract Expressionists and their successors.

From the lowest level of the new pavilion, follow the under-street corridor, passing primitive artworks from Oceania and Africa along the way, and then take the elevator into the original building, with its displays of pre-Columbian ceramics, Inuit carvings, and Amerindian crafts. Across the street, you'll find a street-level store with an impressive selection of quality books, games, and folk art, and a good cafe.

1379–1380 rue Sherbrooke ouest (at rue Crescent). ℰ 514/285-2000. www.mmfa.qc.ca. Free admission to the permanent collection (although donations are happily accepted). Admission to temporary exhibitions varies, but the following are representative: C$15 (US$12) adults, C$7.50 (US$6) seniors and students, C$3 (US$2.40) children 12 and under; half-price Wed 5:30–9pm. AE, MC, V. Tues–Sun 11am–5pm; Wed 11am–9pm (open daily in summer). Métro: Peel or Guy-Corcordia. Bus: 24.

Musée McCord d'Histoire Canadienne   Associated with McGill University, the McCord Museum of Canadian History showcases the eclectic—and not infrequently eccentric—collections of scores of 19th- and 20th-century benefactors. More than 29,000 costumes, numerous artifacts, and 750,000 historical photographs are rotated in and out of storage to be displayed. In general, expect to view furniture, clothing, china, silver, paintings, photographs, and folk art that reveal rural and urban life as it was lived by English-speaking immigrants of the past 3 centuries. The First Nations room displays portions of the museum's extensive collection of objects from Canada's Native population, including jewelry and meticulous beadwork. Exhibits are intelligently mounted, with texts in English and French, although the upstairs rooms are of narrower interest. There's a popular cafe near the front entrance.

690 rue Sherbrooke ouest (at rue Victoria). ℰ 514/398-7100. www.mccord-museum.qc.ca. Admission C$10 (US$8) adults, C$7.50 (US$6) seniors, C$5.50 (US$4.40) students, C$3 (US$2.40) ages 6–12, free for children under 7; free admission Sat 10am–noon. Tues–Fri 10am–6pm; Sat–Sun 10am–5pm (summer daily from 9am). Métro: McGill. Bus: 24.

Parc du Mont-Royal   Montréal is named for the 232m (761-ft.) hill that rises at its heart—the "Royal Mountain." Joggers, cyclists, dog walkers, skaters, and others use it throughout the year. On Sundays, hundreds congregate around the statue of George-Etienne Cartier to listen and sometimes dance to impromptu music. In summer, Lac des Castors (Beaver Lake) is surrounded by sunbathers and picnickers (no swimming allowed, however). In wintertime, cross-country skiers follow the miles of paths and snowshoers tramp along trails laid out for their use. The large, refurbished

Downtown & Vieux-Montréal Attractions

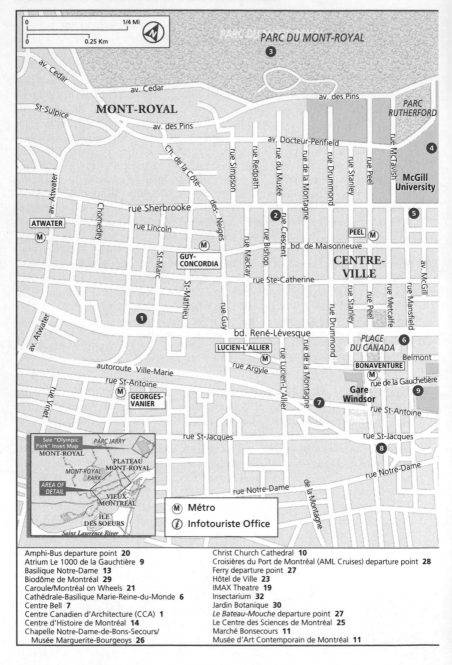

Amphi-Bus departure point **20**
Atrium Le 1000 de la Gauchetière **9**
Basilique Notre-Dame **13**
Biodôme de Montréal **29**
Caroule/Montréal on Wheels **21**
Cathédrale-Basilique Marie-Reine-du-Monde **6**
Centre Bell **7**
Centre Canadien d'Architecture (CCA) **1**
Centre d'Histoire de Montréal **14**
Chapelle Notre-Dame-de-Bons-Secours/
   Musée Marguerite-Bourgeoys **26**

Christ Church Cathedral **10**
Croisières du Port de Montréal (AML Cruises) departure point **28**
Ferry departure point **27**
Hôtel de Ville **23**
IMAX Theatre **19**
Insectarium **32**
Jardin Botanique **30**
Le Bateau-Mouche departure point **27**
Le Centre des Sciences de Montréal **25**
Marché Bonsecours **11**
Musée d'Art Contemporain de Montréal **11**

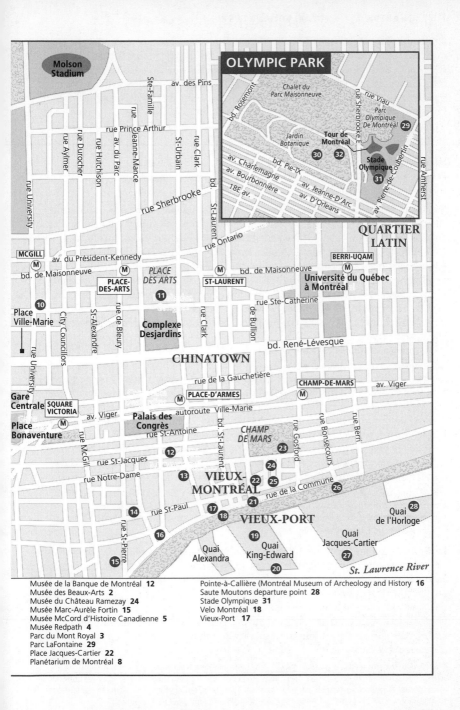

Musée de la Banque de Montréal **12**
Musée des Beaux-Arts **2**
Musée du Château Ramezay **24**
Musée Marc-Aurèle Fortin **15**
Musée McCord d'Histoire Canadienne **5**
Musée Redpath **4**
Parc du Mont Royal **3**
Parc LaFontaine **29**
Place Jacques-Cartier **22**
Planétarium de Montréal **8**

Pointe-à-Callière (Montréal Museum of Archeology and History **16**
Saute Moutons departure point **28**
Stade Olympique **31**
Velo Montréal **18**
Vieux-Port **17**

Chalet du Mont-Royal near the crest of the hill provides a sweeping view of the city from its terrace and the opportunity for a snack. Up the hill behind the chalet is the spot where, tradition says, de Maisonneuve erected his wooden cross to establish the first colony here in 1642. Today the cross is a 30m-high (98-ft.) steel structure visible from all over the city, illuminated at night. See chapter 8 for a walking tour of Mont-Royal.

© 514/844-4928 (general information) or 514/872-6559 (special events). Daily 6am–midnight. Métro: Mont-Royal. Bus: 11; hop off at Lac des Castors.

VIEUX-MONTREAL (OLD MONTREAL)

For further information about this quarter, log on to **www.vieux.montreal.qc.ca**, and try the walking tour in chapter 8.

Basilique Notre-Dame 𝕽𝕽𝕽 Big enough to hold 4,000 worshipers and breath-taking in the richness of its interior furnishings, this magnificent structure was designed in 1824 by James O'Donnell, an Irish-American Protestant architect from New York. So profoundly was O'Donnell moved by the experience that he converted to Catholicism after the basilica was completed. The impact is understandable. Of the hundreds of churches on the island of Montréal, Notre-Dame's interior is the most stunning, with a wealth of exquisite detail, most of it carved from rare woods that have been delicately gilded and painted. O'Donnell, one of the proponents of the Gothic revival style in the early decades of the 19th century, is the only person honored by burial in the crypt.

The main altar was carved from linden wood, the work of Victor Bourgeau. Behind it is the Chapelle Sacré-Coeur (Sacred Heart Chapel), much of it destroyed by a deranged arsonist in 1978 but rebuilt and rededicated in 1982. The altar, with 32 panels repre-senting birth, life, and death, was cast in bronze by Charles Daudelin of Montréal. A 10-bell carillon resides in the east tower, while the west tower contains a single massive bell. Nicknamed "Le Gros Bourdon," it weighs more than 12 tons and has a low, resonant rumble that vibrates right up through your feet. It is tolled only on special occasions.

Although you can go through on your own, guided tours in English are offered at various times throughout the day, beginning with one at 9am. Sound-and-light shows are presented nightly Tuesday through Saturday (see below for times).

110 rue Notre-Dame ouest (on place d'Armes). © 514/842-2925. Basilica C$4 (US$3.20) adults, C$2 (US$1.60) ages 7–17, free for praying. Light show C$10 (US$8) adults, C$9 (US$7.20) seniors, C$5 (US$4) ages 7–17, free for children ages 6 and under. MC, V. Basilica daily 8am–5pm; tours daily 9am–4pm. Light shows Tues–Thurs 6:30pm, Fri 6:30 and 8:30pm, Sat 7 and 8:30pm. Métro: Place d'Armes.

Le Centre des Sciences de Montréal This ambitious complex occupies a new steel-and-glass building running the length of King Edward Pier. Focusing on science and technology, it employs a variety of interactive displays and a cinema, as well as a popular IMAX theater, to enlighten visitors about the life sciences, energy conserva-tion, and 21st-century communications. With its extensive use of computers and elec-tronic visual displays, it is no surprise that youngsters usually take to the exhibits more readily than their elders. Admission fees vary according to combinations of exhibits and movie showings.

King Edward Pier, Vieux-Port. © 514/496-4724. www.montrealsciencecentre.com. C$10–C$22 (US$8–US$18) adults, C$9–C$20 (US$7.20–US$16) ages 13–17 and 60 and over, C$7–C$18 (US$5.60–US$14) ages 4–12, free for children under 4. Summer Sun–Wed 10am–6pm, Thurs–Sat 10am–9pm; rest of year Sun–Thurs 10am–6pm, Fri–Sat 10am–9pm (hours subject to change). Métro: Square Victoria, Place d'Armes, or Champ-de-Mars.

Long May They Wave

With a relatively small population spread over a territory larger than the continental United States, Canadians' loyalties have always tended to be directed to the cities and regions in which they live, rather than to the nation at large. It doesn't help that citizens speak two different languages and that the nation retained a semicolonial relationship with England.

Regional pride and identification grew after World War II. Quebecers began asserting themselves and officially adopted their new "national" flag, the *Fleurdelisé*, in 1950. In contrast to the red ensign with a Union Jack in the upper-left corner that served as the Canadian standard, the Québec flag employs the traditional blue and white of France with four fleurs-de-lis. It wasn't until 1965 that the now-familiar red-and-white maple leaf version of the Canadian flag was introduced. For that matter, it wasn't until the late 1970s that Canadians had a national anthem, *O, Canada!*, and a citizenship oath.

In the face of decades of distrust, hurt, and outright hostilities between French and English Canada, there must be occasional sighs of longing among other Canadians for the diplomatic display that is the flag of the city of Montréal. Adopted way back in 1832, it has red crossbars on a white background. The resulting quadrants have depictions of a rose, a fleur-de-lis, a thistle, and a shamrock. They stand, respectively, for the founding groups of the new nation—the English, French, Scots, and Irish.

Place Jacques-Cartier   Across the street from the Hôtel de Ville (City Hall), this plaza is a focus of summer activity in Vieux-Montréal. The area has two repaved streets bracketing a center promenade that slopes down to the port past venerable stone buildings from the 1700s. Outdoor cafes, street performers, flower sellers, and horse-drawn carriages that gather at the plaza's base recall a Montréal of a century ago. Montrealers insist they would never go to a place so overrun by tourists—which makes one wonder why so many of them do, in fact, congregate here. They take the sun and sip sangria on the bordering terraces on warm days, enjoying the unfolding pageant just as much as visitors do.

Between rue Notre-Dame and rue de la Commune. Métro: Place d'Armes.

Pointe-à-Callière (Montréal Museum of Archaeology and History) 𝔞𝔞𝔞   A first visit to Montréal might best begin here. Built on the very site where the original colony was established in 1642 (Pointe-à-Callière), the modern Museum of Archaeology and History engages visitors in rare, beguiling ways. The triangular new building echoes the Royal Insurance building (1861) that stood here for many years. Go first to the 16-minute multimedia show in an auditorium that actually stands above exposed ruins of the earlier city. The show is accompanied by music and a playful bilingual narration that keeps the history slick and painless (if a little too chamber-of-commerce upbeat).

Pointe-à-Callière was the point where the St-Pierre River merged with the St. Lawrence. Evidence of the many inhabitants of this spot—from Amerindians to

French trappers to Scottish merchants—was unearthed during archaeological digs that took more than a decade. Artifacts are on view in display cases set among the ancient building foundations and burial grounds below street level. Wind your way on the self-guided tour through the subterranean complex until you find yourself in the former Custom House, where there are more exhibits and a well-stocked gift shop. Allow at least an hour for a visit.

New expansion has incorporated the Youville Pumping Station, across from the main building, into the museum. Dating from 1915, it has been restored to serve as an interpretation center. The main building contains L'Arrivage cafe and affords a fine view of Vieux-Montréal and the Vieux-Port.

350 place Royale (at rue de la Commune). ✆ 514/872-9150. www.pacmuseum.qc.ca. Admission C$10 (US$8) adults, C$7.50 (US$6) seniors, C$6 (US$4.80) students, C$3.50 (US$2.80) children 6–12, free for children under 6. AE, MC, V. July–Aug Mon–Fri 10am–6pm, Sat–Sun 11am–6pm; rest of year Tues–Fri 10am–5pm, Sat–Sun 11am–5pm. Métro: Place d'Armes.

Vieux-Port 𝘙𝘙   Montréal's Old Port, a once-dreary commercial wharf area, was transformed in 1992 into a 2km-long (1¼-mile), 53-hectare (131-acre) promenade and park with public spaces, bicycle paths, tram rides, exhibition halls, and a variety of family activities. Harbor cruises also leave from here. To get an idea of all there is to see and do, hop aboard the small, free Balade tram that travels throughout the port. At the far eastern end of the port is a 1922 clock tower, La Tour de l'Horloge, with 192 steps leading past the exposed clockworks to observation decks at three different levels (admission is free). Most cruises, entertainment, and special events take place from mid-May to October. Information booths with bilingual attendants assist visitors during that period. The Vieux-Port stretches along the waterfront from rue McGill to rue Berri. Quadricycles, bicycles, and in-line skates are available for rent.

Information Center/Interpretation Center: 333 rue de la Commune ouest (at rue McGill). ✆ 514/496-7678. www.oldportofmontreal.com. Free admission to port and interpretation center. Information Center/Interpretation Center mid-May to early Sept daily 10am–9pm; hours for specific attractions vary. Métro: Champ-de-Mars, Place d'Armes, or Square Victoria.

ELSEWHERE IN THE CITY

Biodôme de Montréal 𝘙𝘙𝘙   Near Montréal's Botanical Garden and next to the Olympic Stadium, you'll discover the engrossing Biodôme, possibly the only institution of its kind. Originally built as the velodrome for the 1976 Olympics, it has been refitted to house replications of four distinct ecosystems—a Laurentian forest, the St. Lawrence marine system, a tropical rainforest, and a polar environment—that visitors can walk through and explore. All the ecosystems are complete with appropriate temperatures, flora, fauna, and changing seasons, and all four re-creations are allowed a measure of freedom to grow and shift, so the exhibits are never static (for example, fall in the Laurentian forest sees the changing colors of the foliage). With more than 6,000 creatures of 210 species and 4,000 trees and plants, the Biodôme incorporates exhibits gathered from the old aquarium and the modest zoos at the Angrignon and LaFontaine parks. Among the fauna are specimens of certain threatened and endangered species, including macaws, marmosets, and tamarins. The Polar World contains puffins and four kinds of penguins, from both Poles. Biodôme also has a game room for kids called Naturalia, a shop, a restaurant, and a cafeteria. Combination price packages are available for the Biodôme, Olympic Tower, and the Botanical Garden and Insectarium (see Jardin Botanique below for details).

My, what an inefficient way to fish.

Ring toss, good. Horseshoes, bad.

Faster! Faster! Faster!

We take care of the fiddly bits, from providing over 43,000 customer reviews of hotels, to helping you find our best fares, to giving you 24/7 customer service. So you can focus on the only thing that matters. Goofing off.

travelocity
You'll never roam alone.

4777 av. Pierre-de-Coubertin (next to Olympic Stadium). © **514/868-3000.** www.biodome.qc.ca. Admission C$12 (US$9.60) adults, C$9 (US$7.20) seniors and students, C$6 (US$4.80) children 5–17, free for children under 5. AE, MC, V. Jan–Dec daily 9am–5pm (until 6pm in late June, July–Aug). Closed most Mon in Jan–Feb and Sep–Dec. Call ahead for exact hours. Métro: Viau.

Jardin Botanique ⟨⟨⟨   Across the street from the former Olympic sports complex, the Botanical Garden is spread across 75 hectares (185 acres). Celebrating its 75th anniversary in 2005, it has grown to include 22,000 varieties of plants in 31 specialized segments, ensuring something beautiful and fragrant for visitors year-round. Ten large conservatory greenhouses shelter tropical and desert plants, plus bonsai and penjing (Chinese bonsai), from the Canadian winter. Roses bloom here from mid-June to the first frost, May is the month for lilacs, and June is the time for the flowering hawthorn trees. Inaugurated in summer 1991, the 2.5-hectare (6¼-acre) Chinese Garden, a joint project of Montréal and Shanghai, is the largest Chinese garden ever built outside Asia. Meant to evoke the 14th- to 17th-century era of the Ming Dynasty, it incorporates pavilions, inner courtyards, ponds, and myriad plants indigenous to China. The serene Japanese Garden fills 6 hectares (15 acres) and contains a cultural pavilion with an art gallery, a tearoom where ancient tea ceremonies are performed, a stunning bonsai collection, and a Zen garden. The grounds are also home to the Insectarium, displaying some of the world's most beautiful insects, not to mention some of its sinister ones (see "Especially for Kids," later in this chapter). The Insectarium is home to the award-winning "Insect Tasting," in November and December, featuring gourmet snacks made with insects. Birders should bring along binoculars on summer visits to spot some of the more than 130 species of birds that spend at least part of the year in the garden. In summer, an outdoor aviary is filled with butterflies. Year-round, a free shuttle bus links the Botanical Garden and nearby Olympic Park. A small train runs regularly through the gardens and is worth the small fee charged to ride it.

4101 rue Sherbrooke est (opposite Olympic Stadium). © **514/872-1400.** www.ville.montreal.qc.ca/jardin. Admission May 15–Oct 31 to outside gardens, greenhouses, and Insectarium C$12 (US$9.60) adults, C$9 (US$7.20) seniors and students, C$6 (US$4.80) children 5–17, free for children under 5; Nov–May 14 C$8.75 (US$7) adults, C$6.75 (US$5.40) seniors and students, C$4.50 (US$3.60) children 5–17, free for children under 5. Combination tickets for Botanical Garden, Insectarium, Olympic Tower, and Biodôme (good for 30 days) C$29 (US$23) adults, C$22 (US$18) seniors and students, C$15 (US$12) children 5–17, free for children under 5. MC, V. Daily 9am–5pm (until 6pm in summer, until 9pm mid-Sept to Oct). Closed Mon Nov 1–Dec 29 and Jan 4–May 14. Métro: Pie-IX, then walk up the hill to the gardens; or take the free shuttle bus from Olympic Park (Métro: Viau).

Stade Olympique   Centerpiece of the 1976 Olympic Games, Montréal's controversial Olympic Stadium and its associated facilities provide considerable opportunities for both active and passive diversion. The complex incorporates a natatorium with six different pools, including one with competition dimensions and an adjustable bottom, and one that's 15m deep (49-ft.) for scuba diving. The stadium seats 60,000 to 80,000 spectators, who come here to see rock concerts and trade shows. Until recently, the stadium was home to the Montréal Expos, but in 2005, the team relocated to Washington, D.C.

The roof doesn't retract anymore, and never did perform that action well. That's only one reason that what was first known as "The Big O" was scorned as "The Big Owe" after cost overruns led to heavy increases in taxes. Plans for its future have run from total demolition to adding thousands of seats.

The 188m (617-ft.) inclined tower, which leans at a 45-degree angle, also does duty as an observation deck, with a funicular that whisks 90 passengers to the top in 95 seconds. On a clear day, the deck bestows a 56km (35-mile) view over Montréal and into the neighboring Laurentides. A free shuttle bus links the Olympic Park and the Botanical Garden. Combination price packages are available for the Olympic Tower, Biodôme, Botanical Garden, and Insectarium (see Jardin Botanique above for details).

4141 av. Pierre-de-Coubertin (bd. Pie IX). *C* 514/252-4737. www.rio.gouv.qc.ca. Funicular ride C$9 (US$7.20) adults, C$5.50 (US$4.40) students and children. Guided tours of the stadium are available. Public swim periods are scheduled daily, with low admission rates. Funicular mid-June to early Sept Mon noon–6pm, Tues–Thurs 10am–9pm, Fri–Sat 10am–11pm; early Sept to mid-Jan and mid-Feb to mid-June daily noon–6pm. Closed mid-Jan to mid-Feb. Métro: Pie-IX or Viau (choose the Viau station to meet up with the guided tour).

2 More Attractions

DOWNTOWN

Cathédrale-Basilique Marie-Reine-du-Monde   No one who has seen both will confuse Montréal's "Mary Queen of the World" Cathedral with St. Peter's Basilica in Rome, but a scaled-down homage was the intention of Bishop Ignace Bourget, who oversaw its construction after the first Catholic cathedral burned to the ground in 1852. Construction lasted from 1875 to 1894, its start delayed by the bishop's desire to place it not in Francophone east Montréal but in the heart of the Protestant Anglophone west. The resulting structure covers less than a quarter of the area of its Roman inspiration. Most impressive is the 76m-high (249-ft.) dome, about a third of the size of the original. The statues standing on the roofline represent patron saints of the region, providing a local touch. The interior is less rewarding visually than the exterior, but the high altar is worth a look.

Bd. René-Lévesque (at rue Mansfield). *C* **514/866-1661.** Free admission; donations accepted. Mon–Fri 7am–7:30pm; Sat 7:30am–8:30pm; Sun 8:30am–7:30pm. Métro: Bonaventure.

Fun Fact Moving Day

Montréal is an island of renters. About 60% of its 1.8 million residents live in properties owned by others. Every July 1, about 500,000 of them move from old apartments to new ones. That day, and only that day. It coincides with Canada's National Day, ensuring that separatist-minded Francophone Quebecers won't even have time to celebrate a holiday they have no intention of observing anyway.

On that first day of July (all but certain to be miserably hot and humid), families struggle to get furniture down narrow staircases to the curb, burly men struggle with sofas and bedroom sets and large appliances. Sidewalks become obstacle courses of baby cribs, bicycles, TV sets, and overflowing cardboard boxes scrounged in the days leading up to the event. Tempers fray and relationships sour. Moving companies, both legitimate and fly-by-night, double their rates. Streets are clogged with every serviceable van, truck, cab, and SUV that can be mustered for duty.

Arriving at their new digs, often still only partly vacated, hundreds of newly arrived tenants discover that they have been bestowed a gift no long desired by their predecessors—a dog with bowel issues, a cat that claws upholstered chairs to ribbons, an occasional famished boa constrictor.

No one seems certain why reason didn't prevail long ago in the form of a mandated staggered schedule, but it doesn't take much thought for residents and visitors to consider being someplace else on July 1.

Christ Church Cathedral   This Anglican cathedral, which is reflected in the shiny exterior of the postmodernist Tour de Catedral office tower, stands in glorious Gothic contrast to the city's glassy downtown skyscrapers. Sometimes called the "floating cathedral" because of the many tiers of malls and corridors in the underground city beneath it, the building was completed in 1859. The original steeple, too heavy for the structure, was replaced by a lighter aluminum version in 1940. Christ Church Cathedral hosts concerts throughout the year, most frequently from mid-January to August on Wednesdays at 12:30pm.

635 rue Ste-Catherine (at rue University). ℂ 514/843-6577, ext. 369 (recorded information about concerts). www.montreal.anglican.org/cathedral. Free admission; donations accepted. Daily 8am–6pm; services Sun 8am, 10am, and 4pm. Métro: McGill.

Musée d'Art Contemporain de Montréal ℛ   Montréal's Museum of Contemporary Art, the only museum in Canada devoted exclusively to contemporary art, moved into this new facility at the Place des Arts in 1992. "Contemporary" is defined here as art produced since 1939. About 60% of the permanent collection of some 6,000 works is composed of the work of Quebecois artists, but it also includes examples of such international painters as Jean Dubuffet, Max Ernst, Jean Arp, Larry Poons, and Antoni Tàpies, as well as photographers Robert Mapplethorpe and Ansel Adams. A few larger pieces are seen on the ground floor, but most are one flight up, with space for temporary exhibitions to the left and selections from the permanent collection on the right. No single style prevails, so expect to see installations, video displays, and examples of Pop, Op, and Abstract Expressionism. That the works often arouse strong opinions signifies a museum that is doing something right. The museum's restaurant, La Rotonde, has a summer dining terrace.

185 rue Ste-Catherine ouest. ℂ 514/847-6226. www.macm.org. Admission C$6 (US$4.80) adults, C$4 (US$3.20) seniors, C$3 (US$2.40) students, free for children under 12, C$12 (US$9.60) families; free to all Wed 6–9pm. Tues–Sun 11am–6pm (until 9pm Wed). Métro: Place des Arts.

VIEUX-MONTREAL (OLD MONTREAL)
Chapelle Notre-Dame-de-Bon-Secours/Musée Marguerite-Bourgeoys   Just
to the east of Marché Bonsecours, Notre Dame de Bon-Secours Chapel is called the Sailors' Church because of the special attachment that fishermen and other mariners have to the church. The devotion of mariners to the church is manifest in the several ship models hanging from the ceiling inside. In addition to the ship models, a revered 16th-century 6-inch-high carving of the Madonna is once again on display. There's an excellent view of the harbor and the old quarter from the church's tower.

The first church building, which no longer stands, was the project of an energetic teacher named Marguerite Bourgeoys, and was built in 1678. Bourgeoys arrived with de Maisonneuve to undertake the education of the children of Montréal in the latter half of the 17th century. Later on, she and several other teachers founded a nuns' order called the Congregation of Notre-Dame, Canada's first nuns' order. The pioneering Bourgeoys was recognized as a saint in 1982. The present church dates from 1773.

A restored 18th-century crypt houses the museum. Part of the museum is devoted to relating the life and work of Marguerite Bourgeoys. Another section displays artifacts from the archaeological site under the chapel, including ruins and materials from the earliest days of the colony as well as an Amerindian fire pit dated to 400 B.C. In another area, a collection of dolls and miniature furnishings is arranged in 58 scenes depicting life in Québec from the earliest days of European settlement.

400 rue St-Paul est (at the foot of rue Bonsecours). ✆ **514/282-8670**. www.marguerite-bourgeoys.com. Free admission to chapel. Museum C$6 (US$4.80) adults, C$4 (US$3.20) seniors and students, C$3 (US$2.40) ages 6–12, free for children under 6; archaeological site and museum C$8 (US$6.40). May–Oct Tues–Sun 10am–5:30pm; Nov to mid-Jan and Mar–Apr Tues–Sun 11am–3:30pm. Closed mid-Jan to Feb. Métro: Champ-de-Mars.

Hôtel de Ville   City Hall, finished in 1878, is relatively young by Vieux-Montréal standards. The French Second Empire design makes it look as though it was imported stone by stone from the mother country. Balconies, turrets, and mansard roofs decorate the exterior. The details are seen particularly well when the exterior is illuminated at night. It was from the balcony above the awning that an ill-mannered Charles de Gaulle proclaimed, "Vive le Québec Libre!" in 1967, thereby pleasing his immediate audience but straining relations with the Canadian government for years. The Hall of Honour is made of green marble from Campagna, Italy, and houses Art Deco lamps from Paris and a bronze-and-glass chandelier, also from France, that weighs a metric ton. The hall also has a hand-carved ceiling and five stained-glass windows representing religion, the port, industry and commerce, finance, and transportation. The mayor's office is on the main floor.

Fifteen-minute guided tours are given throughout the day on weekdays from May through October.

275 rue Notre-Dame (at the corner of rue Gosford). ✆ **514/872-3355**. Free admission. Daily 8:30am–4:30pm. Métro: Champ-de-Mars.

Marché Bonsecours   Bonsecours Market, an imposing neoclassical building with a long facade, a colonnaded portico, and a silvery dome, was built in the mid-1800s and first used as Montréal's City Hall, then for many years after 1878 as the central market. Its uses have never been decided with finality since then. Essentially abandoned for much of the 20th century, it was restored in 1964 to house city government offices, and in 1992 became the information and exhibition center for the celebration of the city's 350th birthday. It continues to be used as an exhibition space, with shopping stalls and three restaurants with terraces. The architecture alone makes a brief visit worthwhile.

350 rue St-Paul est (at the foot of rue St-Claude). ✆ **514/872-7730**. www.marchebonsecours.qc.ca. Free admission. June 24–Sept 2 Mon–Sat 10am–9pm, Sun 10am–6pm; rest of year daily 10am–6pm (until 9pm Thurs–Fri). Métro: Champ-de-Mars.

Musée du Château Ramezay ⚜   Claude de Ramezay, the 11th governor of the colony, built his residence at this site in 1705. The château was the home of the city's royal French governors for almost 4 decades, but in 1745, Ramezay's heirs sold it to a trading company, who left parts of the original structure but altered others considerably. Fifteen years later, it was taken over by the British conquerors. In 1775, an army of American revolutionaries invaded and held Montréal, using the château as their headquarters. Benjamin Franklin, sent to persuade the Quebecois to rise with the American colonists against British rule, stayed in the château for a time, but failed to persuade the city's people to join his cause. After the American interlude, the house was used as a courthouse, a government office building, a teachers' college, and headquarters for Laval University, before being converted into a museum in 1895. Old coins and prints, portraits, furnishings, tools, a loom, Amerindian artifacts, and other memorabilia related to the economic and social activities of the 18th and first half of the 19th century fill the main floor. In the cellar are the vaults of the original house. Descriptive placards appear in both French and English. After a recent 6-month renovation, it reopened with a restored garden and cafe.

280 rue Notre-Dame (east of place Jacques-Cartier). (C) **514/861-3708**. www.chateauramezay.qc.ca. Admission C$7 (US$5.60) adults, C$6 (US$4.80) seniors, C$5 (US$4) students, C$4 (US$3.20) ages 5–17, free for children under 4, C$15 (US$12) families. MC, V. June–Sept daily 10am–6pm; Oct–May Tues–Sun 10am–4:30pm. Métro: Champ-de-Mars.

MONT-ROYAL & PLATEAU MONT-ROYAL

To further explore this area, try the walking tour in chapter 8.

Oratoire St-Joseph ⋒   This huge basilica with a giant copper dome was built by Québec's Catholics to honor St. Joseph, patron saint of Canada. Dominating the north slope of Mont-Royal, its imposing dimensions are seen by some as inspiring, by others as forbidding. It came into being through the efforts of Brother André, a lay brother in the Holy Cross order who enjoyed a reputation as a healer. By the time he had built a small wooden chapel in 1904 near the site of the basilica, he was said to have performed hundreds of cures. His powers attracted supplicants from great distances, and Brother André performed his work until his death in 1937. His dream of building this shrine to his patron saint became a completed reality in 1967, years after his death. He is buried in the basilica and was beatified by the pope in 1982, a status one step below sainthood. The basilica is largely Italian Renaissance in style, its dome recalling the shape of the Duomo in Florence, but of much greater size and less grace. Inside is a museum where a central exhibit is the heart of Brother André. Outside, a Way of the Cross lined with sculptures was the setting of scenes for the film *Jesus of Montréal.* Brother André's wooden chapel, with his tiny bedroom, is on the grounds and open to the public. Pilgrims, some ill, come to seek intercession from St. Joseph and Brother André and often climb the middle set of 100 steps on their knees. At 263m (863 ft.), the shrine is the highest point in Montréal. A cafeteria and snack bar are on the premises. Ninety-minute guided tours are offered in several languages at 10am and 2pm daily in summer and on weekends in September and October; call for times. There is no fee for the walks, but a donation is requested.

3800 chemin Queen Mary (on the north slope of Mont-Royal). (C) **514/733-8211**. www.saint-joseph.org. Free admission, but donations are requested. Daily 6am–9:30pm; museum daily 9am–5pm; tours 10am and 2pm in summer and weekends Sept–Oct. 56-bell carillon plays Wed–Fri noon–3pm, Sat–Sun noon–2:30pm. Métro: Côtes-des-Neiges. Bus: 165.

Parc Lafontaine   The European-style park in Plateau Mont-Royal is one of the city's oldest. Illustrating the dual identities of the city's populace, half the park is landscaped in the formal French manner, the other in the more casual English style. Among its several bodies of water is a lake used for paddle boating in summer and ice-skating in winter. Snowshoe and cross-country trails wind through the trees and there are tennis courts on the premises. An open amphitheater, the **Théâtre de Verdure,** is the setting for free outdoor theater and movies in summer.

Rue Sherbrooke and av. Parc Lafontaine. (C) **514/872-2644**. Free admission; small fee for use of tennis courts. Park daily 24 hr. Tennis courts summer daily 9am–10pm. Métro: Sherbrooke.

ILE STE-HELENE ⋒

La Biosphère   Not to be confused with the Biodôme at Olympic Park, this facility is located in the geodesic dome designed by Buckminster Fuller to serve as the American Pavilion for Expo '67. A fire destroyed the acrylic skin of the sphere in 1976, and it served no purpose other than as a harbor landmark until 1995. The motivation behind the Biosphère is unabashedly environmentalist, with four exhibition areas, a theater, and an amphitheater, all devoted to promoting awareness of the St. Lawrence–Great Lakes ecosystem. Multimedia shows and hands-on displays invite the active participation of visitors, and there is an exhibition related to the activities of the ocean explorer Jacques-Yves Cousteau. In the highest point of Visions Hall is an observation level with an unobstructed view of the river. Connections Hall offers a "Call to Action" presentation employing six giant screens and three stages. There is a preaching-to-the-choir quality to all this that slips over the edge into zealous philosophizing. But the various displays and exhibits are put together thoughtfully and will engage and enlighten most visitors, at least for a while. Don't make a special trip, but if you're on the island for something else, stop by.

160 chemin Tour-de-l'Isle (Ile Ste-Hélène). ℂ 514/283-5000. http://biosphere.ec.qc.ca. Admission C$8.50 (US$7.05) adults, C$6.50 (US$5.20) seniors and students, C$5 (US$4) ages 7–17, free for children under 7, C$19 (US$15) families. June–Sept daily 10am–6pm; Oct–May Mon and Wed–Fri noon–5pm, Sat–Sun and holidays 10am–5pm. Métro: Parc Jean-Drapeau, then a short walk. Just follow the signs to the park.

Musée David M. Stewart 🏛 After the War of 1812, the British prepared for a possible future American invasion by building a moated fortress, which now houses the David M. Stewart Museum. The duke of Wellington ordered its construction as another link in the chain of defenses along the St. Lawrence. Completed in 1824, it was never involved in armed conflict. The British garrison left in 1870, after confederation of the former Canadian colonies. Today the low stone barracks and blockhouses contain the museum, which displays maps and scientific instruments that helped Europeans explore the New World, as well as military and naval artifacts, weaponry, uniforms, housewares, and related paraphernalia from the time of Jacques Cartier (1535) through 1763, the end of the colonial period. Useful labels appear in both French and English.

From late June through late August, the fort comes to life with reenactments of military parades and retreats by La Compagnie Franche de la Marine and the Olde 78th Fraser Highlanders, daily at 11am, 3pm, and 4:30pm. The presence of the French unit is an unhistorical bow to Francophone sensibilities, because New France had become English Canada almost 65 years before the fort was erected. If you absolutely must be photographed in stocks, they are provided on the parade grounds.

Vieux Fort, Ile Ste-Hélène. ℂ 514/861-6701. www.stewart-museum.org. Admission late May to early Oct C$10 (US$8) adults, C$7 (US$5.60) seniors and students, free for children under 7; mid-Oct to mid-May C$8 (US$6.40) adults, C$6 (US$4.80) seniors and students, free for children under 7. Summer hours typically mid-May to early Sept daily 10am–6pm; early Sept to mid-May Wed–Mon 10am–5pm. Call for exact hours. Métro: Parc Jean-Drapeau, then a 15-min. walk. By car: Take the Jacques-Cartier Bridge to the Parc Jean-Drapeau exit, then follow signs to Vieux Fort.

3 Especially for Kids

IMAX Theatre The images and special effects are larger than life, always visually dazzling and often vertiginous, thrown on a five-story screen in the renovated theater of the Montréal Science Centre. Recent films made the most of Jane Goodall's chimps, and cameras swooping low over glaciers and erupting volcanoes. Running time is usually under an hour. Arrive for shows at least 10 minutes before starting time, earlier on weekends and evenings. Tickets can be ordered online.

Vieux-Port, Quai King Edward (end of bd. St-Laurent). ℂ 877/496-4724 or 514/496-4724 (information and tickets). www.montrealsciencecentre.com. Admission C$10 (US$8) adults, C$9 (US$7.20) seniors and students 13–17, C$7 (US$5.60) ages 4–12. Open daily. Call for current schedule of shows in English. Métro: Place d'Armes.

Insectarium de Montréal 🏛 This two-level structure near the Sherbrooke gate of the Botanical Garden exhibits the collections of two avid entomologists: Georges Brossard (whose brainchild this place is) and Father Firmia Liberté. More than 3,000 mounted butterflies, scarabs, maggots, locusts, beetles, tarantulas, and giraffe weevils are displayed, and live exhibits feature scorpions, tarantulas, crickets, cockroaches, and praying mantises. Needless to say, kids are delighted by the creepy critters and glistening mounted butterflies. During the summer, beautiful live specimens flutter among the nectar-bearing plants in the Butterfly House. In November and early December, check out the award-winning "Insect Tasting" (Croque-insectes), an event which features expertly cooked, spiced, and sauced insects for your eating enjoyment.

Botanical Garden, 4581 rue Sherbrooke est. ℂ **514/872-1400.** www.ville.montreal.qc.ca/insectarium. May 15–Oct C$12 (US$9.60) adults, C$9 (US$7.20) seniors and students, C$5 (US$4) children 6–17, free for children under 6. Nov–May 14 C$8.75 (US$7) adults, C$6.75 (US$5.40) seniors and students, $4.50 (US$3.60) children 6–17, free for children under 6. June 21–Sept 1 daily 9am–6pm; May 19–June 20 and Sept 2–Sept 11 daily 9am–5pm; Sept 12–Nov 2 9am–9pm; Nov 3–May 18 9am–4pm. Closed Mon Jan 29–May 14 and Nov 1–Dec 27. Métro: Pie-IX or Viau.

La Ronde Amusement Park   Montréal's amusement park was run for most of its 35 years by the city. In recent times, that arrangement clearly wasn't working, with the facility sliding into massive disrepair. Then it was sold to the American-owned Six Flags theme park empire. At first, La Ronde under the new management seemed pretty much the same as it had been, minus the threat of insolvency. But seven new rides have now been delivered. Le Vampire, for one, is a suspended coaster, where willing riders experience five loops at over 80km (50 miles) per hour, meaning that they are upside down much of the time.

The park fills the northern reaches of the Île Ste-Hélène with a sailing lagoon, an "Enchanted Forest" with costumed storytellers, and a Western town with a saloon. There are also Ferris wheels, carousels, roller coasters, carnival booths, and plenty of places to eat and drink. Thrill seekers will love rides like Le Boomerang, Le Monstre, and Le Cobra, a stand-up roller coaster that incorporates a 360-degree loop and reaches speeds in excess of 97kmph (60 mph). While many of the 37 rides test adult nerves and stomachs, there are ample attractions for youngsters, such as the Tchou Tchou Train and the Super Volcanozor, which combines 3-D images of dinosaurs with swooping, twirling movement. In 2005, a new section called Le Pays de Ribambelle opened, incorporating 10 family-friendly rides.

A big attraction every year is the **International Fireworks Competition** ✪, held once a week in June and July (postponed in bad weather). The pyromusical displays are launched at 10pm and last at least 30 minutes. Many Montrealers choose to watch them from the Jacques Cartier Bridge, which is closed to traffic during the display. Take along a Walkman to listen to the accompanying music, which is broadcast.

Parc des Îles, Île Ste-Hélène. ℂ **800/797-4537** or 514/872-4537. www.laronde.com. Admission C$35 (US$28) ages 12 and over, C$23 (US$18) ages 3–11, free for children under 3; admission to the grounds but not the rides C$28 (US$22). Parking C$10 (US$8). Last week in May and early Sept to late Oct Sat–Sun only; June to Labor Day daily 10:30am–11pm. Métro: Papineau then bus no. 169, or Parc Jean-Drapeau then bus no. 167.

Planétarium de Montréal   A window on the night sky, with mythical monsters and magical heroes, Montréal's planetarium is right downtown, only 3 blocks south of Centre Bell. It celebrated its 40th anniversary in 2005. Shows under the 20m (66-ft.) dome dazzle and inform kids at the same time. Multimedia presentations change with the seasons, exploring time and space travel and collisions of celestial bodies. The special Christmas show, "Season of Light," can be seen December and early January afternoons, while evenings bring representations of the night sky. Shows in English alternate with those in French.

1000 rue St-Jacques (at Peel). ℂ **514/872-4530.** www.planetarium.montreal.qc.ca. Admission C$7.75 (US$6.20) adults, C$6 (US$4.80) seniors and students, C$4 (US$3.20) children 6–17. MC, V. Show schedule changes frequently, so call ahead. Métro: Bonaventure (Cathédrale exit).

4 Special-Interest Sightseeing

Centre Canadien d'Architecture (CCA)   The understated but handsome Canadian Center of Architecture building occupies a city block, with lawns joining a contemporary structure with an older building, the 1875 Shaughnessy House. The CCA functions as both a study center and a museum, with changing exhibits devoted to the art of architecture and its history, including architects' sketchbooks, elevation drawings, and photography. The collection is international in scope and encompasses architecture, urban planning, and landscape design. Texts are in French and English. Opened in 1989, the museum has received rave reviews from scholars, critics, and serious architecture buffs. That said, it is only fair to note that the average visitor is likely to find it somewhat less enthralling. The bookstore has a special section on Canadian architecture with an emphasis on Montréal and Québec City. The sculpture garden across the Ville-Marie autoroute is part of the CCA, designed by artist/architect Melvin Charney.

1920 rue Baile (at rue du Fort). ℂ **514/939-7026.** http://cca.qc.ca. Admission C$10 (US$8) adults, C$7 (US$5.60) seniors, C$5 (US$4) students, C$3 (US$2.40) ages 6–12, free for children 5 and under and for those with limited mobility. Free Thurs after 5:30pm. June–Sept Tues–Sun 11am–6pm (until 9pm Thurs); rest of year Wed–Fri 11am–6pm (until 8pm Thurs), Sat–Sun 11am–5pm. Guided tours available on request. Métro: Atwater or Guy-Concordia.

Centre d'Histoire de Montréal   Built in 1903 as Montréal's Central Fire Station, this red-brick–and–sandstone building is now the Montréal History Center, which traces the development of the city from its first residents, the Amerindians, to the European settlers who arrived in 1642, to the present day. Throughout its 14 rooms, carefully conceived presentations chart the contributions of the city fathers and mothers and subsequent generations. The development of the railroad, Métro, and related infrastructure is recalled, as is the creation of domestic and public architecture, in imaginative exhibits, videos, and slide shows. On the second floor, reached by a spiral staircase, is memorabilia from the early 20th century.

335 place d'Youville (at St-Pierre). ℂ **514/872-3207.** www.ville.montreal.qc.ca/chm. Admission C$4.50 (US$3.60) adults; C$3 (US$2.40) seniors, students, and children 6–17; free for children under 6. May–Aug Tues–Sun 10am–5pm; Sept–Apr Wed–Sun 10am–5pm. Métro: Square Victoria.

Musée de la Banque de Montréal   Facing Place d'Armes is Montréal's oldest bank building, with a classic facade beneath a graceful dome, a carved pediment, and six Corinthian columns. The outside dimensions and appearance remain largely unchanged since the building's completion in 1847. The interior was renovated from 1901 through 1905 by the famed U.S. firm McKim, Mead, and White, which added Ionic and Corinthian columns of Vermont granite, walls of pink marble from Tennessee, and a counter of Levanto marble. The bank contains a small museum with a replica of its first office (and its first bank teller, Henry Stone, from Boston), gold nuggets from the Yukon, a $3 bill (one of only two known), and a collection of 100-year-old mechanical banks.

119 and 129 rue St-Jacques (at place d'Armes). ℂ **514/877-6810.** Free admission. Mon–Fri 10am–4pm. Métro: Place d'Armes.

Musée Marc-Aurèle Fortin   This is Montréal's only museum dedicated to the work of a single French-Canadian artist. Landscape watercolorist Marc-Aurèle Fortin (1888–1970) interpreted the beauty of the Québec countryside, especially the Laurentians and Charlevoix. The museum also mounts temporary exhibits, usually featuring the work of other Quebecois painters (varied in style, but typically representative rather than nonobjective or abstract).

118 rue St-Pierre (at rue d'Youville). (℃ **514/845-6108**. Admission C$5 (US$4) adults, C$4 (US$3.20) seniors, C$3 (US$2.40) students, free for children under 12. Tues–Sun 11am–5pm. Métro: Square Victoria.

Musée Redpath   If the unusual name seems slightly familiar, think of the wrappings on sugar cubes in many Canadian restaurants. John Redpath was a 19th-century industrialist who built Canada's first sugar refinery and later distributed much of his fortune in philanthropy. This quirky museum, housed in an 1882 building with a grandly proportioned and richly appointed interior, is on the McGill University campus. The main draws are its collection of Egyptian antiquities, the second largest in Canada, and skeletons of whales and prehistoric beasts.

859 rue Sherbrooke ouest (rue University). (℃ **514/398-4086**. Free admission. Sept–June Mon–Fri 9am–5pm, Sun 1–5pm; July–Aug Mon–Thurs 9am–5pm, Sun 1–5pm. Closed holiday weekends. Métro: McGill. Bus: 24.

5 Organized Tours

A generalized guided tour is often the most desirable—or, at least, most efficient—way to begin explorations of a new city. Even a mediocre tour with a guide can provide a timesaving sense of the topography of the city, its history, and which attractions are most likely to reward an in-depth return visit.

For a complete listing of tours and tour operators, check under "Guided Tours" in the annually revised *Montréal Tourist Guide,* available at **Infotouriste Centre** (℃ **877/266-5687** or 514/873-2015; www.bonjourquebec.com). Most of the land tours leave from downtown at Square Dorchester, near the Infotouriste office. Boat tours depart from the Old Port, bordering Vieux-Montréal. Parking is free at the dock, or take the Métro to the Champ-de-Mars or Square Victoria station and walk 6 blocks.

BOAT TOURS

Among numerous opportunities for experiencing Montréal and environs by water, here are a few of the most popular:

Le Bateau-Mouche (℃ **800/361-9952** or 514/849-9952; www.bateau-mouche. com) is an air-conditioned, glass-enclosed vessel reminiscent of those on the Seine in Paris. It plies the St. Lawrence River from mid-May to mid-October. Cruises depart for 60-minute excursions at 10am, 1:30pm, 3pm, and 4:30pm; for a 90-minute cruise at 11:30am; and for a 3½-hour dinner cruise at 7pm (boarding at 6:30pm). The shallow-draft boat takes up to 158 passengers on a route inaccessible by traditional vessels. It passes under several bridges and provides sweeping views of the city, Mont-Royal, the St. Lawrence, and its islands. Daytime snacks are available onboard, and the kitchen of Le Reine Elizabeth hotel prepares dinners. The 60-minute tours cost C$17 (US$14) adults, C$16 (US$13) students and seniors, C$9.50 (US$7.60) children under 12, and C$40 (US$32) families. The 90-minute tour costs C$23 (US$18) adults, C$21 (US$17) students and seniors, and C$9.50 (US$7.60). Dinner cruises cost C$81 to C$136 (US$65–US$109). *Le Bateau-Mouche* departs from the Jacques Cartier Pier, opposite place Jacques-Cartier.

Croisières du Port de Montréal (**AML Cruises;** © **800/667-3131** or 514/842-3871; www.croisieresaml.com) also travels the harbor and the St. Lawrence. The boats depart up to four times a day from May to October from the Clock Tower Pier (Quai de l'Horloge) at the foot of rue Berri in Vieux-Montréal, for 1½-hour sightseeing tours. Fares are C$22 to C$40 (US$18–US$32) adults, C$20 to C$38 (US$16–US$30) students and seniors, C$10 to C$20 (US$8–US$16) children 12 and under, and C$114 (US$91) for families of two adults and two children. AML also offers longer brunch and dinner cruises as well as cruises down the St. Lawrence to Québec City, to Charlevoix for whale-watching, and up the Saguenay River.

Croisière historique sur le canal de Lachine (© **866/846-0448** or 514/846-0428; www.croisierecanaldelachine.ca) is a leisurely Parks Canada trip up the Lachine Canal, which was inaugurated in 1824 so ships could bypass the Lachine Rapids on the way to the Great Lakes. Renovated for C$260 million, the canal was reopened for leisure use in 1997. The guided tours are by a glass-topped *bateau-mouche*, which carries up to 50 passengers. From May 15 to mid-June and early September to mid-October departures are at 1 and 3:30pm on Saturday, Sunday, and holidays; from late June to early September daily departures are at 1pm and 3:30pm. Reservations required. Fares are C$17 (US$14) adults, C$14 (US$11) seniors and students, and C$9.75 (US$7.80) for children 4 to 14. It departs from a dock near the Marché Atwater. Also available at that location through **Ruban Bleu Amérique** (© **514/938-4448**, www.rubanbleu.ca) are rentals of electric boats, kayaks, and pedal boats.

For an exciting—and wet—experience, consider a ride with **Saute Moutons** (© **514/284-9607;** www.jetboatingmontreal.com). Their wave-jumper powerboats take on the roiling Lachine Rapids of the St. Lawrence River. The streamlined hydro-jet makes the 1-hour trip from May to mid-October daily, with departures every 2 hours from 10am to 6pm. It takes half an hour total to get to and from the rapids, which leaves 30 minutes for storming up the river. Arrive 45 minutes early to obtain and don rain gear and a life jacket. Wearing a sweater and bringing a change of clothes are good ideas, because you almost certainly will get splashed or even soaked through. Fares are C$17 to C$46 (US$14–US$37) adults, C$14 to C$37 (US$11–US$30) ages 13 to 18, and C$12 to C$29 (US$9.60–US$23) ages 6 to 12. Kids under 6 ride free. Boats depart from the Clock Tower Pier (Quai de l'Horloge).

A much milder water voyage, with great views, is the **ferry** (© **514/281-8000**) from Jacques-Cartier Pier in Vieux-Montréal to Ile Ste-Hélène, a good way to begin and end a picnic outing or visits to the old fort or La Ronde Amusement Park. The ferry operates from mid-May to mid-October. Rates change frequently, so call for details.

LAND TOURS

Commercial guided tours in air-conditioned buses are offered two to eight times daily year-round by **Gray Line de Montréal** (© **514/934-1222;** www.coachcanada-montreal.com). The basic city tour takes 3 hours; the deluxe 6-hour version includes long stops at the Botanical Garden and the Biodôme. Other tours take you to Île Ste-Hélène, the St. Lawrence Seaway, the Laurentians, and Québec City. Tours depart from Dorchester Square. The basic city tour costs C$35 (US$28) for ages 13 and up, C$20 (US$16) ages 12 and under. Similar but less frequent tours are provided by **Autocar Imperial** (© **514/871-4733**). The 3-hour city tour costs C$35 (US$28) for adults, C$32 (US$26) seniors and students, and C$20 (US$16) ages 5 to 12.

Now for something a little different: **Amphi-Bus** (© 514/849-5181) tours Vieux-Montréal much like any other bus, until it waddles into the waters of the harbor for a dramatic finish. One-hour tours leave on the hour from 10am to midnight in the warmer months and noon to 6pm off-season. Reservations are required. Departures are from Quai King Edward in Vieux-Montréal. The tour costs C$24 (US$19) for adults and C$22 (US$18) seniors and ages 4 to 16.

Montréal's romantic **calèches** (© 514/934-6105) are horse-drawn open carriages whose drivers serve as guides. These carriages operate year-round. In winter some steeds are hitched to old-fashioned sleighs for a ride around the top of Mont-Royal, the horses puffing steam clouds in the cold air, the passengers bundled in lap rugs. Prices are C$60 (US$48) for an hour's tour in the carriage or sleigh, which can seat four comfortably, five if one sits with the driver. In addition to Mont-Royal, calèches depart from Square Dorchester and in Vieux-Montréal from place Jacques-Cartier and rue de la Commune, and Place d'Armes opposite Notre-Dame Basilica. The carriages run year-round, but the schedules vary in the off season; so call first.

WALKING & CYCLING TOURS

Walking tours of Vieux-Montréal, the underground city, or any other section that piques interest are available through **Guidatour** (© 514/844-4021; www.guidatour. qc.ca) or **Visites de Montréal** (© 514/933-6674). Cycling tours in French or English are available through **Vélo Montréal** (© 514/236-8356; www.velomontreal. com), located at 55 rue de la Commune ouest and 3880 rue Rachel est. If you're interested primarily in the city's architecture, landscaping, and urban planning, **Heritage Montréal** (© 514/286-2662; www.heritagemontreal.qc.ca) conducts most of its "Architectours" on foot or on bicycles, and in French and English (just ask when you call). Each has a theme and a different neighborhood to traverse, from the Golden Square Mile to Square St-Louis to Little Italy. Heritage Montréal's summer schedule begins in mid-June and proceeds until late September, rain or shine.

6 Spectator Sports

Montrealers are as devoted to ice hockey as other Canadians are, with plenty of enthusiasm left over for football, soccer, and the other distinctive national sport, curling. They liked baseball too, but not enough. In 2005, the Montréal Expos, plagued by poor attendance, left for Washington, D.C., where the team became the Nationals. There are several prominent annual sporting events of other kinds, such The Player's Ltd. International men's tennis championship in late July and the Montréal Marathon in September.

FOOTBALL

Canadian professional football returned to Montréal after an experimental 3-year league with U.S. teams. The team that was briefly the Baltimore Colts is now in its second incarnation as the **Montréal Alouettes** (French for "larks"), and has enjoyed considerable success since its return, frequently appearing in the Grey Cup, the CFL's Super Bowl. The Als play at McGill University's Molson Stadium on a schedule that runs from June into October. Tickets start at C$20 (US$16). Call © 514/790-1245 or visit www.alouettes.net for information, www.admission.com for tickets.

HARNESS RACING

Popularly known as Blue Bonnets Racetrack, the **Hippodrome de Montréal** at 7440 bd. Décarie, in Jean-Talon (© 514/739-2741; www.hdem.com), is the host facility

The Second Greatest Canadian Pastime

Name That Sport:
"With Ontario leading 6-4 in the 10th end, Manitoba skip Jennifer Jones prepared for her last shot. Manitoba had three rocks in the house, but Ontario had shot rock and had two guards sitting near one another, high atop the house, toward Jones; another guard sat just outside the rings. Jones was left with one option: She hit and rolled off the lone Ontario stone outside the rings to remove Ontario's shot rock near the button."

So was the verbatim report in *The Globe & Mail* of the Canadian women's championship game in February 2005. Manitoba won, 8-6. The sport was curling.

for international harness-racing events, including the Coupe des Elevers (Breeders Cup). Restaurants, bars, a snack bar, and parimutuel betting make for a satisfying evening or Sunday-afternoon outing. There are no races on Tuesday and Thursday. General admission is free. Races begin at 7:30pm on Monday, Wednesday, Friday, and Saturday, and on Sunday at 1:30pm. Métro: Namur, and then take the shuttle bus.

HOCKEY
Fans were beside themselves with frustration over the cancellation of the 2004–05 NHL hockey season, but the contract problems were resolved in 2005. Assuming it returns in the same form, the beloved **Montréal Canadiens** will play at the Centre Bell (formerly Molson Centre), which opened in 1996 at 1260 rue de la Gauchetière, replacing the old Forum. The team has won 24 Stanley Cup championships since 1929, but hasn't enjoyed much success in recent years. The season runs from October into April, with playoffs continuing to mid-June. Tickets range from about C$16 to C$95 (US$13–US$76). Ticket and schedule information can be obtained by phone at (✆ **514/932-2582** (CLUB). Métro: Bonaventure.

7 Outdoor Activities

BICYCLING
Cycling is hugely popular in Montréal, and the city enjoys an expanding network of 349km (216 miles) of cycling paths. Heavily used routes include the nearly flat 15km (9-mile) *piste cyclable* (bicycle path) along the Lachine Canal that leads to Lac St-Louis, the 16km (10-mile) path west from the St-Lambert Lock to the city of Côte Ste-Catherine, and the 6.4km (4-mile) path at Angrignon Park, which has many inviting picnic areas (to get to Angrignon Park take the Métro, which accepts bikes in the last two doors of the last car, to Angrignon station). Bikes can be rented at **CaRoule/Montréal on Wheels,** 27 rue de la Commune est (✆ **514/866-0633**), bordering the Vieux-Port, for C$7 or C$7.50 (US$5.60 or US$6) an hour or C$22 to C$25 (US$18–US$20) a day. CaRoule also rents in-line skates (see below). **Velo Montréal,** 3880 rue Rachel est and 55 rue de la Commune ouest (✆ **514/236-8356;** www.velomontreal.com) is another principal bike rental source, with similar rates. Bikes, along with the popular four-wheel "Q Cycles," may also be rented at the place

Jacques-Cartier entrance to the Vieux-Port. The Q Cycles, for use in the Vieux-Port only, cost C$5 (US$4) per half-hour for adults and C$4 (US$3.20) per half-hour for children.

Cyclists who want to take in a more distant area can arrange for a taxi to take them and up to three bicycles to their desired biking destination, at a fee of C$3 (US$2.40) per bicycle, in addition to the fare. For details, call ⓒ **514/521-8356** or log on to www.velo.qc.ca. A useful booklet, *Pédaler Montréal,* is available at the Infotouriste Centre office on Square Dominion. For additional information, log on to **www.velo. qc.ca.**

CROSS-COUNTRY SKIING

Parc Mont-Royal has a 2.1km (1.3-mile) cross-country course called the *parcours de la croix.* The Botanical Garden has an ecology trail used by cross-country skiers during the winter. The problem with both is that skiers have to supply their own equipment. Just an hour from the city, in the Laurentides, are 19 ski centers, all offering cross-country as well as downhill skiing. See chapter 11.

HIKING

The most popular—and obvious—hike is up to the top of Mont-Royal. Start downtown on rue Peel, which leads north to a stairway, which in turn leads to an 800m (.5-mile) path of switchbacks called Le Serpent. Or opt for the 200 steps that lead up to the terrace lookout of the Chalet du Mont Royal, with the reward of a panoramic view of the city. Figure about 2km (1.3 miles) one-way.

ICE SKATING

One of the most agreeable venues for ice skating is the **Atrium Le 1000 de la Gauchetière** in the downtown skyscraper at that address. For one thing, it's indoors and warm. For another, it's surrounded by cafes and places to relax after twirling around the big rink. It's open all year Sunday and Tuesday through Friday from 11:30am to 6pm, Saturday from 10am to 11am for children and their families, from 11:30am to 7pm for all, from 7 to 10pm for "DJ Nights." Skates are available for rent for C$4.50 (US$3.60). Admission is C$5.50 (US$4.40) for adults 16 and up, C$4.50 (US$3.60) for seniors, C$3.50 (US$2.80) children 12 and under. Call ⓒ **514/395-0555** or log on to www.le1000.com for more information.

IN-LINE SKATING

More than 230 pairs of in-line skates and all the requisite protective gear can be rented from **CaRoule/Montréal on Wheels** (ⓒ **514/866-0633;** www.caroulemontreal.com) at 27 rue de la Commune est, bordering the Vieux-Port. The cost is C$8.50 (US$6.80) weekdays or C$9 (US$7.20) weekends for the first hour, up to a maximum of C$30 (US$24) for a full day. Protective gear is included, and a deposit is required.

JOGGING

There are many possibilities for running. One is to follow rue Peel north to the Le Serpent switchback path on Mont-Royal, continuing uphill on it for 800m (.5 mile) until it peters out. Turn right and continue 2km (1.2 miles) to the monument of George-Etienne Cartier, one of Canada's fathers of confederation. From here, either take a bus back downtown or run back down the same route or along avenue du Parc and avenue des Pins (turn right when you get to it). It's also fun to jog along the Lachine Canal.

8

Montréal Strolls

Cities best reveal themselves on foot, and Montréal is one of the most pedestrian-friendly cities in North America. There's much to see in the concentrated districts—the Old Town, the center city, around rue Crescent, the Latin Quarter, and on "The Mountain"—and the city's layout is fairly straightforward and easily navigated, especially with the aid of the extensive Métro system.

WALKING TOUR 1 VIEUX-MONTREAL

Start:	Place d' Armes, opposite the Notre-Dame Basilica.
Finish:	Vieux-Port.
Time:	2 to 3 hours.
Best Times:	Almost any day the weather is decent. Vieux-Montréal is lively and safe day or night. Note, however, that most of the museums in the area are closed on Monday. On warm weekends and holidays, Montrealers turn out in full force, enjoying the plazas, the 18th- and 19th-century architecture, and the ambience of the most picturesque part of their city. At night, more than a score of the most prominent public buildings are illuminated, including the Basilique Notre-Dame and the Hôtel de Ville, making for a romantic evening stroll.
Worst Times:	Evenings, when museums and historic places are closed.

Take the Métro to the Place d'Armes station (actually beside the newly expanded Palais des Congrès convention center) and follow the signs up the short hill 2 blocks to Vieux-Montréal (Old Montréal) and the Place d'Armes. Turn right on rue St-Jacques. On your immediate right is the domed, colonnaded:

❶ Banque de Montréal

Montréal's oldest bank building dates from 1847. Besides being impressively proportioned and lavishly appointed inside and out, it houses a small banking museum that illustrates its early operations (go in the front door, turn left, then left again). Admission is free. From 1901 to 1905, American architect Stanford White was in charge of extending the original building beyond Ruelle des Fortifications to what is now rue St-Antoine.

In this enlarged space he created a vast chamber with high, green-marble columns topped with golden capitals. The public is welcome to stop in for a look.

Exiting the bank, cross the street to the:

❷ Place d'Armes

The centerpiece of this square is a monument to city founder Paul de Chomedey, sieur de Maisonneuve (1612–76). It marks the spot where the settlers defeated Iroquois warriors in bloody hand-to-hand fighting, with de Maisonneuve himself locked in combat with the Iroquois chief. De Maisonneuve won and lived here another 23 years. The inscription on the monument reads: YOU ARE THE BUCKWHEAT SEED WHICH WILL GROW

Walking Tour: Vieux-Montréal

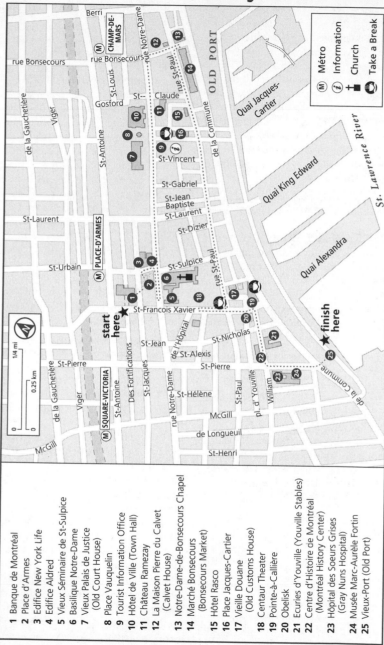

Legend:
- Ⓜ Métro
- ⓘ Information
- ✚■ Church
- ● Take a Break

1 Banque de Montréal
2 Place d'Armes
3 Edifice New York Life
4 Edifice Aldred
5 Vieux Séminaire de St-Sulpice
6 Basilique Notre-Dame
7 Vieux Palais de Justice (Old Court House)
8 Place Vauquelin
9 Tourist Information Office
10 Hôtel de Ville (Town Hall)
11 Château Ramezay
12 La Maison Pierre du Calvet (Calvet House)
13 Notre-Dame-de-Bonsecours Chapel
14 Marché Bonsecours (Bonsecours Market)
15 Hôtel Rasco
16 Place Jacques-Cartier
17 Vieille Douane (Old Customs House)
18 Centaur Theater
19 Pointe-à-Callière
20 Obelisk
21 Ecuries d'Youville (Youville Stables)
22 Centre d'Histoire de Montréal (Montréal History Center)
23 Hôpital des Soeurs Grises (Gray Nuns Hospital)
24 Musée Marc-Aurèle Fortin
25 Vieux-Port (Old Port)

AND MULTIPLY AND SPREAD THROUGHOUT THE COUNTRY. The sculptures at the base of the monument represent three prominent citizens of early Montréal: Charles Lemoyne (1626–85), a farmer; Jeanne Mance, the woman who founded the first hospital in Montréal; and Raphael-Lambert Closse, a soldier and the mayor of Ville-Marie. The fourth sculpture represents an Iroquois brave. Closse is depicted with his dog, Pilote, whose bark once warned the early settlers of an impending Iroquois attack.

Facing the Notre-Dame Basilica from the square, look over to the left. At the corner of St-Jacques is the:

❸ Edifice New York Life

This red-stone Richardson Romanesque building, with a striking wrought-iron door and clock tower, is located at 511 place d'Armes. At all of eight stories, this was Montréal's first skyscraper back in 1888, and it was equipped with a technological marvel—an elevator.

Next to it, on the right, stands the 23-story Art Deco:

❹ Edifice Aldred

If the building looks somehow familiar, there's a reason: Built in 1931, it clearly resembles the Empire State Building in New York, also completed that year. The building's original tenant was Aldred and Co. Ltd., a New York–based multinational finance company with offices in New York, London, and Paris.

From the square, cross rue Notre-Dame, bearing right of the Basilica to the:

❺ Vieux Séminaire de St-Sulpice

The city's oldest building, surrounded by equally ancient stone walls, this seminary was erected by the Sulpician priests who arrived in Ville-Marie in 1657, 15 years after the colony was founded. (The Sulpicians are part of an order founded in Paris by Jean-Jacques Olier in 1641.) The clock on the facade dates from 1701 and has gears made almost entirely of wood.

Unfortunately, the seminary is not open to the public.

After a look through the iron gate, head east on rue Notre-Dame to the magnificent Gothic Revival:

❻ Basilique Notre-Dame (1829)

This brilliantly crafted church was designed by James O'Donnell, a Protestant Irish architect living in New York. Transformed by his experience in building the basilica, he later converted to Roman Catholicism and is the only person buried here. The main altar is made from a hand-carved linden tree. Behind the altar is the Chapel of the Sacred Heart (1982), a perennially popular choice for weddings. The chapel's altar, 32 bronze panels by Montréal artist Charles Daudelin, represents birth, life, and death. The church can seat 4,000 people, and its bell, one of the largest in North America, weighs 12 tons. There's a small museum beside the chapel.

Exiting the basilica, turn right (east) on rue Notre-Dame, crossing rue St-Sulpice. Walk 4 blocks, and then face left to see the:

❼ Vieux Palais de Justice (Old Court House)

Most of this structure was built in 1856. The third floor and dome were added in 1891 (the difference between the original structure and the addition can be easily discerned with a close look). You can explore the Court House, although there are no organized tours. The city's civil cases were tried here until a new courthouse, the Palais de Justice, was built next door in 1978. Civic departments for the city of Montréal are housed here now. The statue beside the Old Court House, called *Homage to Marguerite Bourgeoys* (a teacher and nun), is by sculptor Jules LaSalle.

Next, on the right, is:

❽ Place Vauquelin

This small public square, with a splashing fountain and a view of the Champ-de-Mars park (which lies behind and beneath the city hall), was created in 1858. The statue is of Jean Vauquelin, commander of the French fleet in New France. The statue stares across rue Notre-Dame at Vauquelin's counterpart, the English Admiral Nelson. The two statues are symbols of Montréal's duality.

On the opposite corner is a small but helpful:

❾ Tourist information office

A bilingual staff is ready to answer questions and hand out many useful brochures and maps (daily in warmer months, only Thurs–Sun in winter). The famed Silver Dollar Saloon once stood on this site, though it has long since been torn down. The tavern was named for the 350 silver dollars embedded in its floor.

Around the corner, on the right, is a focus of activity in Vieux-Montréal, a magnet for both citizens and visitors year-round, the Place Jacques-Cartier, which we will visit later in the tour. Rising on the other side of rue Notre-Dame, opposite the top of the square, is the impressive:

❿ Hôtel de Ville (Town Hall)

Built between 1872 and 1878 in the florid French Second Empire style, the edifice is seen to particular advantage when it is illuminated at night. In 1922, it barely survived a disastrous fire. Only the exterior walls remained, and after substantial rebuilding and the addition of another floor, it reopened in 1926.

Take a minute to look inside at the generous use of Italian marble, the Art Deco lamps, and the bronze-and-glass chandelier. The sculptures at the entry are *Woman with a Pail* and *The Sower*, both by Alfred Laliberté.

Cross rue Notre-Dame once again. After passing the recently completed terraced park, with its orderly ranks of trees and a statue honoring the controversial long-time mayor of Montréal, Jean Drapeau, enter the circular drive to:

⓫ Château Ramezay

Built by Claude de Ramezay between 1705 and 1706 in the French Regime style of the period, this was the home of the city's French governors for 4 decades, starting with de Ramezay, before being taken over and used for the same purpose by the British.

In 1775 an army of American rebels invaded and held Montréal, using the house as their headquarters. Benjamin Franklin was sent to persuade Montrealers to join the American revolt against British rule. He stayed in the château but failed to sway Québec's leaders to join his cause.

The house has had other uses over the years. It was a courthouse, government office building, teachers' college, and headquarters for Laval University before becoming a museum in 1895. Inside are furnishings, tools, oil paintings, costumes, and other objects related to the economic and social activities of the 18th century and the first half of the 19th century.

Continue in the same direction (east) along rue Notre-Dame to the corner of rue Bonsecours. Turn right. Near the bottom, at no. 401, on the left, is a house that offers a look at what life was like in Montréal in the late 18th century. This is:

⓬ La Maison Pierre du Calvet (Calvet House)

Built in the 18th century and restored between 1964 and 1966, this appears to be a modest dwelling. In the early days, though, such a house would have been inhabited by a fairly well-to-do family. Pierre du Calvet, believed to be the original owner, was a French Huguenot who supported the American Revolution. Calvet met with Benjamin Franklin here in 1775 and was imprisoned from 1780 to 1783 for supplying money to the Americans. The house, with a characteristic sloped roof meant to discourage snow buildup, and raised end walls that serve as firebreaks, is constructed of Montréal graystone. It is now part of an inn, with an entrance at no. 405.

The next street, rue St-Paul, is the oldest thoroughfare in Montréal, dating from 1672. Across the way is the small:

⑬ Notre-Dame-de-Bon-Secours Chapel (1675)

This chapel, called the Sailors' Church because so many seamen come to worship here, was founded by Marguerite Bourgeoys, a nun and teacher who was made a saint in 1982. Although recent excavations in the basement have unearthed foundations of her original 1675 church, the building has been much altered, and the present facade was built in the late 18th century. A museum (entrance on the left) tells the story of Bourgeoys' life and incorporates a newly opened archaeological site, with discoveries dated to 400 B.C. Sailors saved at sea have made pilgrimages to the church to give thanks. Climb up to the tower for a view of the port and the Old Town.

Just beyond the Sailor's Church, heading west down rue St-Paul, is an imposing building with a colonnaded facade and silvery dome, the limestone:

⑭ Marché Bonsecours (Bonsecours Market)

Completed in 1847, this building was briefly used, in order, as the Parliament of United Canada, the City Hall, the central market, a music recital hall, and the home of the municipality's housing and planning offices. The building was restored in 1992 to serve as a center for temporary exhibitions and musical performances during the city's 350th birthday celebration. It continues to be used for temporary exhibitions, but it is also more of a retail center now, with stalls and shops inside and sidewalk cafes near the entrance.

When the Bonsecours Market was first built, the dome could be seen from everywhere in the city. The Doric columns of the portico were cast of iron in England, and the prominent dome has long served as a landmark for seafarers sailing into the harbor.

Continue down rue St-Paul. At no. 281 is the former:

⑮ Hôtel Rasco

An Italian, Francisco Rasco, came to Canada to manage a hotel for the Molson family and later became successful with this, his own hotel. The 150-room Rasco was the Ritz of its day in Montréal, hosting, among other honored guests, Charles Dickens and his wife in 1842, when the author was directing some of his plays at the theater that used to stand across the street. The hotel lives on in legend if not in fact, as it's devoid of much of its original architectural detail. Rasco left in 1844, and the hotel slipped into decline. Between 1960 and 1981 it stood empty, but the city took it over and restored it in 1982. It has contained a succession of restaurants on the ground floor, but it has seemed jinxed. Laurent Godbout, the chef-proprietor of Chez L'Epicier, a few doors back, isn't put off: he's taken over the space.

Continue heading west on rue St-Paul, turning right when you hit:

⑯ Place Jacques-Cartier

Opened as a marketplace in 1804, this is the most appealing of the Old Town's squares, despite its obviously touristy aspects. Its cobbled cross-streets, gentle downhill slope, and ancient buildings set the mood, while outdoor cafes, street entertainers, itinerant artists, and fruit and flower vendors invite lingering, at least in warm weather. Calèches (horse-drawn carriages) depart from both the lower and the upper ends of the square for tours of Vieux-Montréal.

Walk slowly uphill, taking in the old buildings that bracket the plaza. Plaques in French and English describe some of them: the **Vandelac House** (no. 433), the **del Vecchio House** (nos. 404–410), and the **Cartier House** (no. 407). All these houses were well suited to the rigors of life in the raw young settlement. Their steeply pitched roofs shed the heavy winter snows rather than collapsing under the burden, and small windows with double casements let in light while keeping out wintry breezes. When shuttered, the windows were almost as effective as the heavy stone walls in deflecting hostile arrows or the antics of trappers fresh from raucous evenings in nearby taverns.

At the upper (northern) end of the plaza stands a monument to Horatio Nelson, hero of Trafalgar, erected in 1809. This monument preceded the much larger version in London by several years. However, after years of being subjected to vandalism, presumably by Québec separatists, the original statue was temporarily replaced to permit restoration. The first Nelson once again occupies the crown of the column.

TAKE A BREAK
Most of the old buildings in and around the inclined plaza harbor restaurants and cafes. For a drink or snack, try to find a seat in **Le Jardin Nelson** (no. 407), at the southeast corner, near the bottom of the hill. Sit in the courtyard in back when the weather is good—there often is live music—or on the terrace overlooking the activity of the square.

At the top of the plaza, turn left and descend on the other side back down to rue St-Paul. Turn right. The next few short blocks are given to art galleries and loud souvenir shops, but at 150 rue St-Paul is the neoclassical:

⑰ Vieille Douane (Old Customs House)

Erected from 1836 to 1838, the building was doubled in size to its present proportions when an extension to the south was added in 1882; walk around to the other side of the building for a look at the extension. That end of the building faces Place Royale, the first public square in the early settlement of Ville-Marie. Europeans and Amerindians used to come here to trade.

Continue down rue St-Paul to rue St-François-Xavier. Turn right on a short detour up rue St-François-Xavier. At rue de l'Hôpital, to the right, is the stately:

⑱ Centaur Theater

The home of Montréal's principal English-language theater is a former stock-exchange building. The Beaux Arts architecture is interesting in that the two entrances are on either side rather than in the center of the facade. American architect George Post, who was also responsible for the New York Stock Exchange, designed the building, erected in 1903. It served in its original function until 1965, when it was redesigned as a theater with two stages.

Return back down rue St-François-Xavier, crossing St-Paul. Up ahead, the dramatic wedge-shaped building is the:

⑲ Pointe-à-Callière

Housing the Museum of Archaeology and History, with artifacts unearthed here during more than 10 years of excavation, this site was where Ville-Marie (Montréal) was founded in 1642. The museum also incorporates, via an underground connection, the Old Customs House you just passed.

A fort stood on this spot in 1645. Thirty years later, this same spot became home to the château of a monsieur de Callière, from whom the building and triangular square take their names. At that time, the St. Pierre River separated this piece of land from the mainland. It was made a canal in the 19th century and later filled in.

TAKE A BREAK
One possibility for lunch or an afternoon pick-me-up is the casual, second-floor **L'Arrivage Café** at the museum. Another is the moderately priced **Stash**, 200 rue St-Paul ouest at rue St-François-Xavier, which specializes in Polish fare and is open from 11am until late in the evening.

Proceeding west from Pointe-à-Callière, near rue St-François-Xavier, stands an:

⑳ Obelisk

Commemorating the founding of Ville-Marie on May 18, 1642, the obelisk was erected here in 1893 by the Montréal Historical Society. It bears the names of the city's early pioneers, including de Maisonneuve and Jeanne Mance.

Continuing west from the obelisk 2 blocks, look for the:

㉑ Ecuries d'Youville (Youville Stables)

It's on the left at 296–316 place d'Youville. Despite the name, the rooms in the iron-gated compound, built in 1825 on land owned by the Gray Nuns, were used mainly as warehouses, rather than as horse stables. Like much of the waterfront area, the U-shaped Youville building (the actual stables, next door, were made of wood and disappeared long ago) was run-down and forgotten until the 1960s, when a group of enterprising businesspeople decided to buy and renovate the property. Today the compound contains offices and a popular restaurant, **Gibby's.** Go through the passage to the right of the restaurant for a look at the inner courtyard if the gates are open, as they usually are.

Continue another block west to 335 rue St-Pierre and the:

㉒ Centre d'Histoire de Montréal (Montréal History Center)

Built in 1903 as Montréal's central fire station, this building now houses exhibits, including many audiovisual ones, about the city's past and present. Visitors will learn about the early routes of exploration, the fur trade, architecture, public squares, the railroad, and life in Montréal from 1920 to 1950.

Less than a block away, on the left at 138 rue St-Pierre, pass the former:

㉓ Hôpital des Soeurs Grises (Gray Nuns Hospital)

The hospital was in operation from 1693 to 1851 and served as a novitiate for future nuns. The order, founded by Marguerite d'Youville in 1737, is officially known as the Sisters of Charity of Montréal. The present building incorporates several additions and was part of the city's General Hospital, run by the Charon Brothers but administered by d'Youville, who died here in 1771. The wing in which she died was restored in 1980. The wall of the original chapel remains. Visits inside must be arranged in advance. Call ☏ **514/842-9411** to schedule a visit.

From here, walk down rue St-Pierre to the brown awning at no. 118, which marks the entrance to the:

㉔ Musée Marc-Aurèle Fortin

This museum is devoted to Canadian artist Fortin, who died in 1972. He was known for his watercolors of the Québec countryside, including Charlevoix and the Laurentian Mountains. His depictions of Dutch elms give a glimpse of the time when these giant trees lined rues Sherbrooke and St-Joseph in Montréal, before blight decimated them.

Continue past the museum and cross rue de la Commune and the railroad tracks to enter the:

㉕ Vieux-Port (Old Port)

Montréal's historic commercial wharves have been reborn as a waterfront park frequented by cyclists, in-line skaters, joggers, walkers, strollers, lovers, and picnickers, in good weather. This is the entry to **Parc des Ecluses (Locks Park),** where the first locks on the St. Lawrence River are located.

From there, walk back north along rue McGill to reach **Square Victoria** and its Métro station. Or pick up the beginning of the path along the **Lachine Canal** at Parc des Ecluses and follow it for an hour or less to arrive at Montréal's colorful indoor/outdoor Atwater Market.

WALKING TOUR 2   DOWNTOWN

Start:	Bonaventure Métro stop.
Finish:	Musée McCord.
Time:	1½ hours.
Best Times:	Weekdays in the morning or after 2pm, when the streets hum with big-city vibrancy but aren't too crowded.
Worst Times:	Weekdays from noon to 2pm, when the streets, stores, and restaurants are crowded with businesspeople on lunch-break errands; Monday, when museums are closed; and Sunday, when most stores are closed and the area is virtually deserted (museums, however, are open).

After a tour of Vieux-Montréal, a look around the heart of the new 20th-century city will highlight the ample contrast between these two areas. To see the city at its contemporary best, take the Métro to the Bonaventure stop and start this tour.

Take the Métro to the Bonaventure stop. Emerging from that station, the dramatic skyscraper immediately to the west is:

❶ 1000 rue de la Gauchetière

This young contribution to the already-memorable skyline is easily identified by its copper-and-blue pyramidal top, which rises to the maximum height permitted by the municipal building code. Inside, past an atrium planted with live trees, is a huge indoor skating rink bordered by cafes with seating for more than 1,500 spectators.

Walk west for 1 block on rue de la Gauchetière. On the left is:

❷ Le Marriott Château Champlain

The hotel's distinctive facade of half-moon windows inspired its nickname: the "Cheese Grater."

Turn right on rue Peel, walking north. When you hit boulevard René-Lévesque, bear right and you'll arrive at:

❸ Square Dorchester

The square's tall old trees and benches invite lunchtime brown-baggers. This used to be called Dominion Square, but it was renamed for Baron Dorchester, an early English governor, when the adjacent street, once named for him, was changed to boulevard René-Lévesque. Along the east side of the square is the **Sun Life**

Insurance building, built in three stages between 1914 and 1931, and the tallest building in Québec from 1931 until the skyscraper boom of the post–World War II era. This is a gathering point for tour buses and calèches. In winter, the calèche drivers replace their carriages with sleighs and give rides around the top of Mont-Royal.

At the northeast corner of the square is the main office of:

❹ Infotouriste Centre

Many useful maps and brochures are in stock here, most of them free for the taking. Visitors can ask questions of bilingual attendants, purchase tour tickets, change money, make hotel reservations, connect with the Internet, and rent a car.

From that office, go back to the other end of the square and turn left (east) on:

❺ Boulevard René-Lévesque

Formerly Dorchester Boulevard, this primary street was renamed in 1988 following the death of René-Lévesque, the Parti Quebecois leader who led the movement in favor of Québec independence and the use of the French language. Boulevard René-Lévesque is the city's broadest downtown thoroughfare, and the one with the fastest traffic.

Walking Tour: Downtown Montréal

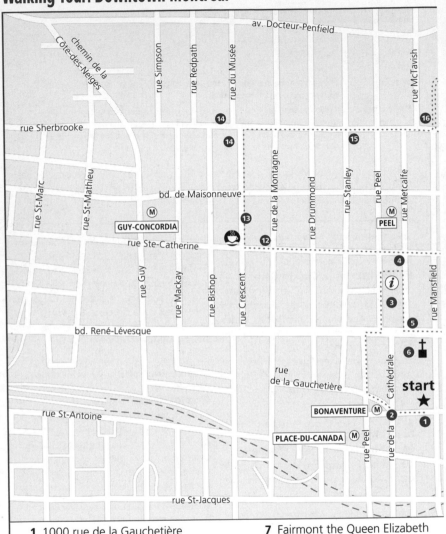

1 1000 rue de la Gauchetière
2 Le Marriott Château
   Champlain
3 Square Dorchester
4 Infotouriste
5 Boulevard René-Lévesque
6 Cathédral Marie-Reine-du-Monde
   (Mary Queen of the World Cathedral)
7 Fairmont the Queen Elizabeth
   (Le Reine Elizabeth)
8 Place Ville-Marie
9 Carré Phillips
10 Cathédrale Christ Church
11 Rue Ste-Catherine
12 Ogilvy
13 Rue Crescent

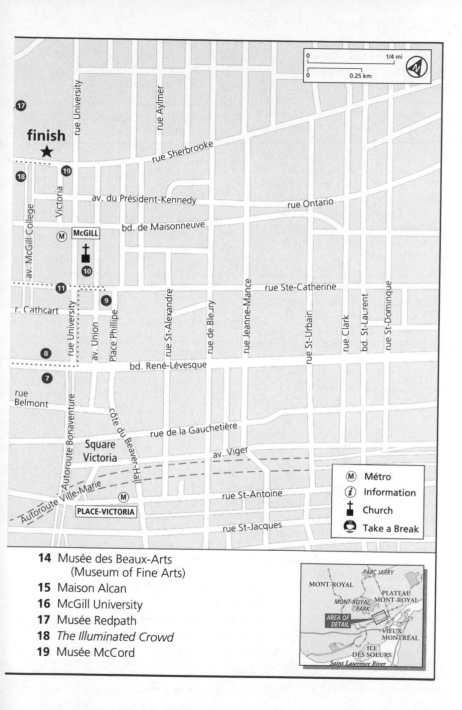

14 Musée des Beaux-Arts
   (Museum of Fine Arts)
15 Maison Alcan
16 McGill University
17 Musée Redpath
18 *The Illuminated Crowd*
19 Musée McCord

On the right is the:

6 Cathédrale Marie-Reine-du-Monde (Mary Queen of the World Cathedral)

Built between 1875 and 1894 as the headquarters for Montréal's Roman Catholic bishop, the cathedral is a copy of St. Peter's Basilica in Rome, built to roughly one-quarter scale. The statue in front of the cathedral is of Bishop Ignace Bourget (1799–1885), the force behind the construction of the basilica. It was sculpted in 1903 by Louis-Philippe Hébert, who is also responsible for the statue of de Maisonneuve in the Place d'Armes in Vieux-Montréal.

Continue past the cathedral and cross rue Mansfield, and you will see:

7 Fairmont The Queen Elizabeth (Le Reine Elizabeth)

Opened in 1958, Montréal's largest hotel stands above **Gare Centrale,** the main railroad station, making it most convenient for people arriving by train. It also has direct access to the underground city, and buses leave for Dorval and Mirabel airports from here.

Across boulevard René-Lévesque from Fairmont Le Reine Elizabeth hotel is:

8 Place Ville-Marie

Known as PVM to Montrealers, this massive structure was the gem of the postwar urban redevelopment efforts in Montréal. The skyscraper, with its cross-shaped floor plan, was designed by I. M. Pei. It is meant to recall Cartier's cross, planted on Mont-Royal to claim the island for France, and for de Maisonneuve's first little settlement, Ville-Marie. The complex, completed in 1962, has a fountain in its plaza called *Feminine Landscape* (1972), executed by Toronto artist Gerald Gladstone.

At the end of the hotel, turn left along rue Université, crossing boulevard René-Lévesque and walking 2 blocks to rue Ste-Catherine. Turn right on rue Ste-Catherine and walk past avenue Union, where you'll see:

9 Carré Phillips

This plaza contains a statue of Edward VII and, during much of the year, a farm stand selling Québec maple products.

Over to the left, across rue Ste-Catherine, is:

10 Cathédrale Christ Church

Built from 1856 to 1859, this neo-Gothic building is the seat of the Anglican bishop of Montréal. The church garden is modeled on a medieval European cloister. The cathedral donated the land on which place de la Cathédrale and the shopping complex underneath it, Promenades de la Cathédrale, were built, in return for eventual ownership of the skyscraper and the underground complex. All those subterranean corridors and levels have caused some to dub it the "floating" or "flying" church.

Turn left on:

11 Rue Ste-Catherine

Head west through the center of Montréal's shopping district. Many of Montréal's department stores are along here, including, to the right of the church, La Baie (or "The Bay," short for Hudson's Bay Company, successor to the famous fur-trapping firm). Movie houses, cafes, shops, and several "adult" emporia line rue Ste-Catherine for several blocks.

At the corner of rue de la Montagne is:

12 Ogilvy

This is the most vibrant of a classy breed of department store that appears to be fading from the scene. Founded in 1866, it strives to maintain its upmarket stature by blending tradition with tasteful marketing strategies. Its Christmas windows are eagerly awaited each year. A bagpiper announces the noon hour.

Continue 1 more block to:

13 Rue Crescent

This and nearby streets are the locus of the center-city social and dining district, largely yuppie Anglo in character, if not necessarily in strict demographics. Pricey boutiques, inexpensive pizza joints, upscale restaurants, and dozens of bars and dance clubs draw enthusiastic consumers looking to spend money and party the night away. This center of gilded youth and glamour was once a run-down slum area slated for demolition. Luckily, buyers with a good aesthetic sense saw the possibilities of these late-19th-century row houses and brought them back to life.

Turn right on rue Crescent and:

TAKE A BREAK

Lively spots for coffee or snacks are abundant along rue Crescent. **Thursday's** (no. 1449, in L'Hôtel de la Montagne) is one, if you can find a seat on the balcony, or walk a little farther up rue Crescent and get a sidewalk table at **Sir Winston Churchill Pub** (no. 1459).

Continue up rue Crescent, past boulevard de Maisonneuve, to the corner of rues Crescent and Sherbrooke. On this left corner, and on the opposite side of Sherbrooke, is the:

⓫ Musée des Beaux-Arts (Museum of Fine Arts)

This is Canada's oldest and Montréal's most prominent museum. The modern annex was added in 1991 and is connected to the original stately Beaux Arts building (1912) across the way by an underground tunnel that doubles as a gallery. Both buildings are made of Vermont marble.

Turn right on rue Sherbrooke, passing, at the next corner, the Holt Renfrew department store, identified on its marquee only as HOLTS. Continue on rue Sherbrooke, passing, on the right, the:

⓰ Maison Alcan

This structure has been frequently lauded for its incorporation of 19th-century houses into its late-20th-century facade.

Step inside the lobby to see the results, especially over to the right.

Walk 4 more blocks in the same direction. On the opposite side of rue Sherbrooke is the entrance to:

⓰ McGill University

The gate is usually open to this, Canada's most prestigious university. Step inside and see, just to the left, a large stone that marks the site of the Amerindian Horchelaga settlement that existed here before the arrival of the Europeans.

Also on the campus is the:

⓱ Musée Redpath

Housed in a building dating from 1882, this museum's main draw is its Egyptian antiquities collection, the second largest of its kind in Canada.

Opposite the university, and just half a block south of rue Sherbrooke, on the left, is a cream-colored resin sculpture called:

⓲ *The Illuminated Crowd* (1979)

Raymond Mason's sculpture is frequently photographed and widely admired for its evocation of the human condition, although its detractors find it sentimental and obvious. Circle it at leisure and then return to rue Sherbrooke, turning right.

One block east on rue Sherbrooke is the:

⓳ Musée McCord

This private museum of Canadian history first opened in 1921 and was substantially renovated and expanded in 1992. Named for its founder, David Ross McCord (1844–1930), the McCord has an eclectic and often eccentric collection of 80,000 artifacts. Furniture, clothing, china, silver, paintings, photographs, and folk art reveal elements of city and rural life from the 18th to the 20th century. Amerindians are represented in the First Nations room.

WALKING TOUR 3   PLATEAU MONT-ROYAL

Start: The corner of avenue du Mont-Royal and rue St-Denis.

Finish: Square St-Louis.

Time: At least 2 hours, but allow more time to linger in and explore this intriguing neighborhood.

Best Times: Monday through Saturday during the day, when the shops are open. Boulevard St-Laurent is at its liveliest on Saturday. For barhopping, evenings work well.

Worst Times: Sunday, when most stores are closed, if shopping is important to you.

This is essentially a window-shopping, browsing, and grazing tour, designed to provide a sampling of the sea of ethnicities that make up Plateau Mont-Royal, north of downtown Montréal and due east of Mont-Royal Park. The neighborhood, which in recent years has seen an unprecedented flourishing of restaurants, cafes, clubs, and shops, is bounded on the south by rue Sherbrooke, on the north by boulevard St-Joseph, on the east by avenue Papineau, and on the west by rue St-Dominique. Monuments and obligatory sights are few along these commercial avenues, and the residential side streets are filled with row houses that are home to students, young professionals, and immigrants old and new. This walk is a glance into the lives of both established and freshly minted Montrealers and the way they spend their leisure time. Be aware that stores and bistros open and close with considerable frequency in this neighborhood, so some of the highlights listed below may not exist when you visit.

To begin, take the Métro to the Mont-Royal station. There's a fruit stand in front of the Métro station. Just beyond the fruit stand turn left, walking west on avenue du Mont-Royal to St-Denis. Turn left. On the left side of the street, at 4481 rue St-Denis, is:

❶ Quai des Brumes

This popular gathering spot for jazz, blues, and beer offers live music most evenings, and even some afternoons. Its name means "Foggy Dock."

Go back to the corner and cross the street to 4430 rue St-Denis, where you'll find:

❷ Requin Chagrin

Check out this retro shop with a good selection of secondhand clothing.

Walk farther along St-Denis to no. 4380:

❸ Champigny

A large bookstore with mostly French stock, it also carries travel guides and literature in English, as well as CDs, magazines, and newspapers in many languages from all over the world. Most of the books are upstairs. There's an extensive children's section. The bookstore is open daily until midnight.

Continue down the right side of St-Denis to no. 4338:

❹ Côté Sud

Here you'll find shelves of distinctive glassware, plus cooking and dining implements, including chef's knives, flatware, china, and related items, such as aluminum canisters and candles. They fill two floors of connecting buildings.

Keep walking down St-Denis and:

TAKE A BREAK
At 4325 rue St-Denis, **Fondue-mentale** specializes in (guess what?) fondue and raclettes—fondues as appetizers, as main courses, as desserts. Excess is not without its virtues. The turn-of-the-20th-century house has a terrace in front and a garden.

Walking Tour: Plateau Mont-Royal

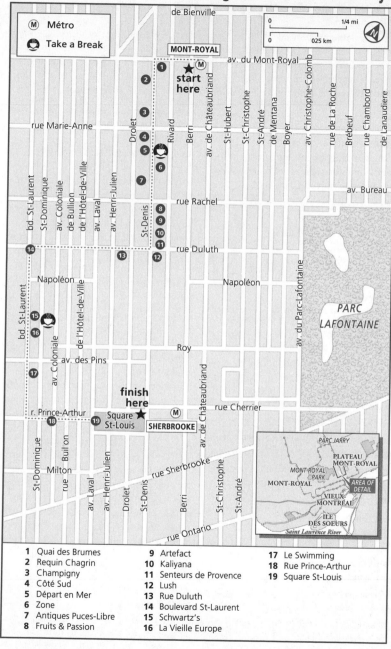

1	Quai des Brumes	**9**	Artefact	**17**	Le Swimming
2	Requin Chagrin	**10**	Kaliyana	**18**	Rue Prince-Arthur
3	Champigny	**11**	Senteurs de Provence	**19**	Square St-Louis
4	Côté Sud	**12**	Lush		
5	Départ en Mer	**13**	Rue Duluth		
6	Zone	**14**	Boulevard St-Laurent		
7	Antiques Puces-Libre	**15**	Schwartz's		
8	Fruits & Passion	**16**	La Vieille Europe		

Not far down the street, at no. 4306, is:

❺ Départ en Mer

A nautical theme prevails at this store, with brass navigation instruments, bells, fisherman shirts, and a variety of ship models ranging in price from a handful of loonies to several hundred dollars. Most of the merchandise is produced in France.

Continue down rue St-Denis to no. 4246:

❻ Zone

This shop purveys contemporary housewares, most of them sleekly monochromatic, and some brightly hued.

Next door, at 4240 rue St-Denis, is the wonderfully cluttered:

❼ Antiques Puces-Libre

This store offers three floors of 19th-century French-Canadian country collectibles—pine and oak furniture, lamps, clocks, vases, and much more.

Continue to rue Rachel, cross to the left side of the street, and continue south to 4159A rue St-Denis, where you'll find:

❽ Fruits & Passion

This company uses "natural extracts" to fabricate their undeniably appealing soaps, aromatherapy, sunscreens, moisturizers . . . and, in the back, olive oils, balsamic vinegars, chutneys, and honey.

Just down the street, at 4117 rue St-Denis, is:

❾ Artefact

Quebecois designers and artists display (and sell) clothing and paintings at this shop.

After that, look for no. 4107:

❿ Kaliyana

This stores sells loose and comfortable clothing by a Czech-born designer who uses hand-printed fabrics.

Next, at 4077 rue St-Denis, you'll come upon:

⓫ Senteurs de Provence

One of a small chain, this store displays hand-painted pottery and printed linens, as well as bath soaps, shower gels, and lotions of high order, all from France.

Shortly, stop in at 4067 rue St-Denis:

⓬ Lush

On the ground floor of one of the prettiest Queen Anne Victorian row houses on the street, Lush is a sort of hippie Body Shop. Featured are soaps and oils with a variety of natural ingredients.

At the corner of St-Denis and rue Duluth, cross over and walk right (west) along:

⓭ Rue Duluth

Along with several small antiques shops, this street is dotted with ever-changing Greek, Portuguese, Italian, North African, Malaysian, and Vietnamese eateries. Many of the restaurants state that you can *"apportez votre vin"*—bring your own wine. Some are fresh and attractive, others not.

Continue along rue Duluth until it arrives at the boulevard St-Laurent, a north–south thoroughfare that's so prominent in the cultural history of the city that it's known to Anglophones, Francophones, and Allophones alike simply as "The Main."

Turn left on:

⓮ Boulevard St-Laurent

Traditionally a beachhead for immigrants to Montréal, St-Laurent has increasingly become a street of chic bistros and clubs. The late-night section runs for several miles, roughly from rue Laurier all the way down to rue Sherbrooke. This bistro and club boom was fueled by low rents and the large number of industrial lofts in this area, a legacy of St-Laurent's heyday as a garment-manufacturing center. Today these cavernous spaces have been converted into restaurants and clubs, many of which have the life spans of fireflies, but some of which pound on for years.

At 3895 bd. St-Laurent you'll find:

⓯ Schwartz's

The language police insisted on the exterior sign with the French mouthful CHEZ SCHWARZ CHARCUTERIE HEBRAIQUE DE MONTREAL, but everyone just calls it

Schwartz's. This narrow, no-frills deli serves smoked meat against which all other smoked meats must be measured. Vegetarians and those who require some distance from their neighbors' elbows will hate it.

TAKE A BREAK
Pop in to **Schwartz's** for some of their famous smoked meat.

Next, a few steps along at no. 3855, is:

⑯ La Vieille Europe

The "Old Europe" delicatessen sells aromatic coffee beans from many nations, plus sausages and meats, cheeses, and cooking utensils.

At no. 3643 you'll find:

⑰ Le Swimming

Here, you'll find a bar downstairs and an upstairs hall with a dozen pool tables.

Continue down boulevard St-Laurent and turn left (east) into:

⑱ Rue Prince-Arthur

Named after Queen Victoria's third son, who was governor-general of Canada from 1911 to 1916, this is a pedestrian street filled with bars and restaurants, most of which add more to the liveliness of the street than to the gastronomic reputation of the city. The older establishments go by such names as La Cabane Grecque, La Caverne Grec, Casa Grecque—no doubt you will discern an emerging theme—but are being challenged by Latino and Asian newcomers. Their owners vie constantly with gimmicks to haul in passersby, including two-drinks-for-the-price-of-one specials and dueling table d'hôte prices that plummet to C$10 (US$8) or lower for three courses. Beer and sangria are the popular drinks at the white resin tables and chairs set out along the sides of the street. Mimes, vendors, street performers, and caricaturists also compete for the tourist dollar.

Five blocks along, rue Prince-Arthur ends at:

⑲ Square St-Louis

This public garden plaza is framed by attractive row houses erected for well-to-do Francophones in the late 19th and early 20th centuries. People stretch out on the grass to take the sun, or sit bundled on benches willing March away. Among them are usually a few harmless derelicts and street people. On occasional summer days, there are impromptu concerts. The square ends at rue St-Denis.

From here, bear left onto rue Cherrier to catch the Métro at the Sherbrooke station, less than half a block away.

WALKING TOUR 4   MONT-ROYAL

Start:	At the corner of rue Peel and avenue des Pins.
Finish:	At the cross on top of the mountain.
Time:	Two hours, allowing for some dawdling. If you're pressed for time, it's possible to get to the lookout in a little more than half an hour and back down the mountain in 15 minutes.
Best Times:	Spring, summer, and autumn mornings.
Worst Times:	Winter, when snow and slush make a sleigh ride to the top of the mountain much more enticing than a hike.

Assuming a reasonable measure of physical fitness, an enjoyable way to explore Parc Mont-Royal is simply to hike up from downtown. Joggers, cyclists, in-line skaters, and anyone in search of a little greenery and space head here in warm weather. In winter, cross-country skiers follow the miles of paths within the park, and snowshoers tramp along trails laid out especially for them. The 200-hectare (494-acre) park was created in 1876 to a plan by American landscape architect Frederick Law Olmsted, who designed Central Park in New York City as well as parks in Philadelphia, Boston, and Chicago. In fact, relatively little of Olmsted's design actually came into being.

Start this tour at the corner of rue Peel and avenue des Pins, at the:

❶ Downtown park entrance

A handy map at the site helps to set bearings. From here, it's possible to ascend the mountain by several routes. Hearty souls can choose the quickest and most strenuous approach—scaling the steep slope directly to the lookout at the top. Those who prefer to take their time and gain altitude slowly can take one short set of stairs followed by a switchback bridle path (turn left onto it) leading to the top. The approach outlined here falls somewhere in between but points out the other alternatives as they present themselves.

Take the gravel path to the right (facing the map of the park). It has intervals of four to six steps, and parallels the wall that separates the park from the outside world. When the path dead-ends, turn left (away from the steep steps seen beside a small lookout).

Those who have chosen the athletic route can take the next:

❷ Stairs on the right

Fair warning: There are more than 250 steps in all, and the last 100 go almost straight up. For a less taxing route, stay on the wide:

❸ Chemin Olmsted (Olmsted Rd.)

The road was named for the park's designer, and it's actually the only part of his design that became a reality (the rest of the park wasn't completed to his scheme). Following this road will bypass a few of this tour's stops (nos. 4 and 5), and get to the next stop (no. 6) in about 45 minutes.

Frederick Law Olmsted designed the road at such a gradual grade not only for pedestrians, but also for horse-drawn carriages. Horses could pull their loads up the hill at a steady pace, and on the way down would not be pushed from behind by the weight of the carriage. Chemin Olmsted is closed to automobiles. Early on, it passes some beautiful stone houses off Redpath Circle, to the left. A couple of paths lead up the mountain to the right. They get walkers to their destination more quickly but aren't as strenuous as the steps recently bypassed.

So if the road begins to seem a little too slow, take the:

❹ Steps

The steps eventually appear on the right. They lead to an old pump station, to the right.

From here, continue in an uphill direction until you arrive at a:

❺ Covered picnic area

Take a snack break if you wish at this open-air stone-and-wood structure with a copper roof.

Then walk around behind the shelter and take the stairway behind it down the hill, which descends again to chemin Olmsted, minus a couple of big loops that you've edited out of the walk by taking the steps. Up ahead is the back of the:

❻ Maison Smith

Regardless of which route you choose at the beginning of the tour, you will end up here. Built in 1858, this structure has been used as a park rangers' station and park police headquarters. From 1983 to 1992 it served as a small nature museum. The house currently serves as an information center, and houses a small exhibit on the park and a gift shop devoted to the park. Nearby is the 90m-high (295-ft.) Radio Canada Tower.

Walking Tour: Mont-Royal

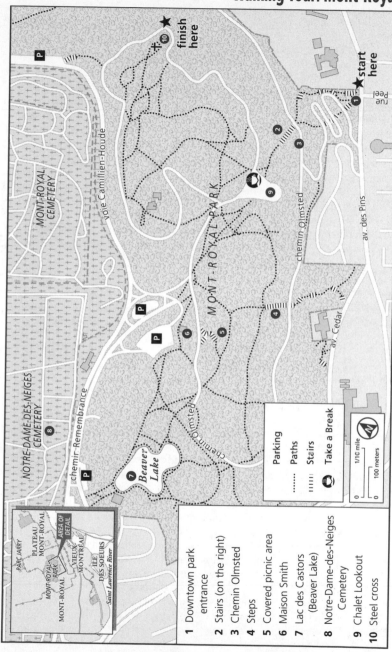

★ start here

rue Peel

★ finish here

1 Downtown park entrance
2 Stairs (on the right)
3 Chemin Olmsted
4 Steps
5 Covered picnic area
6 Maison Smith
7 Lac des Castors (Beaver Lake)
8 Notre-Dame-des-Neiges Cemetery
9 Chalet Lookout
10 Steel cross

Parking
Paths
Stairs
Take a Break

1/10 mile
0   100 meters

MONT-ROYAL CEMETERY

NOTRE-DAME-DES-NEIGES CEMETERY

MONT-ROYAL PARK

Beaver Lake

voie Camillien-Houde

chemin Olmsted

chemin Olmsted

chemin-Remembrance

av. des Pins

av. Cedar

PARC JARRY
PLATEAU MONT-ROYAL
MONT-ROYAL PARK
VIEUX MONTRÉAL
ÎLE DES SŒURS
Saint Lawrence River
AREA OF DETAIL

From the house, walk through the field of sculptures, away from the radio tower, until you reach:

❼ Lac des Castors (Beaver Lake)

The name refers to the once-profitable fur industry, not to the actual presence of the long-gone animals. In summer it's surrounded by sunbathers and picnickers and filled with boaters. In the cold winter months before the snow sets in, it becomes an ice skater's paradise.

There's a small concession stand in the recently renovated pavilion here, but if you're planning to have something to eat or drink on the mountain, wait for the snack bar at the chalet at the nearby lookout. Both the chalet and the pavilion have restrooms and telephones.

Walk across the road, called chemin de la Remembrance (Remembrance Rd.), behind the pavilion, to enter:

❽ Notre-Dame-des-Neiges Cemetery

From this, the city's predominantly Catholic cemetery, you can visit the adjacent Protestant Mount Royal graveyard, and then behind it (to the north), if you're up for a time-consuming walk, see the small adjoining Jewish and Spanish-Portuguese cemetery. Notre-Dame-des-Neiges Cemetery reveals much of the ethnic mix in Montréal. There are headstones, some with likenesses in photos or tiles, for Montrealers with surnames as diverse as Zagorska, Skwyrska, De Ciccio, Sen, Lavoie, Barrett, O'Neill, Hammerschmid, Fernandez, Müller, Giordano, Haddad, and Boudreault.

After wandering through this part of the cemetery, return to chemin Remembrance, pass the Maison Smith again, and continue along the road for a few minutes until you arrive at a water spigot embedded in a granite slab. Take the narrow blacktop path below it through the trees. Along the way, look for a tree trunk carved by artist Jacques Morin in 1986;

part of the inscription reads: an "OLD, SICK TREE, SCULPTED AND TRANSFORMED, NEITHER MALE NOR FEMALE."

This path leads to the:

❾ Chalet Lookout

The chalet was constructed from 1931 to 1932 at a cost of $230,000 and has been used over the years for receptions, concerts, and various other events. Inside the chalet, note the 17 paintings hanging just below the ceiling, starting to the right of the door that leads into the snack bar. They relate the history of the region as well as the story of the French explorations of North America. The front terrace offers a panoramic view of the city and the river. In winter, there's a warming room for skiers here.

TAKE A BREAK
The concession stand in the chalet, usually open daily from 9am to 5pm, sells sandwiches, muffins, apples, ice cream, milk, juice, tea, and coffee. Heed the signs that ask patrons to refrain from feeding the squirrels seen begging so adorably.

Facing the chalet from the terrace, locate the path running off to the right. Follow it for about 8 minutes to a giant:

❿ Steel cross

Legend has it that de Maisonneuve erected a wooden cross here in 1642. The present incarnation, erected in 1924, is lit at night, making it visible from all over the city. Beside the cross is a plaque marking the spot where a time capsule was placed in August 1992, during Montréal's 350th birthday celebration. Some 12,000 children ages 6 to 12 filled the capsule with messages and drawings depicting their visions for the city in the year 2142, when Montréal will be 500 years old and the capsule will be opened.

To return to downtown Montréal, go back along the path to the chalet terrace. On the left, just before the terrace, is another path. It leads to the 250 or so steps that descend to where this tour began, at the entrance to the park. Or catch bus no. 11 at Beaver Lake, hop off at chemin de la Remembrance and Côte-des-Neiges, and pick up bus no. 165, which goes to the Guy Métro station.

9

Montréal Shopping

Shop in Montréal until your feet swell and your eyes cross. Whether you view shopping as the focus of your travels or simply as a diversion, you won't be disappointed. Shopping ranks right up there with dining out as a prime activity among the natives. Most Montréalers are of French ancestry, after all, and seem to believe that impeccable taste bubbles through the Gallic gene pool. The city has produced a thriving fashion industry, from couture to ready-to-wear, with a history that reaches back to the earliest trade in furs and leather. There are more than 1,500 shops in the underground city alone, and many more than that at street level and above. It is unlikely that any reasonable consumer need—or even outlandish fantasy—cannot be met here.

1 The Shopping Scene

American visitors have the advantage of a markdown on all prices encountered in Montréal shops due to the favorable exchange rates between Canadian and U.S. dollars. When traveling with U.S. dollars, go to a bank to exchange cash or traveler's checks for Canadian currency—or, better yet, withdraw Canadian dollars from a local ATM with a credit card, an ATM card, or a debit card. While stores often accept U.S. currency, the exchange is likely to be less favorable than that obtained in a bank. There are exceptions, however, as some stores, in an attempt to attract customers carrying U.S. funds, put out signs offering better exchange rates than might be found in a bank.

Note that you're when making purchases with a credit card, the charges are automatically converted at the going bank rate before appearing on the following monthly statement. In most cases, this is the best deal of all for visitors. Visa and MasterCard are the most popular credit cards in this part of Canada, while shops less frequently accept Discover, and American Express is only accepted reluctantly and sometimes not at all.

THE BEST BUYS

Most items are priced at approximately the same costs as in their countries of origin, including such big international names as Burberry and Ralph Lauren.

Exceptions are British products, including **tweeds, porcelain,** and **glassware,** which tend to cost less. While not cheap, **Inuit sculptures** and 19th- to early-20th-century **country furniture** are handsome and authentic. Less expensive crafts than the intensely collected Inuit works are also available, including quilts, drawings, and carvings by Amerindian and other folk artists. While demand has diminished somewhat, superbly constructed furs and leather goods are high-ticket items, and you can retrieve the high sales tax on these items by filling out paperwork (p. 68). In addition,

Québec's daring clothing designers produce some appealing fashions at prices that are often reasonable.

THE BEST SHOPPING AREAS

Rue Sherbrooke is a major shopping street, with international and domestic designers, luxury items such as furs and jewelry, art galleries, and the Holts department store. **Rue Crescent** has a number of upscale boutiques scattered along its length, plus numerous cafes for a break from shopping. **Boulevard St-Laurent** sells everything from budget practicalities to off-the-wall handmade fashions. Look along **avenue Laurier** between St-Laurent and de l'Epée for French boutiques, home furniture and accessories shops, and young Quebecois designers. **Rue St-Paul** in Vieux-Montréal has a growing number of art galleries, a few jewelry shops, some souvenir stands, and a shop that sells kites.

Antiques can be found along rue Sherbrooke near the Musée des Beaux-Arts and on the little side streets near the museum. More antiques and collectibles, in more than 50 tempting shops one after another, can be found along the lengthening "Antiques Alley" of **rue Notre-Dame,** especially concentrated between Guy and Atwater. In warmer months, artists display and sell their unremarkable but nevertheless competent works along compact **rue St-Amable,** just off place Jacques-Cartier. From there, meander into a walkway called **Le Jardin Amable** to find a courtyard filled with kiosks stocked with eye-catching costume jewelry and items crafted in silver and gold. **Rue St-Denis** north of Sherbrooke has strings of shops filled with fun, funky items.

Some of the best shops in Montréal are found in city museums. Tops among them are shops in **Pointe-à-Callière** (the Montréal Museum of Archaeology and History), which is in Vieux-Montréal; shops in the **Musée des Beaux-Arts** and the **Musée McCord,** both on rue Sherbrooke in the center city; and the shop at the **Musée d'Art Contemporain** in the Place-des-Arts.

Rue Ste-Catherine is home to the city's four top department stores and myriad satellite shops, while **rue Peel** is known for its men's fashions. **Avenue Greene** in Anglophone Westmount has some decidedly English stores. Most of Montréal's big department stores were founded when Scottish, Irish, and English families dominated the city's mercantile class, and most of their names are identifiably English, albeit shorn of their apostrophes. The principal exception is La Baie, French for "The Bay," itself a shortened reference to an earlier name, the Hudson's Bay Company.

Montréal's long history as a center for the fur trade buttresses the many wholesale and retail furriers, with outlets downtown and in Plateau Mont-Royal, but nowhere more concentrated than on the "fur row" of **rue Mayor,** between rue de Bleury and rue City Councillors.

Those who delight in the hunt for bargains—and possess the tenacity to plunge into barely managed chaos to find them—won't want to miss **rue Chabanel.** A long trek north from downtown (nearest Métro station: Crémazie), rue Chabanel is a street that runs west of boulevard St-Laurent and is lined with factory buildings and warehouses. On Saturday mornings from 8:30am to 1pm—very roughly—the clothing manufacturers and importers use ground- and mezzanine-level showrooms and suites to display and sell all manner of men's, women's, and children's clothing at a discount. For those few hours a week (usually not in Jan or July), coats, leather goods, sportswear, suits, and sweaters are all on offer at deeply discounted prices, and diligence and a willingness to bargain are rewarded. Prowl the 8 blocks with buildings numbered 99

Tips   Taxes & Refunds

Visitors can obtain refunds of taxes incurred for lodgings and shop purchases.
See "Fast Facts: Montréal," in chapter 4, for details.

---

to 555; the higher the number, the better the quality, or at least so goes the commonly held conviction.

SHOPPING COMPLEXES

A unique shopping opportunity in Montréal is the **underground city,** a warren of passageways connecting more than 1,500 shops in 10 shopping complexes that have levels both above and below street level. **Complexe Desjardins** (© 514/281-1870) is bounded by rues Jeanne-Mance, Ste-Catherine, St-Urbain, and boulevard René-Lévesque. It has waterfalls and fountains, trees and hanging vines, music, lanes of shops going off in every direction, and elevators whisking people up to one of the four tall office towers. **Les Cours Mont-Royal,** 1455 rue Peel at boulevard de Maisonneuve (© 514/842-7777), is a recycling of the old Mount Royal Hotel. This complex recently added a huge Harry Rosen fashion emporium. The venerable Eaton department store failed, but it spawned **Le Centre Eaton,** 705 rue Ste-Catherine ouest (© 514/288-3708), with more than 175 shops, multiple cinemas, and eateries on five floors. The actual old Eaton department store is now occupied by **Les Ailes de la Mode** (The Wings of Fashion), 677 rue Ste-Catherine ouest, at University (© 514/282-4537), which has five floors of home accessory and fashion retailers, plus eateries, a spa, and more. **Place Bonaventure,** at rues de la Gauchetière and University (© 514/397-2325), has some 125 boutiques beneath the Bonaventure Hilton. **Place Montréal Trust,** at 1500 rue McGill College at rue Ste-Catherine (© 514/843-8000), is a five-story shopping complex, and **Place Ville-Marie,** opposite Le Reine Elizabeth hotel, between boulevard René-Lévêsque and Cathcart (© 514/861-9393), was Montréal's first major postwar shopping complex, known locally simply as "PVM." It has more than 80 boutiques and eateries. **Les Promenades de la Cathédrale,** at the corner of rues University and Ste-Catherine (© 514/849-9925), has more than 70 shops on the levels below the Cathédrale Christ Church. The new **Ruelle des Fortifications,** on rue St-Pierre between St-Antoine and St-Jacques (© 514/982-9888), is in the Centre Mondial du Commerce (World Trade Center), at the edge of Vieux-Montréal. This complex has more than 80 upscale boutiques, centered around two fountains, one modern and one traditional. **Westmount Square,** at rues Wood and Ste-Catherine (© 514/932-0211), combines a shopping center, an office complex, and a condominium complex designed by the famed Mies van der Rohe.

2 Shopping from A to Z

Most **stores** are open from 9 or 10am to 6pm Monday through Wednesday, 9am to 9pm on Thursday and Friday, and 9am to 5pm on Saturday. Many stores are now also open on Sunday from noon to 5pm.

ANTIQUES

The best place to find antiques and collectibles is in the more than 50 storefronts along Rue Notre-Dame between rues Guy and Atwater.

Antiques Puces-Libres   Three fascinatingly cluttered floors are packed with pine and oak furniture, lamps, clocks, vases, and more, most of it 19th- and early-20th-century French-Canadian Art Nouveau. 4240 rue St-Denis (near rue Rachel). ✆ **514/842-5931.**

ARTS & CRAFTS

Also see "Home Design & Housewares," on p. 159, and "Museum Stores," on p. 160.

Boutique Canadiana Worn Doorstep   This shop in the Bonsecours Market sells crafts, children's storybooks, maps, small furniture, and packaged foods, all with a Canadian connection. 350 rue St-Paul est, Vieux-Montréal. ✆ **514/397-0666.**

Guilde Canadienne des Métier d'Art Québec   A small but choice collection of craft items is displayed in a meticulously arranged gallery setting. Among the objects are blown glass, paintings on silk, pewter, tapestries, and ceramics. The store is particularly strong in avant-garde jewelry and Inuit sculpture. A small carving might be had for C$100 to C$300 (US$80–US$240), while the larger, more important pieces go for hundreds, even thousands, more. 1460 rue Sherbrooke ouest (near rue Mackay). ✆ **514/849-6091.**

La Guilde Graphique   More than 200 contemporary artists are represented here, working in a variety of media and with a variety of techniques, but primarily producing works on paper, including drawings, serigraphs, etchings, lithographs, and woodcuts. Some of the artists can often be seen working in the upstairs studio. 9 rue St-Paul ouest, Vieux-Montréal. ✆ **514/844-3438.**

L'Empreinte   This is a *coopérative artisane* (a craftspersons' collective), 1 block off place Jacques-Cartier at the corner of rue du Marché Bonsecours. The ceramics, textiles, glassware, and other items on sale often occupy that vaguely defined territory between art and craft. Quality is uneven but usually tips toward the high end. 272 rue St-Paul est, Vieux-Montréal. ✆ **514/861-4427.**

Les Artisans du Meuble Québécois   A mix of crafts, jewelry, and other objects—some noteworthy, others mediocre—make this an intriguing stop in Vieux-Montréal. Among the possibilities are clothing and accessories for women, greeting cards, woven goods, items for the home, and handmade quilts. 88 rue St-Paul est (near place Jacques-Cartier). ✆ **514/866-1836.**

Poterie Manu Reva   Abandoning a PhD program in biochemistry, the owner opened this shop to sell her work and that of fellow potters. The results are mostly appealing, although not every piece is to every taste. Among the best are wine and water glasses decorated in bright, spiky colors. 5141 rue St-Laurent (near av. Laurier). ✆ **514/948-1717.**

BATH & BODY

See also **Senteurs de Provence** on p. 158 and **Ex Voto** on p. 159.

Lush   Freshly installed on the ground floor of a pretty Queen Anne Victorian in the heart of the St-Denis shopping district, this is a purveyor of soaps and hair and skincare products as they might have been envisioned by the Woodstock Generation. Rough-hewn chunks of soap the size of gold ingots are flavored with olive oil, chocolate, mint, coriander, orange, and whatever other presumably natural ingredients might catch their makers' attention. Prices start at C$7 (US$5.60) and go up, substantially. 4067 rue St-Denis (near rue Duluth). ✆ **514/849-5333.**

BOOKS

Canadian Centre for Architecture Bookstore   This bookstore may be the Centre's most engrossing department. It features a comprehensive selection of books on architecture, with an emphasis on Montréal in particular and Canada in general. Volumes are also available on landscape and garden history, photography, preservation, conservation, design, and city planning. 1920 rue Baile (rue du Fort). ℭ 514/939-7020.

Champigny   For those who know the language or want to brush up, this two-level bookstore with a primarily French-language stock is a valuable resource. It also sells tapes, CDs, and newspapers and magazines from all over the world. Most English-language books are on the upper floor. There's a large children's section. 4380 rue St-Denis (at rue Marie-Anne). ℭ 514/844-2587.

Chapters   This is the flagship store of a chain with many branches, the result of a merger between Smithbooks and Coles booksellers. Thousands of titles are available in French and English on both general and specialized subjects. 1171 rue Ste-Catherine ouest (at rue Stanley). ℭ 514/849-8825.

Indigo   Occupying a street-level space in the Place Montréal Trust, this very complete store sells music, books, magazines, and gifts, and has a cafe upstairs. 1500 rue McGill College (at rue St-Catherine). ℭ 514/281-5549.

Paragraphe   Prowl the rows of shelves in this long storefront, then take your purchases to the adjoining Second Cup cafe, popular with students from the McGill campus, which is a block away. The store hosts frequent autograph parties and author readings, and occasional musical performances. 2220 av. McGill College (south of rue Sherbrooke). ℭ 514/845-5811.

Ulysse   Travelers are served by this good stock of guidebooks, many in English, as well as accessories, including maps, day packs, money pouches, electrical adapters, sewing kits, coffeemakers, and pill cases. 4176 rue St-Denis. ℭ 514/843-9447.

CLOTHING
FOR MEN
Boutique Hugo   Hugo Boss, that is, with stylings for those with the fit frames to carry these clothes and the discretionary income to purchase them. 1407 rue Crescent (near bd. de Maisonneuve). ℭ 514/843-3687.

Eccetera & Co.   Favoring ready-to-wear from such higher-end manufacturers as Hugo Boss and Canali, this store lays out the goods in a soothing setting with personalized service. 2021 rue Peel (near rue Sherbrooke). ℭ 514/845-9181.

Harry Rosen   This well-known retailer of designer suits and accessories purveys goods by Armani, Versace, Dolce & Gabbana, and their ilk. Les Cours Mont-Royal, 1455 rue Peel (at bd. de Maisonneuve). ℭ 514/284-3315.

L'Uomo   This store mostly deals in Italian menswear by such forward-thinking designers as Cerruti, Missoni, Ungaro, Versace, Armani, and Dolce & Gabbana. 1452 rue Peel (near rue Ste-Catherine). ℭ 514/844-1008. A branch of the store, Via Uomo, can be found down the street at 1478 rue Peel (ℭ 514/284-0104).

FOR WOMEN
Ambre   Sonia Kozma is the star designer here, creating fashionable suits, cocktail dresses, and dinner and casual wear made of linen, rayon, and cotton. And to go with the clothes, there are bold complementary accessories. 201 rue St-Paul ouest (at place Jacques-Cartier). ℭ 514/982-0325.

Artéfact Montréal   Browse here among moderate to expensive articles of clothing and paintings by up-and-coming Quebecois designers and artists. 4117 rue St-Denis (near rue Rachel). ℭ **514/842-2780.**

Kyoze   The eye-catching creations of Quebecois and other Canadian designers, including jewelry and accessories, are featured here. Items are moderate to expensive. There's a downtown outlet at 1455 rue Peel in Les Cours Mont-Royal. ℭ **514/849-6552.** There's also a store at Centre Mondial du Commerce, 393 rue St-Jacques ouest, 2nd floor (ℭ **514/847-7572**).

La Cache   Clothes designed and manufactured in India are the principal offerings of this national chain, augmented by housewares and bedding. The downtown outlets are at 2185 rue Crescent (near rue Sherbrooke; ℭ **514/842-0276**) and Place Montréal Trust, 1500 rue McGill College (at rue Sherbrooke; ℭ **514/847-5307**). There's another at 3941 rue St-Denis (near rue Roy; ℭ **514/842-7693**).

FOR MEN & WOMEN

Aritmetik   This fun shop features sportswear of a sort you don't see everywhere, created by young, forward-looking Toronto and California designers. 2011 rue St-Denis. ℭ **514/847-8965.** There are also branches in the Cours Mont-Royal mall downtown (ℭ **514/286-0565**) and at 3688 bd. St-Laurent (north of Sherbrooke; ℭ **514/985-4130**).

Club Monaco   Awareness of this expanding Canadian-owned international chain is growing, as is appreciation of its minimalist, largely monochromatic garments for men and women, along with silver jewelry, eyewear, and cosmetics. Think Prada but affordable, with a helpful young staff. 1455 rue Peel (north of rue Ste-Catherine). ℭ **514/499-0959.**

EnrgXchange   If you're young and sleek, male or female, the stretchy garments purveyed here shouldn't put you off, nor will the substantial discounts on items from terminated lines by Dolce & Gabbana, Moschino, Helmut Lang, and the like. Les Cours Mont-Royal, 1455 rue Peel. ℭ **514/282-0912.**

Le Château   Now you see it, now you don't. The merchandizing philosophy here is to move it, then move it out. That jittery motion encourages inveterate shoppers to drop by regularly to see what's in each week. Mostly what they find are affordable shirts, pants, dresses—mostly sportswear, but also suits and ties for businesspeople. 1310 rue Ste-Catherine (near rue de la Montagne). ℭ **514/866-2481.**

Roots   The company whose berets and uniforms were such a hit at the 2002 Winter Olympics has a three-floor store here, in addition to their other locations throughout Canada. In addition to clothing, they also offer table settings, furniture, perfume, books, and CDs. 1035 rue Ste-Catherine ouest (at rue Peel). ℭ **514/845-7995.**

Terra Nostra   Part of a chain with stores exclusively in Québec, this spiffy new shop features mostly casual ware for men and women in deceptively simple shapes—sort of an upscale Gap. 900 rue Ste-Catherine ouest. ℭ **514/861-6315.**

Urban Outfitters   This outpost of the sizable North American chain used to offer an unpredictable stock that ranged from off-kilter lamps and glassware to such life essentials as the *Star Wars Cookbook.* Now it emphasizes young-end clothes, mostly female. A regretted casualty of the change is the nun doll that breathed fire. 1246 rue Ste-Catherine ouest (near rue de la Montagne). ℭ **514/874-0063.**

COFFEES & TEAS

Brulerie St-Denis   This enticingly aromatic shop has an international selection of coffees from more than two dozen countries, whole or ground to order. There are tables at which to try a cup of the selections, and some desserts to go with it. 3965 rue

St-Denis (at Duluth). ℂ **514/286-9158.** There are several branches, including one in the Maison Alcan, at 2100 rue Stanley (ℂ **514/985-9159**).

DEPARTMENT STORES

Montréal's major shopping emporia stretch along rue Ste-Catherine (except for Holt Renfrew), from rue Guy eastward to Carré Phillips at Aylmer. An excursion along this 12-block stretch can keep a diligent shopper busy for hours, even days. Most of the stores mentioned below have branches elsewhere, including in the underground city.

Henry Birks et Fils   Across from Christ Church Cathedral stands Henry Birks et Fils, a highly regarded jeweler since 1879. This beautiful old store, with its dark wood display cases, stone pillars, and marble floors, is a living part of Montréal's Victorian heritage. Valuable products on display go well beyond jewelry to encompass pens and desk accessories, watches, ties, leather goods, belts and other personal accessories, glassware, and china. 1240 Carré Phillips (at av. Union). ℂ **514/397-2511.**

Holt Renfrew   This store began as a furrier in 1837, and is now a showcase for the best in international style, focusing on fashion for men and women. Such prestigious names as Giorgio Armani, Prada, Gucci, and Chanel are displayed with a tastefulness bordering on solemnity. The marquee outside reads only HOLTS. An actual human operates the elevator. 1300 rue Sherbrooke ouest (at rue de la Montagne). ℂ **514/842-5111.**

La Baie   No retailer has an older or more celebrated name than that of the Hudson's Bay Company, a name shortened in recent years to "The Bay," then transformed into "La Baie" by the language laws. The company has done business in Canada for the better part of 300 years. Its main store focuses on clothing, but also offers crystal, china, and Inuit carvings. Its Canadiana Boutique features historical souvenir items and wool merchandise, including their famous Hudson's Bay blankets. 585 rue Ste-Catherine ouest (near rue Aylmer). ℂ **514/281-4422.**

Maison Simons   This branch was the first foray out of its home area for Québec City's long-established family-owned department store. Most Montréalers had never heard of it, but that changed fast as attention was quickly captured by the fashions that fill the refurbished first three floors of a building that once housed the venerable Simpson's department store. One guidebook describes the store as "swanky," but the actuality is closer to the "softer side of Sears," with good prices. 977 rue Ste-Catherine ouest (at rue Mansfield). ℂ **514/282-1840.**

Ogilvy   Established in 1866, Ogilvy has been at this location since 1912. Besides having a reputation for quality merchandise, the store is known for its eagerly awaited Christmas windows. Once thought of as hidebound with tradition—a bagpiper still announces the noon hour and special events—it now contains more than 50 boutiques, including such high-profile purveyors as Dior, Escada, Louis Vuitton, Anne Klein, Aquascutum, and Rodier Paris. Wide aisles and glowing chandeliers enhance the shopping experience. 1307 rue Ste-Catherine ouest (at rue de la Montagne). ℂ **514/842-7711.**

EDIBLES

The food markets described in "Picnic Fare: Where to Get It, Where to Eat It" (p. 110) carry abundant assortments of cheeses, wines, and packaged food products that can serve as gifts or delicious reminders of your visit when you get home.

HOME DESIGN & HOUSEWARES

Also see "Arts & Crafts," on p. 155; "Museum Stores," on p. 160; **Henry Birks et Fils,** on p. 158; **La Baie,** on p. 158; and **Roots,** on p. 157.

Arthur Quentin   Doling out household products of quiet taste and discernment for over 25 years, this St-Denis stalwart is divided into departments specializing in tableware, kitchen gadgets, and home decor. That means lamps and Limoges china, terrines and tea towels, mandolins and mezzalunas, and just about any related items that might be imagined. Clay jugs for making vinegar? *Naturellement.* 3960 rue St-Denis (south of rue Duluth). ℭ 514/843-7513.

Caban   While it doesn't slide easily into a pigeonhole, think of this as a place that sells "life . . . with style." It's a newborn sibling to the Club Monaco chain, whose classy minimalist standards are applied to an eclectic stock that includes lawn furniture, glassware, flowerpots, deck chairs, and simple summery clothing. It's one of only three outlets, the others in Toronto and Vancouver—to date, at least. 777 rue Ste-Catherine ouest. ℭ 514/844-9300.

Collection Méli Mélo   Quality shops like this one continue to challenge Vieux-Montréal's purveyors of mock moccasins, trashy T-shirts, and related doodads. The stock is never quite the same as on your last visit, but always with a mix of exotica originating in the band of nations reaching from Morocco to Thailand down into sub-Saharan Africa. You'll find carpets, jewelry, carved chests, mirrors, and objects made of polished camel bone. With the drifting essences of sandalwood and incense, the store even smells good. 205 St-Paul ouest (at rue St-François-Xavier). ℭ 514/285-5585.

Ex Voto   After a bagel brunch at the St-Viateur Café down the street, drop in here for a look at the many varieties of candles, aromatic soaps, decorative and functional Moroccan oil lamps, and, for some reason, watering cans and hand puppets. 1254 rue Mont-Royal est. ℭ 514/525-1012.

Les Touilleurs   Kitchenware of the highest order, meticulously arranged in a minimalist setting, earned this shop design honors soon after it opened. The stock includes only superior versions of cooking essentials, including small appliances that strike high new standards. Check the toasters with slots so wide they can accept whole uncut bagels. 152 rue Laurier ouest. ℭ 514/278-0008.

Senteurs de Provence   The sunny south of France is evoked in pottery that's hand-painted in the creamy-bright colors of Provence, complemented by cunning collections of bath soaps and gels, printed linens, and lightly perfumed lotions and creams. 4077 rue St-Denis. ℭ 514/845-6867. There are also branches at 4859 rue Sherbrooke (ℭ 514/369-7888) and 363 rue St-Paul est, Vieux-Montréal (ℭ 514/395-8686).

12° en Cave   A store dedicated to the good life, with an emphasis on the oenophilist aspect. They contract to build custom wine cellars anywhere in North America, but if that's a stretch, they also sell Reidel crystal, Laguiole sutlery, espresso machines, and a variety of decidedly high-end wine-related paraphernalia. 367 rue St-Paul est, Vieux-Montréal ℭ 514/866-5722.

JEWELRY & ACCESSORIES

See the reviews under "Museum Stores" on p. 160 and "Department Stores" on p. 158. Also see **Collection Méli Mélo** on p. 159, **Guilde Canadienne des Métier d'Art Québec** on p. 155, **L'Empreinte** on p. 155, **Les Artisans du Meuble Québécois** on p. 155, **Ambre** on p. 156, **Kyoze** on p. 157, and **Club Monaco** on p. 157.

bleu comme le ciel   Costume jewelry here is flashy, often startling, and decidedly worth a visit for women looking to shake up their image. There are strings of fat faux pearls, often with tiny ceramic pigs attached, but the bulk of the stock reveals a clear Middle Eastern/North African influence with silvery strands of orange stones. Prices for most objects are in the reasonable C$100 to C$300 (US$80–US$240) range. 2000 rue Peel (near rue Ste-Catherine). ✆ 514/847-1128.

Clio Blue   This rue Peel outlet is quite different from other branches of the small chain, with spare displays in a narrow modernist storefront, a design competition winner. The custom jewelry tastefully incorporates Middle Eastern and South Asia motifs, often with carefully spaced semiprecious stones on silver strands and more festively designed bracelets. 1468 rue Peel (near rue Sherbrooke). ✆ 514/281-3116.

LEATHER GOODS

Les Cuirs Danier   This coast-to-coast national chain became so well respected by selling quality leather garments, belts, bags, and such—mostly for women, but men aren't ignored. Place Ville Marie. ✆ 514/874-0472. Also at 730 rue Ste-Catherine ouest (near av. McGill College; ✆ 514/392-0936).

Tag Cuirs   You have to check this out: *suede* jeans that are *washable!* They're manufactured by a Québec firm and, at this writing, aren't yet available in the States. Also on display are leather jackets and other leather items. 1325 rue Ste-Catherine ouest (at rue Crescent). ✆ 514/499-1180.

MUSEUM STORES

Musée d'Art Contemporain   The boutique of the contemporary art museum sells much of what might be expected, including poster-sized reproductions of paintings and prints, postcards, and art books. Added to the mix are tasteful design pieces and unusual gifts as well as souvenirs that eschew the lowest common denominator standards of too many Vieux Montréal shops. 185 rue Ste-Catherine ouest (at rue Jeanne-Mance). ✆ 514/847-6904.

Musée des Beaux-Arts Boutique   Next to the annex of the Museum of Fine Arts, this unusually large and impressive shop sells everything from folk art to furniture. The expected art-related postcards and prints are at hand, along with ties, jewelry, watches, scarves, address books, toys, games, clocks, and even designer napkins and paper plates. The boutique is to the right of the entrance, and a large bookstore is to the left. 380 rue Sherbrooke ouest (at rue Bishop). ✆ 514/285-1600.

Musée McCord Shop   Part of the newly expanded museum that relates the history of the province, this shop has a small, carefully chosen selection of cards, books with an emphasis on history, coloring books, jewelry, and handcrafts. 690 rue Sherbrooke ouest (at rue Victoria). ✆ 514/398-3142.

Pointe-à-Callière Gift Shop   Located in the Old Customs House at the end of the underground tour of the Museum of Archaeology and History (but with a separate entrance on rue St-Paul), this boutique sells collectibles for the home, gift items, paper products, souvenirs, toys, and books (in French). Some are worthwhile, some not. 150 rue St-Paul ouest (at place Royale). ✆ 514/872-9150.

MUSIC

Archambault Musique   French-Canadian singers are gaining fans across the border—Céline Dion only the most popular among them—and their music can be found here, along with recordings by the Montréal Symphony Orchestra, Ensemble I Musici, and other groups. Some of the recordings may be hard to find outside of Québec. 500 rue Ste-Catherine est (across the park from the Voyageur bus terminal). © 514/849-6201. A new outlet is located at Place des Arts (© 514/281-0367).

Inbeat   Decor is storefront plain, but the stock includes CDs and vinyl that just aren't available anywhere else. The staff describes the store's offerings as "deep house, progressive, tribal, techno, trance, old skool, Afro-Latin nu jazz, US & UK garage," and there are things that don't even fit into *those* categories. 3814 bd. St-Laurent. © 514/499-2063.

Marché du Disque et du Video   In response to the escalating cost of CDs, a number of shops specializing in previously owned CDs have made appearances, especially along avenue Mont-Royal. This one has thousands of different CDs, plus vinyl collectibles, DVDs, and videos. 793 av. Mont-Royal est (at St-Hubert). © 514/526-3575.

SHOES

Terra Firma   The sign reads T. FIRMA, but everyone knows the store by its full name, which is the only way you'll get directions in Le Centre Eaton (it's toward the back on the ground floor). Men's and women's shoes are the products, with labels that include Ecco, Stonefly, Rockport, Bostonian, Hush Puppies, Cole Haan, and pricey Mephisto. 705 rue Ste-Catherine ouest. © 514/288-3708. There's another outlet in Les Cours Mont-Royal (© 514/845-3007).

TOYS

Franc Jeu   Expectant parents (and new grandparents) will want to make a detour to browse through this store's expansive collection of Corolle dolls, which are known for their realistic look. The store also sells the clothes, jewelry, and accessories with which to dress the dolls. 4152 rue St-Denis (near rue Rachel). © 514/849-9253.

La Cerf-Volanterie   This Vieux-Montréal shop, long in business, is filled with sturdy, dazzling cloth kites created by the owner, who is often seen at his workbench in back. 4428 rue Berri. © 514/845-7613.

WINES & SPIRITS

Although wine and beer are sold in supermarkets and convenience stores, liquor and other spirits can only be sold in shops operated by the provincial Société des Alcools du Québec (SAQ). Though it was once as bureaucratic as most state-run agencies, successful efforts have made the stores more inviting. Some serve particular needs, others strive to be comprehensive. One of the largest is the **SAQ Selection** at 440 bd. de Maisonneuve ouest at rue City Councillors (© 514/873-2274), a virtual supermarket of wines and liquors, with more than 3,000 labels from some 55 countries. Prices run from C$10 to C$1,000 (US$8–US$800) for some bordeaux vintages. **SAQ Selection** at 998 bd. de Maisonneuve ouest at rue Metcalf (© 514/282-9445) specializes in single-malt scotches, whiskeys, brandies, and liqueurs, and has a bar for tastings. Smaller and less fancy, the **SAQ Express** at 1108 rue Ste-Catherine ouest is meant for quick in-and-out purchases; it's open daily and later than the other stores, 11am to 10pm.

   In addition, the food markets described in "Picnic Fare: Where to Get It, Where to Eat It" (p. 110) shouldn't be overlooked for wine purchases.

10

Montréal After Dark

Montréal's reputation for effervescent nightlife reaches back to the Roaring Twenties, specifically to the 13-year experiment with Prohibition in the United States. Canadian distillers and brewers made fortunes—few of them with meticulous regard for legalistic niceties—and Americans streamed into Montréal for temporary relief from alcohol deprivation. The city already enjoyed a sophisticated and slightly naughty reputation as the Paris of North America, which added to the allure. Clubbing and barhopping remain popular activities, with nightspots keeping much later hours in Montréal than in archrival Toronto, which still heeds Calvinist notions of propriety and early bedtimes.

Montréalers' nocturnal pursuits are often as cultural as they are social. The city boasts its own outstanding symphony, more than 65 French- and English-speaking theater companies, and the incomparable performance company Cirque du Soleil. It's also on the standard concert circuit that includes Chicago, Boston, and New York, so internationally known entertainers, rock bands, orchestra conductors and classical virtuosos, and ballet and modern-dance companies pass through frequently. A decidedly French enthusiasm for film, as well as the city's ever-increasing reputation as a movie-production center, ensures support for cinemas showcasing experimental, offbeat, and foreign films, as well as the usual Hollywood blockbusters.

And in summer, the city becomes even livelier than usual with several enticing and often overlapping events: the Festival de Théâtre des Amériques, the flashy Montréal International Fireworks Competition, the renowned Festival International de Jazz, the humor-packed Juste pour Rire/Just for Laughs Festival, and the Festival International Nuits d'Afrique. To this bursting roster, the city has added the Montréal Highlights Festival/Festival Montréal en Lumière, held for 11 days in February and dedicated to the arts, which, by this gastronomic city's measure, includes chefs the caliber of Paul Bocuse and Charlie Trotter; and Les Franco Folíes de Montréal, presenting artists and musicians from French-speaking nations during 10 days in July and August.

Concentrations of pubs and discos underscore the city's linguistic dichotomy. While there's a great deal of crossover mingling, the parallel blocks of **rue Crescent,** rue Bishop, and rue de la Montagne north of rue Ste-Catherine have a pronounced Anglophone character, while Francophones dominate the **Quartier Latin,** with college-age patrons most evident along the lower reaches of rue St-Denis and their yuppie elders gravitating to the nightspots of the slightly more uptown blocks of the same street. **Vieux-Montréal (Old Montréal),** especially along rue St-Paul, has a more universal quality, and many of the bars and clubs there feature live jazz, blues, and folk music. In the **Plateau Mont-Royal** area, boulevard St-Laurent, parallel to St-Denis and known locally as "The Main," has become a miles-long haven of hip restaurants and clubs, roughly from rue Laurier

---

⟨*Tips*⟩ **Finding Out What's On**

For details on performances or special events that are on when you're in town, pick up a free copy of *Montréal Scope,* a weekly ads-and-events booklet usually available at hotel reception desks, or the free weekly newspapers *Mirror* and *Hour* (in English) or *Voir* and *Ici* (in French), available all over town. (If you don't know what a "rave" is, you won't need to know that their upcoming dates, locations, and phone numbers can be found in *Ici.*) *Fugues,* available at the tourist information office opposite the Beaudry Métro station or online (www.fugues.com), provides news and views of gay and lesbian events, clubs, restaurants, and activities. For extensive listings of largely mainstream cultural and entertainment events, log on to **www.canada.com/english** or **www.montrealplus.ca.** A similar service is provided by *Hour* at **www.afterhour.com.** Also try the official website of Tourisme Montréal: **www.tourisme-montreal.org.**

---

to rue Sherbrooke. Boulevard St-Laurent is a good place to wind up in the wee hours, as there's always someplace with the welcome mat still out, even after the official 3am closing.

Most bars and clubs don't charge cover, and when they do, it's rarely more than

C$10 (US$8). Depending on the venue, beer is usually in the C$4 to C$7 (US$3.20–US$5.60) range, while cocktails and highballs are typically C$6 to C$12 (US$4.80–US$9.60).

1 The Performing Arts

CLASSICAL MUSIC & OPERA

L'Opéra de Montréal   Founded in 1980, this outstanding opera company mounts six productions a year in Montréal, with artists from Québec and abroad participating in such shows as *La Traviata, Carmen, Aida, Otello,* and *Mefistofele.* Video translations are provided from the original languages into French and English. The box office is open Monday to Friday 9am to 5pm. Performances are held from September to June in three theaters at Place des Arts and occasionally at other venues. Salle Wilfrid-Pelletier, Place des Arts, 260 bd. de Maisonneuve ouest. ⓒ 514/985-2222. www.operademontreal.com. Tickets from C$41 (US$33). Métro: Place des Arts.

L'Orchestre Symphonique de Montréal (OSM)   This world-famous orchestra performs at Place des Arts and the Notre-Dame Basilica, as well as around the world, and may be heard on numerous recordings. The orchestra's balanced repertoire continues to run from Elgar to Rabaud to Saint-Saëns, in addition to Beethoven and Mozart. The box office is open Monday to Saturday noon to 8pm. The full season runs September to May, supplemented by Mozart concerts in Notre-Dame Basilica on 6 evenings in June and July, interspersed with free performances at three parks in the metropolitan region. People under 25 can purchase tickets for only C$10 (US$8) on the day of a concert. Salle Wilfrid-Pelletier, Place des Arts, 260 bd. de Maisonneuve ouest. ⓒ 514/842-9951 (for tickets, Mon–Fri 9am–5pm). www.osm.ca. Tickets from C$19 (US$15). Métro: Place des Arts.

Orchestre Métropolitain du Grand Montréal   This orchestra has a regular season at Place des Arts, where it works with L'Opera de Montréal, but it also performs concerts in the St-Jean-Baptiste Church and tours regionally. The box office is open

Monday to Saturday noon to 8pm. Performances are held mid-October to early April and outdoors in Parc Lafontaine in August. Maisonneuve Theatre, Place des Arts, 260 bd. de Maisonneuve ouest. ✆ **514/598-0870.** Tickets from C$19 (US$15). Métro: Place des Arts.

CONCERT HALLS & AUDITORIUMS

Montréal has a score of venues, so check the papers upon arrival to see who's playing where during your stay. Big-name rock bands and pop stars that used to play at the Forum now show up at the new downtown arena, Centre Bell (below).

Le Centre Bell This is the home of the Montréal Canadiens and hosts big international rock and pop stars on the order of Avril Lavigne, Billy Idol, Sarah McLachlan, and Velvet Revolver, as well as such dissimilar attractions as Disney's On Ice. These stars used to be booked into the old Forum but are now diverted to this sparkling facility, which opened in 1996. Most people agree that it's vastly superior to the old Forum on all but the nostalgia scale, and the location is better. More than 21,000 can be seated. The box office is open Monday through Friday 10am to 6pm (or to 9pm on days of events). Ticket prices vary greatly, depending on the attraction. 1260 rue de la Gauchetière ouest. ✆ **514/932-2582.** www.centrebell.ca. Métro: Bonaventure.

Metropolis A prime showplace for traveling rock groups, it competes with its sister facility, **Spectrum** (see below) for those bands on the way up or retracing their steps down. It has recently hosted Billy Idol and Garbage. While it is primarily a concert venue that can hold up to 2,300 customers, there is a small attached cabaret, the Savoy. The building started life as a skating rink in 1884, and has served through various periods and reconstructions as a theater, a cinema, a porn house, and a disco. 59

A Circus Extraordinaire

Through the exposure generated by its frequent tours across North America, Europe, and Australia, the **Cirque du Soleil,** 8400 2e ave., St-Michel (✆ **800/361-4595** or 514/722-2324; www.cirquedusoleil.com), is enjoying an ever-widening following. One reason is the absence of animals in the troupe, which means no one need be troubled by the possibility of mistreated lions and elephants. Linear descriptions and even photographs can't begin to do justice to what is presented during a Cirque du Soleil performance. The experience is nothing less than magical, a celebration of pure skill and theater. There are plenty of acrobats, clowns, trapeze artists, tightrope walkers, and contortionists, but there is dance, too, and people costumed to look like creatures not of this world—iguanas crossed with goblins, say, or peacocks born of trolls. There are even storylines, of a sort. This is truly for children of all ages. Since 1984, more than 15 million people in more than 120 cities have seen the Cirque du Soleil in action. The troupe is so much in demand it's difficult to track from year to year how long it will alight in its hometown, although most recently it has stayed from mid-April to late May most years. Check ahead to discover its current plans. Ticket prices range unpredictably, but at a recent production in the tent in Montréal's Vieux-Port, the top price was C$76 (US$61). It was truly worth it.

Ste-Catherine est. 𝒞 **514/844-3500.** www.spectrumdemontreal.ca/metropolis. Tickets C$16 (US$13) (for most attractions). Métro: St-Laurent or Berri-UQAM.

Place des Arts   Founded in 1963 and in its striking present home in the heart of Montréal since 1992, Place des Arts mounts performances of musical concerts, opera, dance, and theater in five halls: **Salle Wilfrid-Pelletier** (2,982 seats), where the Orchestre Symphonique de Montréal often performs; the **Théâtre Maisonneuve** (1,460 seats), where the Orchestre Métropolitain de Montréal and the McGill Chamber Orchestra perform; the **Théâtre Jean-Duceppe** (755 seats); the **Cinquième Salle** (350 seats); and the small **Studio-Théâtre Stella Artois** (138 seats). Traveling productions of Broadway classics have limited runs at the center, and portions of the city's arts festivals are staged here. The box office is open Monday through Saturday noon to 8pm. Ticket prices vary according to hall and the group performing. 175 rue Ste-Catherine ouest. 𝒞 **514/285-4200** for information, **514/842-2112** for tickets, or www.pda.qc.ca for tickets online. Métro: Place des Arts.

Pollack Concert Hall   In a landmark building dating from 1899 and fronted by a statue of Queen Victoria, this hall is in nearly constant use, especially during the university year. Among the attractions are concerts and recitals by McGill students or professionals from McGill's music faculty. Recordings of some of the more memorable concerts are available on the university's own label, McGill Records. Box office hours are Monday to Friday noon to 6pm. Concerts are also given in the campus's smaller **Redpath Hall,** 3461 rue McTavish (𝒞 **514/398-4547**). Performances are often free, but tickets for some events can cost up to C$25 (US$20). On the McGill University campus, 555 rue Sherbrooke ouest. 𝒞 **514/398-4547.** www.music.mcgill.ca. Métro: McGill.

Spectrum de Montréal   A broad range of Canadian and international performers, usually second-tier celebrities unlikely to fill the larger Centre Bell, use this converted movie theater. Rock groups are the usual fare, comedians are sometimes booked, and the space also hosts segments of the city's annual jazz festival. Seats are available on a first-come, first-served basis. Tickets are priced according to attraction. Long-term construction is underway to expand the Spectrum into a major cultural complex, with a concert hall, 13 cinemas for mainstream and art-house films, a jazz club, a book-and-music store, and restaurants, so call ahead to ascertain the current status. 318 rue Ste-Catherine ouest (at rue de Bleury). 𝒞 **800/361-4595** or 514/861-5851. www.spectrumdemontreal. ca/spectrum. Métro: Place des Arts; then take the Bleury exit.

Théâtre de Outremont   As with many of the numerous performance spaces in the city, this venue has endured a history of rising and falling fortunes. Opened in 1929, it had its moments of greatest glory in the 1970s, then closed in the late 1980s. After 8 years of repairs and reconstruction, it started a new life in 2001, with a larger stage and terraced seating. Its calendar incorporates all manner of music, comedy, dance, theater, and film. While most of this is addressed to French-speaking audiences, others can find entertainment in obvious nonverbal performances. 1249 av. Bernard ouest (at av. McEachran). 𝒞 **514/495-9944.** www.spectrumdemontreal.ca/outremont. Métro: Outremont.

Théâtre de Verdure   Nestled in a popular park in Plateau Mont-Royal, this open-air theater presents free music and dance concerts and theater, often with well-known artists and performers. Sometimes free outdoor movies are shown. Many in the audience pack picnics. Performances are held from June to August; call for days and times. In Lafontaine Park. 𝒞 **514/872-2644.** Métro: Sherbrooke.

Théâtre St-Denis Recently refurbished, this theater in the heart of the Latin Quarter hosts a variety of shows, including pop singers, rock groups, and comedians, as well as segments of the Juste pour Rire (Just for Laughs) Festival in late July. It's actually two theaters, one seating more than 2,000, the other almost 1,000. The box office is open daily noon to 9pm. 1594 rue St-Denis (at Emery). ℭ **514/790-1111.** Métro: Berri-UQAM.

DANCE

Frequent appearances by notable dancers and troupes from other parts of Canada and the world—among them Paul Taylor, the Feld Ballet, and Le Ballet National du Canada—augment the accomplished resident companies. During the summer, Les Grands Ballets Canadiens sometimes performs at the outdoor Théâtre de Verdure in Parc Lafontaine. In winter, it's scheduled at various venues around the city, but especially in the several halls at the Place des Arts.

Les Grands Ballets Canadiens This prestigious company, performing both a classical and a modern repertoire, has developed a following far beyond national borders over more than 35 years. In the process, it has brought prominence to many gifted Canadian choreographers and composers. It tours internationally and was the first Canadian ballet company to be invited to the People's Republic of China. The troupe's production of *The Nutcracker* during the last couple of weeks in December is always a big event in Montréal. The box office is open Monday to Saturday noon to 8pm. Performances are held late October to early May. Place des Arts, 175 Ste-Catherine ouest. ℭ **514/842-2112.** www.grandsballets.qc.ca. Tickets from C$25 (US$20). Métro: Place des Arts.

THEATER

The **Festival de Théâtre des Amériques** (ℭ **514/842-0704;** www.fta.qc.ca), held every spring from late May to early June, presents innovative dramatic and musical stage productions that are international in scope, not simply North American as the name suggests. There have been works from Vietnam and China as well as from Canada, the United States, and Mexico. As many as 20 plays are performed in their original languages, with simultaneous translations in French and/or English when appropriate. The festival is held at various venues in the city.

Centaur Theatre A former stock-exchange building (1903) is home to Montréal's principal English-language theater. A mix of classics, foreign adaptations, and works by Canadian playwrights is presented. A sampling of past productions includes *Proof, Copenhagen, Cabaret,* and *The Cripple of Inishmaan.* Off season, the theater is rented out to other groups. Performances are held October to June. Box-office hours are Monday to Friday noon to 5pm. 453 rue St-François-Xavier (near rue Notre-Dame). ℭ **514/288-3161.** www.centaurtheatre.com. Tickets from C$24 (US$19). Métro: Place d'Armes.

Saidye Bronfman Centre for the Arts Montréal's Yiddish Theatre, founded in 1937, is housed in the Saidye Bronfman Centre for the Arts, not far from St. Joseph's Oratory. The 300-seat theater hosts dance and music recitals, occasional lectures, and plays in both Yiddish and English. Among recent productions were *Tuesdays with Morrie, Fiddler on the Roof,* and *The Tempest.* There's also an art gallery on the premises, with exhibits that change almost monthly. Across the street, in the Edifice Cummings House, is a small Holocaust museum and the Jewish Public Library. The center takes its name from late philanthropist Saidye Bronfman, widow of Samuel Bronfman, founder of the Seagram Company. Note that the Centre is at a considerable distance from downtown, and the taxi fare is considerable. The box office is usually open

Monday through Thursday 11am to 8pm and Sunday noon to 7pm. Call ahead. 5170 Côte-Ste-Catherine (near bd. Décarie). © 514/739-7944. www.saidyebronfman.org. Tickets from C$15 (US$12). Métro: Côte-Ste-Catherine. Bus: 29 ouest.

2 The Club & Music Scene

COMEDY

The once-enthusiastic market for comedy clubs across North America has long since cooled, but Montréal still has a couple of laugh spots, mostly because it's the home to the highly regarded **Juste pour Rire (Just for Laughs) Festival** held every summer (for information, call © **514/845-2322**). Those who have so far eluded the comedy-club experience should know that profanity, bathroom humor, and assorted ethnic slurs are common fodder for performers. If patrons wish to avoid becoming objects of the comedians' barbs, it's wise to sit well back from the stage. Performances are in French or English (about 50/50, it seems) or both.

Comedyworks   There's a full card of comedy every night at this long-running club situated on a jumping block of rue Bishop south of rue Ste-Catherine. Monday is usually open-mic night, while on Tuesday and Wednesday, improvisational groups work off the audience's suggestions. Headliners—usually from Montréal, Toronto, New York, or Boston—take the stage Thursday through Sunday. No food is served, just drinks. Reservations are recommended, especially on Friday, when early arrival may be necessary to secure a seat. Shows are nightly at 9pm, and also at 11:15pm on Fridays and Saturdays. 1238 rue Bishop (at rue Ste-Catherine). © 514/398-9661. Cover from C$5 (US$4). Métro: Guy-Concordia.

DANCE CLUBS

As elsewhere, Montréal's dance clubs change in popularity in mere eye blinks; new ones sprout like toadstools after a heavy rain, and wither as quickly. For the latest feverish spots, quiz concierges, guides, waiters—all those who look as if they might follow the scene. Here are a few that appear more likely to survive the whims of night owls and landlords. At some, you'll encounter steroid abusers with funny haircuts guarding the doors. Usually they'll let you inside; the admittance game is rarely as strict or as arbitrary as the "hipper than thou" criteria encountered at some New York and Los Angeles clubs.

In addition to the dance clubs listed below, also see the reviews for **Café Campus/Petit Campus** (p. 169), **Hard Rock Cafe** (p. 169), **Laïka** (p. 173), **Le Tour de Ville** (p. 172), **Jello Bar** (p. 174), **Sir Winston Churchill Pub** (p. 172), **Sky Club & Pub** (p. 176), **Thursday's** (p. 172), **Club Chez Mado** (p. 175), and **Complexe Bourbon** (p. 175).

Blizzarts   Remnants of '50s modern, much of it mismatched, fill the space around the small dance floor. Most nights, heavy-beat dance music is designed to get the 20-ish crowd up and moving. Next to the DJ booth is a full bar with an espresso machine. On weekends, there's usually a band. Last we saw, the bartender on duty poured with a generous tilt of the bottle. 3956a bd. St-Laurent (near rue Duluth). © 514/843-4860. Cover up to C$5 (US$4). Métro: Mont-Royal.

Club Balattou   An infectious, sensual tropical beat issues from this club-with-a-difference on The Main, a hot, happy variation from the prevailing grunge and murk that seeps out of what might be described as mainstream clubs. Things get going about 10pm every night but Monday. 4372 bd. St-Laurent (at rue Marie-Anne). © 514/845-5447. Cover charge of C$5–C$10 (US$4–US$8) includes a beer or glass of wine. Métro: Mont-Royal.

FunkyTown   For most of the vivacious crowd that swirls through this downtown disco, the '70s are the *really* old days, yet much of the music is of that era, with supporting decor. Think mirrored balls, floors lit from below, and a setting resembling that in which John Travolta committed The Hustle in his ice-cream suit. Go too late and you'll most likely encounter a line and a wait. The club opens at 10pm, Thursday through Saturday. 1454 rue Peel. ✆ 514/282-8387. www.clubsmontreal.com. Cover C$8 (US$6.40) Fri–Sat. Métro: Guy-Concordia.

Les Foufounes Electriques   On the scene for more than a decade, this multilevel disco–rock club has mellowed somewhat from its outlaw days, although it still features hardcore rock and industrial bands. An occasional one-hit wonder puts in an appearance—Vanilla Ice, anyone? With three dance floors and a couple of beer gardens in back, there's plenty to keep customers busy, starting with cheap brews and shooters during the 4 to 6pm happy hour. Look for the rocket ship over the door. Open 7 days a week, 3pm to 3am. 87 Ste-Catherine est (near rue St-Denis). ✆ 514/844-5539. www.foufounes. qc.ca. Cover C$8–C$15 (US$6.40–US$12). Métro: Berri-UQAM.

Newtown   Huge fanfare trumpeted the summer 2001 opening of this tri-level club in the white-hot center of rue Crescent nightlife. One of the owners is Formula One race car driver and local hero Jacques Villeneuve, whose last name can be translated as "New Town." Adjoining town houses were scooped out to make one big trendy nightspot at a reported cost of US$5.3 million at the time, with a disco in the basement, big barroom on the main floor, restaurant one floor up, and rooftop terrace in summer. Reservations are usually required for the restaurant, but admission to the bar and dance floor should-n't be a problem. The bar and restaurant are open daily, and the disco is open Friday and Saturday. 1476 rue Crescent (at de Maisonneuve). ✆ 514/284-6555. Métro: Peel.

Orchid   As if to underscore the odds against success for fledgling nightspots, this club took over the site of what used to be Kokino, one of the hottest-of-the-hot clubs a scant few years ago. That hasn't bothered the droves of gorgeous gals and hunky guys—500 total on most nights—who eye each other across the thumping dance floor. Five bars attend to them. House is big, mixed with soul and salsa. Get there before the glow fades, and dress right to get past the door. The club is open Tuesday to Saturday from 10pm; Tuesday has been Gay Men's Night. 3556 bd. St-Laurent (north of rue Sherbrooke). ✆ 514/848-6398. Cover is usually C$10 (US$8). Métro: Sherbrooke.

Time Supper Club   This is yet another creation of the high-profile chef-entrepreneur David McMillan, who is also responsible for the restaurants Globe (p. 100) and Rosalie (p. 92). The club is as popular with the beautiful and powerful folk as McMillan's other establishments, which are primarily eateries. Though this place also serves food, Time gives the fabulous crowd a chance to get up from their tables and work off the calories to rock, house, and hip-hop that pounds on 'til closing at 3am. The waitstaff is startlingly attractive. Dress well, look good, and approach the door with confidence. They are open Wednesday through Saturday, starting at 7pm; dancing usually gets going around 11pm. 997 rue St-Jacques (at rue Catédrale). ✆ 514/392-9292. Métro: Place d'Armes.

Upperclub   At one point—no guarantees about next week—this was probably the most exclusive club in Montréal. They still don't have a public telephone number. Allowing for whatever changes in policy might occur when the heat cools, don't even *think* of showing up at the guarded portal in baseball caps, sneaks, or jeans. A Brooks Brothers suit might not cut it, either . . . Sean Jean stylish should work, though. Once inside, almost everyone, from patrons to staff, will look as great as you do, gathering around the three bars and out on the dance floor. DJs spin progressive house Thursday through Monday nights. 3519 bd. St-Laurent (north of rue Sherbrooke). Cover C$10 (US$8). Métro: Sherbrooke.

FOLK, ROCK & POP

Montréal has become a hotbed of innovative alternative rock, a place to hear bands that might be the next big thing. Critics point approvingly to such homegrown outfits as Arcade Fire, Bionic, the Stills, the Unicorns, Stars, The Dears, Wolf Parade, Les Georges Leningrad, and Pony Up!

Scores of bars, cafes, theaters, clubs, and even churches present live music on at least an occasional basis, even if only at Sunday brunch. The performers, local or touring, draw from every idiom, from metal to funk to reggae to grunge and unvarnished Vegas. Here are a few places that focus their energies on music.

Barfly   The offhandedly scruffy facade is covered with crude posters of upcoming appearances. Late teens and 20s constitute the clientele, with the average individual quota of visible piercings and body ink running about three and two respectively. They crowd around the small pool table in front and spill out onto the sidewalk. Beer is the mood elevator of choice; music is unpredictable. 4062a bd. St-Laurent (near rue Duluth). ✆ 514/284-6665. Métro: Mont-Royal.

Brutopia   This pub pulls endless pints of its own microbrews to go with rock/pop at least 5 nights a week. With several rooms on two levels, a terrace in back, and a streetside balcony, it anchors the raucous southern end of rue Crescent. Chances are you haven't heard of any of the bands, but they keep the tempo up. Sunday is usually open mic; Monday, "Trivia Night." 1219 rue Crescent (north of bd. René-Lévesque). ✆ 514/393-9277. Métro: Lucien L'Allier.

Café Campus/Petit Campus   When anyone over 25 shows up inside this bleak club on touristy rue Prince-Arthur, he or she is probably a parent of one of the musicians. Alternative rock prevails, but blues and retro-rock bands also make appearances. Groups such as The Dears, The Von Bondies, and White Cowbell Oklahoma have hit the stage here. Disco parties are often scheduled Wednesday nights, and a smaller room, Petit Campus, usually has DJ'd hip-hop. 57 rue Prince-Arthur est (near bd. St-Laurent). ✆ 514/844-1010. www.cafecampus.com. Cover usually C$8–C$15 (US$6.40–US$12). Métro: Sherbrooke.

Club Soda   This long-established club's new quarters are even larger than its old location on avenue du Parc. It remains one of the prime destinations for performers just below the megastar level and is a principal venue for the Just for Laughs festival. Performers are given a stage in a hall that seats several hundred fans. Five bars pump audience enthusiasm. Musical choices hop all over the charts—folk, rock, blues, country, Afro-Cuban, heavy metal—you name it. Acts for the annual jazz festival are booked here, too. 1225 bd. St-Laurent (at rue Ste-Catherine). ✆ 514/286-1010. www.clubsoda.ca. Cover up to C$25 (US$20). Métro: St-Laurent.

Hard Rock Cafe   No surprises here, not with clones around the world. The hamburgers are good enough and not overly expensive. The formula still works, and the place gets crowded at lunch and on weekend evenings. There's a terrace seating about 30 patrons. Open Sunday to Thursday from 11:30am to midnight, Friday to Saturday from 11:30am to 3am; the disco is up and going from 11:30pm to 1am. 1458 rue Crescent (near bd. de Maisonneuve). ✆ 514/987-1420. Métro: Guy-Concordia.

Hurley's Irish Pub The Irish have been one of the largest immigrant groups in Montréal since the famine of the 1840s, and their musical tradition thrives here. In front is a street-level terrace, with several semisubterranean rooms in back. Celtic instrumentalists and dancers perform every night of the week, often both on the ground floor and upstairs, usually starting around 9:30pm. 1225 rue Crescent (at rue Ste-Catherine). *ⓒ* 514/861-4111. Métro: Peel or Guy-Concordia.

Les Bobards Why call this heavy-duty music venue "Tall Stories"? You'll get no good answer, but the reasons to go are nights that feature a wide variety of distinct forms. By management's reckoning, that includes reggae, salsa, Afro-funk, Latino, syncpop, and anything else that takes its fancy. Live shows are Wednesday through Saturday (usually), starting around 9:30pm. Foosball and pool can fill the time until then. 4348 bd. St-Laurent (at rue Marie-Anne). *ⓒ* 514/987-1174. www.lesbobards.qc.ca. Cover up to $5 (US$4). Métro: Mont-Royal.

Les Deux Pierrots Perhaps the best known of Montréal's *boîtes-à-chansons*—song clubs—this is an intimate French-style cabaret. The singers interact animatedly with the crowd, often bilingually. It's open daily from early June to late September, Thursday through Sunday the other months, with music into the wee hours. The terrace is open on Friday and Saturday nights in summer. 104 rue St-Paul est (west of place Jacques-Cartier). *ⓒ* 514/861-1270. www.lespierrots.com. Cover from C$5 (US$4). Métro: Place d'Armes.

Le Divan Orange This is a *cooperative de travail,* or worker's cooperative, which means, in part, that it is a not-for-profit operation, with the "suggested" cover charge going into the pot to pay the musicians. Bands and combos have been known to include fusion jazz, country, indie rock, reggae, world, swing, traditional North African, and undertakings that might best be described as performance art. Shows start around 9:30pm. It's open every night and food is served. 4234 bd. St-Laurent (near rue Rachel). *ⓒ* 514/840-9090. www.ledivanorange.org. Cover C$5–C$10 (US$4–US$8). Métro: Mont-Royal.

Le Swimming A nondescript entry and a stairway that smells of stale beer lead to a trendy pool hall that attracts an equal number of drinkers/socializers and pool players (*le swimming,* get it?). Many Montréal bars have a pool table, but this one has 11, along with foosball games, two bars, nine TVs, and a terrace. At least 3 nights of the week they have bands churning out ska, funk, reggae, or jazz. There may be someone sleeping on the floor near the entrance. Open daily 1pm to 3am; pool is free until 5pm. 3643 bd. St-Laurent (north of rue Sherbrooke). *ⓒ* 514/282-7665. www.leswimming.com. Cover from C$5 (US$4) Thurs–Sat (when live bands are booked). Métro: Sherbrooke.

JAZZ & BLUES

The respected and heavily attended **Festival International de Jazz,** held every summer in the city, caters to the public's interest in this original American art form. During the 12 days of the event, more than 2,500 musicians perform on 10 stages for an average total audience of 1.7 million. Scores of events are scheduled, indoors and out, more than 350 of them free. "Jazz" is broadly interpreted to include everything from Dixieland to reggae, world beat, and the unclassifiable experimental. In 2005, for example, Pat Methany and Sonny Rollins were featured, as were Bobby McFerrin, the Neville Brothers, John Mayall, Roberta Flack, and Paul Anka (*Paul Anka?*). Such jazz stalwarts as Gil Evans, Dave Brubeck, Wynton Marsalis, and B. B. King have appeared in the past. Piano legend Oscar Peterson grew up here and has sometimes returned to perform in his hometown. For information on the festival, call *ⓒ* **888/515-0515** or 514/871-1881, or visit www.montrealjazzfest.com.

There are many more clubs featuring jazz and related forms than the sampling that follows. Pick up a copy of *Mirror* or *Hour,* distributed free everywhere, or buy the Friday or Saturday editions of the *Gazette* for the entertainment section. These publications have full listings of the bands and stars appearing during the week.

Casa del Popolo   This scruffy storefront might seem an unlikely place to launch an increasingly visible summer music festival, but that it has. While jazz and blues dominate the regular schedule, there's plenty of room for hip-shakin' dance party sounds, for percussion specialists, jazz bagpipe, calypso, folkies, reggae, and whatever else grabs their attention. The festival takes up most of June, sharing performance space with La Sala Rossa, across the street. The rest of the year brings an equally diverse musical menu, with DJs Monday and Tuesday and live music the rest of the week. Food is available—strictly vegetarian—and draft beer by the pint is the beverage preferred by the leftie Bohemian clientele. Don't overdress. 4873 bd. St-Laurent (near bd. St-Joseph). ℂ 514/ 284-3804. www.casadelpopolo.com. Cover C$5–C$10 (US$4–US$8).Métro: Laurier.

Maestro S.V.P.   Good eats and live music aren't strangers in Montréal. Although this bistro is best known for seafood, especially its oyster bar (p. 103), the owner brings in a jazz trio on Sunday nights at 6:30pm. That justifies the name and the musical instruments that constitute most of the decor. 3615 bd. St-Laurent (north of rue Sherbrooke). ℂ 514/842-6447. Métro: Sherbrooke.

Maison de Jazz   Right downtown, this jazz venue has been on the scene for decades. It was redecorated in mock Art Nouveau style after the 2003 death of the owner-founder, Charlie Biddle. Lovers of barbecued ribs and jazz, most of them well past the bloom of youth, start filling the room early. Live music starts around 7pm and continues until closing time. The ribs are okay and the jazz is of the swinging mainstream variety, with occasional digressions into more esoteric forms. 2060 rue Aylmer (south of rue Sherbrooke). ℂ 514/842-8656. Cover is C$3 (US$2.40) Sun–Wed, C$5 (US$4) Thurs–Sat. Métro: McGill.

Modavie   In the winter, set aside Friday or Saturday night for dinner with jazz at this popular Vieux-Montréal bistro-bar-lounge (p. 98); come in any night during the summer at 7pm for dinner and jazz. Bar snacks are free during happy hour and single-malt scotches and cigars are at the ready. Music is usually mainstream jazz, by trios. It's a friendly place, and the food is good, too. 1 rue St-Paul ouest (corner of rue St-Laurent). ℂ 514/287-9582. Métro: Place d'Armes.

Upstairs   Name aside, the club is *down* a few steps from the street. Big names are infrequent, but the jazz groups appearing 5 nights a week are more than competent. Performances most weeks are Tuesday through Saturday. Decor is largely vintage record album covers and fish tanks. Pretty good food ranges from bar snacks to more substantial meals, including table d'hôte offerings. Most patrons are edging toward their middle years or are already there. 1254 rue Mackay (near rue Ste-Catherine). ℂ 514/931-6808. Cover C$10 (US$8). Métro: Guy-Concordia.

3 The Bar & Cafe Scene

An abundance of restaurants, bars, and cafes line the streets near the downtown commercial district, from rue Stanley to rue Guy between rue Ste-Catherine and boulevard de Maisonneuve. **Rue Crescent,** in particular, hums with activity from late afternoon until far into the evening, especially after 10pm on cool summer weekend nights, when the street swarms with people careening from bar to restaurant to club. **Boulevard St-Laurent,** or The Main, as it's known, is another nightlife strip, abounding in bars and clubs, most with a distinctive European—particularly French—personality, as opposed to the Anglo flavor of the rue Crescent area. **Rue St-Paul,** west of place Jacques-Cartier in Vieux-Montréal, falls somewhere in the middle on the Anglophone-Francophone spectrum. In all cases, bars tend to open around 11:30am and stay open late. Many of them have *heures joyeuses* (happy hours) from as early as 3pm to as late as 9pm, but usually for a shorter period within those hours. At those times, two-for-one drinks are the rule. Otherwise, given the high taxes on alcoholic beverages, the beverage of choice is most often beer. Look for a sign reading BIERES EN FUT—beer on draft. Last call for orders is 3am, but patrons are often allowed to dawdle over those drinks until 4am.

DOWNTOWN/RUE CRESCENT

Le Cabaret   Within sight of the trademark lobby fountain with its nude bronze sprite sporting stained-glass wings, this appealing piano bar draws a crowd of youngish to middle-aged professionals after 5:30pm. In summer the hotel opens the terrace bar on the roof by the pool. In L'Hôtel de la Montagne, 1430 rue de la Montagne (north of rue Ste-Catherine). ℂ 514/288-5656. Métro: Guy-Concordia.

Le Tour de Ville   Memorable. Breathtaking. The view, that is, from Montréal's only revolving restaurant and bar (the bar doesn't revolve, but you still get a great view). The best time to go is when the sun is setting and the city lights are beginning to blink on. In the bar, one floor down from the restaurant, the same wonderful vistas are visible from the dance floor, which has a band Thursday through Saturday 9pm to 1 or 2am. There's no cover, but drinks range from C$6 to C$12 (US$4.80–US$9.60). Eat somewhere else. In the Delta Centre-Ville Hôtel, 777 rue University. ℂ 514/879-1370. Métro: Square Victoria.

Ritz Bar   A mature, prosperous crowd seeks out the quiet Ritz Bar in the Ritz-Carlton, adjacent to the semilegendary Café de Paris restaurant. Anyone can take advantage of the tranquil room and the professionalism of its staff, but because the atmosphere is rather formal, most men will be more at ease with a jacket. Piano music flutters softly around conversation during cocktail hour Monday through Friday 5 to 8pm and at dinnertime (5–11pm) from September to mid-May. The bar is just off the hotel lobby, to the right. In the Ritz-Carlton Hôtel, 1228 rue Sherbrooke ouest (at rue Drummond). ℂ 514/842-4212. Métro: Peel.

Sir Winston Churchill Pub   The three levels of bars and cafes incorporated in the Sir Winston Churchill Pub are rue Crescent landmarks. One reason is the sidewalk terrace (open in summer and enclosed in winter), which makes a perfect vantage point for checking out the pedestrian traffic. Inside and down the stairs, the pub, with English ales on tap, attempts to imitate a British public house. The burgers and such have to look up to see mediocrity. A mixed crowd of questing young professionals mills around a total of 17 bars and two dance floors. Winnie, on the second floor, is a restaurant with a terrace of its own. Open daily noon to 2am. During the 5 to 8pm happy hour, drinks are two for one. 1459 rue Crescent (near rue Ste-Catherine). ℂ 514/288-0623. Métro: Guy-Concordia.

Thursday's   This is a prime watering hole for Montréal's young professional set—especially those who are ever alert for possibilities of companionship. The pubby bar spills out onto a terrace that hangs over the street, and there's a glittery disco in back. Both the bar and the disco are in L'Hôtel de la Montagne. Thursday's presumably takes its name from the Montréal custom of prowling nightspots on Thursday evening in search of the perfect date for the weekend. In L'Hôtel de la Montagne, 1430 rue de la Montagne (north of rue Ste-Catherine). ℂ 514/288-5656. Métro: Guy-Concordia.

VIEUX MONTREAL

Cluny ArtBar   The loft and factory district west of avenue McGill, at the edge of Vieux-Montréal, is showing signs of rebirth. Artists are moving in, although only empty buildings, galleries, offbeat enterprises, and possibly illegal living spaces are much in evidence. Among the pioneers is the Quartier Éphémère, a large exhibition space that occupies a partially converted former foundry. Room is provided for Cluny, which puts on parties for exhibition openings in the adjacent gallery. The rest of the time, Cluny serves antipasti, sandwiches like tuna melts and smoked salmon *panini*, and, on Thursday and Friday nights, light dinners. These are frequently underscored by the sometimes-deafening sound system, which is lowered on request. 257 rue Prince (near rue Ottawa). ℂ 514/866-1213. Métro: Square Victoria.

Le Jardin Nelson   Near the foot of place Jacques Cartier, a passage leads into a tree-shaded garden court in back of a stone building dating from 1812. A pleasant hour or two can be spent attending to jazz most nights and weekend afternoons. Classical chamber groups perform Monday to Friday during lunch hours in the warm-weather months. Food takes second place, but the kitchen does well with its pizzas and crepes, the latter with both sweet and savory fillings (including lobster). There's a covered people-watching porch in front (with effective heat lamps in cold weather), and dining rooms and a bar inside. Closed December through March. 407 place Jacques-Cartier (at rue St-Paul). ℂ 514/861-5731. Métro: Place d'Armes or Champ de Mars.

PLATEAU MONT-ROYAL

Champs   Montréalers are no less enthusiastic about sports, especially hockey, than other Canadians, and fans both avid and casual drop by this three-story sports emporium to catch up with their teams and hoist a few. Games from around the world are fed to 35 TV monitors through 20 satellites, so they don't miss a goal, run, or TD. Food is what you expect—burgers, steaks, and such. 3956 bd. St-Laurent (near rue Duluth). ℂ 514/987-6444. Métro: Mont-Royal.

Korova   There was a J. Lo look-alike behind the bar when we last stopped by. She made up for the trudge up the grungy staircase to the second floor. A dragonhead overlooks the fully stocked bar, although the drinks most ordered are beer by the pitcher (C$12/US$9.60) or pint (C$4.75/US$3.80). An acoustic jam occupies Tuesday nights, and ladies get two-for-one drinks Fridays. There's usually a DJ, and foosball and a pool table are at the ready. 3908 bd. St-Laurent (near rue Duluth). ℂ 514/848-0343. Métro: Mont-Royal.

Laïka   Amidst the plethora of St-Laurent watering stops, this bright little boîte stands out for its open front in summer and the fresh flowers on the bar and some of the tables. Tasty sandwiches and tapas are served, and the Sunday brunch is popular. The DJ spins house and funk from 8pm to 3am for the mostly 18- to 35-year-old crowd. Drinks range from C$4 to C$9 (US$3.20–US$7.20). 4040 bd. St-Laurent (near rue Duluth). ℂ 514/842-8088. Métro: Mont-Royal.

Le Bifteck   Even on the most dismal of Mondays, this place jumps, with a roistering grunge crowd aging from barely legal to early 30s. Most of them quaff beer by the pitcher, but attention is also given to shooters, including such tasteful evergreens as Kamikazi and Windex. Despite the name, food isn't served, apart from popcorn. The front opens on warm nights, the bar is in the middle, and foosball and two pool tables take up space in back. The second floor is opened Wednesday through Saturday to accommodate the overflow. 3702 bd. St-Laurent (near rue Prince Arthur). ✆ **514/844-6211.** Métro: Guy Concordia.

Le Pistol   Get here early, because this newcomer on The Main gets packed in no time. There are ample attractions: a high-definition plasma TV to follow hockey and the occasional alternative sports event. A kitchen that assembles some tasty salads and unusual sandwiches, several of which are named for Bond flicks—Goldfinger, Moonraker. A stereo system moves from jazz to house to rock. The ground-floor front is thrown open in decent weather. Drinks and eats are mostly in the C$5 to C$9 (US$4–US$7.20) range. 3723 bd. St-Laurent (near rue Prince Arthur). ✆ **514/847-2222.** Métro: Sherbrooke.

Oasis Oxygène   As New Age-y as all get-out, this unclassifiable . . . refuge . . . is neither bar nor nightclub. The activities here include receiving massages in chairs and inhaling purified oxygen, simultaneously usually. While you wait, there are fruit drinks, nonstandard sandwiches, and fresh salads. The starship interior has pussy willows in vats of blue water. Prices for oxygen therapy run from C$10 (US$8) for 10 minutes to C$18 (US$14) for 20 minutes, while massages are C$24 (US$19) for 20 minutes and C$46 (US$37) for 40 minutes. They're open Tuesday through Friday from 11am to 9pm and Saturday and Sunday from 9am to 6pm. 4059 bd. St-Laurent (near rue Duluth). ✆ **514/284-1196.** Métro: Mont-Royal.

Shed Café   This bar/restaurant, in a lively stretch of The Main near rue Sherbrooke, used to look as if the ceiling was caving in. Now it's been transformed into a Gothic dungeon hangout, and it's not a whit less frenetically popular. There are local *bieres en fût* as well as good fries and oversize portions of cake. The crowd skews young, but with enough diversity to make an hour or two interesting. 3515 bd. St-Laurent (north of rue Sherbrooke). ✆ **514/842-0220.** Métro: Sherbrooke.

MILE END

Mile End Bar   Walk into this designer bar before 10pm and you might be drinking in scant company. While food isn't its *raison d'etre,* there's a compact menu of nibbles categorized as tapas, pinchos (skewered tapas), and *amuses gueles.* Tasting plates of tapas, including meats, seafood, and vegetarian items, can constitute light meals, priced from C$25 to C$35 (US$20–US$28). Such eating happens between 5 and 10pm, which is when the three floors really start to fill up. A DJ works the crowd into a lather on Thursday through Saturday nights. Closed Sunday and Monday. 5322 bd. St-Laurent (north of rue Labadie). ✆ **514/279-0200.** Métro: Laurier.

Whisky Café   Those who enjoy scotch, particularly single-malts like Laphraoig and Glenfiddich, will find dozens of different labels to sample here. Trouble is, the Québec government applies stiff taxes for the privilege, so many of the patrons (suits to grad students) seem to stick to beer. The decor is sophisticated, with exposed beams and vents, handmade tiled tables, and large wood-enclosed columns, but the real decorative triumph is the men's urinal, with a waterfall acting as the *pissoir.* Women are welcome to have a look. The bar opens at 5pm most evenings. 5800 bd. St-Laurent (at rue Bernard). ✆ **514/278-2646.** Métro: Outremont.

QUARTIER LATIN

Jello Bar   Lava lamps and other fixtures make it look like the rumpus room of a suburban ranch house in the 1960s, but central to the rep of this goofy throwback is the menu of more than 50 kinds of martinis. Most are flavored excuses for people who don't really like liquor, but the classic gin and vodka versions are stalwarts to be savored. Live music—groove, swing, salsa—usually played on Tuesday, Wednesday, Friday, and Saturday, helps fuel dancing and the rollicking good mood that pervades the bar. Other times, there's a DJ. 151 rue Ontario est (near bd. St-Laurent). © 514/285-2621. Métro: St-Laurent or Berri-UQAM.

4 The Gay & Lesbian Scene

The city's lively **Quartier Gai (Gay Village)** comprises a stretch of rue Ste-Catherine from rue St-Hubert to rue Papineau. One of the largest gay and lesbian communities in North America, it is action central for both natives and visitors, especially during such annual events as the 10 days celebrating sexual diversity known as **Divers/Cité** in late July and early August (www.diverscite.org). Much excitement has attended the announcement that Montréal will host the **1st World Outgames** in 2006 (www. montreal2006.org). The gay games are expected to attract more than 16,000 athletes from more than 100 countries. Already established is the **Black & Blue Festival** (www.bbcm.org), probably the world's largest circuit party, a 6-day event involving extended entertainments, dancing to music spun by circuit DJs, and featuring shows by often big-name performers.

Tourisme Québec has launched the website, www.bonjourquebec.com/anglais/ idees_vac. Select "Gay-Friendly Québec" for information and resources of interest to gay and lesbian travelers. In addition, the **Québec Gay Chamber of Commerce** has a website at www.tourismegai.com. Of several targeted local publications, the most useful magazine is *Fugues,* describing current and future events as well as listing gay-friendly lodgings, clubs, saunas, and other resources. Get a copy at the tourist office (© 514/522-1885) opposite the Beaudry Métro station, or check www.fugues.com.

Area   While this is at the edge of the Gay Village, it doesn't have a particularly gay identity, nor is it a club or disco, as are the establishments described below. But it is arguably the best restaurant in the neighborhood and ranks well in the entire city. The chef-proprietor deftly manipulates techniques and ingredients found in a couple dozen countries around the Pacific and Mediterranean rims, in precociously assured concoctions that challenge taste assumptions. He changes his menu every couple of months; be assured that convention will be disregarded. There are two seatings nightly, the times varying according to demand and time of the year. It's open every night for dinner, Tuesday through Friday for lunch. Reservations are recommended. 1429 rue Amherst (north of rue Ste-Catherine). © 514/890-6691. Métro: Beaudry.

Club Chez Mado   Relatively new on the Village scene, this determinedly trendy place has both cabaret performances and dancing to DJ tracks. Every night of the week has a different theme, from Monday's karaoke and Wednesday's variety shows to Thursday's live dancers and Friday and Saturday's drag shows. Check ahead to see what's on. Happy hour is from 4 to 9pm. 1115 rue Ste-Catherine est (near rue Amherst). © 514/525-7566. Cover up to C$5 (US$4) on weekends. Métro: Beaudry.

Complexe Bourbon   Stop early in the evening at this block-long, block-wide compound, billed as "the largest gay complex in the world," and you might never get to the Village's other attractions. Open 24 hours, it incorporates a 37-room hotel, a sauna, Le Zone disco, a theater, a wedding chapel, an ice-cream parlor, and several bars and restaurants. One of the latter is the 24-hour Le Club Sandwich, a hyperventilating take on a 1950s diner with lots of neon and glass block. The signature edibles are huge, with slabs of bread as thick as a couple of fingers and fillings just as thick. The large terrace is a prominent Village gathering place. Rooms in the Hôtel Bourbon cost from C$95 to C$230 (US$76–US$184), depending on the season. 1574 rue Ste-Catherine est (at rue Plessis). ✆ 514/523-4679. Métro: Papineau.

Le Drugstore Both men and women can find their respective comfort zones in one of eight bars in this multilevel complex. There are cafes, restaurants, and shops, too, as well as pool tables and video games to pique meeting and greeting. In size and diversity of attractions, it rivals even Unity II and Sky Club & Pub (below) in popularity. 1360 rue St-Catherine est (near rue Beaudry). ✆ 514/524-1960. Métro: Beaudry.

Le Parking Open Wenesday through Sunday, the first 2 nights of the week invite a mix of gay men and women as well as bi and trans-genders. With a notable sound-and-light system and DJ tracks, dancing ensues, mostly to hip-hop and house. Friday and Saturday are for male-only cruising, except for "Femme Fridays" in the Traffic Lounge. Special themes often apply—obligatory leather and such—so it's a good idea to call ahead for a heads-up. 1296 rue Amherst (north of rue Ste-Catherine). ✆ 514/522-2766. Métro: Beaudry.

Sauna Centre-Ville Handily located just across the street from the Sky Club, here's a place to either chill out after a hot evening or continue the action in a more intimate setting. There are 60 rooms on two levels, all with TV and mirrors, and both saunas and steam rooms, as well as a snack bar. Their dress code stipulates that "less is more." 1465 Ste-Catherine est (between rue Beaudry and ave. Papineau). ✆ 514/524-3486. Métro: Papineau.

Sky Club & Pub Thought by many to be the city's best gay club, Sky continues to thrive after its expensive recent renovations. Spiffy decor and pounding (usually house) music in the upstairs disco contribute to the popularity. Up to six transvestite performers present a cabaret show Friday and Saturday nights. Also on the second floor is a male strip club called Nirvana. On the third floor is a spacious disco. In addition to a restaurant, which serves dinner Monday through Saturday and brunch on weekends, there are an outdoor terrace and frequent two-for-one beer hours. 1474 rue Ste-Catherine est (near rue Amherst). ✆ 514/529-6969. Métro: Beaudry.

Stéréo One of a growing number of after-hours clubs, this hyper-hip disco doesn't crank up the jaw-dropping sound system until 2am. If you remember Richard Nixon, you'll feel like grandpa in this crowd, which stays on until dawn and beyond. 858 rue Ste-Catherine est (near rue Berri). No phone. Métro: Berri-UQAM.

Unity II Yet another three-floor mega-club and one of the biggest discos in town, this hotter-than-hot club draws mixed crowds Wednesday through Saturday. A rotating roster of DJs kicks things into gear each night from 10pm, pulling from libraries of everything from house to dance pop. Nightly entertainment includes karaoke and drag shows. Things keep rolling past the usual closing. 1500 rue Montcalm (north of Ste-Catherine). ✆ 514/523-2777. Métro: Beaudry.

5 More Entertainment

CINEMA

In Montréal, English-language films are usually presented with subtitles in French. However, when the initials "VF" (for *version française*) follow the title of a non-Francophone movie, it means that the movie has been dubbed into French. Policies vary on English subtitles on non–English-language films—the best idea is to ask at the box office. Besides the many first-run movie houses that advertise in the daily newspapers, Montréal is rich in "ciné-clubs," which tend to be slightly older and show second-run, foreign, and art films at reduced prices.

In first-run movie houses, admission is usually about C$10 (US$8) for adults in the evening, C$6 or C$7 (US$4.80 or US$5.60) for adults on some afternoons (usually Tues and Wed). The **Centre Eaton,** 705 rue Ste-Catherine ouest, near the corner of rue McGill, has a multiplex cinema with six modern theaters.

Foreign-language and independent films are the menu at **Ex-Centris,** 3536 bd. St-Laurent (© 514/847-2206; www.ex-centris.com), and the architectural surroundings are at least as interesting—sort of a post–machine-age spaceship. A hip bar-cafe is also on the premises. The films are in English about half the time. Call and ask. Similar fare, without the jazzy setting, is presented at the repertory **Cinéma du Parc,** 3575 av. du Parc (© **514/281-1900;** www.cinemaduparc.com). It has three screens. The **National Film Board of Canada (Cinema ONF),** 1564 rue St-Denis (© **514/496-6887**), shows Canadian and international films, primarily in English and French, particularly classics. Shows are Tuesday through Sunday; call for times.

Imposing, sometimes visually disorienting images confront viewers of the seven-story screen in the **IMAX theater** in the Interactive Science Centre in the Vieux-Port (Old Port; © **514/496-4629**), and at **Imax Paramount Montréal,** 977 rue Ste-Catherine (© **514/842-5828**). Efforts are made to create IMAX films suitable for the entire family. See "Especially for Kids," in chapter 7, for more details.

GAMBLING

The **Casino de Montréal** (© **800/665-2274** or 514/392-2746; www.casino-de-montreal.com), Québec's first, is in the former French Pavilion, left over from the 1967 Expo World's Fair, on Ile Notre-Dame. The adjacent Québec Pavilion was incorporated into the complex in 1996. Several floors contain more than 120 game tables, including roulette, craps, blackjack, and baccarat, and more than 3,000 slot machines. Its four restaurants get good reviews, especially **Nuances** (p. 105). There are also four bars and live shows. No alcoholic beverages are served in the gambling areas. Patrons must be 18 or over. The casino is open around the clock. Tickets to the cabaret can be purchased at the casino or on the Internet at **www.admission.com**. They are priced from C$39 (US$31) for the show alone, or from C$65 (US$52) for the show and dinner. The originally strict dress code has been relaxed somewhat, but the following items of clothing are still prohibited: "cut-off sweaters and shirts, tank tops, jogging outfits, cut-off shorts and bike shorts, beachwear, work or motorcycle boots, and clothing associated with violence or with an organization known to be violent." To get to the casino, take the Métro to the Île Ste-Hélène stop, which is adjacent to Île Notre-Dame, and walk or take the shuttle bus from there. There's also an hourly shuttle bus *(navette)* from the Infotouriste Centre at 1001 rue du Square-Dorchester.

11

Side Trips from Montréal

For respite from urban stresses and demands, Montrealers need only drive 30 minutes or so to the north or east of the city to find themselves in the hearts of the resort regions of the Laurentides or the Cantons-de-l'Est. The lakes and mountains of both areas have invited development of year-round vacation retreats and ski centers. The pearl of the Laurentides is Mont-Tremblant, the highest peak in eastern Canada, but the region has 18 other ski centers with scores of trails at every level of difficulty, many of them less than an hour from Montréal.

The bucolic Cantons-de-l'Est, known as the Eastern Townships when it was a haven for English Loyalists and their descendants, is blessed with a trio of memorable country inns on beautiful Lake Massawippi. The region promotes four seasons of outdoor diversions. Many of the same trails and settings developed for winter sports are used for parallel activities in summer. Bromont, for example, has 100km (62 miles) of marked trails for mountain biking, and Mont-Orford Park is the focal point for another 160km (99 miles) of hiking trails linking six regional parks. Rock climbing, white-water kayaking, sailing, and fishing are additional options. Appropriate equipment is readily available for rent on-site, wilderness shelters and trail cabins are at hand, and even meals can be catered in the woods. So, though it has fewer ski centers than the Laurentides, and the resort hotels that serve them are generally smaller and less extensive in their facilities, the Cantons-de-l'Est's many lakes and year-round pastimes give it the edge for warm-weather vacations.

Because the people of both regions rely heavily on tourism for their livelihoods, knowledge of at least rudimentary English is widespread, even outside such obvious places as hotels and ski resorts.

1 North into the Laurentians (Laurentides)

55–129km (34–80 miles) N of Montréal

Don't expect spiked peaks or high ragged ridges. The rolling hills and rounded mountains of the Laurentian Shield are among the oldest in the world, worn down by wind and water over eons. They average between 300m and 520m (984 ft. and 1,706 ft.) in height, with the highest being Mont-Tremblant, at 968m (3,175 ft.). In the lower area, nearer to Montréal, the terrain resembles a rumpled quilt, its folds and hollows cupping a multitude of lakes large and small. Farther north the summits are higher and craggier, with patches of snow persisting well into spring, but these are still not the Alps or the Rockies. They're welcoming and embracing rather than awe-inspiring.

Half a century ago the first ski schools, rope tows, and trails began to appear. Today there are 19 ski centers within a 40-mile radius, and cross-country skiing has as enthusiastic a following as downhill. The best cross-country trails are at Far Hills in Val-Morin, at L'Esterel in Ville d'Esterel, and on the grounds of a monastery called

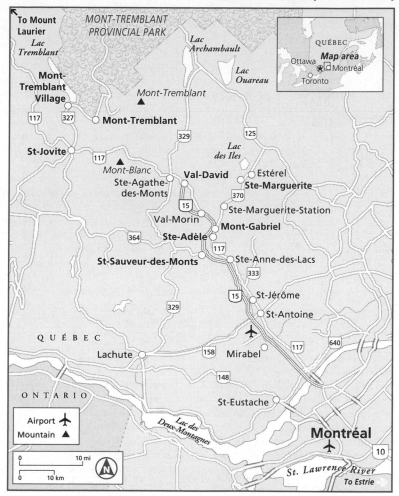

Domaine du St-Bernard near Villa Bellevue in Mont-Tremblant. Sprawling resorts and modest lodges and inns are packed in winter with skiers, some of them through April. Trails for advanced skiers typically have short pitches and challenging moguls, with broad, hard-packed avenues for beginners and the less experienced.

But skiing is only half the story. As transportation improved, people took advantage of the obvious opportunities for watersports, golf (courses in the area now total over 30), tennis, mountain biking, hiking, and every other kind of summer sport. Before long, the region had gained a sometimes-deserved reputation for fine dining and a convivial atmosphere that survives to this day. Bird-watchers of both intense and casual bent are fully occupied. Loon lovers, in particular, know that the lakes of Québec province's mountains are home to an estimated 16,000 of the native water-fowl that gives its name to the dollar coin. Excellent divers and swimmers, the birds are unable to walk on land, which makes nesting a trial. They're identified by a distinctive call that might be described as an extended mournful giggle.

At any time of the year, a visit to any of the villages and resorts in the Laurentians is likely to yield pleasant memories. The busiest times are in February and March, in July and August, and during the Christmas to New Year holiday period. Other times of the year, reservations are easier to get, prices of virtually everything are lower, and crowds are less dense. May and September are often characterized by warm days, cool nights, and just enough people that the streets don't seem deserted. In May and June, it must be said, the indigenous black flies and mosquitoes can seem as big and as ill-tempered as buzzards, so be prepared for them. Some of the resorts, inns, and lodges close down for a couple of weeks in the spring and the fall; a handful are open only for a few winter months.

March and April are the months when the maple trees are tapped, and *cabanes à sucre* ("sugar shacks") open up everywhere, some selling only maple candies and syrup, others serving full meals featuring the principal product and even staging entertainment.

July and August bring glorious summer days to the Laurentians, and during the last 2 weeks in September the leaves put on a stunning show of autumnal color. Skiers can usually expect reliable snow from early December to mid-April.

As for prices, they can be difficult to pin down: The large resorts have so many types of rooms, suites, cottages, meal plans, discounts, and packages that you may need a travel agent to pick through the thicket of options. In planning, remember that Montrealers fill the highways when they "go up north" on weekends, particularly during the top skiing months of February and March, so plan ahead when making reservations. An unfortunate note for pet owners: Few Laurentian resorts accept animals.

ESSENTIALS
GETTING THERE
BY CAR   The fast and scenic Autoroute des Laurentides, also known as Autoroute 15, goes straight from Montréal to the Laurentian mountains. Just follow the signs to St-Jérôme. The exit numbers are actually the distance in kilometers that the village is from Montréal. Although the pace of development is quickening, crowding the highway with water parks, condos, and chain restaurants, this is still a pretty drive, once you're out of the clutches of the tangle of expressways surrounding Montréal. The Autoroute des Laurentides gives a sweeping, panoramic introduction to the area, from the rolling hills and forests of the lower Laurentians to the mountain drama of the upper Laurentians.

Those with the time to meander can exit at St-Jérôme and pick up the older, parallel Route 117, which plays tag with the autoroute all the way to Ste-Agathe-des-Monts, where the autoroute ends. Most of the region's more appealing towns are strung along or near Route 117. Approaching each town, signs direct drivers to the local tourism information office, where attendants provide helpful tips on lodging, restaurants, and things to do. North of Ste-Agathe, the autoroute ends and Route 117 becomes the major artery for the region, continuing deep into Québec's north country and finally ending at the Ontario border hundreds of miles from Montréal.

Québec's equivalent of the Highway Patrol maintains a presence along the stretch of Autoroute 15 between St-Faustin and Ste-Adèle. While enforcement of speed limits is loose, if you are pulled over, remember that radar detectors are illegal in the province (even if they're not turned on) and can be confiscated.

BY BUS   **Limocar Laurentides** buses depart Montréal's **Terminus Voyageur,** 505 bd. de Maisonneuve est, stopping in the larger Laurentian towns, including Ste-Agathe, Ste-Adèle, St-Jovite, and Mont-Tremblant; call ℂ **514/842-2281** or 450/435-6767 or check www.limocar.ca for schedules. An express bus can make the run to St-Jovite and Mont-Tremblant in less than 2 hours, while a local bus, making all the stops, takes almost 3 hours. From Montréal to Ste-Adèle takes about 1½ hours, 15 minutes more to Val-Morin and Val-David. Some of the major resorts provide their own bus service from Montréal at an additional charge, so ask when booking.

BY LIMOUSINE   Taxis and limousines await arrivals at Trudeau Airport in Montréal, where all domestic and international commercial flights arrive, and will take you to any Laurentian hideaway—for a price. While the fare for the 1-hour trip by limo from Trudeau is steep, four or five people can share the cost and lessen the pain. Ask for the standard fare to your inn or lodge when calling to make accommodation reservations. The inn will usually take responsibility for seeing that a taxi or limo is waiting at the airport and may even help to find other guests arriving at the same time to share the cost.

VISITOR INFORMATION

For an orientation to the entire region, stop at **La Maison du Tourisme des Laurentides,** La Porte du Nord (ℂ **450/224-700**), a regional tourist information office located at Exit 51 off Autoroute 15. It shares a building with a McDonald's restaurant, and there is a gas station next door. In addition to its racks of helpful brochures, the staff can make reservations for lodging throughout the Laurentides, and the service is free. It's open daily June 24 to Labor Day from 8:30am to 5pm (until 6 Fri), with shorter hours the rest of the year. For information about the entire region, log on to **www.laurentides.com.**

ST-SAUVEUR & ST-SAUVEUR-DES-MONTS

Only 60km (37 miles) north of Montréal, the adjacent villages of St-Sauveur and St-Sauveur-des-Monts (pop. 5,864) can easily be visited on a day trip. The village square is dominated by a handsome church, and the streets around it bustle with activity much of the year; so be prepared to have difficulty finding a parking place in season (try the large lot behind the church). Dining and snacking on everything from crepes to hot dogs are big activities here, evidenced by the many beckoning cafes. In season, there's a tourist kiosk on the square.

The area is well-known for its night skiing—23 well-lit trails, only 3 fewer than those available during the day. The mountain is wide, with a 213m (700-ft.) vertical drop and a variety of well-groomed trails, making it a good choice for families. In summer, the **Parc Aquatique du Mont St-Sauveur,** 350 rue St-Denis (ℂ **800/363-2426** or 450/227-4671; www.montsaintsauveur.com), Canada's largest water park, features rafting, a wave pool, a "tidal wave" river, and slides, including a mountain slide where you go up in chairlifts and ride down the slide in tubes. Ten days in late July and early August are dedicated to the annual **Festival des Arts** (ℂ **450/227-0427;** www.artssaintsauveur.com), with an emphasis on music and dance, including jazz and chamber concerts and ballet troupes as celebrated as the Kirov Ballet and the José Greco Flamenco Group.

The **tourist information office** serving the area is located at Exit 60 of Autoroute 15, at 605 chemin des Frênes, Piedmont, PQ J0R 1K0 (ℂ **450/227-3417;** www.tourismepdh.org), and is open year-round daily from 9am to 5pm, with longer hours in summer. There is also a seasonal booth (☎ **450/227-2564**) in St-Sauveur in the park in front of the church.

WHERE TO STAY & DINE

If the idea of a picnic appeals—and in this town of ordinary restaurants, it well might—drive west on the main street to **Chez Bernard,** 411 rue Principale (☎ **450/240-0000**). Inside the pretty little house behind the iron fence, you'll find a store selling fragrant cheeses, crusty breads, wines, savory tarts, pâtés, sausages, smoked meats, and a variety of prepared meals. Prices range from about C$4 to C$15 (US$3.20–US$12). The store opens daily at 11am.

Manoir Saint-Sauveur   This is one of the region's several large resort hotels, with a monster outdoor pool and a comprehensive roster of four-season activities. Racquetball, squash, and in-house movies are among the offerings. Rooms are spacious and comfortable, blandly modern with light-wood furnishings that hint vaguely of 19th-century Gallic inspirations. Units in the condo section have kitchenettes. The main building, with its green roof and many dormers, is easily spotted from the road. The front desk adjusts room prices up or down according to season, demand, and the occupancy rate on any given night, so ask if they have anything cheaper when you book or arrive. The hotel cuts 10% off the rack rates if you book online.

246 chemin du Lac-Millette, St-Sauveur-des-Monts, PQ J0R 1R3. ☎ **800/361-0505** or 450/227-1811. Fax 450/227-8512. www.manoir-saint-sauveur.com. 300 units. C$219–C$289 (US$175–US$231) double; from C$289 (US$231) suite. Children 17 and under stay free in parent's room. Packages available. AE, DC, MC, V. Take Exit 60 off Autoroute 15. **Amenities:** Restaurant (Continental); bar; large indoor and outdoor pools; golf nearby; tennis courts (2 lit for night play); substantial health club w/Jacuzzi and sauna; limited room service; massage; babysitting; laundry service; same-day dry cleaning. *In room:* A/C, TV, dataport, minibar, coffeemaker, hair dryer.

MONT-GABRIEL

Mont-Gabriel is only 4km (2½ miles) from St-Sauveur. To get there, follow Autoroute 15 to Exit 64 and turn right at the stop sign. Although popular in summer, Mont-Gabriel comes into its own each winter when guests schuss down its 21 trails and slopes and then slide back up again on the seven T-bar lifts, the triple-chair, or the quadruple-chair lift. Eight trails are lit for night skiing. Cross-country trails wrap the mountain and range through the surrounding countryside.

Mont-Gabriel ☆ *(Kids*   Perched high above the highways and the valley, and looking like the rambling log "cottages" of the turn-of-the-20th-century wealthy, this desirable, kid-friendly resort is only 32km (20 miles) from Montréal's Trudeau Airport. Set on a 480-hectare (1,186-acre) forest estate, the resort complex features golf and tennis programs in summer and ski packages in winter. The spacious rooms in the Tyrol section are the most desirable and modern, many with views of the surrounding hills. Those called Rustique are constructed of logs and have views of either the pool or the mountains. Some units have fireplaces and/or whirlpool tubs. With the Club Package come three meals and unlimited access to all sports facilities, and prices include tax and service charge. Rates drop for stays of 2 to 5 nights. Meals are served poolside as well as in the resort's dining rooms.

1699 chemin Montée Gabriel, PQ J8B 1A5. ☎ **450/229-3547,** 514/861-2852 in Montréal, or 800/668-5253 in Canada. Fax 450/229-7034. www.montgabriel.com. 129 units. C$96–C$276 (US$77–US$221) double. Meal plans and packages available. Children under 16 stay free in parent's room. AE, DC, MC, V. Take Exit 64 from Autoroute 15. **Amenities:** Restaurant (Continental); bar; heated indoor and outdoor pools; 18-hole golf course; 6 night-lit tennis courts; exercise room; spa; Jacuzzi; sauna; children's programs; small business center; massage; babysitting. *In room:* A/C, TV, dataport, coffeemaker, hair dryer.

Tips **On the Road**

Canada is on the metric system, so distances are measured in kilometers (1 kilometer = .62 miles). Many American cars have a secondary speedometer that gives speed in kilometers. The maximum posted speed limit on most highways is 100kmph (62 mph). Few drivers observe it.

At service stations, *AVEC SERVICE* means FULL SERVICE, and *LIBRE SERVICE* means SELF SERVICE. The directions on the pump are usually only in French, but educated guesses will probably get you through the menu without too much trouble. Gas is sold by the liter, and 3.78 liters equals 1 gallon, 37.85 liters equals 10 gallons, and 56.78 liters equals 15 gallons.

Road signs are always in French, only sometimes in English as well. *ARRET* means STOP, while *CONTRÔLE RADAR* means what you think. Those mysterious green-and-white signs declaring only CLSC refer to the presence nearby of a *Centre locale de services communautaires,* or Local Center of Community Services, where you can go for assistance with any problems on the road.

STE-ADELE

Route 117 swings directly into Ste-Adèle to become its main street, boulevard Ste-Adèle; if you're on Autoroute 15 north take Exit 67. The village (pop. 9,710), only 67km (42 miles) north of Montréal, is a near-metropolis compared to the other Laurentian villages that line the upper reaches of Route 117. What makes it seem big are its services: police, doctors, ambulances, a shopping center, cinemas, art galleries, and a larger collection of places to stay and dine than is found elsewhere in the Laurentians. As rue Morin mounts the hill to Lac Rond, Ste-Adèle's resort lake, it's easy to see why the town is divided into a lower part *(en bas)* and an upper part *(en haut).*

EXPLORING STE-ADELE

The main street of Ste-Adèle, **rue Valiquette,** is a busy one-way thoroughfare lined with cafes, galleries, and bakeries, but **Lac Rond** is the center of activities during the Ste-Adèle summer. Canoes, sailboats, and *pédalos* (pedal-powered watercraft), rented from several docks, glide over the placid surface, while swimmers splash and play near shoreside beaches.

In winter the surrounding green hills are swathed in white, and the **ski trails** descend to the shores of the frozen lake. Downhill ski equipment can be rented and lessons obtained at **Le Chantecler** resort (see below), which has 22 trails served by six chairlifts and two T-bars. Some of the trails end right by the main hotel. At the town's **Centre Municipal,** Côtes 40/80, 1400 rue Rolland (② **450/229-2921**), the trails are good for beginners: Three T-bar lifts carry skiers up the slopes for runs down five different trails. Ste-Adèle has a **cinema** showing first-run English-language movies all year.

WHERE TO STAY & DINE

L'Eau à la Bouche ✦✦   The owners leave no doubt where their priorities lie. While the hotel is entirely satisfactory, even charming, the restaurant is their beloved baby, and it has the glowing reviews to prove its prowess (those stars up there are for the dining). False modesty isn't a factor—*l'eau à la bouche* means "mouthwatering"—and the kitchen delivers. Native ingredients and ample portions are meshed with nouvelle presentations, and the menu changes often. Full advantage is taken of seasonal products, as with one summer starter of a poached half-lobster with chanterelles and gathered wild vegetables. Game dishes arrive in fall. Desserts are impressive, but the cheese plate—pungent nubbins delivered with warm baguette slices—is truly special. Main courses are C$36 to C$48 (US$29–US$38). A meal here might well be the most memorable (and pricey) dining experience of a Laurentian visit.

The bedrooms in the hotel have reproductions of Québec country furniture, and six have fireplaces and balconies or patios. There are no elevators and no porters, but help with luggage can be obtained if necessary. The hotel faces Mont-Chantecler and its ski trails.

3003 bd. Ste-Adèle (Rte. 117), Ste-Adèle, PQ J8B 2N6. © **450/229-2991.** Fax 514/229-7573. www.leaualabouche. com. 25 units. C$165–C$245 (US$132–US$196) double; from C$270 (US$216) suite. Packages and meal plans available. AE, DC, MC, V. **Amenities:** Restaurant (Contemporary French); bar; heated outdoor pool; golf nearby; limited room service; babysitting; laundry service; dry cleaning. *In room:* A/C, TV, dataport, hair dryer, iron, safe.

WHERE TO STAY

Le Chantecler 🥾 Sprawled across steep slopes cupping Lac à la Truite, this resort is composed of several stone buildings of varying heights, its roofs bristling with steeples and dormers. It has 23 runs (13 lit at night) on four mountains for all levels of skiers, including a 190m (623-ft.) vertical drop, plus a ski school. Cross-country skiing and ice skating are available. A chalet up top has a cafeteria and bar. There's a disco in the main lodge in winter and a vast dining terrace for sunset drinks and frequent barbecues. Warm weather brings the possibilities of windsurfing and boating on the lake. The rooms have pine furniture; most have air-conditioning. Many of the suites have fireplaces, and most have Jacuzzis. A bountiful buffet breakfast is served in the glass-enclosed dining room, which overlooks the slopes and the lake, with its small beach. Recent upgrading has taken care of most of the dings and dents that routinely afflict family resorts, and new rooms have been added.

1474 chemin Chantecler, Ste-Adèle, PQ J8B 1A2. © **888/916-1616** or 450/229-3555. Fax 450/229-5593. www.le chantecler.com. 211 units. C$190–C$235 (US$152–C$188) double. Rates include breakfast. Children 17 and under stay free in parent's room. Packages and meal plans available. AE, DC, DISC, MC, V. Take Exit 67 off Autoroute 15, turn left at the 4th traffic light onto rue Morin, then turn right at the top of the hill onto chemin Chantecler. **Amenities:** Restaurant (Regional); bar; indoor pool; lake beach; 18-hole and lit 9-hole golf courses; 6 lit tennis courts; health club w/squash, racquetball, and badminton; watersports equipment; bike rental; children's programs; massage; babysitting; coin-op washers and dryers; dry cleaning. *In room:* A/C in most rooms, TV, dataport.

STE-MARGUERITE & ESTEREL

To get to Ste-Marguerite (pop. 2,250) or the less populous Estérel, only 3km (2 miles) away, follow Autoroute 15 north to Exit 69. Or if driving from Ste-Adèle, look for a street heading northeast named chemin Ste-Marguerite (Rte. 370). It becomes a narrow road that crosses the Laurentian Autoroute (at Exit 69), bridges the Rivière du Nord, and leads into an area of many lakes bordered by upscale vacation properties.

Ste-Marguerite and Estérel are 85km (53 miles) and 88km (55 miles) north of Montréal, respectively. In summer, information about the area is available from Pavillon du Parc, 74 chemin Masson, in Ste-Marguerite-du-Lac-Masson (© **514/228-3525**).

WHERE TO STAY IN ESTEREL

L'Estérel 🥾🥾 One of the more prominent Laurentian resorts lies a few miles past Ste-Marguerite in the hamlet of Estérel. This year-round complex is capable of accommodating 300 guests on its 2,000-hectare (4,940-acre) estate with three linked lakes. Occupying an expanse of otherwise vacant lakeshore, L'Estérel offers conventionally furnished rooms, many with balconies. Those with a view of the lake are more expensive.

For a special winter experience, inquire about the dogsled trips through the woods and over the frozen lake. There are 115km (71 miles) of cross-country trails, 18km (11 miles) of groomed snowshoe hiking trails, nearby downhill skiing, and ice skating on a rink; in summer, horseback riding, sailing, parasailing, and water-skiing are options. Also in summer, there is a dining terrace with a barbecue menu.

39 bd. Fridolin-Simard, Ville d'Estérel, PQ J0T 1E0. © 888/378-3735 or 450/228-2571. Fax 450/228-4977. www. esterel.com. 124 units. C$210–C$260 (US$168–US$208) double, including full breakfast and dinner and use of most facilities. Lower rates Dec–May. Discounts for stays of 3 or more nights. Packages available. AE, DC, MC, V. Take the Limocar bus from Montréal into Ste-Adèle; the hotel picks up guests there. **Amenities:** Restaurant (Eclectic); coffee shop; bar; heated indoor pool; golf; 7 tennis courts; spa; Jacuzzi; sauna; watersports equipment; bike rental; children's programs (summer); concierge; small business center; limited room service; babysitting; laundry service. In room: A/C, TV w/pay movies, coffeemaker.

WHERE TO DINE IN STE-MARGUERITE

Le Bistro à Champlain ☞☞ FRENCH   On the shore of Lac Masson is one of the most honored restaurants in the Laurentians. Its 1864 building used to be a general store, and it retains the exposed beams and cash register. Abstract paintings and prints, some of them by prominent artists, adorn the rough-hewn board walls. The 35,000-bottle cellar is the reason that many people make gastronomic pilgrimages here from Montréal. In fact, it can be fairly said that the tail wags the dog—this is a place to have some food with your wine. The wine list is as thick as the A–D volume of an encyclopedia, and everyone is invited to visit the cellar. An unusually large number of wines can be sampled by the glass, including a 2-ounce pour of Château d'Yquem with a serving of seared duck foie gras (C$82/US$66). Waiters are ready and equipped to discuss even the humblest bottles at length. It must be said, though, that recent visits suggest that the kitchen places greater emphasis on presentation than taste.

75 chemin Masson. © 450/228-4988. Reservations recommended. Main courses C$22–C$46 (US$18–US$37); table d'hôte C$42 (US$34); menu degustation C$79 (US$63). AE, DC, MC, V. Summer daily 6–10pm, Sun noon–10pm; rest of year Wed–Sun 6–10pm.

VAL-DAVID

Follow Route 117 north to reach Val-David. To those who know it, the faintly bohemian enclave (pop. 3,800), 80km (50 miles) north of Montréal, conjures up images of cabin hideaways set among hills rearing above ponds and lakes, and creeks tumbling through fragrant forests. The village celebrated its 75th anniversary in 1996.

The **tourist office** is on the main street at 2501 rue de l'Eglise (© **888/322-7030** or 819/322-2900 ext. 235; www.valdavid.com). It's open June 20 to Labor Day daily 9am to 7pm, and September 5 to June 19 daily 10am to 4pm. Another possibility for assistance is **La Maison du Village,** a cultural center that mounts art exhibits in a two-story wooden building at 2495 rue de l'Eglise (© **819/322-2900,** ext. 237). Note that this far north into the Laurentians, the telephone area code changes to 819.

EXPLORING VAL-DAVID

Val-David is small, so park anywhere and meander at leisure. Visiting the studios of local artists is a possible activity, and the village sponsors an annual **art festival** in the first 2 weeks of August, when painters, sculptors, ceramicists, jewelers, pewter smiths, and other craftspeople display their work. There are concerts and other outdoor activities at the same time.

Val-David sits astride a 200km (124-mile) parkway called the **Parc Linéaire le P'Tit Train du Nord,** a former railroad right-of-way. It is now a trail that runs from St-Jérôme to Mont-Laurier, heavily used for cycling in summer and for cross-country skiing and snowmobiling in winter. Have a picnic beside the North River in the **Parc des Amoureax,** which is 4km (2½ miles) from the main road through town. It has plenty of benches, and some parking spaces on the approach to the park. Watch for the sign SITE PITTORESQUE and turn at chemin de la Rivière.

WHERE TO STAY & DINE

Edelweiss   Business is good at this intimate hostelry hidden in the woods east of town, enough to underwrite the new building next to the original Tyrolean structure. That makes a total of 14 bedrooms that stay full of admirers of the inn's kitchen. Despite the Austro-Germanic appearance of the place, the Belgian chef and co-owner (his wife, the manager, is from Québec) draws from the French canon. His graceful touch is drawing more and more notice from serious eaters. Don't miss his foie gras terrine. Waterzooi (fish stew) and lamb are other specialties. Twelve of the rooms have gas fireplaces, eight have Jacuzzis. Deer are kept in a pen behind the inn.

3050 chemin Doncaster, Val-David, J0T 2N0. (C) 866/355-7800 or 819/322-7800. Fax 819/322-1550. www.ar-edelweiss.com. 14 units. C$100–C$180 (US$80–US$144). Rates include breakfast. Packages available. AE, MC, V. Drive through downtown and watch for the sign on the left, about 2.8km (1¾ miles). **Amenities:** Restaurant (French); heated outdoor pool w/Jacuzzi; golf nearby. In room: TV, hair dryer.

STE-AGATHE-DES-MONTS

With a population over 10,300, Ste-Agathe-des-Monts, 85km (53 miles) north of Montréal, has surpassed St-Adele for the title of largest town in the Laurentians. It marks the end of Autoroute 15.

Early settlers and vacationers flocked here in search of land fronting on Lac des Sables, and entrepreneurs followed the crowds. Ste-Agathe's main street, **rue Principale,** is the closest you'll get to citification in these mountains, but it's only a touch of urbanity. Follow rue Principale from the highway through town and end up at the town dock on the lake. Watch out for four-way stops along the way.

The dock and surrounding **waterfront park** make Ste-Agathe a good place to pause for a few hours. One possibility is renting a bicycle from **Jacques Champoux Sports,** 74 rue St-Vincent ((C) 819/326-3480), for the 5km (3-mile) ride around the lake; another is **Sports Denis Parent,** 217 chemin Lac Millette ((C) 450/227-2700). Lake cruises, beaches, and watercraft rentals seduce many visitors into lingering for days.

The **Bureau Touristique de Ste-Agathe-des-Monts,** 24 rue St-Paul ((C) 819/326-0457; www.sainte-agathe.org), is open daily 9am to 8:30pm in summer, 9am to 5pm the rest of the year.

Croisières Alouette ((C) 819/326-3656; www.croisierealouette.com) offers cruises on the lake that depart from the dock at the foot of rue Principale from mid-May to late October. It's a 50-minute, 19km (12-mile) voyage on a boat equipped with a bar. There is a running commentary on the sights that you'll observe, and a discussion of the water-ski competitions and windsurfing that Ste-Agathe and the Lac des Sables are famous for. The cost for the Alouette cruise is C$12 (US$9.60) adults, C$10 (US$8) seniors and students, and C$5 (US$4) for children 5 to 15. Children under 5 go free. There are regular departures from mid-May to late June 11:30am to 3:30pm, with additional departures until 7:30pm late June to late August. Call for departure times in September and October.

ST-JOVITE & MONT-TREMBLANT

Follow Route 117 about 37km (23 miles) north from Ste-Agathe to the St-Jovite exit. It's 122km (76 miles) north of Montréal. To get to Mont-Tremblant, turn right on

Route 327 just before the church in St-Jovite. Most vacationers make their base at one of the resorts or lodges scattered along Route 327. Mont-Tremblant is 45km (28 miles) north of Ste-Agathe and 130km (81 miles) north of Montréal.

A few words of clarification about the use of the name Tremblant, a subject of considerable confusion to first-time visitors: First, there is Mont-Tremblant, the mountain. On its slope is Tremblant, the growing resort village described below. At the base of the mountain is Lac (Lake) Tremblant, and on the opposite shore is Club Tremblant, also described below, an independently owned resort that has no connection to Tremblant resort village (although its guests ski the mountain). And, finally, there is the village of Mont-Tremblant, about 5km (3 miles) west, with its own market, post office, restaurants, and inns that have no specific affiliation with any of the aforementioned properties and geographical features.

Mont-Tremblant, at 650m (2,132 ft.), is the highest peak in the Laurentians. In 1894 the provincial government set aside almost 386 sq. km (151 sq. miles) of wilderness as **Parc Mont-Tremblant,** and the foresight of this early conservation effort has yielded outdoor enjoyment to skiers and four-season vacationers ever since. The mountain's name comes from a legend of the area's first inhabitants. Amerindians named the peak after the god Manitou. When humans disturbed nature in any way, Manitou became enraged and made the great mountain tremble—*montagne tremblante.*

St-Jovite (pop. 4,118), about 12km (7½ miles) south of Mont-Tremblant, is the commercial center for this most famous and popular of Laurentian districts. A pleasant community, it provides most of the expected services. The main street, **rue Ouimet,** is lined with cafes and shops, including **Le Coq Rouge,** which sells folk art and country antiques.

Tourist information, including maps of local ski trails, is available at the **Tourisme de Mont-Tremblant,** 5080 Montée Ryan (© **819/425-2434**), open daily 8:30am to 6pm (until 7pm Fri and Sat) in summer and daily 9am to 5pm the rest of the year; and from the **Tourisme de Saint-Jovite/Mont-Tremblant,** 48 chemin Brébeuf (© **819/425-3300**), open daily in summer 9am to 8pm, the rest of the year daily 9am to 5pm. You can also log on to www.tourismemonttremblant.com.

SKIING, WATERSPORTS & MORE

Watersports in summer are almost as popular as the ski slopes and trails in winter, because the base of Mont-Tremblant is surrounded by no fewer than 10 lakes: Lac Tremblant, a gorgeous stretch of water 16km (10 miles) long, and also Lac Ouimet, Lac Mercier, Lac Gelinas, Lac Desmarais, and five smaller bodies of water, not to mention rivers and streams. From June to October, **Croisières Mont-Tremblant,** 2810 chemin Principale, in Mont-Tremblant (© **819/425-1045**), offers a 70-minute narrated cruise of Lac Tremblant, focusing on its history, nature, and legends. Fares are C$15 (US$12) adults, C$12 (US$9.60) seniors, C$6 (US$4.80) children ages 6 to 15, and free for children under 6. Twilight cruises are given Tuesday through Thursday, June 24 to August 20.

Mont-Tremblant, which has a vertical drop of 650m (2,132 ft.), draws the biggest downhill ski crowds in the Laurentians. Founded in 1939 by the Philadelphia millionaire Joe Ryan, Mont-Tremblant is one of the oldest ski areas in North America, the first to create trails on both sides of a mountain and the second in the world to install a chairlift. There are higher mountains with longer runs and steeper pitches, but something about Mont-Tremblant compels people to return time and again.

Today Mont-Tremblant has the snowmaking capability to cover 131 hectares (324 acres), making skiing possible from early November to late May, and keeping at least 30 of the trails open at Christmastime (as opposed to 9 in 1992). There are now a total of 92 downhill runs and trails, including the recently opened Dynamite and Verige trails, with 245m (804-ft.) and 225m (738-ft.) drops, respectively, and the Edge, a peak with two gladed trails. The 13 lifts are mostly gondolas (one of which is heated) and quad chairs, no T-bars. There is plenty of cross-country action on 90km (56 miles) of maintained trails. And in summer, choose from golf, tennis, horseback riding, boating, swimming, biking, and hiking—for starters.

A new diversion, introduced in the summer of 2003, is the downhill dry-land luge run. The engineless sleds are gravity-propelled, reaching speeds of up to 30 mph on the 1.4km (¾-mile) course. Rides cost C$8 (US$6.40).

WHERE TO STAY & DINE

A source for bed-and-breakfast lodgings in the area is **www.bbtremblant.com**.

Auberge La Porte Rouge *Value*   This unusual motel is in the middle of everything, across the road from the Hôtel de Ville (Town Hall). Wake to a view of Lake Mercier through the picture windows, or gaze at the lake from your little balcony. Some rooms have both fireplaces and Jacuzzis. Later in the day, take lunch on the terrace facing the lake or wind down in the cocktail lounge. Deluxe rooms with kitchens and fireplaces accommodate 3 to 10 people. The dining room serves all three meals, including a four-course table d'hôte dinner. Rowboats, canoes, and pedal boats are available, and the motel is directly on the regional bike and cross-country ski linear park, Le P'tit Train du Nord. Note that rates include breakfast and dinner.

1874 chemin Principale, Mont-Tremblant. ⓒ 800/665-3505 or 819/425-3505. Fax 819/425-6700. www.aubergela porterouge.com. 26 units. C$100–C$250 (US$80–US$200) double. Rates include breakfast. Packages available. MC, V. **Amenities:** Restaurant (Regional); bar; heated outdoor pool; golf nearby; tennis nearby; watersports equipment rentals; bike rental. *In room:* A/C, TV.

Fairmont Mont Tremblant *ⓡⓡ*   This 1996 luxury lodging stands on a crest above the village, as befits its stature among the Tremblant hostelries. Although young compared with the chain's Château Frontenac in Québec City and Le Reine Elizabeth in Montréal, it hews closely to the high standards of its siblings across Canada. The enlarged lobby area has a north-woods look, with a monster fireplace and antiques and folk art prominently placed around the public areas. Guests use the outdoor pool right through the winter, and they can ski out and ski in to the hotel, which is close to the bottom of the chairlift. Even visitors staying elsewhere in the resort troop past the tantalizing buffet lines of in-house Windigo for nightly dinner and brunches 4 days a week. The concierge can arrange bike, blade, and ATV rentals, as well as plane tours and horseback rides.

3045 chemin de la Chapelle, Mont-Tremblant, PQ J8E 1B1. ⓒ 800/441-1414 or 819/681-7000. Fax 819/681-7099. www.fairmont.com. 316 units. C$539–C$769 (US$431–US$615) double. Packages available. AE, DC, DISC, MC, V. **Amenities:** Restaurant (International); cafe; bar; indoor lap pool and heated outdoor pools; golf nearby; tennis nearby; health club and spa; watersports equipment; bike rental; children's programs; concierge; business center; shopping arcade; limited room service; in-room massage; babysitting; laundry service; same-day dry cleaning. *In room:* A/C, TV w/pay movies, dataport, fridge, coffeemaker, hair dryer, iron.

Gray Rocks *ⓡ*   The area's dowager resort has been under new management since 1993, and its ongoing ministrations are evident. The accommodations—rooms and condos—are in a huge rambling main building, in the cozier Le Château lodge, or in one of the resort's four-person cottages. (Ask for a room in the redecorated Center or Pavilion wings of the main building.) Condos have full kitchens and washers and dryers. The family-friendly resort covers most of the recreational bases, including, for summer, two 18-hole golf courses, junior and adult tennis schools, horseback riding, and boating. In winter, it has its own mountain, Sugar Hill, with 22 trails, four lifts, and a ski school. Guests also have access to 90km (56 miles) of cross-country trails. And there is not only a private airport for guests who fly in, but also a seaplane base for joy rides over Lac Ouimet. A complete playground has attendants to provide child-care, as well as a program of free swimming lessons. The bar has piano and other music 4 nights a week.

525 chemin Principale, Mont-Tremblant, PQ J0T 1Z0. © 800/567-6767 or 819/425-2771. Fax 819/425-9156. www. grayrocks.com. 277 units, including 62 condos. C$145–C$425 (US$116–US$340) double; from C$655 (US$524) condo (4–8 persons). Rates include breakfast and dinner in hotel, but not in condos. Discounts for children sharing parent's room. Meals optional in condos. Ski-school packages available. AE, DISC, MC, V. **Amenities:** Restaurant (Continental); bar; large indoor pool; 36 holes of golf; 22 tennis courts; health club; sauna; watersports equipment; bike rental; business center; babysitting; coin-op laundry; same-day laundry and dry cleaning. *In room:* A/C, TV, coffeemaker, hair dryer, iron.

Hôtel Club Tremblant 🏃🏃

Terraced into a hillside sloping steeply to the shore of Lac Tremblant, this attractive property consists of several lodges in muted alpine style. Essentially a concentration of privately owned apartments operated by a single management, the accommodations represent excellent value and that greatest of luxuries: space. Most of the rental units are suites of one to three bedrooms, which go for prices equivalent to a single room at many other resorts in the region, and rates include both breakfast and dinner (although it must be conceded that the food is no more than adequate). A typical suite has a fireplace, balcony, sitting room with cable TV and a dining table, full kitchen with cookware and dishwasher, one or two bathrooms with Jacuzzi, and clothes washer and dryer. Nearly all accommodations have views of the lake and Mont-Tremblant, which rises from the opposite shore. This is a family resort, so expect childish squeals in the dining rooms in peak months—July, August, February, and March. During ski season, a 22-passenger bus shuttles between the lodge and the slopes.

Rue Cuttle, Mont-Tremblant, PQ J0T 1Z0. © 800/567-8341 or 819/425-2731. Fax 819/425-5617. www.clubtremblant. com. 100 units. C$239–C$528 (US$191–US$422) suite. Rates include full breakfast and dinner. Rates are lower for stays of 2 days or more. Packages available. AE, DC, MC, V. Turn left off Montée Ryan, then right on Lac Tremblant North and follow signs for less than a mile. **Amenities:** 2 restaurants in summer (French/Continental), 1 in winter; 2 bars in summer, 1 in winter; heated indoor and outdoor pools; 6 golf courses nearby; 4 tennis courts; exercise room; spa w/therapeutic baths; Jacuzzi; watersports equipment rental; children's programs; massage; babysitting. *In room:* TV, kitchen, fridge, coffeemaker, hair dryer, iron.

Hôtel Mont-Tremblant *Value*

One of the first things the new owners did was banish the pink-and-purple color scheme of the 1902 inn, a big improvement right there. The restaurant, now called Le Bernardin after a restaurant they had in Montréal, was made larger, incorporating the covered front terrace, and a canopied separate entrance was added. All meals are served, with dinner main courses from C$16 to C$24 (US$13–US$19). Upstairs rooms all have private bathrooms; most have twin or double beds, a few have sitting areas. The hotel is popular with skiers who want to avoid Tremblant's higher prices, and there's a mountain shuttle bus stop across the street. Cyclists like the location on Le P'tit Train du Nord linear park.

1900 chemin du Village, Mont-Tremblant, PQ J8E 1K4. © 888/887-1111 or 819/425-3232. Fax 819/425-9755. www.hotelmonttremblant.com. 25 units. C$90–C$120 (US$72–US$96). Rates include breakfast. MAP available. MC, V. **Amenities:** Restaurant (Mediterranean); bar; game room; golf, tennis, beach nearby. *In room:* A/C, TV, hair dryer, no phone.

Le Grand Lodge ⭐⭐   Replacing the old Villa Bellevue on the bank of Lake Ouimet, this handsome all-suites hotel was built with the palatial log construction of the north country. The atmosphere here is adult and sophisticated. The suites leave little to be desired—all come with full kitchens, fireplaces, and balconies—and, because the hotel is fairly new, the furniture is fresh, without the battering of many ski seasons. Canoeing and kayaking on the lake, float-plane tours, dog sledding, horseback riding, snowshoeing, and snowmobiling flesh out the more obvious skiing and golfing pursuits. But with lodgings this comfortable, you might pass much of the time with a bottle of wine in front of the fire. This is a highly desirable addition to Mont-Tremblant's housing stock, at a quiet distance from the frequent clamor of the main resort.

845 chemin Principale, Mont-Tremblant, PQ J0T 1Z0. ⓒ 800/567-6763 or 819/425-2734. Fax 819/425-9360. www. legrandlodge.com. 112 units. C$440–C$700 (US$352–US$560) suite. Children under 14 stay free in parent's room. Packages available. AE, DC, MC, V. Small pets accepted (C$25/US$20 a night). **Amenities:** Restaurant (International); bar; large heated indoor pool; golf nearby; 4 tennis courts; exercise room; spa; watersports equipment rental; children's programs; concierge; activities desk; limited room service; in-room massage; babysitting; coin-op laundry; same-day dry cleaning. *In room:* A/C, TV w/pay movies, dataport, kitchen, fridge, coffeemaker, hair dryer, iron.

Le Westin Resort Tremblant ⭐⭐⭐   Easily one of the most attractive hotels in the ever-expanding resort, this turn-of-this-century addition to the complex competes for king of the hill. Restrained corporate decor prevails, applied to rooms that have every convenience you might expect and some you might not. In the latter category are gas fireplaces, wet bars, video games, and Internet access through the TV with wireless keyboards. All units have at least small kitchenettes with microwaves, toasters, fridges, and enough plates and flatware for four. Many have balconies. The outdoor pool is open all year.

100 chemin Kandahar, Mont-Tremblant, PQ J0T 1Z0. ⓒ 877/873-6252 or 819/681-8000. Fax 819/681-8001. www. tremblant.ca. 126 units. C$395–C$795 (US$316–US$636) double; from C$659 (US$527) suite. Packages available. AE, DC, MC, V. **Amenities:** 2 restaurants (Japanese, International); bar; heated outdoor saltwater pool w/Jacuzzi; golf nearby; tennis; health club and spa; watersports equipment rental; children's programs; concierge; business center; shopping arcade; 24-hr. room service; massage; babysitting; laundry service; same-day dry cleaning; executive floors. *In room:* A/C, TV w/pay movies, dataport, kitchen or kitchenette, fridge, coffeemaker, hair dryer, iron, safe.

Quintessence ⭐⭐⭐   Go in assuming that virtually every service you might find in a 300-room deluxe will be available to you . . . then concentrate on the extras. Check-in is in your room—make that "suite"—so you don't have to stand around at a reception desk. Check out the hugely comfortable bed with the 4-inch-thick feather mattress cover and the wood-burning fireplace. Note that the bathroom floors are heated, that the jets in the tub are controlled by a remote, and that the shower is of the drenching rainforest variety. Be advised that you can order a massage in your room, in front of a blazing fire. Every suite has a view of the lake, which may well inspire you to book a picnic and a ride on the gorgeous 1910 mahogany powerboat. Yoga classes can be arranged, followed by a steam and a sauna. Anticipate a lavish dinner with a goblet of wine from the 5,000-bottle cellar. No sacrifice is made by booking one of the least expensive units. There's even a separate honeymoon cottage.

3004 chemin de la Chapelle, Mont-Tremblant, PQ J8E 1E1. ⓒ 866/425-3400 or 819/425-3400. Fax 819/425-3480. www.hotelquintessence.com. 30 units. C$389–C$739 (US$311–US$591) double. Rates include breakfast. Packages available. AE, DC, MC, V. **Amenities:** Restaurant (Contemporary French); bar; heated outdoor pool and hot tubs; golf and tennis nearby; health club and spa; concierge; business center; 24-hr. room service; massage; babysitting; laundry service; same-day dry cleaning. *In room:* A/C, TV/VCR w/pay movies, dataport, minibar, hair dryer, iron, safe.

WHERE TO STAY

Ermitage du Lac ✿✿   Find this new entry in the resort's lodging-go-round slightly to the right and behind the 19th-century church located at the main entrance. Just the place for families on long stays, all its units are large studios or one- to three-bedroom suites. Fireplaces and balconies are standard, as are kitchens fully equipped with oven-ranges, microwaves, dishwashers, unstocked fridges, and necessary cookware and crockery. TVs are supplemented with PlayStations and stereo systems. High-speed Internet access is provided. There is a secure underground parking garage. The entire property is nonsmoking.

Lodging at Tremblant Resort

Not merely a hotel with a pool, Tremblant is a complete and growing resort village stretching from the mountain's skirts to the shores of 16km-long (10-mile) Lac Tremblant and beyond. It'll be a pretty nice place if they ever finish it, but this is the kind of enterprise that always has another "phase" to go. It has the prefabricated look of a theme park, but at least they used the Quebecois architectural style of pitched or mansard roofs in bright colors, not ersatz Tyrolean or Bavarian Alpine flourishes. At recent count, there were several hotels and condo complexes, an 18-hole golf course (with another on the way), and 14 shops, including a liquor store, as well as more than 30 eateries and bars. When the snow is deep, skiers here like to follow the sun around the mountain, making the run down slopes with an eastern exposure in the morning and down the western-facing ones in the afternoon.

To get to the resort, drive 5km (3 miles) north of St-Jovite on Route 117; then take Montée Ryan and follow the blue signs for about 10km (6¼ miles). The Limocar bus from Montréal stops at the entrance, and there's door-to-door shuttle service from Trudeau Airport; reservations are required (© 800/471-1155).

Reservations for lodgings at the resort can be made through the central number (© 888/289-8888), on www.tremblant.com, or by contacting the establishments directly. The more prominent hotels, some of which incorporate privately owned condominium units, are described in this section.

Several of the less expensive lodgings have only limited facilities. Pools and health clubs are provided at centers located around the resort. Supervision is provided for children ages 1 to 12 in the Kidz Club, with excursions, crafts, games, and activities. They and their older siblings can also get blissfully waterlogged at the AquaClub, with indoor and outdoor pools and Jacuzzis. The facility also has a well-equipped fitness area. Chairs and gondola lifts take you to various points on the slopes.

In summer, extensive possible diversions include lake swimming, boat cruises, chairlift rides to the top of Mont-Tremblant, playing on 1 of the 11 lighted Har-Tru tennis courts, minigolfing, and biking and in-line skating (rentals are readily available). In winter, shops rent and repair ski equipment and provide information about access to the cross-country trails.

150 chemin du Cure-Deslauriers, Mont-Tremblant, PQ J8E 1C9. ② **800/461-8711** or 819/681-2222. Fax 819/681-2223. www.tremblant.ca/ermitage. 69 umits. C$389–C$839 (US$311–US$671) double. Rates include breakfast. AE, DC, MC, V. **Amenities:** Wine and cheese bar; outdoor pool and hot tub; exercise room; concierge; business center; babysitting; laundry service; same-day dry cleaning. *In room:* A/C, TV/VCR, dataport, kitchen, coffeemaker, hair dryer, iron.

Homewood Suites by Hilton   Taking up the interiors of several buildings meant to look like separate row houses, the most desirable rooms are those that overlook the Place St-Bernard, the central gathering space of the village. Many of the resort's restaurants and shops form the perimeter of the plaza. Ski lockers are available to guests, who have ready access to the slopes. Indoor parking and a laundromat are provided. All accommodations are crisply furnished suites, with fireplaces and equipped kitchens.

3035 chemin de la Chapelle, Mont-Tremblant, PQ J8E 1E1. ② **888/288-2988** or 819/681-0808. Fax 819/681-0331. www.hiltontremblant.com. 102 units. C$295–C$715 (US$236–US$572) suite. Rates include breakfast and afternoon snack (Mon–Thurs). AE, DC, DISC, MC, V. **Amenities:** Access to health club, golf, tennis, skiing all nearby; laundromat. *In room:* A/C, TV, coffeemaker, hair dryer, iron.

WHERE TO DINE

Although most Laurentian inns and resorts have their own dining facilities and often require that guests use them (especially in winter), Mont-Tremblant and St-Jovite have several decent independent dining options for casual lunches or the odd night out. Note that restaurants in the area open and close with irritating unpredictability, so call ahead before setting out. Those recommended below are among the more reliable.

Antipasto ITALIAN   Housed in an old train station moved to this site, there is the expected railroad memorabilia on the walls, but the owners have resisted the temptation to play up the theme aspect to excess. Captain's chairs are drawn up to big tables with green Formica tops. Almost everyone orders the César salad (their spelling), which is dense and strongly flavored—the half-portion is more than enough as a first course. Individual pizzas emerge from the brick ovens. An enormous range of possible toppings, scallops and crabmeat among them, are baked on a choice of regular or whole-wheat crust. Pastas are available in even greater variety; those with shellfish are among the winners. The sauces are savory, if a bit thin. There are outdoor tables in summer.

855 rue Ouimet, St-Jovite. ② **819/425-7580.** Main courses C$11–C$30 (US$8.80–US$24); table d'hôte lunch C$11–C$13 (US$8.80–US$10). MC, V. Daily 11am–11pm.

Aux Truffes ✻ FRENCH CONTEMPORARY   Small hurricane lamps flicker on each table, which are set with tablecloths and silver. That includes those out on the terrace, but any time but deepest summer is likely to be chilly out there. The management and kitchen are more ambitious than just about any on the mountain, evidenced by a wine cellar that sails through Canadian, Californian, Chilean, Australian, Spanish, and many admirable French bottlings, up to a Château Latour '90 for well over C$1,000 (US$800). Put yourself in the hands of the knowledgeable wine steward. The meal proceeds from a heartier-than-usual *amuse-bouche* to a very good salad to such imaginative mains as a succulent slab of bison filet on black rice sprinkled with cashews and capped by slices of duck foie gras. Ostrich carpaccio with truffle oil is worth trying, too. Follow with selections from the *plateau* of four raw milk Québec cheeses.

3035 chemin Principale, Mont-Tremblant. ② **819/681-4544.** Main courses C$29–C$40 (US$23–US$32). AE, MC, V. Daily 6–11pm.

Dining at Tremblant Resort

In addition to the bars and restaurants at the hotels of the Tremblant resort village described above, there are more than 30 free-standing places at which to get a meal or a snack in the pedestrian areas of the resort. That isn't to say they are especially satisfying, for few restaurants in the village rise above mediocrity. A notable exception is Aux Truffes, reviewed below. Otherwise, my recommendation is to do the ski and aprés-ski thing, sport about, have cocktails, and hear some music in the resort, but take serious meals off the premises (if your hotel permits).

That said, there are plenty of eating options for the exhausted or car-less. Serving a variety of kinds of food implicit in their names are La Pizzateria, Coco Pazzo (Italian), Créperie Catherine, La Savoie (fondues), and Mexicali Rosa's. Le Grappe a Vin, at the lower end of the pedestrian concourse, edges most of its competitors in quality, with dishes featuring game, such as wapiti, duck, and caribou. Popular Les Artistes, in the village center, has four loud levels and a menu that scrupulously avoids challenges to convention. On the summit of the mountain is Le Rendezvous Café, with a circular fireplace, and the 1,000-seat Le Grand Manitou restaurant complex, with a dining room called La Légende, plus a bistro and cafeteria. On the food-with-entertainment front, Le Shack opens for breakfast at 7am and doesn't close the bar until 3am. La Diable pours craft beers to accompany live jazz on weekends, and Le P'tit Caribou brings in pop performers weekly.

Patrick Bermand *☞* MEDITERRANEAN   If you cherish seafood and have been disappointed by the paucity of finned fish offered by local restaurants, reserve for dinner here on Friday or Saturday night. The kitchen receives deliveries of anything fresh from the depths at the end of each week, appearing as unlisted specials until supplies run out. Come here any other night and you'll still find a marked improvement over other eateries in the lackluster Tremblant dining scene. Opened in 2003 in a roadside log-cabin–style house, the restaurant is also more likely to be open during slow off-season periods. Appetizers are especially satisfying, among them garlicky, buttery escargot served in individual ceramic pots and cool chunks of tuna rolled in black sesame seeds accompanied by a swirl of cold sesame noodles. Main courses are good, too, but wastefully large—a lot of leftovers walk out the door.

2176 chemin du Village, Mont-Tremblant. *©* **819/425-6475.** Main courses C$24–C$39 (US$19–US$31). AE, MC, V. Daily 6–10pm.

2 East into the Cantons-de-l'Est

24–77km (15–48 miles) SE of Montréal

Until recently called Estrie or the Eastern Townships, the Cantons-de-l'Est served as breadbasket to Montréal and the rest of the province. It is a largely pastoral region marked by billowing hills and the 792m (2,598-ft.) peak of Mont-Orford, centerpiece of a provincial park and the district's premier downhill ski area. A short distance from Mont-Orford is Sherbrooke, the industrial and commercial capital of the region.

Throughout the Mont-Orford–Sherbrooke area are serene glacial lakes that attract summer fishing enthusiasts, sailors, and swimmers from all over. In terms of tourism, the Cantons are one of Québec's best-kept secrets, for it's mostly Quebecois who occupy rental houses to ski, fish, cycle, or launch their boats. Follow their lead: Once out of Montréal, drive east along arrow-straight Autoroute 10 past silos and fields, clusters of cows, and meadows strewn with wildflowers. Clumps of mountains rise with improbable suddenness from the rolling terrain that flattens as it approaches the St. Lawrence. Cresting the hill at kilometer 100, there's an especially beguiling view of countryside stretching toward New England, not far over the horizon.

Unlike the Laurentides, which virtually close down in "mud time," when spring warmth thaws the ground, the Cantons-de-l'Est kick into gear as crews penetrate every "sugar bush" (stand of sugar maples) to tap the sap and "sugar off." The result? Maple festivals and farms hosting "sugaring parties"—guests wolfing down prodigious country repasts capped by traditional maple syrup desserts. One popular example of a maple sugar sweet is created when hot maple syrup is poured on the fast-melting winter snow and cooled instantly to produce a kind of maple-sugar taffy. Montréal newspapers and local tourist offices and chambers of commerce keep up-to-date lists of what's happening where and when during the sugaring.

Autumn has its special attractions, too, for in addition to the glorious fall foliage (usually best in the weeks on either side of the third weekend in Sept), the orchards of Cantons-de-l'Est sag under the weight of apples of every variety, and cider mills hum day and night to produce what has been described as Québec's "wine." Visitors are invited to help with the harvest, paying a low price for the baskets of fruit they gather for themselves. Cider mills open their doors for tours and tastings.

English town names such as Granby, Waterloo, and Sherbrooke are vestiges of the time when Americans loyal to the Crown migrated here during and shortly after the Revolutionary War. The region was long known as the Eastern Townships. Now, however, the Cantons-de-l'Est are about 90% French-speaking, with a name to reflect that demographic. A few words of French and a little sign language are sometimes necessary outside hotels and other tourist facilities, since the area draws fewer Anglophone visitors than do the Laurentides.

For extended stays in the region, consider making your base in one of the several inns along the shores of Lac Massawippi, especially in and around **North Hatley,** and take day trips from there.

ESSENTIALS
GETTING THERE
BY CAR   Leave Montréal by the Champlain Bridge, which funnels into Autoroute 10, in the direction of Sherbrooke, the grungy metropolis of the region. People in a hurry can remain on Autoroute 10—and plenty of express buses do this, too—but to get to know the countryside, turn off the autoroute at Exit 37 and go north the short distance to join Route 112 east.

BY BUS   Local buses leave Montréal to follow Route 112 more than a dozen times a day, arriving in Sherbrooke, 160km (99 miles) away, 3 hours, 15 minutes later. Express buses use Autoroute 10, making a stop in Magog and arriving in Sherbrooke in 2 hours and 10 minutes (2½ hr. from Québec City). Call © **450/842-2281** at the Terminus Voyageur in Montréal for information.

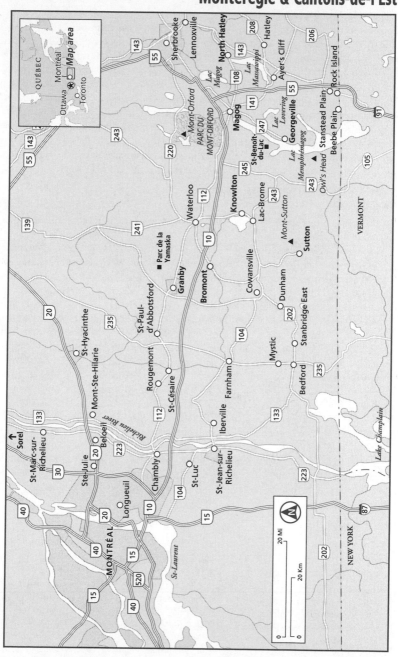

VISITOR INFORMATION

La Maison du Tourisme (Tourism House), at Exit 68 off Autoroute 10 (© **866/ 472-6292** or 450/375-8774; fax 450/375-3530; www.granby-bromont.com), which represents the **Cantons-de-l'Est,** is open Monday through Thursday and Sunday 8:30am to 5pm, Friday 8:30am to 8pm, and Saturday 8:30am to 6pm (shorter hours in winter). Or contact **Tourisme Cantons-de-l'Est,** 20 rue Don Bosco sud, Sherbrooke, PQ J1L 1W4 (© **800/355-5755;** fax 819/566-4445; www.easterntownships.ca or www.cantonsdelest.com), for more information. The Sherbrooke tourist information bureau is at 2964 rue King ouest (© **819/821-1919**), open late June to Labor Day daily 8:30am to 7:30pm, and the rest of the year 9am to 5pm.

The **telephone area codes** are 450 or 819, depending on the part of the region that you're calling (towns with a 450 area code are closer to Montréal).

EXPLORING CANTONS DE L'EST

GRANBY

North of the Autoroute at Exit 68, this largely unbeguiling city (pop. 56,856) does have a couple of surprises.

First is the **Zoo de Granby,** 525 rue St-Hubert (© **877/472-6299;** www.zoode granby.ca). Take Exit 68 or 74 off Autoroute 10 and follow the signs. The zoo's 28 wooded hectares (69 acres) harbor more than 1,000 mammals, exotic birds, reptiles, and amphibians of 225 species from around the world. Founded in 1953, the zoo has an educational program for children and presents shows every day in summer, including demonstrations of and explanations about raptors—birds of prey. Among the newer exhibits are a nocturnal cave, a display of robotic whales, a Siberian tiger pavilion, and the "Afrika" pavilion, notable for its group of gorillas. There are restaurants, picnic areas, gift shops, free rides, and a water park with what is said to be the largest heated wave pool in Québec. The zoo is open weekends in May and September, daily June through August. Open times vary but are usually 10am to 6pm in high season, until 5pm in shoulder periods. Admission is C$24 (US$19) for ages 13 and older, C$18 (US$14) for seniors and children ages 5 to 12, and C$11 (US$8.80) for children 2 to 4. Parking is C$4 (US$3.20). The visitor entrance is on boulevard David-Bouchard nord.

Granby is also home to **Parc de la Yamaska** (© **450/776-7182;** www.sepaq.com), with swimming on the longest beach in the area, a 3km (1.9-mile) hiking trail, 40km (25 miles) of cross-country ski trails, and 22km (14 miles) of cycling trails along an old railroad track between Granby and the towns of Bromont and Waterloo.

BROMONT

Take Exit 78 off Autoroute 10.

Founded in 1964 primarily to accommodate an industrial park and other commercial enterprises, this town of 5,000 is now a popular destination for day and night skiing, mountain biking (rent bikes at the entrance to the town opposite the tourist office), golf, hiking, and horseback riding. Shoppers have two of the largest **factory outlets** in Canada—Versants de Bromont and Les Manufacturiers de Bromont—and the area's largest **flea market,** with more than 350 stalls set up in the local drive-in from 9am to 5pm every Sunday from the first Sunday in May to the last Sunday in October.

Where to Stay & Dine

Hôtel Château Bromont ✿   All the rooms at the château have rocking chairs, Internet connections, and Nintendo games; half have fireplaces. A landscaped terrace looks up at the ski mountain across the way, a most attractive setting. The interior decor gets a trifle gaudy here and there, but not jarring. The staff is young and bilingual. In addition to squash and racquetball courts, there's a European spa featuring mud and algae baths (use of the spa facilities costs extra).

90 rue Stanstead, Bromont, PQ J2L 1K6. ℂ 800/304-3433 or 450/534-3433. Fax 450/534-0514. www.chateau bromont.com. 152 units. C$156–C$318 (US$125–US$254) double; from C$320 (US$256) suite. Rates include breakfast. Free for children under 12 in parent's room. Packages available. AE, DC, DISC, MC, V. **Amenities:** 2 restaurants (French, Continental); bar; heated indoor and outdoor pools; 4 golf courses nearby; exercise room; spa; Jacuzzi; sauna; massage; babysitting. *In room:* A/C, TV w/pay movies, minibar, coffeemaker, iron, safe.

KNOWLTON

Those who shop for amusement, not mere necessity, will want to make this a destination. Knowlton is compact, but its two main shopping streets have a number of clothing and antiques stores that reveal a creeping chic influenced by refugees and day-trippers from Montréal. Ralph Lauren is here, and a shop that replaced a Liz Claiborne outlet sells outdoor gear and clothing and whimsically refers to itself as "L.L. Brome." The main shopping streets are **Lakeside Street** and **Knowlton Road.**

Knowlton is at the southeast corner of Brome Lake and is part of the seven-village municipality known as **Lac Brome** (pop. 5,073). It is one of the last towns in the region where a slim majority of the residents have English as their mother tongue. The first settler here was Paul Holland Knowlton, a Loyalist from Vermont. He arrived in 1815 and established a farm where the golf course stands today. By 1834, he had added a sawmill, a blacksmith shop, a gristmill, and a store. He also founded the first high school.

The **tourist information office** is at 696 rue Lakeside (ℂ **450/242-2870;** www.cc lacbrome.qc.ca). The major local sight is the **Musée Historique du Comté de Brome (Brome County Historical Museum)** at 130 rue Lakeside (Rte. 243), ℂ **450/243-6782.** It occupies five historic buildings, including the town's first school. Exhibits focus on various aspects of town life, with re-creations of a schoolroom, bedroom, parlor, and kitchen. The Martin Annex (1921) is dominated by a 1917 Fokker single-seat biplane, the foremost German aircraft in World War I. Also on premises are collections of old radios and 18th- to early-20th-century weapons. The museum sells books about the area. Admission is C$5 (US$4) adults, C$3 (US$2.40) seniors, and C$2.50 (US$2) ages 16 and under. It's open mid-May to mid-September Monday to Saturday 10am to 4:30pm, Sunday 11am to 4:30pm, and closed the rest of the year.

Where to Stay & Dine

Auberge Lakeview   The core structure of this Victorian inn dates from 1874, and a 19th-century flavor has been sustained through many renovations. Leather chairs are arranged around the fireplace in the lobby, tin ceilings prevail, and Spencer's, the brass-and-mahogany pub that is a replica of the London original, is a nice place to settle in for an evening. On weekends, there's dancing to live music. The bedrooms come in four categories of relative comfort—go for the best ones and get two robes, a sitting area, access to the veranda, and a heart-shaped Jacuzzi. Much of the furniture is crafted in Québec country style. Rooms in the least expensive category lack TVs, but the rest have cable. Since rates include dinner, this is the place to sample the area's important gourmet treat, Lake Brome duck. Make sure to try the duck wings served as a bar snack.

50 rue Victoria, Knowlton (Lac Brome), PQ J0E 1V0. ℂ 800/661-6183 or 450/243-6183. Fax 450/243-0602. www.aubergelakeviewinn.com. 28 units. C$252–C$360 (US$202–US$288) double. Rates include breakfast, dinner, and service. Packages available. AE, MC, V. 1 block south of the town hall. **Amenities:** Restaurant (Continental); bar; heated outdoor pool. *In room:* A/C, TV in most units.

Auberge West Brome   Out in the country, beyond the town limits, drivers first notice the creamy yellow 1898 farmhouse at roadside. That's where reception and the restaurant are located. About 100 yards back are three grey modern structures (two are nonsmoking) where the bedrooms are located. The fitness center is in the middle one, and there's an outdoor pool with a hot tub. Rooms are in three categories: Classic, on the small side but not cramped; Deluxe, with full kitchens, fireplaces, and decks; and Suite, with or without whirlpool tubs. The suites can accommodate four. All beds are new, with feather mattresses. Only dinner and Sunday brunch are served in the dining room.

129 Route 139, West Brome, PQ J0E 2P0. ℂ 888/902-7663. Fax 450/266-2040. www.aubergewestbrome.ca. 24 units. C$149–C$169 (US$119–US$135); from C$180 (US$144) suite. Rates include breakfast. Packages available. AE, MC, V. **Amenities:** Restaurant (Regional); bar; heated outdoor pool; sparsely equipped fitness room. *In room:* A/C, TV, coffeemaker, hair dryer, iron.

Cantons-de-l'Est: Wine Country?

Canada is known more for its beers and ales than its wines, and rightly so. But that hasn't stopped a few stouthearted agriculturists from attempting to plant vines and transform the fruit into approximations of drinkable clarets, chardonnays, and sauternes. So far, the most successful efforts have blossomed along the Niagara Frontier in southern Ontario and in the relatively warmer precincts of British Columbia. The Cantons-de-l'Est enjoy the mildest microclimates in Québec, and where apples grow, as they do in these parts, so will other fruits, including grapes.

Most vintners are concentrated around **Dunham,** about 29km (18 miles) west of Sutton, with several vineyards along Route 202. No winemaker in the valleys of Napa or the Gironde is feeling the hot breath of competition from the Cantons-de-l'Est. Still, a stop for a snack or a tour of vineyard facilities makes for an agreeable break from driving.

One possibility is the family-owned and -run **Les Blancs Coteaux,** at 1046 Route 202 (ℂ **450/295-3503**), which opened in 1990. They serve picnic baskets and welcome visitors all year, daily 9am to 5pm. The vineyard's shop sells its Seyval Blanc and Vendange de Bacchus white wines, hard cider, apple liqueur, and syrup. The area's oldest and best-regarded vineyard, **l'Orpailleur,** 1086 Route 202 (ℂ **450/295-2763**), opened in 1982. They serve meals, have picnic tables, offer wine tastings, and conduct tours; call ahead to determine schedules and hours. Look, too, for the similar **Domaine des Côtes d'Ardoise,** at 879 Route 202 (ℂ **450/295-2020**), and **Les Trois Clochers,** at 341 Route 202 (ℂ **450/295-2034**).

The most credible wines in the region come out of **Le Cep d'Argent,** outside Magog, at 1257 chemin de la Rivière (ℂ **819/864-4441**). They produce several wines, their prizewinners being the Le Cep d'Argent dry white made from the Seyval varietal, the aperitif Mistral, and L'Archer, a portlike fortified wine. They're open all year and offer frequent guided tours daily May to August, weekends only the rest of the year. Tours cost C$5 (US$4) for visitors over age 14.

MONT-ORFORD

Exit 115 north off the autoroute leads into one of Québec's most popular provincial parks. From mid-September to mid-October, **Parc du Mont-Orford** blazes with autumn color. Visitors come to try the 18-hole golf course in summer; in winter, they visit for the more than 40km (25 miles) of ski trails and slopes, with a vertical drop of more than 488m (1,601 ft.), or for the extensive network of cross-country ski and snowshoe trails.

Mont-Orford is a veteran ski area compared to Bromont (see above) and has long provided slopes of choice for the moneyed families of the Cantons-de-l'Est and Montréal. It is composed of contiguous Mont-Giroux, Mont-Desrochers, and Mont-Orford itself, the second highest peak in Québec after Mont-Tremblant. Children enjoy special treatment with "Kinderski," where some 100 instructors conduct a ski-and-snowboard school and supervise a tube slide. Aprés-ski drinks, dinner, and entertainment are provided by the Slalom Pub.

The area's other ski resorts—Owl's Head and Mont-Sutton—are more family-oriented and less glitzy than Mont-Orford. These resorts, and the centers at Bromont and Mont-Glen, have banded together in the Ski-dans-l'Est program to offer a multiday pass good at all five areas. For prices and other information, call © **800/355-5755.** Rental equipment is available.

Orford has another claim to fame in the **Centre d'Arts Orford,** 3165 chemin du Parc (© **800/567-6155** or 819/843-3981), set on an 89-hectare (220-acre) estate within the park and providing music classes for talented young musicians every summer. From early July to the middle of August, a series of more than 30 classical and chamber music concerts is given in connection with **Festival Orford.** Prices usually are C$20 to C$50 (US$16–US$40) for professional concerts, free for student performances. Concerts are held Thursday to Sunday. A complete luncheon is served outside following each week's Saturday concert. Visual-arts exhibitions at the center are open to the public, and walking trails connect the center to a nearby campground.

Where to Stay

Manoir des Sables 🎿🎿   This thoroughly contemporary facility is one of the most complete resort hotels in the region, serving business groups, couples, families, golfers, skiers, skaters, fitness enthusiasts, tennis players, and kayakers. And, as the pitchmen say, that's not all! Add snowshoeing trails, snowmobiling, toboggan rides, tube slides, fishing in the hotel's lake, and Saturday-night horse-drawn sleigh rides to the list of activities. Bedrooms have all the big-city gadgets and niceties, which is to be expected since the hotel began life as a Sheraton. All rooms have either one queen or two double beds and sitting areas. About half have fireplaces. The new Château section contains 24 upscale suites and its own lounge.

90 av. des Jardins, Orford, PQ J1X 6M6. © 800/567-3514 or 819/847-4747. Fax 819/847-3519. www.manoirdes sables.com. 141 units. C$166–C$380 (US$133–US$304) double. AE, DC, MC, V. Packages and meal plans available. Take Exit 118 from Autoroute 10 and follow Rte. 141 north to the hotel, on the right. **Amenities:** 2 restaurants (International); bar; indoor and outdoor pools; golf course on property; 4 lit tennis courts; health club and spa; bike rental; children's programs; game room; secretarial services; limited room service; massage; babysitting; laundry service; dry cleaning. *In room:* A/C, TV, dataport, coffeemaker, hair dryer, iron.

MAGOG & LAC MEMPHREMAGOG

Orford is where people visit, but Magog (pop. 23,085) is where people live. As with countless other North American place names, Magog came by its handle through corruption of a Native Canadian word. The Abenaki name *Memrobagak* (Great Expanse

Moments Sugaring Off

For a purely Québec experience that shouldn't be missed, get yourself to sugar shack. Called in French *cabanes à sucre* or *érablières,* they were once (and often still are) places that merely processed sap from maple trees.

Essential to the operation is a rendering room, where the sap gathered from taps in hundreds, even thousands, of maple trees is boiled in a trough called the evaporator, then cooked further on a stove. After that, the syrup is filtered and poured into cans. One popular sales device is to set up a long narrow tray of snow and pour a wiggly stream of syrup down the middle. This forms a sort of maple taffy, which is then rolled up on Popsicle sticks and eaten.

Once producers realized that they were drawing larger and larger audiences, they began to offer wider experiences to keep the customers reaching for their wallets. They put in bars and dining rooms where bountiful spreads of simple country food were served at long communal tables. Some even put in dance floors and live entertainment. Originally open only during sugaring-off season, roughly February through April, a few now stay open much longer, even all year.

There usually isn't a menu. Sit down at table, and the food starts coming. Thick pea soup is standard, as are loaves of fragrant bread, sausages, ham slices, home fries, baked beans, coleslaw, and stacks of pancakes. At the ready are preserves, pickles, and all the maple syrup you can ingest. You won't be considered a bad person if you can't finish it all; few diners can. Total cost rarely exceeds C$25 (US$20) per person. If you can't move afterward, basic bedrooms are sometimes available for rent.

Signature products are available in several sizes and forms, primarily syrup and candy. Keep in mind that the best syrup is from the first run of sap and is clear and light in color. It gets darker as the weeks of the season proceed.

Québec Province has more than 400 sugar shacks. Small directional signs are often positioned at roadsides. A website concerned with sugar shacks is **www.Erabliere.com.**

---

of Water) somehow became Memphrémagog, which was eventually shortened to Magog (pronounced *May*-gog). The town is positioned at the northernmost end of Lac Memphrémagog (pronounced Mem-*phree*-may-gog), *not* on Lac Magog, which is about 13km (8 miles) north of Magog. The lake spills across the U.S.-Canadian border into Vermont.

The helpful **Bureau d'Information Touristique Memphrémagog,** at 55 rue Cabana (via Rte. 112), Magog, PQ J1X 2C4 (© **800/267-2744** or 819/843-2744; fax 819/847-4036; www.tourisme-memphremagog.com), is open daily in summer 8:30am to 8pm, and the rest of the year daily from 9am to 5pm.

Magog has a fully used waterfront, and in July each year the **Lac Memphrémagog International Swimming Marathon** (© **818/843-5000;** www.traversee-memphremagog.com)

creates a big splash. Participants start out in Newport, Vermont, at 6am and swim 24 miles to Magog, arriving in midafternoon around 3:30 or 4pm. To experience the lake without such soggy exertion, take a 1¾-hour **lake cruise** aboard the 70-passenger *Aventure I* or 100-passenger *Aventure II* (© **819/843-8068;** www.croisiere-memphremagog.com). The cost for the 1 hour, 45 minute cruise is C$18 (US$14) for adults and C$8.75 (US$7) for children 3 to 11; a daylong cruise to Newport, Vermont, and back is C$59 (US$47). The boats leave from Point Merry Park, the focal point for many of the town's outdoor activities. Cruises off-season depend upon demand, so call ahead.

Several firms rent sailboats, motorboats, kayaks, and windsurfers, among them **Boutique Nautique 30 Degrés,** 201 rue Merry sud (© **819/843-2102;** www.30degres.com); **Marina Le Merry Club,** 201 rue Merry sud (© **819/843-2728**); and **Voile Memphrémagog,** Plage des Cantons (© **819/847-3181**). And while you're on the water, scan the ripples for Memphre, the lake's own legendary sea creature, which supposedly surfaced for the first time in 1798. It will come as no surprise that other sightings have been claimed since then.

A 19km (12-mile) bike path links the lake with Mont-Orford; in winter it is transformed into a **cross-country ski trail,** and a 2.5km-long (1½-mile) **skating rink** is created on the shores of the lake. Snowmobiling trails crisscross the region.

Other popular activities in the area include golf, tennis, and horseback riding. A **Grape Harvest Festival** is held over 4 days at the end of August and start of September.

Abbaye de Saint-Benoît-du-Lac

There's no mistaking the abbey, with its granite steeple that thrusts into the sky above the lake and with Owl's Head Mountain in the background. Although Saint-Benoît-du-Lac dates only from 1912, the serenity of the site is timeless. Some 40 monks help keep the art of Gregorian chant alive in their liturgy, which can be attended by outsiders. For the 45-minute service, walk to the rear of the abbey and down the stairs; follow signs for the *oratoire* and sit in back to avoid a lot of otherwise obligatory standing up and sitting down. The abbey receives 7,000 pilgrims a year, most of them between the ages of 16 and 25. It maintains separate hostels for men and women (© **819/843-4080** for men, © **819/843-2340** for women). You can find out more at www.st-benoit-du-lac.com. Make room reservations in advance, figuring about C$35 (US$28) per person.

A blue cheese known as L'Ermite, among Québec's most famous, is produced at the monastery, along with a creamy version and Swiss and cheddar types. They are on sale in the little shop, which also sells chocolate from Oka (a small town in an Amerindian reserve about a dozen miles southwest of Montréal), honey, a nonalcoholic cider, and tapes of religious chants. Peek into the tiny stone chapel to the left at the entrance to the property, opposite the small cemetery. Visitors during the last 2 weeks of September or the first 2 weeks of October may want to help pick apples in the orchard.

Chemin Fisher. © **819/843-4080**. Free admission; donations accepted. Daily 5am–9pm; Mass with Gregorian chant daily at 11am, vespers with Gregorian chant at 5pm (7pm Thurs). No vespers Tues July–Aug. Shop: June–Oct Mon–Sat 9–10:45am and 11:45am–4:30pm; Nov–May Mon–Fri 9–10:45am and 1:30–4:30pm, Sat 9–10:45am and 11:45am–4:30pm. Driving west from Magog on Rte. 112, watch for the 1st road on the left on the far side of the lake; take chemin Bolton est 19km (12 miles) south to the turnoff to the abbey.

Where to Stay

Lodging choices in Magog aren't beguiling. However, if you must spend the night here, there are a number of modest B&Bs and small hotels located along the blocks of rue Merry, immediately north and south of its intersection with the main street, rue

Principale. Otherwise, the recommendation here is to look for accommodations in one of the nearby towns described in this section.

LAKE MASSAWIPPI

Southeast of Magog, reachable by Routes 141 or 108, east of Autoroute 55, is Lake Massawippi, easily the most desirable resort area in the Cantons-de-l'Est. Set among rolling hills and fertile farm country, the 19km-long (12-mile) lake, with its scalloped shoreline, was discovered in the early years of the 20th century by people of wealth and power, many of whom were American Southerners trying to escape the sultry summers of Virginia and Georgia. (They came up by train and are said to have pulled down their window shades while they crossed through Yankee territory.) They built grand "cottages" on slopes in prime locations along the lakeshore, with enough bedrooms to house their extended families and friends for months at a time. Several of these have now been converted to inns. Boating, fishing, golf, and cross-country skiing are all readily available. For a few days' escape from work or intensive travel, it's difficult to do better than Lake Massawippi.

The jewel of Lake Massawippi (which means "deep water" in Abenaki) is the town of **North Hatley** (pop. 704). Only half an hour from the United States border and 138km (86 miles) from Montréal, the town has a river meandering through it that empties into the lake. Apart from impressive sunsets over the lake, the town has a variety of lodgings and restaurants, shops, golf, a marina, and an unlabeled laundromat between the general store and the post office. Horse lovers will want to know about **Randonnées J. Robidas** at 32 chemin McFarland (℃ **819/563-0166**). Guides lead trail rides through forest and meadow beside the Massawippi in summer, with rates around C$25 (US$20) per hour. Buggy and winter sleigh rides are possibilities, and packages that include longer rides, meals, and vineyard visits are also available.

At noon on Sundays from mid-April to mid-June, **Le Festival du Lac Massawippi** (℃ **819/823-7810**) brings recitals by soloists and groups playing jazz, ethnic, and new music to North Hatley at the Ste-Elisabeth Church on chemin Capelton.

Where to Stay

Le Tricorne While the core of the main house is 125 years old, it looks as if it were erected only a few years ago. The exterior is shocking pink and white, the interior decked out in perfect *Good Housekeeping* manner, with lots of duck decoys and tartans. That decorative scheme is quite different from the one that informs the brand-new structure 45m (148 ft.) up the hill. The five bedrooms there are much larger and have a more sophisticated corporate style. Eight rooms have fireplaces, 10 have Jacuzzis. No phones or TVs, but those are available in common rooms. There are spectacular views of Lake Massawippi from the property.

50 chemin Gosselin, North Hatley, PQ J0B 2C0. ℃ 819/842-4522. Fax 819/842-2692. www.manoirletricorne.com. 17 units. C$105–C$250 (US$84–US$200) double. Rates include full breakfast. AE, MC, V. Take Rte. 108 west out of North Hatley and follow the signs. Children over 8 years are welcome. **Amenities:** Heated outdoor pool; golf nearby. *In room:* A/C, no phone.

Where to Stay & Dine

While the full-service inns of this region won't refuse children, they have serious dining rooms that may test youngsters' patience to the limits. Other meal arrangements should be made for young kids.

Auberge Hatley ✿✿✿ This acclaimed gastronomic resort, occupying a hillside above the lake, exudes a sense of well-being, felt as soon as you enter the front door.

It was purchased in 2002 by the owners of four superb designer hotels in Québec and Ontario, including the Germain in Montréal (p. 75) and the Dominion 1912 in Québec City (p. 225). There was some concern about how that very urban sensibility would mesh with the sophisticated but countrified tone of the *auberge*, but it hasn't presented a conflict. The rooms thus far are a tasteful blend of urbanity and rusticity, and more than half have Jacuzzis and/or fireplaces. Antiques, many of them sizable Quebecois pieces, have been retained. A new wing is to be added by summer 2006, bringing the total of rooms to 38, and they are talking about planting grapevines on 16 adjoining acres.

There's no arguing that the previous owners placed their priorities on the pleasures of the table, and that emphasis hasn't been subdued. Reserve a table—set with Rosenthal china, thin-stemmed glasses, and fresh flowers—overlooking the lake. It's a necessarily soothing environment, since dinner can easily extend over 3 hours. Updated but essentially classical French techniques are applied to such ingredients as salmon, red deer, halibut, partridge, bison, and wild boar. The wine cellar holds more than 15,000 bottles, and provides interesting wines by the glass and enough half-bottles to satisfy lighter imbibers. Table d'hôte menus start at C$58 (US$46) and top out with the gastronomic spectacular at C$95 (US$76), and are worth every last loonie. This dining room is second to none in all Québec, and its equals can be counted on one hand.

325 chemin Virgin, North Hatley, PQ J0B 2C0. ℂ 800/336-2451 or 819/842-2451. Fax 819/842-2907. www.auberge hatley.com. 25 units. C$250–C$590 (US$200–US$472) double. Rates include breakfast, dinner, and gratuities. Packages available. AE, MC, V. Closed 2 weeks in Jan. Take Exit 29 from Autoroute 55 and follow Rte. 108 east, watching for signs. **Amenities:** Restaurant (French contemporary); bar; heated outdoor pool; golf nearby; in-room massage. *In room:* A/C, TV, hair dryer.

Auberge Ripplecove ☆☆☆

A warm welcome is extended by the staff of this handsome inn, and impeccable housekeeping standards are observed throughout. The core structure dates from 1945, but subsequent expansions have added rooms, suites, cottages, and, recently, a spa with exercise room and outdoor hot tub. About half the rooms have gas fireplaces, balconies, and Jacuzzis, and the suites add kitchenettes and stocked minibars to the list of amenities. Check out the elegant lobby lounge and its ornate 4.2m-high (14-ft.) breakfront built in 1880. This 4.8-hectare (12-acre) property beside Lake Massawippi has two private beaches and a night-lit tennis court, and instruction and equipment are available for sailing, sailboarding, water-skiing, canoeing, kayaking, and cross-country skiing. The inn's award-winning lakeside restaurant fills up most nights in season with diners drawn to the kitchen's reputation for creativity. "Seafood *pot au feu* perfumed with cilantro" or "Townships duck confit with onion compote," anyone? The gastronomic menu is C$85 (US$68). Innkeeper Jeffrey Stafford is the brother of the owner of Manoir Hovey in North Hatley. Taste and energy run in the family.

700 chemin Ripplecove (P.O. Box 26), Ayer's Cliff, PQ J0B 1C0. ℂ 800/668-4296 or 819/838-4296. Fax 819/838-5541. www.ripplecove.com. 25 units. C$210–C$520 (US$168–US$416) double; from C$410 (US$328) suite. Rates include breakfast and dinner, gratuities, and the use of most recreational facilities. AE, MC, V. Take Rte. 55 to Exit 21; follow Rte. 141 east, watching for signs. **Amenities:** Restaurant (French Contemporary); pub; heated outdoor pool; golf nearby; tennis court; free watersports equipment; free bikes; children's programs; concierge; secretarial services; limited room service; massage; babysitting; laundry service; dry cleaning. *In room:* A/C, TV, dataport, coffeemaker, hair dryer, iron.

Manoir Hovey ☆☆☆

Named for Capt. Ebenezer Hovey, a Connecticut Yankee who came upon Lake Massawippi in 1793, this columned manor was built in 1899.

Encompassing 8 hectares (20 acres) and 488m (1,601 ft.) of lakefront property, it's one of eastern Canada's most complete resort inns. It has not only closed the gap with its friendly rival, the Auberge Hatley (see above), in the excellence of its cuisine, but also trumped with its sumptuously appointed rooms, especially in the 25 that were accorded extensive renovations most recently and the two lavishly rustic suites in a separate building above the main inn. All have been rendered even more desirable than before—ravishingly luxurious, in some cases—with fireplaces, balconies, and Jacuzzis. The library lounge is as beckoning a room as can be found, with floor-to-ceiling bookshelves, deep chairs and sofas, and a stone fireplace, with the daily newspapers laid out. Free touring bikes, two beaches, and the use of canoes, kayaks, and rowboats add to the appeal. Water-skiing is available at extra charge. In winter, they push a heated cabin out onto the lake for ice fishing. The menu in the paneled dining room features fresh herbs, vegetables, and edible flowers from the kitchen garden. Meals are brought and explained in as much detail as patrons desire. Dishes are fragrant and full-bodied, in attractive presentations. Lunch is served alfresco in summer. Steve and Kathy Stafford are the gracious hosts.

Chemin Hovey (P.O. Box 60), North Hatley, PQ J0B 2C0. © 800/661-2421 or 819/842-2421. Fax 819/842-2248. www.manoirhovey.com. 40 units. C$230–C$540 (US$184–US$432) double; from C$410 (US$328) suite. Rates include full breakfast, dinner, tax, gratuities, and use of most recreational facilities. Packages available. AE, DC, MC, V. Take Exit 29 off Autoroute 55 and follow Rte. 108 east, watching for signs. **Amenities:** Restaurant (French Contemporary); bar; heated outdoor pool; golf nearby; lit tennis court; exercise room; concierge; limited room service; massage; dry cleaning. *In room:* A/C, TV, coffeemaker, hair dryer.

Where to Dine

Café Massawippi ✪ FRENCH CONTEMPORARY   Contained in a small roadside house with a plain, unassuming interior hung with inept abstract paintings, newcomers can be excused if their expectations are low. They discover, along with the regulars and other tourists whose cars fill the parking lot by 7pm nightly, that the true art appears on the plate. Although the menu is fairly short, you can be forgiven if you change your mind two or three times. The declared house specialties—foie gras and venison tartare—might be bypassed, but how to choose between snowy halibut with shrimp guacamole and mango-tequila sauce or rack of lamb and truffle spätzle dressed with balsamic vinegar and tamari sauce? Appetizers are equally appealing, enough to ask to have two or three of them instead of the conventional first and main course. It took daring to open an ambitious restaurant in the same small town as the multi-starred inns described above, but chef-owner Tremblay pulled it off.

3050 chemin Capelton. © 819/842-4528. Reservations recommended. Main courses C$40–C$48 (US$32–US$38). AE, MC, V. June 1–Labor Day, daily 6–10pm, rest of year Wed–Sat 6–10pm.

Pilsen INTERNATIONAL   For food less grand and less expensive than that at the four entries listed above, check out this pub and restaurant in the center of North Hatley. There are a terrace in front and a narrow deck overhanging the river that feeds the lake. The place fills up quickly on warm days, the better to watch boats setting out or returning. Patrons snaffle up renditions of nachos and burgers, pastas, and fried calamari, as well as more adventurous fare, such as chipotle and lime tilapia with tomato-cilantro salsa. The menu is changed weekly. There's an extensive choice of beers, including local microbrews Massawippi Blonde and Townships Pale Ale. Park behind the restaurant.

55 rue Principale. © 819/842-2971. Reservations recommended on weekends. Main courses C$10–C$24 (US$8–US$19); table d'hôte lunch C$14–C$16 (US$11–US$13), dinner C$23–C$34 (US$18–US$27). AE, MC, V. Daily 11:30am–10:30pm (closed Mon–Tues late Oct to late Apr). The bar stays open until 3am Fri–Sat.

STANSTEAD PLAIN, ROCK ISLAND & BEEBE PLAIN

For a briefly diverting detour on the way south to Vermont, follow Route 143 as far as possible without actually crossing into the United States, and turn west to explore the three border villages that compose the town of Stanstead.

In 1995, **Stanstead** (pop. 3,162) incorporated the village of **Rock Island,** which is the commercial center of the area. Fans of geographical oddities will love the **Haskell Opera House.** Dating from 1904, it's literally and logistically half Canadian and half American: The stage and performers are in Canada, and the audience is in the United States.

Also gathered into the township was **Beebe Plain,** west of Rock Island, a center for quarrying granite. What makes this town notable is 1km-long (⅗-mile) **Canusa Street.** The north side is in Canada, the south side in the United States—thus its name, CAN-USA. Check the car license plates on either side. Here, it's long distance to call a neighbor across the street, and while they're free to walk across the street for a visit, they are expected, at least technically, to report to the authorities if they decide to drive.

12

Getting to Know Québec City

Québec City is the soul of New France. It was the first significant settlement in Canada, and today it is the capital of politically prickly Québec, a province larger than Alaska. The old city, a tumble of slate-roofed granite houses clustered around the dominating Château Frontenac, is a haunting evocation of a coastal town in the motherland, as romantic as any on that continent. The St. Lawrence makes a majestic sweep beneath the palisades on which the capital stands, as gray as gunmetal under dark skies, but silvered by sunlight when the clouds pass. Because of its history, beauty, and unique stature as the only walled city north of Mexico, the historic district of Québec City was named a UNESCO World Heritage Site in 1985—the only area so designated in North America.

Québec City is almost entirely French in feeling, in spirit, and in language; 95% of the population is Francophone. But many of its 167,000 citizens speak some English, especially those who work in hotels, restaurants, and shops where they deal with Anglophones every day. Québec City and adjoining Sainte-Foy are also college towns, and thousands of resident young people study English as a second language. So although it is often more difficult in Québec City than in Montréal to understand and be understood, the average Quebecois goes out of his or her way to communicate—in halting English, sign language, simplified French, or a combination of all three. Most of the Quebecois are an uncommonly gracious lot, and it is a pleasure to spend time in their company and in their city.

In the following chapters are tips on where to stay, where to dine, and what to do in the city itself. After exploring Québec City, consider such excursions as a day trip around the Île d'Orléans, an agricultural and resort island within sight of the Château Frontenac, extended, perhaps, by a drive along the northern coast past the shrine of Ste-Anne-de-Beaupré to the provincial park and ski resort at Mont Ste-Anne, and on to Charlevoix and the dramatic Saguenay River, where whales come to play.

1 Orientation

Almost all of a visit to Québec City can be spent in the old upper and lower towns, because many accommodations, restaurants, and tourist-oriented services are based there. The colonial city was first built right down by the St. Lawrence at the foot of rearing Cap Diamant (Cape Diamond). It was here that the earliest merchants, traders, and boatmen earned their livelihoods; but due to unfriendly fire from the British and Amerindians in the 1700s, residents moved to safer houses atop the steep cliffs that form the rim of Cap Diamant, and the Basse-Ville (Lower Town) became primarily a district of wharves and warehouses. That trend has been reversed of late, with several new *auberges* (inns) and small hotels, and many attractive bistros and shops bringing new life to the area.

Haute-Ville, or Upper Town, the Quebecois later discovered, was not immune to cannon fire either, as the British General Wolfe was to prove. Nevertheless, the division into Upper and Lower Towns persisted for obvious topographical reasons. The Upper Town remains enclosed by fortification walls, and several ramplike streets and a cliffside elevator (funiculaire) connect it to the Lower Town.

ARRIVING

BY PLANE   **Jean-Lesage International Airport** (© 418/640-2700; www.aeroport dequebec.com) is small, despite the grand name. It is served by **Air Canada** and **Air Canada Jazz** (© 888/247-2252; www.aircanada.com and www.flyjazz.ca), **Continental** (© 800/231-0856; www.continental.com), **American** (© 800/433-7300; www.aa.com), and **Northwest/KLM** (© 800/225-2525; www.nwa.com). Bus service is no longer available between the airport and the city. A taxi to downtown Québec City is a fixed-rate C$25 (US$20).

BY TRAIN   The handsome train station in Québec City, **Gare du Palais,** 450 rue de la Gare-du-Palais (© **418/692-3940**), was designed by Bruce Price, who is also responsible for the fabled Château Frontenac. The Lower Town location isn't central, though, so plan on a moderately strenuous uphill hike or a C$6 to C$8 (US$4.80– US$6.40) cab ride to the Upper Town. That's per trip, incidentally, not per passenger, as an occasional cabbie may pretend.

BY BUS   The bus station, **Gare d'Autobus de la Vieille Capitale,** at 320 rue Abraham-Martin (© **418/525-3000**), is near the train station. From the train station, it is an uphill climb or quick cab ride to Château Frontenac and the Upper Town. A taxi should cost about the same as from the train station, C$6 to C$8 (US$4.80–US$6.40) per trip, not per passenger.

BY CAR   From New York City, follow I-87 to Autoroute 15 to Montréal, picking up Autoroute 20 to Québec City. Take 73 nord across the Pont Pierre-Laporte and exit onto boulevard Champlain immediately after crossing the bridge. This skirts the city at river level. Turn left at Parc des Champs-de-Bataille (Battlefields Park) and right onto the Grande-Allée. Alternatively, take Autoroute 40 from Montréal, which follows the north shore of the St. Lawrence.

From Boston, take I-89 to I-93 to I-91 in Montpelier, Vermont, which connects with Autoroute 55 in Québec to link up with Autoroute 20. Or follow I-90 up the Atlantic coast, through Portland, Maine, to Route 201 west of Bangor, then Autoroute 173 to Lévis. A car-ferry there, **Traverse Québec-Lévis** (© **418/644-3704**), provides a 10-minute ride across the St. Lawrence River. Although the schedule varies substantially according to time of day, week, and season, the ferry leaves at least every hour (more often during rush hours) from 6am to 2am. One-way, it costs C$5.10 or C$5.60 (US$4.10 or US$4.50) for the car, and C$8.50 or $C9.85 (US$6.80 or US$7.90) for up to six passengers. Passengers without vehicles pay C$2 or $C2.50 (US$1.60 or US$2) for ages 12 to 64, C$1.40 or US$1.75 (US$1.15 or US$1.40) for ages 5 to 11, C$1.80 or C$2.25 (US$1.45 or US$1.80) for each passenger over 65, free for those under 5. Prices shown reflect low- and high-season rates.

VISITOR INFORMATION

The Greater Québec Area Tourism and Convention Bureau operates two useful provincial information centers in and near the city. One is in the Discovery Pavilion at 835 av. Wilfrid-Laurier (© **418/641-6290**), bordering the Plaines d'Abraham, and

Québec City Orientation

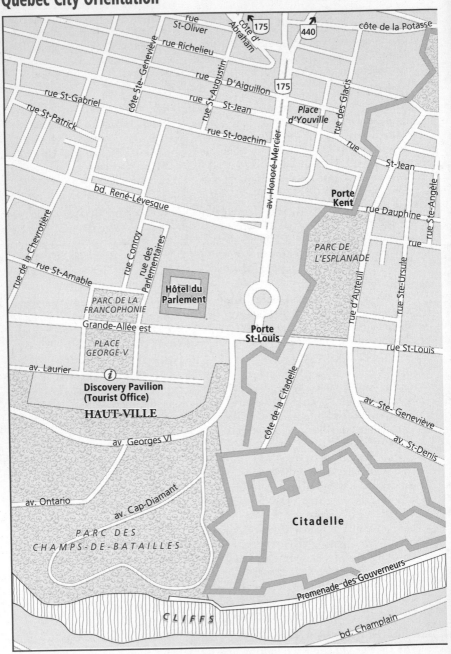

rue St-Oliver

rue Richelieu

rue St-Gabriel

rue St-Patrick

côte Ste-Geneviève

rue St-Augustin

D'Aiguillon

St-Jean

rue St-Joachim

côte d'Abraham

175

440

175

côte de la Potasse

Place d'Youville

rue des Glacis

rue

St-Jean

av. Honoré-Mercier

bd. René-Lévesque

Porte Kent

rue Dauphine

rue Ste-Angèle

rue

rue de la Chevrotière

rue St-Amable

rue Conroy

rue des Parlementaires

Hôtel du Parlement

PARC DE L'ESPLANADE

rue d'Auteuil

rue Ste-Ursule

PARC DE LA FRANCOPHONIE

Grande-Allée est

PLACE GEORGE-V

Porte St-Louis

rue St-Louis

av. Laurier

Discovery Pavilion (Tourist Office)

HAUT-VILLE

côte de la Citadelle

av. Ste- Geneviève

av. St-Denis

av. Georges VI

av. Ontario

av. Cap-Diamant

PARC DES CHAMPS-DE-BATAILLES

Citadelle

Promenade-des-Gouverneurs

CLIFFS

bd. Champlain

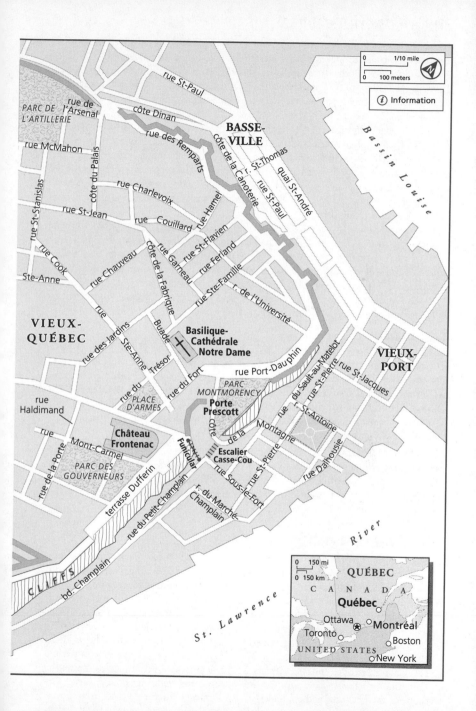

rue St-Paul

PARC DE
L'ARTILLERIE

rue de l'Arsenal

côte Dinan

BASSE-
VILLE

Bassin Louise

rue McMahon

rue des Remparts

côte de la Canoterie

r. St-Thomas

quai St-André

rue St-Paul

rue St-Thomas

côte du Palais

rue Charlevoix

rue St-Stanislas

rue St-Jean

rue Couillard

rue Hamel

rue St-Flavien

rue Ferland

rue Cook

rue Chauveau

rue Garneau

côte de la Fabrique

rue Ste-Famille

r. de l'Université

Ste-Anne

VIEUX-
QUÉBEC

rue des Jardins

Ste-Anne

Buade

Trésor

Basilique-
Cathédrale
Notre Dame

rue Port-Dauphin

VIEUX-
PORT

rue du Sault-au-Matelot

rue St-Pierre

rue St-Jacques

rue du Fort

PARC
MONTMORENCY

rue
Haldimand

PLACE
D'ARMES

Porte
Prescott

côte de la Montagne

r. St-Antoine

rue
Mont-Carmel

Château
Frontenac

Funicular

Escalier
Casse-Cou

rue St-Pierre

rue Dalhousie

rue de la Porte

PARC DES
GOUVERNEURS

terrasse Dufferin

rue du Petit-Champlain

rue Sous-le-Fort

r. du Marché
Champlain

CLIFFS

bd. Champlain

St. Lawrence

River

Information

1/10 mile

100 meters

QUÉBEC

150 mi

150 km

CANADA

Québec

Ottawa

Montréal

Toronto

Boston

UNITED STATES

New York

the other is in suburban Ste-Foy, at 3300 av. des Hôtels (© **418/651-2882**). They have rack after rack of brochures and attendants who can answer questions and make hotel reservations. Both offices are open daily 8:30am to 7:30pm from June 24 to Labor Day; 8:30am to 6:30pm Labor Day to Thanksgiving; the rest of the year 9am to 5pm Monday through Saturday, 10am to 4pm Sunday. The website for the bureau is www.quebecregion.com.

The Québec Government's tourism department operates an **Infotouriste de Québec** office on place d'Armes, down the hill from the Château Frontenac, at 12 rue Ste-Anne (© **877/266-5687; www.bonjourquebec.com**). It's open from 9am to 5pm daily, late June to early September, and from 10am to 5pm the rest of the year. The office has many brochures, information about cruise and bus tour operators, a souvenir shop, a 24-hour ATM *(guichet automatique),* a currency-exchange office, and a free lodging reservation service.

From early June through Labor Day, university students pilot motorscooters through the tourist districts of Old Québec and near tourist sites in the Upper and Lower Towns, making themselves available to offer information to visitors. In French, it's called the *service mobile d'information touristique,* and their scooters fly flags bearing a large "?". Just hail them as they approach; they're bilingual.

Parks Canada operates an information kiosk in front of the Château Frontenac; it's open daily 9am to noon and 1 to 5pm.

CITY LAYOUT

MAIN AVENUES & STREETS   Within the walls of the **Haute-Ville (Upper Town),** the principal streets are rues St-Louis (which becomes the Grande-Allée outside the city walls), Ste-Anne, and St-Jean, and the pedestrians-only Terrasse Dufferin, which overlooks the river in front of the Château Frontenac. In the **Basse-Ville (Lower Town),** major streets are St-Pierre, Dalhousie, St-Paul, and, parallel to St-Paul, St-André. There are good maps of the Upper and Lower Towns and the metropolitan area available at any tourist office.

FINDING AN ADDRESS   If it were larger, the historic district, with its winding and plunging streets, might be confusing to negotiate. However, it's very compact, so most visitors have little difficulty finding their way around. Most streets are only a few blocks long, so when the name of the street is known, it is fairly easy to find a specific address.

THE NEIGHBORHOODS IN BRIEF

Haute-Ville   The Upper Town, surrounded by thick ramparts, occupies the crest of Cap Diamant and overlooks the Fleuve Saint-Laurent (St. Lawrence River). It includes many of the sites for which the city is famous, among them the Château Frontenac, Place d'Armes, Basilica of Notre-Dame, Québec Seminary and Museum, and the Terrasse Dufferin. At a higher elevation, to the south of the Château, is the Citadel, a partially star-shaped fortress begun by the French in the 18th century and augmented often by the English well into the 19th century. Since most buildings are at least 100 years old, made of granite in similar styles, the Haute-Ville is visually harmonious, with few jarring modern intrusions. When they added a new wing to the Château Frontenac a few years ago, they modeled it after the original—standing policy here. The Terrasse Dufferin is a pedestrian promenade that attracts crowds in all seasons for its magnificent views of the river and the land to the south, ferries gliding back and forth, cruise ships and Great Lakes freighters putting in at the harbor below.

Basse-Ville The Lower Town encompasses the restored Quartier du Petit-Champlain, including pedestrian-only rue du Petit-Champlain; Place Royale and the small Notre-Dame-des-Victoires church; and, nearby, the impressive Museum of Civilization, a highlight of any visit. Basse is linked to Haute by the funicular on Terrasse Dufferin and by several streets and stairways, including one near the entrance to the funicular. Petit-Champlain is undeniably touristy, but not unpleasantly so: T-shirt vendors have been held in check, though hardly banned. It contains several agreeable cafes and shops. Restored Place Royale is perhaps the most attractive of the city's many squares, upper or lower.

Grande-Allée This boulevard is the western extension of rue St-Louis, from the St-Louis Gate in the fortified walls to avenue Taché. It passes the stately Parliament building, in front of which the Winter Carnival takes place every year (the ice sculptures are installed across the street), as well as the numerous terraced bars and restaurants that line both sides from rue de la Chevrotière to rue de Claire-Fontaine. Later, it skirts the Musée des Beaux-Arts and the Plains of Abraham, where one of the most important battles in the history of North America took place between the French and the British for control of the city. The city's large modern hotels are also on or near the Grande-Allée.

2 Getting Around

Once you're within or near the walls of the Haute-Ville, virtually no place of interest, hotel, or restaurant is beyond walking distance. In bad weather, or when you're traversing between opposite ends of Lower and Upper Towns, a taxi might be necessary, but in general, walking is the best way to explore the city.

BY BUS

Local buses run quite often and charge C$2.50 (US$2) in exact change. One-day passes cost C$5.45 (US$4.35), and discounts are available for seniors and students. Bus no. 7 travels up and down rue St-Jean; no. 11 shuttles along Grande-Allée/rue St-Louis and, along with nos. 7 and 8, also goes well into suburban Ste-Foy, for those who want to visit the shopping centers there.

BY FUNICULAR

Although there are streets and stairs between the Château Frontenac on the top of the cliff and Place Royale in the Lower Town, there is also a funicular, which has long operated along an inclined 63m (207-ft.) track between the Terrasse Dufferin and the Quartier du Petit-Champlain. It was closed for a couple of years after a fatal accident in 1996. Repaired now, the **upper station** is near the front of the Château Frontenac and Place d'Armes, while the **lower station** is actually inside the Maison Louis-Jolliet, on rue du Petit-Champlain. It runs year-round daily from early morning until 11:30pm. Wheelchairs are accommodated. The one-way fare is C$1.50 (US$1.20).

BY TAXI

Taxis are everywhere, cruising and parked in front of the big hotels and in some of the larger squares of the Upper Town. In theory, they can be hailed, but they are best obtained by locating one of their stands, as in the Place d'Armes or in front of the

Hôtel-de-Ville (City Hall). Restaurant managers and hotel bell captains will also summon them if you ask. Fares are the same as in Montréal, meaning they're somewhat expensive given the short distances of most rides. The starting rate is C$2.75 (US$2.20), and each kilometer costs C$1.30 (US$1). Tip 10% to 15%. A taxi from the train station to one of the big hotels is about C$6 to C$8 (US$4.80–US$6.40) plus tip. To call a cab, try **Taxi Coop** (© **418/525-5191**) or **Taxi Québec** (© **418/ 525-8123**).

BY CAR

See "By Car" under "Getting Around," in chapter 4, for information on gasoline and driving rules in Canada. Unlike in Montréal, drivers are permitted to turn right at red traffic lights, but only after coming to a full stop and yielding to pedestrians in the crosswalk.

RENTALS   Car-rental companies include **Avis,** at the airport (© **800/879-2847** or 418/872-2861; www.avis.com) and in the city (© 418/523-1075); **Budget,** at the airport (© **800/268-8900** or 418/872-9885; www.budget.com) and in the city (© 418/ 687-4220); **Hertz Canada,** at the airport (© **800/654-3131** or 418/871-1571; www. hertz.ca) and in the city (© 418/697-4949); **Thrifty,** at the airport (© **800/367-2277** or 418/877-2870; www.thrifty.com) and in the city (© 418/648-7766); and **Tilden National,** at the airport (© **418/871-1224;** www.nationalcar.com) and in the city (© 418/692-1727).

PARKING   On-street parking is very difficult in the cramped quarters of old Québec City. When you find a rare space on the street, be sure to check the signs for the hours when parking is permissible. When meters are in place, the charge is C25¢ (US20¢) per 15 minutes up to 120 minutes. Metered spots are free on Sundays, before 9am and after 6pm Monday through Wednesday and on Saturday, and before 9am and after 9pm Thursday and Friday.

Many of the smaller hotels have special arrangements with local garages, resulting in discounts for their guests of three or four dollars less per day than the usual C$10 (US$8) or more per day. Check at the hotel first before parking in a lot or garage.

If a particular hotel or *auberge* doesn't have access to a garage or lot, plenty are available, clearly marked on the foldout city map available at tourist offices. Several convenient lots include the one next to the Hôtel-de-Ville (City Hall), where parking is free in the evening and on weekends; Complexe G, off the Grande-Allée on rue St-Cyrille, with twice-daily in-and-out privileges at no extra charge; and in the Lower Town across the street from the Musée de la Civilisation, on rue Dalhousie, where discounts are often offered on weekends.

BY BICYCLE

Given the hilly topography of the Upper Town, cycling isn't a particularly attractive option for most. But pedal and motorized bicycles are available at a shop in the flatter Lower Town. Bikes are C$10 (US$8) an hour or C$18 (US$14) for 4 hours. The shop, **Cyclo Services,** 160 quai Saint-André (© **418/692-4052;** www.microtec. net/cyclo), also rents tandems, child trailers, and in-line skates, and it's open daily throughout the year. Up in the Haute-Ville, near rue St-Jean, is **Vélo Passe-Sport Plein Air,** at 22 côte du Palais (© **418/692-3643;** www.velopasse-sport.com). They rent bikes and scooters in summer, skis and snowshoes in winter. Prices are similar.

FAST FACTS: Québec City

American Express There is no office right in town, but for lost traveler's checks or credit cards, call ✆ **418/692-0997.** American Express keeps a customer-service desk in two shopping centers in Ste-Foy, a bus or taxi ride away: Les Galeries de la Capitale, 5401 bd. des Galeries (✆ **418/627-2580**), and Place Laurier, 2740 bd. Laurier (✆ **418/658-8820**).

ATMs ATMs are not as ubiquitous in Québec City as they are in Montréal. The most conveniently located cash machine in the Haute-Ville is at the corner of rues Ste-Anne and des Jardins.

Business Hours Banks are open from Monday to Friday 10am to 3pm, with most also having hours on Thursday and Friday evenings. Several banks have Saturday hours, but the ones that do are mostly located outside of the old town. Most stores are open Monday through Wednesday from 9 or 10am to 6pm, Thursday and/or Friday from 9am to 9pm, and Saturday from 9am to 5pm. Many stores are now also open on Sunday from noon to 5pm.

Consulate The U.S. Consulate is near the Château Frontenac, facing Jardin des Gouverneurs at 2 place Terrasse Dufferin (✆ **418/692-2095**).

Currency Exchange Conveniently located near the Château Frontenac, the Bureau de Change at 19 rue Ste-Anne and rue des Jardins is open Monday, Tuesday, and Friday from 10am to 3pm, and Wednesday and Thursday from 10am to 6pm. On weekends, it's possible to change money in hotels and shops, but you'll get an equal or better rate at an ATM.

Dentists Call ✆ **418/524-2444** Monday through Saturday or ✆ **418/656-6060** for weekend emergencies. Both numbers are hot lines that refer callers to available dentists.

Doctors For emergency treatment, call **Info-Santé** (✆ **418/648-2626**) 24 hours a day, or the **Hôtel-Dieu de Québec** hospital emergency room (11 Côte du Palais; ✆ **418/691-5151**). Call ✆ **911** for an ambulance.

Drugstores **Caron & Bernier,** in the Upper Town, 38 Côte du Palais (at rue Charlevoix; ✆ **418/692-4252**), is open 8:15am to 8pm Monday through Friday, and 9am to 3pm on Saturday. In an emergency, it's necessary to travel to the suburbs to **Pharmacie Brunet,** in Les Galeries Charlesbourg, 4250 Première Ave. (1ère or First Ave.), in Charlesbourg (✆ **418/623-1571**), open 24 hours, 7 days a week.

Electricity As in the United States, Canada uses 110–120 volts AC (60 cycles) compared to 220–240 volts AC (50 cycles) in most of Europe, Australia, and New Zealand. If your small appliances use 220–240 volts, you'll need a 110-volt transformer and a plug adapter with two flat parallel pins to operate them here.

Emergencies For police or ambulance, call ✆ **911.** Marine Search and Rescue (Canadian Coast Guard), 24 hours a day, ✆ **418/648-3599** (Greater Québec area) or ✆ **800/463-4393** (St. Lawrence River). The number for the Poison Control Center is ✆ **800/463-5060** or 418/656-8090.

Internet **Tribune Café,** 950 rue St-Jean (✆ **418/694-0051**), serves sandwiches, coffee, and ice cream, but the main attraction is several computers available to passersby. The fee is C$3.50 (US$2.80) for 30 minutes, C$6 (US$4.80) for an hour.

Liquor & Wine A supermarket-sized **Société des Alcools** store is located at 1059 av. Cartier. Wine and beer can be bought in grocery stores and supermarkets. The legal drinking age in the province is 18.

Mail All mail posted in Canada must bear Canadian stamps. That might seem painfully obvious, but apparently large numbers of visitors use stamps from their home countries, especially the United States.

Newspapers & Magazines Major Canadian and American English-language newspapers and magazines are available in the newsstands of the large hotels, at vending machines on tourist corners in the old town, and at **Maison de la Presse Internationale**, at 1050 rue St-Jean. The leading French-language newspapers are *Le Soleil* and *Le Journal de Québec.*

Pets For emergency pet illnesses or injuries, call ✆ **418/872-5355** 24 hours a day. Pet owners must by law pick up after their animals, and animals must be kept on leashes.

Police For the Québec City police, call ✆ **911.** For the Sûreté du Québec, comparable to the state police or highway patrol, call ✆ **800/461-2131.**

Post Office The main post office *(bureau de poste)* is in the Lower Town, at 300 rue St-Paul near rue Abraham-Martin, not far from Carré Parent (Parent Square) by the port (✆ **418/694-6175**). Hours are 8am to 5:45pm Monday through Friday. A convenient branch in the Upper Town, half a block down the hill from the Château Frontenac at 5 av. du Fort (✆ **418/694-6102**), keeps the same hours. They sell postcards and souvenirs, and have a computer terminal available free to customers (the use of which will almost always involve a wait).

Safety Canadian cities are far safer than most of their U.S. counterparts. Still, tourists are particular targets of street criminals, so the usual caveats pertain. Avoid leaving possessions in plain view in your car and stay aware of the behavior of people in your vicinity.

Taxes Most goods and services in Canada are taxed 7% by the federal government. On top of that, the province of Québec has an additional 8% tax on goods and services, including those provided by hotels. In Québec, the federal tax appears on the bill as the TPS, and the provincial tax is known as the TVQ. Tourists may receive a rebate on both the federal and provincial tax on items they have purchased but not used in Québec, as well as on lodging. To take advantage of this refund, request the necessary forms at duty-free shops and hotels, and submit them, with the original receipts, within a year of the purchase. Contact the Canadian consulate or Québec tourism office for up-to-the-minute information about taxes.

Telephones The telephone system, operated by Bell Canada, closely resembles the American model. All operators (dial ✆ **00** to get one) speak French and English, and respond in the appropriate language as soon as callers speak to them. Directory information calls (dial ✆ **411**) are free of charge. Both local and long-distance calls usually cost more from hotels—sometimes a lot more, so check. Directories *(annuaires des téléphones)* come in White Pages (residential) and Yellow Pages (commercial). Some, not all, U.S. cellphone companies cover Canada as well—check before departure.

Time Québec City is on Eastern Standard Time. Daylight saving time is observed as in the U.S., moving clocks ahead an hour in the spring and back an hour in the fall.

Tipping Practices are similar to those in the United States: 15% to 20% of restaurant bills, 10% to 15% for taxi drivers, C$1 (US80¢) per bag for porters, C$1 (US80¢) per night for the hotel room attendant. Hairdressers and barbers expect 10% to 15%. Hotel doormen should be tipped for calling a taxi or other services.

Transit Information Call © 418/627-2511 for the transit authority.

Useful Telephone Numbers For Alcoholics Anonymous, call © 418/529-0015, daily 8am to midnight. For Health Info, a 24-hour hot line answered by nurses, call © 418/648-2626. For Tel-Aide, for emotional distress including anxiety and depression, call © 418/686-2433.

13

Where to Stay in Québec City

Staying in one of the small hotels or inns within the walls of the Upper Town can be one of Québec City's most memorable experiences. That isn't a guarantee, however, that it will be enjoyable. Standards of comfort, amenities, and prices fluctuate so wildly from one small hotel to another—even within a single establishment—that it is wise to shop around and examine any rooms offered before registering. From rooms with private bathrooms, minibars, cable TVs, and high-speed Internet connections, to walk-up budget accommodations with linoleum floors and toilets down the hall, Québec City has a wide enough variety of lodgings to suit most tastes and wallets.

If cost is a prime consideration, note that prices drop significantly from November to April, except for such events as the Winter Carnival in February. As a rule, the prices given in the listings below are rack rates. That means you'll rarely, if ever, have to pay that much, unless it's the middle of Winter Carnival and everything else is booked. The higher rates given apply during the warmer months, the Christmas season, and the Winter Carnival. The cheapest rooms are usually found in smaller establishments, typically converted residences or lodgings carved out of several row houses. Often family-run, they offer fewer of the usual electronic gadgets—air-conditioning and TVs are far from standard at this level—and may have four or five floors but no elevator. In the budget category, even with an advance reservation, always ask to see two or three rooms before making a choice. Unless otherwise noted, all rooms in the lodgings listed below have private bathrooms—*en suite,* as they say in Canada.

Similar in atmosphere and price band to these small hotels are the more than 30 bed-and-breakfasts in and around Vieux-Québec. With rates in the C$70 to C$160 (US$56–US$128) range, they don't represent substantial savings over the small hotels, but will give you the opportunity to get to know some of the city dwellers.

When calling to make arrangements at a B&B, be very clear about your needs and requirements. A deposit is typically required, and minimum stays of 2 nights are common. Credit cards may not be accepted. A very useful *Accommodation Guide,* revised annually, is available at the tourist offices. It lists every member of the Greater Québec Area Tourism and Convention Bureau, from B&Bs to five-star hotels, providing details about number of rooms, prices, and facilities.

If you prefer the conveniences of large chain hotels and the Fairmont Le Château Frontenac is fully booked, you can go outside the ancient walls to the younger part of town. The handful of high-rise hotels out there are within walking distance of the attractions in the old city, or are only a quick bus or taxi ride away. In recent years, a clutch of new boutique hotels and small inns in the Lower Town has greatly enhanced the lodging stock.

Best Hotel Bets
For a roundup of my favorite Québec City hotels, see chapter 1.

1 Haute-Ville (Upper Town)

VERY EXPENSIVE

Fairmont Le Château Frontenac ✹✹✹ *Kids* Québec City's magical "castle" turned 100 years old in 1993. To celebrate, the management added a new 66-room wing, and because the hotel serves as the very symbol of the city, care was taken to replicate the original architectural style throughout. The hotel has hosted Queen Elizabeth and Prince Philip, and during World War II, Winston Churchill and Franklin D. Roosevelt had the entire place to themselves for a conference. It was built in phases, following the landline, so the wide halls take crooked paths. Luxurious rooms are outfitted with regal decor and elegant château furnishings. The highly variable room prices depend on size, location, view or lack of one, and how recently the room was renovated. That makes the rates given below no better than a very rough guide, because day of the week, time of the year, and even the weather, if it has influenced bookings, can determine the range of prices at which the rooms are offered. The casual Café de la Terrasse has dancing on Saturday nights. Two bars overlook the Terrasse Dufferin. If you have occasion to use the concierges, you are likely to be delighted with the experience. The 55 Entrée Gold rooms and suites have separate concierge and reception and a lounge with honor bar where breakfast is served. Children under 18 stay free in parent's room, and meals are free for kids under 5 and half-price for ages 6 to 12.

1 rue des Carrières (at rue St-Louis), Québec City, PQ G1R 4P5. ℂ 800/828-7447 or 418/692-3861. Fax 418/692-1751. www.cphotels.ca. 618 units. May–Oct C$503–C$699 (US$402–US$559) double; Nov–Apr C$301–C$349 (US$241–US$279) double; from C$699 (US$559) suite year-round. AE, DC, DISC, MC, V. Valet parking C$25 (US$20) per day. **Amenities:** 3 restaurants (Fusion, International); 2 bars; new indoor pool and kiddie pool; expansive health club; spa; Jacuzzi; children's programs; video arcade; concierge; car-rental desk; courtesy limo; business center; shopping arcade; 24-hr. room service; in-room massage; babysitting; laundry service; same-day dry cleaning; executive floors. *In room:* A/C, TV w/pay movies, dataport, minibar, coffeemaker, hair dryer, iron, safe.

EXPENSIVE

Manoir Victoria ✹ The sprawling lobby isn't especially beguiling, even though a C$4-million renovation was completed in 2004. But there are a new wing (ask for a room there) and two serviceable restaurants on the premises, and the proximity to the rue St-Jean restaurant and bar scene is a plus for many. An added extra is the indoor pool, rare in this city. The hotel sprawls all the way from the main entrance on Côte de Palais to adjacent St-Jean, zigzagging around a couple of stores. A long staircase reaches the lobby, but elevators make the trip to most of the rooms. All 156 rooms, half of which are nonsmoking, have been redecorated; all have Nintendo games and high-speed Internet access. Upping its appeal, the hotel installed a spa in 2004, with packages including mud or algae body wraps, hour massages, facials, exfoliations with sea salt, and pressotherapy at prices ranging from as little as C$60 (US$48) to as much as C$455 (US$364) for 2-day full treatments.

44 Côte du Palais (rue St-Jean), Québec City, PQ G1R 4H8. ℂ 800/463-6283 or 418/692-1030. Fax 418/692-3822. www.manoir-victoria.com. 156 units. June to mid-Oct C$215–C$285 (US$172–US$228) double, from C$285 (US$228) suite; late Oct to May C$109–C$169 (US$87–US$135) double, from C$285 (US$228) suite. Packages available. AE, DC, DISC, MC, V. 2 children under 18 stay free in parent's room. Valet parking C$18 (US$14). **Amenities:** 2

Where to Stay in Québec City

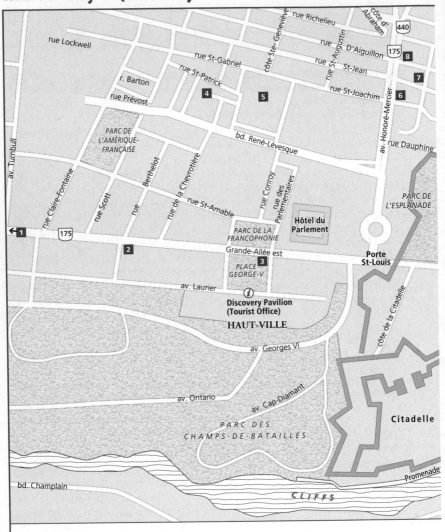

Auberge Saint-Antoine **19**
Auberge Saint-Pierre **18**
Château Bellevue **12**
Château Laurier **3**
Courtyard by Marriott **6**

Delta Québec **4**
Dominion 1912 **16**
Fairmont Le Château Frontenac **14**
Hilton Québec **5**
Hôtel Place Royal **8**

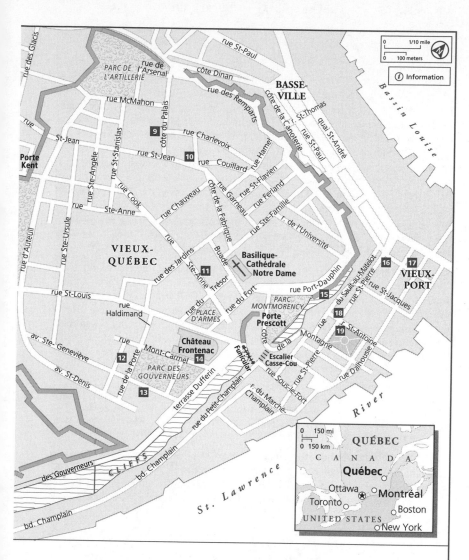

Hôtel Sainte-Anne **11**
Le Capitole **7**
Le Port Royale **17**
Le Priori **15**
L'Hôtel du Vieux-Québec **10**

Loews Le Concorde **2**
Manoir Sur-le-Cap **13**
Manoir Victoria **9**
Relais Charles-Alexander **1**

restaurants (French); 2 bars; heated indoor pool; health club w/sauna; concierge; car rental; limited room service; babysitting; laundry service; dry cleaning. *In room:* A/C, TV w/pay movies, minibar, hair dryer, iron.

MODERATE

Château Bellevue   Occupying several row houses at the top of the Jardin des Gouverneurs, this minihotel has a pleasant lobby with leather couches and chairs, and a helpful staff, as well as some of the creature comforts that smaller inns in the neighborhood lack. Although the rooms are small and often suffer from unfortunate decorating choices, they are quiet for the most part and have private bathrooms. A few higher-priced units overlook the park. The hotel's private parking is directly behind the building, a notable convenience in this congested part of town, although there are only a few spaces. Free coffee and other beverages are available in the lobby. If you're searching for a room on the spot and this place is full, there are 10 other lodgings within a block in any direction.

16 rue de la Porte, Québec City, PQ G1R 4M9. ⓒ 800/463-2617 or 418/692-2573. Fax 418/692-4876. www.vieux-quebec.com/bellevue. 58 units. Winter Carnival and May to late Oct C$149–C$189 (US$119–US$151) double; late Oct to June 30 C$99–C$159 (US$79–US$127) double. AE, DC, MC, V. Free valet parking. *In room:* A/C, TV.

Hôtel Sainte-Anne   Housed in a 19th-century row house in the very center of the historic district of the Upper Town, the interior has been transformed into a European-style design hotel (economy division). Exposed brick walls are common, and to avoid complicated construction, each room has a tall, narrow, free-standing cabinet containing a TV near the top, an unstocked fridge, a coffeemaker, and a wardrobe. The effect is quite spare, but unusual light fixtures add drama. Beds are comfortable and bathrooms feature satisfyingly drenching showers. The hotel fronts on a pedestrian block of rue Ste-Anne, and the nearest parking is over a block and several staircases away, in an underground garage.

32 rue Sainte-Anne (near rue des Jardins), Québec City, PQ G1R 3X3. ⓒ 877/222-9422 or 418/694-1455. Fax 418/692-4096. www.hotelste-anne.com. 28 units. May–Sept C$149–C$229 (US$119–US$183) double, from C$204 (US$163) suite; Oct–Apr C$124–C$164 (US$99–US$131) double, from C$194 (US$155). Rates include breakfast. AE, MC, V. **Amenities:** Restaurant (summer only); bar; laundry service. *In room:* TV, coffeemaker, hair dryer.

L'Hôtel du Vieux-Québec *Kids*   This century-old brick hotel has been renovated with care. Guest rooms are equipped with sofas, two double beds, and modern bathrooms. Most have kitchenettes. Ask for one of the 24 rooms recently redone with new carpeting and furniture; 2 of these are junior suites with Jacuzzis. With these homey

---

Kids Family-Friendly Hotels

Delta Québec (p. 223)   The rooftop swimming pool is a treat, with its indoor water route to the outside. Winter Carnival activities are a quick and easy walk away.

Fairmont Le Château Frontenac (p. 217)   Most kids love sleeping in a fairytale castle with an indoor pool and street performers just outside the door.

L'Hôtel du Vieux-Québec (p. 220)   Popular with families and school groups due to its comfortable rooms with kitchenettes, this is a good base for exploring Upper or Lower Town.

The Coldest Reception in Town

It takes all kinds. Winter visitors clamor to spend the night—at over C$522 (US$418) per couple—in a hotel carved from ice. Under contract with the creators of the first such undertaking in Sweden, Québec's own first ice hotel was carved to order in December 2000 for occupancy from January through March of 2001. Erected in Montmorency Falls Park, 10 minutes north of the capital, there was a 16-foot vaulted ceiling over the main hall, with an ice chandelier. In the bar, vodka was served in thick square shot glasses made of ice. And the beds in the six bedrooms were made of . . . you guessed it! Mattresses and deer skins insulated sleepers. No showers, but toilets were provided in an adjoining heated building.

It was a huge success. By 2003, the square footage of the hotel was tripled, allowing for 32 rooms and suites, a wedding chapel, a bar, and a cinema. To find out the plans for next winter, check **www.icehotel-canada.com**.

layouts, the hotel is understandably popular with families, skiers, and the groups of visiting high-school students who descend upon the city in late spring. In addition to Les Frères de la Côte on the ground floor, there are many moderately priced restaurants and nightspots nearby.

1190 rue St-Jean (at rue de l'Hôtel Dieu), Québec City, PQ G1R 1S6. *©* **800/361-7787** or 418/692-1850. Fax 418/692-5637. www.hvq.com. 41 units. July to mid-Oct C$159–C$239 (US$127–US$191) double; late Oct to June C$99–C$159 (US$79–US$127) double. Discount with stays of 3 nights or more. DC, MC, V. *In room:* A/C, TV, fridge, hair dryer.

INEXPENSIVE

Manoir Sur-le-Cap   All was fresh, painted, and shellacked a few years ago at this inn on the south side of the Parc des Gouverneurs, opposite the Château Frontenac. It still looks good, with gleaming floors and many exposed stone or brick walls. Obviously the price is right, unless you require air-conditioning or a phone. Know, too, that these four floors have no elevator. Upgrade to what they call their "condo"—an apartment in a separate building in back—and get a lodging with a working fireplace, a phone, a VCR, and a kitchenette with microwave oven, coffeemaker, and basic crockery. When booking, request parking at one of the nearby lots. This is a non-smoking lodging.

9 av. Ste-Geneviève (near rue Laporte), Québec City, PQ G1R 4A7. *©* **418/694-1987.** Fax 418/627-7405. www.manoir-sur-le-cap.com. 14 units. May–Oct C$105–C$195 (US$84–US$156) double, from C$265 (US$212) suite (condo); Nov–Apr C$80–C$95 (US$64–US$76) double, from C$165 (US$132) suite. Additional person C$15 (US$12). AE, MC, V. *In room:* TV, coffeemaker, hair dryer, iron.

2 Outside the Walls

EXPENSIVE

Château Laurier 👁👁   Anchoring the east end of the action-filled Grande-Allée, you'd never guess this was once a dowdy old-timer utterly lacking in distinction. A few years ago, the owners took over an adjoining building and added 65 newer, larger, jazzier units. Some of them have working fireplaces, Jacuzzis, and king beds; all enjoy the comforts and doodads of a first-class hotel, including free Internet access. The new rooms are clearly more desirable than those in the plainer and more cramped original wing. A bar and bistro remain in front, down a few steps from Grande-Allée, while the expansive new lobby is located on the Georges V side. The hotel is only 2 blocks west of the St-Louis Gate and across the way from Parliament Hill. Parking is free.

1220 place Georges V ouest (near corner of Grande-Allée), Québec City, PQ G1R 5B8. (⌀ **800/463-4453** or 418/522-8108. Fax 418/524-8768. www.vieuxquebec.com/laurier. 154 units. May to mid-Oct C$189–C$325 (US$151–US$260) double; mid-Oct to April C$134–C$275 (US$107–US$220). AE, DC, MC, V. Parking C$18 (US$14). **Amenities:** Restaurant (Bistro); bar; concierge; limited room service; laundry service; dry cleaning. *In room:* A/C, TV w/pay movies, dataport, coffeemaker, hair dryer.

Courtyard by Marriott ⍟

By sidestepping the conventional template of the parent chain, this fresh entry makes a substantial contribution to the ongoing enhancement of place d'Youville as a day-and-night gathering place for visitors and natives alike. A handsome building from the 1930s was converted into Marriott's first hotel in Québec City. The lobby impresses with a balustraded second floor above a carved marble fireplace flanked by leather sofas. A bar is to the right, the full-service restaurant beyond. A pianist plays at mealtimes. Bedrooms are Courtyard-simple, without flourishes, but perfectly comfortable, and with free high-speed Internet access. Two washing machines for guest use stand ready next to the small exercise room.

850 place d'Youville (at rue St-Joachim), Québec City, G1R 3P6. (⌀ **800/321-2211** or 418/694-4004. Fax 418/694-4007. www.marriott-quebec.com. 111 units. Summer C$309–C$358 (US$247–US$286) double; winter C$111–C$199 (US$89–US$159) double. AE, DC, DISC, MC, V. Parking C$18 (US$14). **Amenities:** Restaurant (Continental); bar; exercise room w/whirlpool; business center; limited room service; self-service laundry; dry cleaning. *In room:* A/C, TV w/pay movies, dataport, unstocked fridges, coffeemaker, hair dryer, iron.

Hilton Québec ⍟⍟

Superior on virtually every count to the other mid-rise contemporary hotels outside the old town (excluding Le Capitole, below), this Hilton is entirely true to the breed, the clear choice for executives and those leisure travelers who can't bear to live without their gadgets. The location—across the street from the city walls and near the Parliament—is excellent. It is also connected to the Place Québec shopping complex, which has 75 shops, two cinemas, a 1,000-car parking garage, and the convention center. The public rooms are big and brassy, Hilton-style. Most of the guest rooms have one or two large beds. Upper-floor views of the St. Lawrence River and old Québec are grand. Small pets are accepted.

1100 bd. René-Lévesque est, Québec City, PQ G1K 7K7. (⌀ **800/447-2411** or 418/647-6508. Fax 418/647-2986. www.hilton.com. 571 units. Summer C$289–C$349 (US$231–US$279) double; winter C$129–C$229 (US$103–US$183). Children stay free in parent's room. Packages available. AE, DC, DISC, MC, V. Valet parking C$25 (US$20). Head east along Grande-Allée, and just before the St-Louis Gate in the city wall, turn left on rue Honoré-Mercier, then left again as you pass the Parliament building; the hotel is 1 block ahead. Small pets accepted. **Amenities:** Restaurant (International); bar; heated outdoor pool (year-round); well-equipped health club w/Jacuzzi and sauna; children's programs; concierge; activities desk; car rental; courtesy limo; substantial business center; limited room service; in-room massage; babysitting; laundry service; same-day dry cleaning; executive floors. *In room:* A/C, TV w/pay movies, dataport, minibar, coffeemaker, hair dryer.

Hôtel Palace Royal ⍟⍟

The newest and most luxurious addition to a small, family-owned Québec hotel group, this hotel elevates the standards of the business hotels outside the city walls. Admittedly, it lacks a distinctive personality, perhaps because it's still young. Shooting for a Parisian ambience, lots of bronze statuary and marble are lavished on the lobby areas, while the kidney-shaped pool is at the heart of a virtual tropical garden. Over two-thirds of the units are suites, with unstocked fridges, extra

TV sets, and, in many cases, Jacuzzis meant for two. Secure underground garage parking is provided.

775 av. Honoré-Mercier (at place d'Youville), Québec City, PQ G1R 6A5. © 800/567-5276 or 418/694-2000. Fax 418/380-2553. www.jaro.qc.ca. 234 units. C$140–C$320 (US$112–US$256) double; from C$455 (US$364) suite. AE, DC, MC, V. Valet parking C$25 (US$20). **Amenities:** Restaurant (Steakhouse); bar; indoor pool; decently equipped health club; Jacuzzi; concierge; limited room service; laundry service; same-day dry cleaning. *In room:* A/C, TV w/pay movies, dataport, coffeemaker, hair dryer.

Le Capitole ⟨⟨★ Le Capitole is as gleefully eccentric as the four business hotels described elsewhere in this section are conventional. The entrance to this hotel is squeezed almost to anonymity between a restaurant and two theaters on place d'Youville. Rooms, which are all curves and obtuse angles, borrow from Art Deco and feature stars on the carpets and clouds on the ceiling. Most bathtubs have Jacuzzi jets, and beds have down comforters. All rooms are equipped with VCRs and CD players, with more than 100 videos available free of charge.

972 rue Saint-Jean (1 block west of Porte Saint-Jean), Québec City, PQ G1R 1R5. © 800/363-4040 or 418/694-4040. Fax 418/694-1916. www.lecapitole.com. 40 units. June to mid-Oct C$189–C$209 (US$151–US$167) double; late Oct to May C$129–C$165 (US$103–US$132) double. Packages available. AE, MC, V. Valet parking C$18 (US$14). **Amenities:** Restaurant (Italian/International); bar; concierge; limited room service; laundry service; dry cleaning. *In room:* A/C, TV/VCR, dataport, minibar, coffeemaker, hair dryer.

Loews Le Concorde ⟨★ From outside, the skyscraper that houses this hotel is a visual insult to the skyline, rising from a neighborhood of late-Victorian town houses. Inside, the modernist decor increasingly looks dated. Those affronts might be forgotten, at least by those who can't be bothered with architectural aesthetics. Standard rooms have marble bathrooms and three telephones. There are spectacular views of the river and the old city, even from the lower floors. L'Astral is a revolving rooftop restaurant, with a bar and live piano music most nights. It has better food than usually can be expected of such sky-high venues. Of all the hotels listed here, this is the farthest from the old town, about a 10-minute walk to the walls, and then another 10 minutes to the center of the Haute-Ville.

1225 cours du Géneral de Montcalm (at Grande-Allée), Québec City, PQ G1R 4W6. © 800/463-5256 or 418/647-2222. Fax 418/647-4710. www.loewshotels.com. 404 units. May–Oct C$190–C$220 (US$152–US$176) double; Nov–Apr C$124–C$154 (US$99–US$123) double; from C$245 (US$196) suite year-round. Children under 17 stay free in parent's room. Children 7–12 receive 50% discount on meals. Ski and weekend packages available. AE, DC, MC, V. Self-parking C$15 (US$12), valet parking C$18 (US$14). **Amenities:** Restaurant (International); 2 bars; heated outdoor pool (Apr–Nov); well-equipped health club w/sauna; concierge; car-rental desk; business center; shopping arcade; limited room service; in-room massage; babysitting; laundry service; same-day dry cleaning; executive floors. *In room:* A/C, TV w/pay movies, fax, dataport, minibar, coffeemaker, hair dryer, iron.

MODERATE

Delta Québec ⟨★ *(Kids* Part of Place Québec, a multiuse complex, this hotel is also connected to the city's convention center. It is 2 blocks from Porte (Gate) Kent in the city wall, and not far from the Québec Parliament building, a location likely to fit almost any businessperson's needs. It is, however, an uphill climb from the old city (like all the hotels and inns along or near the Grande-Allée). All rooms have minibars and video game stations. While the exterior and parts of the interior public spaces are formed by ugly concrete blocks, the bedrooms and service areas benefited from a renovation completed in 2000. Reception is two levels up.

690 bd. René-Lévesque est, Québec City, PQ G1R 5A8. © 888/884-7777 in Canada, 800/333-3333 from elsewhere, or 418/647-1717. Fax 418/647-2146. www.deltaquebec.com. 377 units. May–Oct C$165–C$189 (US$132–US$151)

double; Nov–Apr C$145–C$181 (US$116–US$145). Children under 16 stay free in parent's room. AE, DC, DISC, MC, V. Parking C$18 (US$14). Turn left off Grande-Allée, and then left again onto Dufferin, just before the St-Louis Gate in the city wall. Once past the Parliament building, take the 1st left. The hotel is 2 blocks ahead. **Amenities:** Restaurant (American/Continental); bar; heated outdoor pool (open year-round); fully equipped health club w/sauna and Jacuzzi; concierge; business center; limited room service; babysitting; laundry service; same-day dry cleaning; executive floors. *In room:* A/C, TV w/pay movies, dataport, minibar, coffeemaker, hair dryer, iron.

INEXPENSIVE

Relais Charles-Alexander *Value*   On the ground floor of this charming brick-faced B&B is an art gallery, which also serves as the breakfast room. This stylish use of space extends to the bedrooms as well, which are crisply maintained and decorated with eclectic antique and wicker pieces and reproductions. Rooms in front are larger; most have showers, not tubs; and some have phones. They are quiet, for the most part, because the inn is just outside the orbit of the sometimes-raucous Grande-Allée terrace bars. Yet the St-Louis Gate is less than a 15-minute walk away from the hotel. This place is totally nonsmoking.

91 Grande-Allée est, Québec City, PQ G1R 2H5. ⓒ 418/523-1220. Fax 418/523-9556. www.quebecweb.com/rca. 23 units. Summer C$119–C$128 (US$95–US$102) double; winter C$89–C$99 (US$71–US$79). Parking C$7 (US$5.60). Rates include breakfast. MC, V. **Amenities:** Same-day dry cleaning. *In room:* A/C, TV, hair dryer.

3 Basse-Ville (Lower Town)

EXPENSIVE

Auberge Saint-Antoine 𝓡𝓡𝓡   There isn't enough space here to chart the evolution of this uncommonly attractive property from charming waterfront inn to landmark luxury hotel. It began with an 1830 maritime warehouse with soaring ceiling, dark beams, and a stone floor. A modern wing and a remodeled 1727 annex then were added. They are connected by a copper-mansard central structure and underground garage erected in the former parking lot. During the course of excavation, ancient walls were uncovered and remain in view, and artifacts unearthed in the process are now on display throughout the hotel. These include clay pipes, keys, glassware, and pottery shards, seen in niches in public areas and used to identify bedrooms. A striking new lounge serves breakfast, lunch, snacks, and drinks, and a restaurant took over the original warehouse lobby. Clever mixtures of antique and reproduction furniture are found in both public and private areas. All rooms have two robes, CD players, and free high-speed Internet access. Public rooms are now wireless hot spots. Many rooms have balconies or terraces, about a tenth have fireplaces, and a number of suites have kitchenettes and wet bars. There's a small cinema, and a spa is planned.

8 rue St-Antoine (at rue Dalhousie), Québec City, PQ G1K 4C9. ⓒ 888/692-2211 or 418/692-2211. Fax 418/692-1177. www.saint-antoine.com. 94 units. May–Oct C$149–C$369 (US$119–US$295) double; Nov–Apr C$149–C$279 (US$119–US$223) double; C$229–C$499 (US$183–US$400) suite year-round. Children under 12 stay free in parent's room. AE, DC, MC, V. Valet garage parking C$18 (US$14). Follow rue Dalhousie around the Lower Town to rue St-Antoine. The hotel is next to the Musée de la Civilisation. **Amenities:** Restaurant (New Quebecois); concierge; business center; limited room service; in-room massage; babysitting; laundry service; same-day dry cleaning. *In room:* A/C, TV, dataport, coffeemaker, hair dryer, iron, safe.

Auberge Saint-Pierre 𝓡   The doors had barely opened in 1997, the paint still drying, when this hotel expanded into the adjacent building to add another 13 rooms. The full breakfasts (included in the price) are special, cooked to order by the chef in the open kitchen. Most of the rooms are surprisingly spacious, and the even more commodious suites are a luxury on a longer visit, especially since they have modest kitchen facilities. All rooms and suites have whirlpool tubs. The made-to-order furnishings are meant to suggest, rather than replicate, traditional Québec styles. Robes are provided. The new wing is nonsmoking.

79 rue Saint-Pierre (behind the Musée de la Civilisation), Québec City, PQ G1K 4A3. © **888/268-1017** or 418/694-7981. Fax 418/694-0406. www.auberge.qc.ca. 41 units. May–Oct C$235–C$265 (US$188–US$212) double; Nov–Apr C$179–C$205 (US$143–US$164) double. Rates include full breakfast. AE, DC, DISC, MC, V. Valet parking C$18 (US$14). **Amenities:** Bar; access to nearby health club; concierge; breakfast room service; in-room massage; babysitting; laundry service; same-day dry cleaning. *In room:* A/C, TV, dataport, coffeemaker, hair dryer, iron.

Dominion 1912 ✹✹✹   For many years, this was the most appealing boutique hotel in the city. That honor must now pass to the Auberge Saint-Antoine (above), but that doesn't make the Dominion a bit less desirable. To begin, the owners stripped the inside of the 1912 Dominion Fish & Fruit building down to the studs and pipes and started over. Even the least expensive rooms are large. If you require a rock-hard mattress, look elsewhere; these beds are deep, soft, and enveloping, heaped with linen-covered pillows and covered with feather duvets. Custom-made bedside tables swing into place or out of the way. A fruit basket awaits your arrival. Modem outlets are at handy desktop level, near the CD players. Robes and an umbrella are provided. About a third of the rooms have showers, but not tubs. A hearty continental breakfast is set out near the fireplace in the handsome lobby along with morning newspapers, and you can munch and read out on the terrace in back.

126 rue Saint-Pierre (at rue Saint-Paul), Québec City, PQ G1K 4A8. © **888/833-5253** or 418/692-2224. Fax 418/692-4403. www.hoteldominion.com. 60 units. May–Oct C$205–C$305 (US$164–US$244) double; Nov–Apr C$189–C$260 (US$151–US$208) double. Rates include breakfast. AE, DC, MC, V. Parking C$18 (US$14). **Amenities:** Bar; access to nearby health club; concierge; limited room service; in-room massage; babysitting; laundry service; same-day dry cleaning. *In room:* A/C, TV/VCR, dataport, minibar, coffeemaker, hair dryer, iron, safe.

MODERATE

Le Port-Royal   This newcomer wasn't finished at the time we had a look around, but there was enough to declare that it will be giving serious competition to the best boutique hotels of the Basse-Ville. The first customers arrived in mid-spring 2005. The preexisting 18th-century structure was hollowed out to make a total of 40 suites, the smallest of which has 37 sq. m (398 sq. ft.). They all have well-equipped kitchenettes with microwave ovens, and some have rangetops and dishwashers as well. Up to four people can be accommodated in each unit, making this an excellent choice for families as well as long-stay businesspeople. Wireless Internet access is free and DVD and CD players are provided. A fitness center and roof garden are planned. **Le 48,** a restaurant under separate management with an entrance from the lobby, provides room service and a snack-y menu of tapas, burgers, wraps, and such. The hotel is nonsmoking throughout. Go quickly—these low prices won't last.

1144 rue Saint-Pierre (rue St-Andre), Québec City, PQ G1K 4A8. © 418/692-2777. Fax 418/692-2778. www.hotel portroyalsuites.com. Nov–Apr C$155–C$245 (US$124–US$196) suite; May–Oct C$175–C$345 (US$140–US$276) suite. 40 units. AE, DC, MC, V. Parking C$15 (US$12). **Amenities:** Restaurant (International); bar; limited room service; laundry service; same-day dry cleaning. *In room:* A/C, TV/DVR, dataport, coffeemaker, hair dryer.

Le Priori   A forerunner of the burgeoning Basse-Ville hotel scene, Le Priori provides a playful postmodern ambience behind the somber facade of a 1726 house. Designer Philippe Starck inspired the original owners, who installed versions of his conical stainless-steel sinks in the bedrooms and sensual multinozzle showers in the small bathrooms. In some rooms, a claw-foot tub sits beside the queen-size beds, which are covered with duvets. New table lamps help enliven the formerly dim lighting. Suites have sitting rooms with wood-burning fireplaces, kitchens, and Jacuzzis. The restaurant **Toast!,** off the lobby, draws good notices, including mine (p. 234).

15 rue Sault-au-Matelot (at rue St-Antoine), Québec City, PQ G1K 3Y7. Ⓒ **800/351-3992** or 418/692-3992. Fax 418/692-0883. www.hotellepriori.com. 26 units. Summer C$189–C$305 (US$151–US$244) double; winter C$119–C$209 (US$95–US$167). Rates include breakfast. Packages available. AE, DC, MC, V. Self-parking C$10 (US$8) per day. **Amenities:** Restaurant (Fusion); bar; concierge; limited room service; laundry service; same-day dry cleaning. *In room:* A/C, TV, dataport, coffeemaker, hair dryer, iron.

4 A Resort Hotel in the City

Château Bonne Entente 𝕽𝕽   Cast a line for trout in the pond in front, twirl around the skating rink, get swaddled in seaweed—and still be only a 15-minute drive from Vieux-Québec. Bushels of dollars have elevated this hotel far beyond the folksy boarding house that it was a half-century ago. For romantics, the choice has to be Art Deco room no. 358, with a monster tub two steps away from the king-size bed. There's a "Fun Club" for kids ages 2 to 14, and the "AmeriSpa," where guests are pampered by the hour with a list that only begins with body scrubs and foot massage. The tennis courts, alas, have been lost to the expanded man-made lake, but guests have access to a new private golf course 20km (12 miles) away. A new 28-suite wing opened in summer 2005.

3400 chemin Saint-Foy, Ste-Foy, PQ G1X 1S6. Ⓒ **800/463-4390** or 418/653-5221. Fax 418/653-3098. www.chateau bonneentente.com. 165 units. C$169–$499 (US$135–US$400) double. Packages available. AE, DC, MC, V. Free parking. From Montréal on Rte. 40, take the exit onto Autoroute Duplessis, shortly turning onto chemin Sainte-Foy; at the light, make a right, go straight, and turn right again at the next traffic light. **Amenities:** 3 restaurants (California, only in summer; French; Quebecois); 2 bars; large outdoor pool; golf nearby; extensive health club and spa; limited room service; massage; babysitting; laundry service; same-day dry cleaning. *In room:* A/C, TV w/pay movies, dataport, minibar, coffeemaker, hair dryer, iron, safe.

14

Where to Dine in Québec City

Not long ago, it was fair to say that this gloriously scenic city had no *temples de cuisine* comparable to those of Montréal or Manhattan. That has changed. At least two restaurants are comparable in every way to the most honored establishments of any North American city. What's more, the appearance of surprising numbers of creative and ambitious young chefs and restaurateurs are bidding to achieve similar status. It is now easy to eat well in the capital—*quite* well, in an increasing number of cases.

By sticking to any of the many competent bistros, the handful of *nuovo Italiano* trattorie, and a couple of jazzy fusion eateries, you will likely be more than content. Another step up, a half-dozen or so ambitious enterprises tease the palate with hints of higher achievement. Even the blatantly touristy restaurants along rue St-Louis and around the Place d'Armes, many of them with hawkers outside and showy tableside presentations inside, can produce decent meals. The less extravagant among them, in fact, are entirely satisfactory for breakfast or simple lunches, a useful fact to keep in mind if you're staying in one of the many old town guesthouses that serve no meals.

As throughout the province, the best dining deals are the table d'hôte—fixed-price—meals. Virtually all full-service restaurants offer them, if only at lunch. As a rule, they include at least soup or salad, a main course, and a dessert. Some places add in an extra appetizer and/or a beverage, all for the approximate a la carte price of the main course alone.

Curiously, seafood is not given as much attention as might be expected, considering all that water out there. Mussels and salmon are on most menus, but look for those places that go beyond those staples. Game is popular, and everything from venison, rabbit, and duck to more exotic quail, goose, caribou, and wapiti (North American deer) is available.

At the better places, and even at some of those that might seem inexplicably popular, reservations are all but essential during traditional holidays and the festivals that pepper the social calendar. Other times, it's usually necessary to book ahead only for weekend evenings. In the listings below, where no mention is made of reservations, they aren't necessary. Dress codes are rarely stipulated, but "dressy casual" works almost everywhere. Remember that for the Quebecois, *dîner* (dinner) is lunch, and *souper* (supper) is dinner, though the word *dinner* below is used in the common American sense. Also note that an *entrée* in Québec is an appetizer, while a *plat principal* is a main course. The evening meal tends to be served earlier in Québec City than in Montréal, at 6 or 7pm rather than 8pm.

Smoking in restaurants, bars, and most other public places in the province was banned as of January 1, 2006.

For a more extended discussion of Québec dining, see "Cuisine Haute, Cuisine Bas: Smoked Meat, Fiddleheads & Caribou," in the appendix.

1 Restaurants by Cuisine

The prices within each review refer to the cost in U.S. dollars of individual main courses, using the following categories: Very Expensive, main courses at dinner average more than $30; Expensive, $21 to $30; Moderate, $10 to $20; and Inexpensive, $10 and under.

ECLECTIC

Voodoo Grill ⋆ (Grande-Allée, $$$, p. 232)

FRENCH BISTRO

Café du Clocher Penché (Downtown/St-Roch, $$, p. 236)

L'Ardoise (Basse-Ville, $$, p. 235)

L'Echaudé ⋆ (Basse-Ville, $$$, p. 233)

Le Marie-Clarisse ⋆ (Basse-Ville, $$$, p. 234)

FRENCH CONTEMPORARY

Initiale ⋆⋆⋆ (Basse-Ville, $$$$, p. 232)

Le Paris-Brest ⋆ (Grande-Allée, $$$, p. 229)

Le Saint-Amour ⋆ (Haute-Ville, $$$, p. 229)

Panache (Basse-Ville, $$$$, p. 233)

FRENCH/INTERNATIONAL

Le Café du Monde ⋆ (Basse-Ville, $$, p. 235)

FUSION

Laurie Raphaël ⋆⋆⋆ (Basse-Ville, $$$$, p. 232)

Toast! ⋆ (Basse-Ville, $$$, p. 234)

Utopie ⋆ (Downtown/St-Roch, $$$, p. 235)

Versa (Downtown/St-Roch, $$, p. 236)

JAPANESE

Yuzu ⋆ (Downtown/St-Roch, $$$, p. 235)

LIGHT FARE/CREPES

Le Casse-Crêpe Breton (Haute-Ville, $, p. 229)

QUEBECOIS

Aux Anciens Canadiens ⋆ (Haute-Ville, $$$, p. 228)

SEAFOOD

Le Marie-Clarisse ⋆ (Basse-Ville, $$$, p. 234)

Poisson d'Avril (Basse-Ville, $$$, p. 234)

SUSHI

Yuzu ⋆ (Downtown/St-Roch, $$$, p. 235)

Key to Abbreviations: $$$$ = Very Expensive $$$ = Expensive $$ = Moderate $ = Inexpensive

2 Haute-Ville (Upper Town)

EXPENSIVE

Aux Anciens Canadiens ⋆ QUEBECOIS   Smack in the middle of the tourist swarms and inundated by travelers during peak months, this venerable restaurant is in what is probably the oldest (1677) house in the city. Surprisingly, the food at this famous establishment is both fairly priced (at least at lunch) and well prepared. In addition, it's one of the best places in La Belle Province to sample cooking that has its roots in the earliest years of New France. Don't count on ancient Quebecois recipes tasting this good anywhere else. Caribou and maple syrup figure in many of the dishes, including the meat pie, Lac Brome duck, and a definitive rendering of luscious sugar pie. Servings are large enough to ward off winter for a week. Servers are in costume and there are carved wooden bas-reliefs of regional scenes. Beware menu supplements on the table d'hôte meals.

34 rue St-Louis (at rue Haldimand). ℂ 418/692-1627. Reservations recommended. Main courses C$22–C$39 (US$18–US$31); table d'hôte lunch C$15 (US$12), dinner C$33–C$49 (US$26–US$39). AE, DC, MC, V. Daily noon–10pm.

Le Saint-Amour ℱ FRENCH CONTEMPORARY   This is for the coolly attractive and the amorously inclined. Patrons pass through a front room with lace curtains into a covered terrace lit by flickering candles. Easily the most romantic setting for dining in a city that knows about seductive atmosphere, the glass roof reveals splashes of stars. The courtyard has been re-created with mirrors and polished wood paneling. Caribou filet comes with a wild mushroom crust, enhanced by dried berries in a pepper sauce. The lobster presented out of its shell looks as good as it tastes, and desserts are dazzlers—maple sugar and blackberry crème brûlée in a pastry shell, for one. Having come this far back to its previous levels of achievement, a final enhancement would be to move the pace of the meal along a little more expeditiously.

48 rue Ste-Ursule (near rue St-Louis). ℂ 418/694-0667. www.saint-amour.com. Reservations recommended for dinner. Main courses C$28–C$38 (US$22–US$30); table d'hôte dinner C$46 (US$37); tasting dinner (10 courses) C$90 (US$72). AE, DC, MC, V. Mon–Fri 11am–2pm and 6–11pm; Sat–Sun 6–11pm.

INEXPENSIVE

Le Casse-Crêpe Breton ⟨Value⟩ LIGHT FARE/CREPES   Eat at the bar and watch the crepes being made, or attempt to snag one of the 14 tables. These aren't those sissy crepes named for Suzette; they're pizza-sized monsters. Main-course versions come with two to five ingredients of the customer's choice, usually a combo of ham, cheese, sweet peppers, mushrooms, eggs, and/or pepperoni. Dessert types are stuffed with jams or fruit and cream. Soups, salads, and sandwiches are as inexpensive as the crepes. It's open 18 hours a day, which is useful, but when it gets busy, the service is glacial and occasionally rude. Beer is served in bottles or on tap.

1136 rue St-Jean (near rue Garneau). ℂ 418/692-0438. Most items under C$8 (US$6.40). MC, V. Daily 7am–1am.

3 On or Near the Grande-Allée

EXPENSIVE

Le Paris-Brest ℱ FRENCH CONTEMPORARY   Named for a French dessert, this is one of the best restaurants outside the walls, tendering a polished performance from greeting to check. Within minutes after the doors are opened at lunchtime, a happy noise ensues, drowning out the cellphone users. Dinner is quieter. A fashionable crowd comes in wearing everything from bespoke suits to designer jeans—tacky T-shirts, as well as children, are out of place. They are attended by a comely waitstaff dressed in black who convey as much warmth as the rushed process permits. One sparkling recent appetizer was snow crab tagliatelle. Game and seafood are featured, often including pheasant with honey caramelized pears, crawfish étouffée, and Dover sole. The menu doesn't change much, so pay attention to the daily specials, which are more likely to demonstrate the kitchen's creativity. Find the entrance on rue de la Chevrotière. There are outdoor tables and free valet parking is available after 5:30pm.

590 Grande-Allée est (at rue de la Chevrotière). ℂ 418/529-2243. Reservations recommended. Main courses C$15–C$32 (US$12–US$26); table d'hôte lunch C$15 (US$12), dinner C$24–C$35 (US$19–US$28). AE, DC, MC, V. Mon–Fri 11:30am–2:30pm; Mon–Sat 6–11:30pm; Sun 5:30–11:30pm.

Where to Dine in Québec City

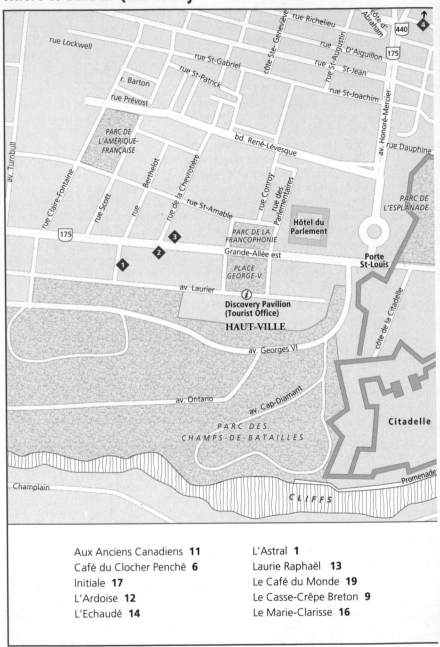

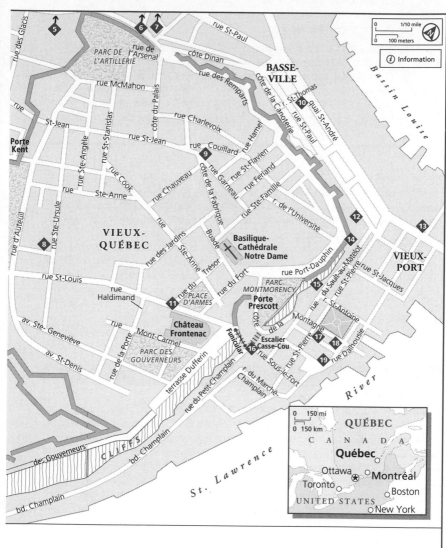

Tips **A Place for Picnic Fare**

Les Halles du Petit-Cartier is, in effect, a mall for foodies, containing a collection of merchants in open-fronted shops purveying fresh meats and fish, cheeses, sushi, pâtés and terrines, glistening produce, deli products, pastries, confections, and fancy picnic items. There are a few fast-food counters and delis that make up sandwiches to order. How about a cooked lobster for your picnic? The mall is open 7 days a week. It's located at 1191 av. Cartier (near rue Fraser).

Voodoo Grill ❀ ECLECTIC   Of all the unlikely places to expect a decent meal, let alone one that surpasses most of what can be found at more conventional local restaurants, this takes the laurels. African carvings adorn the walls, and a trio of conga drummers circulate nightly, beating out rapid, insistent rhythms on bongos—a tremendous distraction. It is all loud, young, and extremely casual. The menu swings around the Pacific Rim, with stops in Hawaii, Thailand, and Indonesia. Authenticity isn't the point, taste is. Ravioli, for only one example, is stuffed with veal, garnished with baby corn and other vegetables, touched with a sesame sauce, and braced with plantain chips. If you're interested, the cover charge for the disco upstairs is waived with proof that you ate at Voodoo. Pick an appetizer and a main course and get soup, salad, or dessert for an extra C$6 (US$4.80).

575 Grande-Allée est (corner of rue de la Chevro tiére). ✆ **418/647-2000.** Reservations recommended. Main courses C$19–C$44 (US$15–US$35). AE, DC, MC, V. Mon–Fri 11:30am–2:30pm and 6–11pm; Sat–Sun 6–11pm.

4 Basse-Ville (Lower Town)
VERY EXPENSIVE

Initiale ❀❀❀ FRENCH CONTEMPORARY   No more waffling: Initiale is not only one of the capital's elite restaurants, but it holds that status among the best of the entire province. The palatial setting of tall windows, columns, and a deeply recessed ceiling sets a gracious tone, and the welcome is both cordial and correct. Subdued lighting and the muffled noise level help, too. Cast economy to the winds, choosing from prix-fixe menus of three to six courses. They are changed often, because the chef values freshness of ingredients over novelty. As an example, a recent dinner started with a buckwheat crepe folded around an artichoke, a round of crabmeat with a creamy purée of onions, and a flash-fried leaf of baby spinach that added a delicate crackle, all arrayed on the plate as on an artist's palette. It continued with grilled tuna supported by sweet garlic, salsify, and lemon marmalade, and a swirl of pasta with marguerite leaves. The veal is tender, young, pink beef, selected on the hoof by the chef. Québec cheeses are an impressive topper. This is a place to celebrate important events. Men should wear jackets.

54 rue St-Pierre (corner of Côte de la Montagne). ✆ **418/694-1818.** www.restaurantinitiale.com. Reservations recommended on weekends. Main courses C$30–C$39 (US$24–US$31); table d'hôte lunch C$14–C$20 (US$11–US$16), dinner C$45–C$82 (US$36–US$66). AE, DC, MC, V. Mon–Fri 11:30am–2pm and 6–9pm; Sat–Sun 6–9pm.

Laurie Raphaël ❀❀❀ FUSION   The owners, who named this place after their two children, tinker relentlessly with their creation. Energized by the emergence of a challenging cadre of sharp young chefs and restaurateurs in the city, they overhauled their quarters so completely last year as to be unrecognizable, ensuring a suitable arena for what has long been one of the city's most accomplished kitchens. Living up to the even more sophisticated setting of slate grays and taupes, the platings are prettier and more sophisticated than ever. A painter's palette is suggested by the layouts of the appetizers, as with the one that joins a small cup of foie gras mousse in one corner of the square plate with a tumble of delicate mixed greens in a fruity vinaigrette in the other. Main courses run to caribou, quail, rabbit, arctic char, sea bass, and scallops in unconventional guises, often with Asian touches. One example is the square of cod cooked to a precise silken turn resting atop a nest of noodle-like strips of carrots, squash, sweet peppers, and rice, mini–baby bok choy to the side. A concern for "healthy" saucing and exotic combinations is evident throughout. Service falls within the friendly/correct range. With all the vigorous new competition, this is still at the top of the order.

117 rue Dalhousie (at rue St-André). ✆ 418/692-4555. Reservations recommended. Main courses C$32–C$42 (US$26–US$34); table d'hôte lunch (Tues–Fri) C$14–C$25 (US$11–US$20); gourmet dinner menu C$89 (US$71). AE, DC, MC, V. Tues–Fri 11:30am–2pm and 5:30–10pm; Sat 6–10pm.

Panache FRENCH CONTEMPORARY   The new restaurant of the superb Auberge Saint-Antoine started life with a big advantage: It is housed in the original lobby of the inn, a former 19th-century warehouse delineated by massive wood beams and rough stone walls. A wrought-iron staircase winds up to a second dining level. Flickering candles and glowing coals in the center fireplace enhance the inherent romantic aura. Still in its formative months, there were some understandable hiccups and bumps in food and service—a waiter changing a diner's silverware three times between the first and second courses, for one. Five scallops in lobster sauce were correctly cooked but bland, though the accompanying takes on asparagus were considerably more interesting—a demitasse of cream of asparagus, four dainty spears with cheese, and a mini-timbale of rice with shaved almonds. Nothing was wrong with the food, it's simply that the price-to-quality was out of whack. Panache was not yet at the level of the top competition (see Initiale, a block away, for comparison), yet prices were. (The six-course "Signature" menu is C$139/US$111.) There's every reason to believe that these early wobbles will be eliminated. Panache is headed in the right direction.

10 rue St-Antoine (in Auberge Saint-Antoine). ✆ 418/692-2211. Main courses C$32–C$45 (US$26–US$36); tasting menu C$139 (US$111). AE, DC, MC, V. Mon–Fri 11:30am–2pm and 6–10pm; Sat–Sun 6–10pm.

EXPENSIVE

L'Echaudé ✿ FRENCH BISTRO   The most polished of the necklace of restaurants adorning this Basse-Ville corner, L'Echaudé has a zinc-topped bar and tables covered with butcher paper inside and out. Bowls of flowers add color, and the businessman's lunch is written on the mirror, Parisian style. The grilled meats and fishes and the seafood stews blaze no new trails, but they are very satisfying and an excellent value. Good lunch deals range from cheese omelets to steak tartare, served with appetizer, dessert, and coffee. Among many classics on the menu are steak frites, ravioli with blue cheese, lamb mixed grill, and salmon tartare. They keep 24 brands of beer on ice. The owner has a weekly radio show about wine, and he keeps an important cellar, with 125 varieties of wine, a generous 8 of which are available by the glass. This place is frequented mostly by locals, aged from their 20s to forever, attended by a highly efficient staff.

73 rue Sault-au-Matelot (near rue St-Paul). © **418/692-1299.** Reservations suggested on weekends. Main courses C$16–C$35 (US$13–US$28); table d'hôte lunch C$14–C$21 (US$11–US$17), dinner C$27–C$45 (US$22–US$36). AE, DC, MC, V. Mon–Wed 11:30am–2:30pm and 5:30–10pm; Thurs–Fri 11:30am–2:30pm and 5:30–11pm; Sat 5:30–11pm; Sun 10am–2:30pm and 5:30–10pm. Closed 2 weeks in Jan.

Le Marie-Clarisse 🐟 FRENCH BISTRO/SEAFOOD   This spot, at the bottom of Breakneck Stairs, sits where the streets are awash with day-packers and shutterbugs. It serves what many consider to be the best seafood in town, chosen by a finicky owner who makes his selections personally at the market. The result of daily fish deliveries is a menu that changes often, so listen to the specials. A more pleasant hour cannot be passed anywhere in Québec City than here, over a platter of shrimp or pâtés, out on the terrace on a summer afternoon. In January, cocoon by the stone fireplace inside, indulging in bouillabaisse—a stew of mussels, scallops, tuna, tilapia, and shrimp, with a boat of saffron mayo to slather on croutons. Try a Québec wine to wash it down, maybe the l'Orpailleur from Dunham. The two rooms are formed of stone, brick, and rafters that are over 200 years old.

12 rue du Petit-Champlain (at rue Sous-le-Fort). © **418/692-0857.** Main courses C$29–C$33 (US$23–US$26); table d'hôte dinner is the price of the main course plus C$18 (US$14). AE, DC, MC, V. Mon–Sat 11:30am–2:30pm and 6–10pm; terrace open daily Apr 15–Oct 31 11:30am–10pm.

Poisson d'Avril SEAFOOD   Whoever christened this place was having a little joke: its name means both "April Fool" and "April Fish." Nevertheless, nautical trappings that include model ships, marine prints, and mounted sailfish make the real intent clear. The dinner menu, which changes daily, is packed with seafood, including some combinations of costly crustaceans responsible for the stiffer prices noted below. Two of these are the crowded bouillabaisse, which comes with half a lobster, and a special platter called *L'assiette du commodore* laden with snow crabs, giant shrimp, glossy sea scallops, mussels, and another half lobster. Mixed grill and pastas are also on the menu. Lunch is a more modest event, with land-based dishes, pastas, and individual pizzas. In good weather, there's a covered dining terrace.

115 quai Saint-André (in Vieux-Port, near rue St-Thomas). © **418/692-1010.** Reservations suggested. Main courses C$13–C$40 (US$10–US$32); table d'hôte lunch C$10–C$18 (US$8–US$14), dinner C$25–C$52 (US$20–US$42). MC, V. Mon–Fri 11am–2pm; daily 5–10pm.

Toast! 🐟 FUSION   This bright new spot adjoins Hôtel Le Priori, occupying the space where Laurie Raphaël started before it went on to become the city's gastronomic flag bearer. Toast! has all the signs of following the same trajectory.

As is true of most restaurants in the province, the kitchen has its base in the French idiom, but takes off in many directions. See that in the appetizer of galantine of chicken, mushrooms, and spinach on corn kernels and slivers of jalapeño, perhaps followed by pecan-crusted rack of rabbit with a cold purée of potato, cream, and horseradish, perked with a basil foam and Parmesan. Every dish is like that—audacious, sprightly, attentive to joined tastes and textures.

A large dining terrace in back supplements the stone-walled interior splashed with crimson and furnished with retro-modern lights and chairs. Because it is attached to a hotel, breakfast is also served.

17 rue Sault-au-Matelot (at rue St-Antoine). © **418/692-1334.** Reservations suggested on weekends. Main courses C$26–C$39 (US$21–US$32); table d'hôte lunch C$12–C$19 (US$9.60–US$15), dinner C$32–C$38 (US$26–US$30). AE, DC, MC, V. Daily 7–10am, noon–2pm, and 6–10:30pm.

MODERATE

L'Ardoise FRENCH BISTRO   This is one of several bistros that wrap around the intersection of rues St-Paul and Sault-au-Matelot. The success of this one is attested by its expansion into the building next door. Mussels are staples at Québec restaurants, prepared in the Belgian manner, with bowls of frites on the side. Here, they come with 14 different sauces and, with soup or salad, cost only C$19 (US$15)—with free seconds. That the chef cares about what he sends out of his kitchen is evident. His food is vibrant and flavorful, served at banquettes along the walls and at tables both inside and out on the sidewalk. Piaf and Aznavour clones warble laments on the stereo. This is a place to leaf through a book, sip a double espresso, and meet the neighbors.

71 rue St-Paul (near rue des Navigateurs). ⓒ 418/694-0213. Reservations recommended at dinner. Main courses C$14–C$27 (US$11–US$22); table d'hôte lunch C$15–C$18 (US$12–US$14), dinner C$35 (US$28). AE, DC, MC, V. Mon–Thurs 11am–10pm; Fri–Sat 11am–10:30pm; Sun 9am–10pm.

Le Café du Monde ⓡ FRENCH/INTERNATIONAL   A relentlessly convivial spot, the Café du Monde enjoyed long popularity at its prominent address near the Musée de la Civilisation. In late 2002, it moved to this new site on the edge of the river, adjoining Le Terminal de Croisières—the cruise terminal. It's a much larger, fancier space, seating three times as many people, not counting the terrace. The staff is as amiable as ever, the food a touch more creative but still within bistro conventions. The short menu continues to feature classic pâtés, quiches, cassoulet, duck confit, and six versions of mussels with frites, with pastas and paella among some of the less French preparations. Imported beers are the favored beverages, along with wines by the glass. Service is friendly, but easily distracted, given the lively atmosphere.

84 rue Dalhousie (near rue de la Barricade). ⓒ 418/692-4455. www.lecafedumonde.com. Reservations recommended. Main courses C$10–C$25 (US$8–US$20); table d'hôte (after 3pm) the price of your main course plus C$8 or C$11 (US$6.40 or US$8.80). AE, DC, MC, V. Mon–Fri 11:30am–11pm; Sat–Sun brunch 9:30am–11pm.

5 Downtown/St-Roch

EXPENSIVE

Utopie ⓡ FUSION   It was iffy to recommend a place so soon after it opened in May 2004, but it proved to have the essential ingredients. The clientele has a stylish sheen, the interior is almost painfully chic, the food isn't same-old, and the location is sufficiently out of the way to require that customers have to be those in the know. Stands of birch trunks march down the middle of the high-ceilinged space, and blown-up photos of bark line the right wall. The chef is an owner, along with three others who run the front; all are young and clearly ambitious. Sautéed *lotte* (monkfish) is joined with translucent baby bok choy and wild asparagus no thicker than bean sprouts. A menu staple is the crisp-fried crab ravioli on avocado purée, as is the duck confit with braised endive and onion compote. All is calm and refined, leaving some dishes somewhat listless, but with no startling clashes of flavor.

226 rue St-Joseph (near rue Caron). ⓒ 418/523-7878. Reservations recommended on weekends. Main courses C$19–C$29 (US$15–US$23); table d'hôte lunch C$17–C$30 (US$14–US$24). AE, MC, V. Tues–Fri 11:30am–2pm; Tues–Sat 6–9:30pm.

Yuzu ⓡ SUSHI/JAPANESE   For just a while, this was the hottest restaurant in town, offering evenings of astonishingly good food. Then the original chef left for Montréal, where he expects to open his own restaurant. His replacement is young, with a wild punk haircut. Though his food is entirely competent, it demonstrates little of the same audacity. "Good" has replaced "brilliant," but the restaurant is still worth finding. It's in the downtown district of St-Roch, an area of office buildings and low-key retail that tourists rarely see. Sushi and Japanese preparations are the focus, but authenticity isn't sought, not with foie gras and caviar on the card (and as expensive as you expect). Individual sushi run C$3.75 to C$6.50 (US$3–US$5.20) each, and there are tasting menus of C$65 (US$52) for five courses and C$85 (US$68) for seven.

438 rue de L'Eglise (at rue Charest). ⒸⒻ **418/521-7253.** Reservations essential. Main courses C$27–C$36 (US$22–US$29). AE, DC, MC, V. Mon–Thurs 11:30am–2:30pm and 5–10pm; Fri 11:30am–2:30pm and 5–11pm; Sat 5–11pm; Sun 5–10pm.

MODERATE/INEXPENSIVE

Café du Clocher Penché FRENCH BISTRO   This high-energy bistro doesn't need any extra business these words might bring. Arrive on the first Tuesday of the month and the only personal space you can count on is that which your bottom can occupy. That's tapas and entertainment night. The eats are brought in little bowls on wood slat trays, and the roof-raising performers have included flamenco troupes and rock bands. No music the other nights, but the crowds are hardly diminished. It looks like a student hangout and plenty of patrons are under 25, but the 40-plus set is well represented. They indulge in a menu that runs to venison, osso buco, and sea trout. Descriptions are stripped to essentials—"pan-roasted halibut with dumplings," for one. Dishes emerging from the kitchen have ample dash, and less precision, which doesn't demean for a minute their robust desirability. Service reflects the food—amiable and without flourishes. Lunch specials (Mon–Fri) cost only C$9 to C$15 (US$7.20–US$12).

203 rue St-Joseph est (at rue Caron). ⒸⒻ **418/640-0597.** Reservations essential. Main courses C$14–C$21 (US$11–US$17). MC, V. Mon–Fri 11:30am–2:30pm; Sat–Sun 8:30am–2pm; daily 6–10pm.

Versa FUSION   Looking more like a club than a restaurant, this is a destination to remember when with a group in a partying mood. A communal table sits beneath a teak oval ceiling illuminated by pinlights, just the arena for friendly extroverts. Seatings have a '60s Swedish mien, and the windows along the front open in good weather. The translucent panels behind the back bar pulse with a rainbow of colors, highlighting the inventions of the kinetic barman. He prides himself on his cocktails—over a dozen martinis, yes, but also his specials. One begins with muddled grapes and fresh ginger before two ounces of icy vodka are poured over. He also takes orders for the oyster bar, suggesting that the humungous Albas are better cooked a la Rockefeller than eaten raw. Dinners might feature mussels four ways, soufflé of black crab, leg of lamb with maple syrup, or, for the less hungry or demanding, a "Diablo dog" or tartare burger.

432 rue de l'Eglise (at rue St-Françoise). ⒸⒻ **418/523-9995.** Main courses C$14–C$24 (US$11–US$19), table d'hôte lunch C$9–C$18 (US$7.20–US$14). MC, V. Mon–Fri 11:30am–3pm and 4:30pm–1am; Sat–Sun 5pm–1am.

Exploring Québec City

Wandering at random through the streets of Vieux-Québec is a singular pleasure, comparable to exploring a provincial capital in Europe. On the way, you can happen upon an ancient convent, blocks of gabled houses with steeply pitched roofs, a battery of 18th-century cannons in a leafy park, and a bistro with a blazing fireplace on a wintry day. The old city, upper and lower, is so compact that it's hardly necessary to plan precise sightseeing itineraries. Start at the Terrasse Dufferin and go off on a whim, down Breakneck Stairs (Escalier Casse-Cou) to the Quartier du Petit-Champlain

and Place Royale, or up to the Citadel and onto the Plains of Abraham, where Wolfe and Montcalm fought to their mutual deaths in a 20-minute battle that changed the destiny of the continent.

Most of what there is to see is within the city walls or in the Lower Town. It's fairly easy walking. While the Upper Town is hilly, with sloping streets, it's nothing like San Francisco, and only people with physical limitations are likely to experience difficulty. If rain or ice discourages exploration on foot, tour buses and horse-drawn calèches are options.

1 The Top Attractions

BASSE-VILLE (LOWER TOWN)

Musée de la Civilisation ★★★   Try to set aside at least 2 hours for a visit to this special museum, one of the most engrossing in all of Canada. Designed by Boston-based, McGill University–trained Moshe Safdie and opened in 1988, the Museum of Civilization is an innovative presence in the historic Basse-Ville, near Place Royale. A dramatic atrium-lobby sets the tone with a representation of the St. Lawrence with an ancient ship beached on the shore. Through the glass wall in back you can see the 1752 Maison Estèbe, now restored to contain the museum shop. It stands above vaulted cellars, which can also be viewed.

In the galleries upstairs are five permanent exhibitions, supplemented by up to six temporary exhibits on a variety of themes, many of them interactive. The precise mission of the museum has never been entirely clear. For example, recent exhibits ran the gamut from a display on the color blue to an exhibit about the Middle Ages. But never mind. Through highly imaginative display techniques, hands-on devices, computers, holograms, videos, and even an ant farm, the curators have ensured that visitors will be so enthralled by the experience that they won't pause to question its intent. If time is short, definitely use it to take in "Memoires," the permanent exhibit that is a sprawling examination of Québec history, moving from the province's roots as a fur-trading colony to the present. Furnishings from frontier homes, tools of the trappers' trade, worn farm implements, religious garments from the 19th century, and old campaign

Québec City Attractions

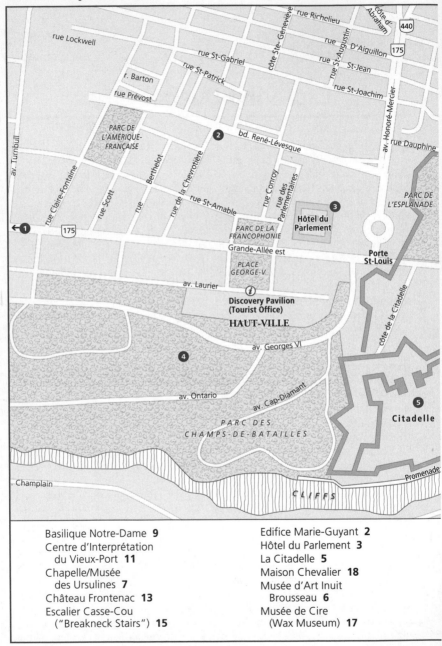

Basilique Notre-Dame **9**
Centre d'Interprétation
  du Vieux-Port **11**
Chapelle/Musée
  des Ursulines **7**
Château Frontenac **13**
Escalier Casse-Cou
  ("Breakneck Stairs") **15**

Edifice Marie-Guyant **2**
Hôtel du Parlement **3**
La Citadelle **5**
Maison Chevalier **18**
Musée d'Art Inuit
  Brousseau **6**
Musée de Cire
  (Wax Museum) **17**

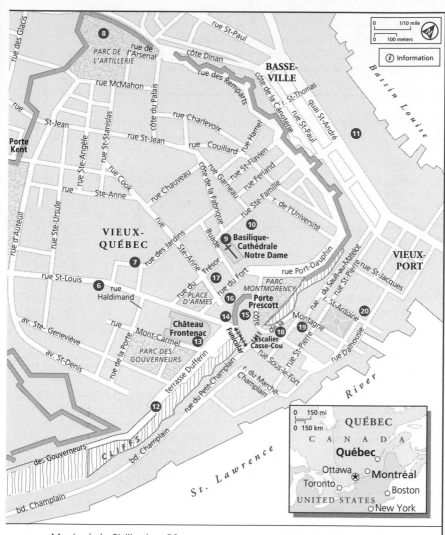

Impressions

The old world rises in the midst of the new in the manner of a change of scene on the stage . . . on its rocky promontory sits the ancient town, belted with its hoary wall and crowned with its granite citadel. . . .

—Henry James, "Québec," 1871, in Portraits of Places, 1883

posters endow visitors with a rich sense of Québec's daily life from generation to generation. A permanent exhibition called "Encounter with the First Nations" examines the products and visions of the aboriginal tribes that inhabit Québec.

Exhibit texts are in French and English. There's a cafe on the ground floor.

85 rue Dalhousie (at rue St-Antoine). (☎) **418/643-2158.** Admission C$8 (US$6.40) adults, C$7 (US$5.60) 65 and over, C$5 (US$4) students over 16, C$3 (US$2.40) children 12–16, free for children under 12. Tues free to all June 1–Oct 31. Late June to Labor Day daily 9:30am–6:30pm; day after Labor Day to late June Tues–Sun 10am–5pm.

Place Royale 𝕬𝕬𝕬   This picturesque plaza is the literal and spiritual heart of Basse-Ville. Royal Square is a short walk from the bottom of Breakneck Stairs, via rue Sous-le-Fort. In the 17th and 18th centuries, it was the town marketplace and the center of business and industry. The Eglise Notre-Dame-des-Victoires—the oldest stone church in Québec, built in 1688 and restored in 1763 and 1969—dominates the enclosed square. The paintings, altar, and large model boat suspended from the ceiling were votive offerings brought by early settlers to ensure safe voyages. The church is usually open to visitors during the day, unless a wedding is underway.

Folk dances, impromptu concerts, and other festive gatherings are often held near the bust of Louis XIV in the center of the square.

All the buildings on the square have been restored. For years, there was only an empty lot behind the stone facade at the northeast corner, but now it is a whole building again. On the ground floor is the new **Centre d'Interprétation de Place-Royale.** Inside, a multimedia show and other exhibitions detail the nearly 4-century history and development of the plaza. Guided tours of the plaza and surrounding area are available from the interpretation center in both English and French.

Centre d'Interprétation de Place-Royale: 27 rue Notre-Dame. (☎) **418/646-3167.** www.mcq.org/place_royale. Admission to Centre d'Interprétation de Place-Royal C$4 (US$3.20) adults, C$3.50 (US$2.80) seniors, C$3 (US$2.40) ages 17 and over, C$2 (US$1.60) ages 12–16, free for children under 12. June 24 to Labor Day daily 9:30am–5pm; day after Labor Day to June 23 Tues–Sun 10am–5pm.

 HAUTE-VILLE (UPPER TOWN)

La Citadelle 𝕬𝕬   The duke of Wellington had this partially star-shaped fortress built at the south end of the city walls in anticipation of renewed American attacks after the War of 1812. Some remnants of earlier French military structures were incorporated into the Citadel, including a 1750 magazine. Dug into the Plains of Abraham, the fort has a low profile that keeps it all but invisible until walkers are actually upon it. Never having exchanged fire with an invader, it continues its vigil from the tip of Cap Diamant. British construction of the fortress, now a national historic site, was begun in 1820 and took 30 years to complete. As events unfolded, it proved to be an exercise in obsolescence. Since 1920, it has been home to Québec's Royal 22e Régiment, the only fully Francophone unit in Canada's armed forces. That makes it the largest fortified group of buildings still occupied by troops in North America.

As part of a guided tour only, the public may visit the Citadel and its 25 buildings, including the small regimental museums in the former powder house and prison. Despite a couple of spectacular overlooks, the length of the tour and the dry narration are likely to test the patience of younger visitors and the legs of many older people. In those cases, it might be better to attend the ceremonies of the changing of the guard or beating the retreat (see times and dates for those events in the information listing below). Walk or drive up the Côte de la Citadelle (entrance near the St-Louis Gate); there are many parking spaces inside the walls.

1 Côte de la Citadelle (enter off rue St-Louis). ✆ **418/694-2815**. www.lacitadelle.qc.ca. Admission C$8 (US$6.40) adults, C$7 (US$5.60) seniors and students over 17, C$4.50 (US$3.60) children 7–17, free for persons with disabilities and children under 7. Guided 55-min. tours daily roughly on the hour: Apr 10am–4pm; May–June 9am–5pm; July to Labor Day 9am–6pm; Sept (after Labor Day) 9am–4pm; Oct 10am–3pm; Nov–Mar group reservations only. Changing of the guard (30 min.) June 24 to Labor Day daily at 10am; beating the retreat (20 min.) July and Aug Wed–Sat at 6pm. May be canceled in the event of rain. Walk up the Côte de la Citadelle from the St-Louis Gate.

NEAR THE GRANDE-ALLEE

Musée des Beaux-Arts du Québec 𝔾𝔾   Toward the southern end of the Parc des Champs-de-Bataille (Battlefields Park), just off the Grande-Allée and a half-hour walk or a short bus ride from the Haute-Ville, the Museum of Québec is an art museum that now occupies two buildings, one a former prison, linked together by a soaring glass-roofed "Grand Hall" housing the reception area, a stylish cafe, and a shop.

The original 1933 Gérard-Morisset Pavilion houses the permanent collection—the largest aggregation of Quebecois art in North America, filling eight galleries with works from the beginning of the colony to the present. Famed Québec Abstract-Expressionist Jean-Paul Riopelle has a permanent exhibition. On the top floor are regional landscapes and canvases of other Québec themes, with some works by North American and British painters. On the ground floor is a splendid assortment of African masks, carvings, musical instruments, and ceremonial staffs. Connected to the museum is the 1867 Charles-Baillairgé Pavilion, a former prison, which in the 1970s became a youth hostel nicknamed the "Petite Bastille." One cell block has been left intact as an exhibit. In this building, four galleries house temporary shows, and the tower contains a provocative sculpture called *Le Plongeur* (The Diver) by the Irish artist David Moore. Also incorporated in the building is the Parc des Champs-de-Bataille Interpretation Centre. There is a children's playroom stocked with toys and books. An accomplished cafe-restaurant serves table d'hôte lunches Monday through Saturday, brunch Sunday, and dinner Wednesday and Saturday nights. Traveling exhibitions and musical events are often arranged.

1 av. Wolfe-Montcalm (near av. George VI). ✆ **418/643-2150**. www.mnba.qc.ca/english. Free admission to permanent collection. Admission for special exhibitions C$10 (US$8) adults, C$9 (US$7.20) seniors, C$5 (US$4) students over 16, C$3 (US$2.40) ages 12–16, free for children under 12. June 1 to Labor Day daily 10am–5pm (until 9pm Wed); early Sept to May 31 Tues–Sun 10am–5pm (until 9pm Wed). Bus: 11.

Parc des Champs-de-Bataille 𝔾𝔾   Covering 107 hectares (264 acres) of grassy hills, sunken gardens, monuments, fountains, and trees, Québec's Battlefields Park stretches over the Plains of Abraham, where Wolfe and Montcalm engaged in their short but crucial battle in 1759, resulting in the British defeat of the French troops. It is a favorite place for all Quebecois when they want some sunshine or a bit of exercise. Free concerts are given during the summer at the bandstand in the park, the Kiosque Edwin-Bélanger. Be sure to see the Jardin Jeanne d'Arc (Joan of Arc Garden), just off avenue Laurier between Loews le Concorde Hôtel and the Ministry of Justice. The statue of Joan of Arc was a gift from anonymous Americans, and it was here that "O Canada," the country's national anthem, was sung for the first time. Within the park are two Martello towers, cylindrical stone defensive structures built between 1808 and 1812, when Québec feared an invasion from the United States.

Today, Battlefields Park contains almost 5,000 trees representing more than 80 species. Prominent among these are sugar maple, silver maple, Norway maple, American elm, and American ash. There are frequent special activities, including theatrical and musical events, presented in the park during the summer.

Year-round, the park's **Centre d'Interprétation du Parc des Champs-de-Bataille (Battlefields Park Interpretation Centre),** at 1 av. Wolfe-Montcalm (*©* **418/648-5641**), provides insights into the significance of the Plains of Abraham to Québec over the years, employing effective multimedia techniques. For C$5 (US$4) for adults and C$4 (US$3.20) for students and seniors, visitors are provided with wireless headsets and directed through several chambers—actually corridors and cells in what was once a prison—to witness dramatic presentations in sound and pictures of episodes in Québec's long history. The narration doesn't fail to describe some of the racier components of that tenure, including a number of elaborate executions and tales of the prostitutes who serviced the garrison at the Citadelle. It also discusses the landing of Charles Lindbergh on the Plains in 1928. Allow 30 minutes for the audiovisual tour.

The Interpretation Centre is in the Baillairgé Pavilion of the Musée des Beaux-Arts du Québec. It also serves as a starting point for bus and walking tours of the park. In summer, a shuttle bus tours the park in 45 minutes, with narration in French and English (prices given below).

Battlefields Park Interpretation Centre, 1 av. Wolfe-Montcalm (near av. George VI). *©* **418/648-5641.** Free admission to park. Shuttle bus tours: C$3.50 (US$2.80) ages 18–64, C$2.75 (US$2.20) ages 13–17 and 65 and over, free for children 12 and under. Discovery Pavilion open in summer daily 10am–5:30pm; winter Tues–Sun 10am–5pm. Park is open at all times. Bus: 3 or 11.

Room with a View

For a panoramic look at the city, seek out the building that houses Québec's Education Ministry, the **Edifice Marie-Guyart** at 1037 rue de la Chevrotière (*©* **418/644-9841;** www.observatoirecapitale.org). Enter the tower at the corner of de la Chevrotière and René-Lévesque, and look for signs and elevators directing you to the OBSERVATOIRE DE LA CAPITALE, on the 31st floor. It's the highest overlook in the city. Open late June to mid-October daily 10am to 5pm, and late October to late June Tuesday to Sunday 10am to 5pm. Admission is C$5 (US$4) adults, C$4 (US$3.20) seniors and students, and free for ages 12 and under.

Another place for a vista of the city is **L'Astral,** the revolving restaurant atop the Loews le Concorde hotel. It isn't necessary to plan a meal there (although the food and prices are more than acceptable), since the bar is as good a vantage point as any. See p. 223 for details.

2 More Attractions

HAUTE-VILLE (UPPER TOWN)

Basilique Notre-Dame ✿ Notre-Dame Basilica, representing the oldest Christian parish north of Mexico, has weathered a tumultuous history of bombardment, reconstruction, and restoration. Parts of the existing basilica date from the original 1647 structure, including the bell tower and portions of the walls, but most of today's exterior is from the reconstruction completed in 1771. The interior, a re-creation undertaken after a fire in 1922, is flamboyantly neo-baroque, with shadows wavering by the fluttering light of votive candles. Paintings and ecclesiastical treasures still remain from the time of the French regime, including a chancel lamp given by Louis XIV. In summer, the basilica is the backdrop for a 30-minute multimedia sound-and-light show called "Feux Sacrés" (Acts of Faith), which dramatically recalls 5 centuries of Québec's history, as well as the history of this building. The basilica is connected to the group of old buildings that make up Québec Seminary. To enter that complex, go to 7 rue de l'Université, a block away.

20 rue Buade (at Côte de la Fabrique). ② 418/694-0665. Free admission to basilica and guided tours. "Feux Sacrés" sound-and-light show C$7.50 (US$6) adults; C$5 (US$4) 65 and over, students with ID, and children 6 and over; free for children under 6. Cathedral daily 7:30am–4:30pm. Guided tours May 1–Nov 1 daily 9am–4:30pm, on the half-hour. "Feux Sacrés" sound-and-light show May–Oct 15 Mon–Fri 3:30, 4:30, 5:30, 6:30, 7:30, and 8:30pm, Sat–Sun 6:30, 7:30, and 8:30pm; Oct 16–Apr 30, group reservations only.

Chapelle/Musée des Ursulines This chapel is notable for the sculptures in its pulpit and two richly decorated altarpieces. They were created by Pierre-Noël Levasseur between 1726 and 1736. Although the present building dates only from 1902, much of the interior decoration is nearly 2 centuries older. The tomb of the founder of the Ursulines teaching order, Marie de l'Incarnation, who arrived in Québec City in 1639 at the age of 40, is to the right of the entry. Marie de l'Incarnation was declared blessed by Pope John Paul II in 1980. A museum on the premises displays accouterments of the daily and spiritual life of the Ursulines. On the third floor are exhibits of vestments woven with gold thread by the Ursulines. A cape made of the drapes from the bedroom of Anne of Austria, which was given to Marie de l'Incarnation when she left for New France in 1639, is on display. There are also musical instruments and Amerindian crafts, including the flèche, or arrow sash, still worn during Winter Carnival. Some of the docents are nuns of the still-active order. The Ursuline convent, built originally as a girls' school in 1642, is the oldest in North America.

12 rue Donnacona (des Jardins). ② 418/694-0694. Free admission to chapel. Museum C$6 (US$4.80) adults, C$5 (US$4) seniors, C$4 (US$3.20) students 17 and over, C$3 (US$2.40) ages 12–16, free for children under 12. Museum Oct–Nov and Feb–Apr Tues–Sun 1–4:30pm; May–Sept Tues–Sat 10am–noon and 1–5pm, Sun 1–5pm. Closed Dec–Jan except to groups with reservations. Chapel May–Oct same days and hours as museum.

Château Frontenac ✿ Opened in 1893 to house railroad passengers and encourage tourism, this monster version of a Loire Valley palace is the city's emblem, its Eiffel Tower. The hotel can be seen from almost every quarter, commanding its majestic position atop Cap Diamant. Franklin D. Roosevelt and Winston Churchill held two important summit conferences here in 1943 and 1944. Visitors curious about the interior may wish to take one of the 50-minute guided tours offered. To make reservations, which are required, call ② 418/691-2166.

1 rue des Carrières, Place d'Armes. ② 418/691-2166. C$8 (US$6.40) adults, C$7.25 (US$5.80) for seniors, C$5.50 (US$4.40) children ages 6–16. May 1–Oct 15 Mon–Fri 10am–6pm; Oct 16–Apr 30 Sat–Sun 1–5pm (departures on the hour).

Musée de l'Amérique Française   Located at the site of the Québec Seminary, which dates from 1663, the Museum of French America focuses on the beginnings and evolution of French culture and civilization in North America. Its extensive collections include paintings by European and Canadian artists, engravings and parchments from the early French regime, old and rare books, coins, early scientific instruments, and even mounted animals and an Egyptian mummy. The mix makes for a mostly engrossing visit, although parts of the museum can be rather dry.

The museum is located in three parts of the large seminary complex, the Guillaume-Couillard and Jérôme-Demers wings, and the beautiful François-Ranvoyze section, with its *trompe l'oeil* ornamentation, which served as a chapel for the seminary priests and students. Recent construction has added an annex to the chapel, an underground passage, and a new entrance lobby. Concerts are often held in the chapel.

2 Côte de la Fabrique. ⓒ 418/692-2843. www.mcq.org. Admission C$5 (US$4) adults, C$4 (US$3.20) seniors and students over 16, C$2 (US$1.60) children 12–16, free for children under 12. Late June to Labor Day daily 9:30am–5pm; Sept to mid-June Tues–Sun 10am–5pm. Guided tours (call for reservations) of exhibitions and some buildings daily in summer, Sat and Sun rest of the year.

Musée du Fort   A long-running but still effective multimedia show combines film, light, stirring music, and a 36-sq.-m (400-sq.-ft.) scale model of the city and environs to tell the story of the several battles that flared here in the 18th century. At under 25 minutes, it is a sufficiently engrossing presentation during which only the very young are likely to grow restless. Shows in English are every hour on the hour during the summer season, but variable the rest of the year.

10 rue Ste-Anne (Place d'Armes). ⓒ 418/692-4161. Admission C$7.50 (US$6) adults, C$5.50 (US$4.40) seniors, C$4.50 (US$3.60) students. Apr 1–June 30 and Sept 16–Oct 31 daily 10am–5pm; July 1–Sept 15 daily 10am–7pm; Dec 26–Jan 2 daily noon–4pm; Feb and Mar Thurs–Sun noon–4pm; open to groups upon reservation the rest of the year.

Parc de l'Artillerie   Fortifications erected by the French in the 17th and 18th centuries enclose Artillery Park. In addition to protecting the garrison, the defensive works contained an ammunition factory that was functional until 1964. On view are the old officers' mess and quarters, an iron foundry, and a scale model of the city created in 1806. Costumed docents give tours. From July 1 to September, there are daily musket demonstrations; schedule varies.

It may be a blow to romantics and history buffs to learn that the nearby St-Jean Gate in the city wall was built in 1940, the fourth in a series that began with the original 1693 entrance, which was replaced in 1747, and then replaced again in 1867.

2 rue d'Auteuil (near Porte St-Jean). ⓒ 418/648-4205. www.parcscanada.gc.ca/artillerie. Admission C$4 (US$3.20) adults, C$3.50 (US$2.80) seniors and students 17 and over, C$2.75 (US$2.20) ages 6–16, free for children under 6. Early May to mid-Oct Wed–Sun 10am–5pm; rest of year call for hours.

BASSE-VILLE (LOWER TOWN)

The **Escalier Casse-Cou** connects the Terrasse Dufferin at the top of the cliff with rue Sous-le-Fort at the base. The name translates to "Breakneck Stairs," which is self-explanatory as soon as you see them. They lead from Haute-Ville to the Quartier du Petit-Champlain in Basse-Ville. A stairway has existed here since the settlement began. In fact, in 1698 the town council forbade citizens from taking their animals up or down the stairway. If they didn't comply they were punished with a fine.

Centre d'Interprétation du Vieux-Port   A unit of Parks Canada, the four floors of the Old Port Interpretation Center depict the Port of Québec as it was during its maritime zenith in the 19th century. Exhibits illustrate the shipbuilding and lumbering enterprises, employing animated figures and docents in costumes appropriate to the era. The modern port and city can be viewed from the top level, where reference maps identify landmarks. Guided tours of the harbor are available. Texts accompanying the displays are in French and English, and most exhibits invite tactile interaction. Guided tours of the Old Port in French and English leave from the center from mid-June to mid-October. Tour prices are C$8 (US$6.40) adults and C$7 ($5.60) for children 6 to 16. Kids under 6 are free.

100 quai St-Andre (at rue Rioux). ☎ 418/648-3300. www.parkscanada.gc.ca/vieuxport. Admission C$3.50 (US$2.80) adults, C$3 (US$2.40) seniors and students over 17, C$2 (US$1.60) children 5–17, free for children under 5. May–Aug daily 10am–5pm; Sept to mid-Oct 1–5pm.

Maison Chevalier Built in 1752 for ship owner Jean-Baptiste Chevalier, the existing structure incorporated two older buildings, dating from 1675 and 1695. It was run as an inn throughout the 19th century. The Québec government restored the house in 1960, and it became a museum 5 years later. The interior has exposed wood beams, wide-board floors, and stone fireplaces. There are changing exhibits on Québec history and civilization, focusing especially on the 17th and 18th centuries. While exhibit texts are in French, guidebooks in English are available at the sometimes-unattended front desk. *Note:* The house also serves as an air-conditioned refuge on hot days.

50 rue du Marché-Champlain (near rue Notre-Dame). ☎ 418/643-2158. Free admission. Late June to Labor Day daily 9:30am–5pm; Sept to mid-Oct Tues–Sun 10am–7pm; late Oct to Apr and May to mid-June Tues–Sun 10am–5pm, Sat–Sun 10am–7pm. Closed mid-Dec to Jan 2.

NEAR THE GRANDE-ALLEE

Hôtel du Parlement Since 1968, what the Quebecois choose to call their "National Assembly" has occupied this imposing Second Empire château constructed in 1886. Twenty-two bronze statues of some of the most prominent figures in Québec's tumultuous history gaze out from the facade. Highlights are the Assembly Chamber, and the Room of the Old Legislative Council, where parliamentary committees meet. Throughout the building, representations of the fleur-de-lis and the initials VR (for Victoria Regina) remind visitors of Québec's dual heritage. The building can now be toured unaccompanied, but there are free 30-minute guided tours in both French and English. Tour times change without warning so call ahead.

The Restaurant Le Parlementaire (☎ **418/643-6640**) is open to the public. Featuring Québec products and cuisine, it serves breakfast and lunch Monday through Friday most of the year, and dinner Tuesday through Friday in June and December.

Entrance at corner of Grande-Allée est and av. Honoré-Mercier. ☎ 418/643-7239. Free admission. Guided tours: Mon–Fri 9am–4:30pm; Sat, Sun, and holidays 10am–4:30pm.

3 Especially for Kids

Children who have responded to Arthurian tales of fortresses and castles or to the adventures of Harry Potter often delight in simply walking around this storybook city. As soon as possible, head for **Terrasse Dufferin,** which has those coin-operated telescopes that kids find so engaging. In decent weather, there are always street entertainers, ranging from Peruvian musical groups to men who play saws or wine glasses. A few steps away at Place d'Armes are **horse-drawn carriages,** and not far in the same direction are the **Musée de Cire (Wax Museum),** on Place d'Armes at 22 rue Ste-Anne, and the **Musée du Fort,** at 10 rue Ste-Anne (p. 244).

Also at Place d'Armes is the top of **Breakneck Stairs.** Halfway down, across the road, are giant **cannons** ranged along the battlements on rue des Ramparts. The gun carriages are impervious to the assaults of small humans, so kids can scramble over them at will. At the bottom of the Breakneck Stairs, on the left, is a **glass-blowing workshop,** the Verrerie la Mailloche. In the front room, craftsmen give intriguing and informative glass-blowing demonstrations. The glass is melted at 2,545°F (1,396°C) and is worked at 2,000°F (1,093°C). Also in the Lower Town, at 86 rue Dalhousie, the playful **Musée de la Civilisation** (p. 237) keeps kids occupied for hours in its exhibits, shop, and cafe. Military sites are usually a hit, too. **La Citadelle** has tours of the grounds and buildings, but the distances covered and the dry narration are apt to give kids the fidgets. Better still, take them to the colorful changing of the guard and beating retreat ceremonies (p. 240).

The **ferry** to Lévis across the St. Lawrence is inexpensive, convenient from the Lower Town, and exciting for kids. The crossing, over and back, takes less than an hour. To run off the kids' excess energy, head for **Battlefields Park (Parc des Champs-de-Bataille),** which is also called the **Plains of Abraham.** To get there, take rue St-Louis, just inside the St-Louis Gate, or, more vigorously, the walkway along Terrasse Dufferin and the Promenade des Gouverneurs, which has a long set of stairs. Acres of grassy lawn give children room to roam and provide the perfect spot for a family picnic.

Even better is the **Village Vacances Valcartier (*(C)* 418/844-2200;** www.valcartier. com) at 1860 bd. Valcartier in St-Gabriel-de-Valcartier, about 20 minutes' drive north of downtown. In summer, it's a water park, with 25 slides, a huge wave pool, and diving shows. In winter, those same facilities are put to use for snow rafting on inner tubes, sliding down ice slides, and skating.

4 Organized Tours

Québec City is small enough to get around quickly and easily with a good map and a guidebook, but a tour is helpful for getting background information on the history and culture of the city, grasping the lay of the land, and seeing those attractions that are a bit of a hike or require wheels to reach, such as the Musée du Québec. **Kiosque Frontenac,** facing the Château Frontenac near the upper terminal of the funicular, can make reservations for most city tours, whether by bus, boat, or foot, and is also a currency exchange. Here are some agencies and organizations that have proved reliable in the past.

BUS TOURS
Buses are obviously convenient if extensive walking is difficult for individual visitors, especially in the hilly and steeply sloping Upper Town. Among the established tour operators, **Gray Line** (*(C)* 888/558-7668 or 418/649-9226) offers English-only tours, which are preferable since twice as much information is imparted in the same amount of time as on a bilingual tour. The company's city tours are in small coaches that carry 24 or fewer people, while day trips out of the city, to the casino at Charlevoix and along the south shore, for example, are in full-size buses. Gray Line also offers a 9½-hour whale-watching excursion by bus to Tadoussac and boat into the St. Lawrence. **Maple Leaf Sightseeing Tours** (*(C)* 877/622-3677 or 418/622-3677) picks up passengers at their hotels in a 25-passenger "trolley bus" and embarks on a comprehensive tour of Québec, old and new, Upper and Lower Towns. They also provide walking

tours and individual guides—your car or theirs. **La Tournée du Québec Métro** (© **418/836-8687** or 800/672-5232) has tours of the city and excursions to Île d'Orléans and Ste-Anne-de-Beaupré, with hotel pickup.

City tours usually last 2 to 2½ hours and cost from about C$19 to C$28 (US$15–US$22) for adults, about half-price for children ages 3 to 12. Many of the tour operators offer half- or full-day (lunch included) tours to Ste-Anne-de-Beaupré, Montmorency Falls, and Ile d'Orléans. These usually cost around C$37 (US$30) for adults.

For more information about bus tours of the ity, read the "City Tours" section of the *Greater Québec Area Tourist Guide,* supplied ι ʳ the tourist office.

HORSE-DRAWN CARRIAGE TOURS

A romantic but expensive way to tour the city is in a horse-drawn carriage, called a calèche. They can be hired at Place d'Armes or on rue d'Auteuil, just within the city walls near the St-Louis Gate. The 35-minute guided tour in either French or English costs C$50 (US$40) per carriage, plus tax and tip. Each carriage typically holds up to five people. Carriages operate all summer, rain or shine. For information call © **418/683-9222** or 418/624-3062.

RIVER CRUISES

A variety of cruise possibilities are offered by **Croisières AML** (© **800/563-4643** or 418/692-1159; www.croisieresaml.com). Weighing in at 900 tons, M/V *Louis Jolliet* is a three-deck 1930s ferry–turned–excursion vessel. It can carry 1,000 passengers, and has bilingual guides, full dining facilities, and a bar. Cruises last 1½ hours in the late morning and afternoon, with three daily departures, 4-hour "Love Boat" and "Buffet and Martini" cruises in the evening, when dancing and dining are part of the experience. Prices start at C$25 (US$20) for adults, C$23 (US$18) for seniors and students, and C$10 (US$8) for children 6 to 16, but are higher for evening cruises. Meals on the "Love Boat" cruises are extra, from C$24 to C$38 (US$19–US$30) per person over the cruise fare, tax and tip not included. Most times, board the boat at quai Chouinard, 10 rue Dalhousie, near Place Royale in the Lower Town, but some cruises depart from Lévis, on the south shore, from late June to Labor Day.

Croisières AML also has 3-hour **whale-watching cruises** from Baie Ste-Catherine, at the mouth of the Saguenay River. Departures are at 9:45am and cost C$52 (US$42) for adults 17 and over, C$47 (US$38) for seniors and students, and C$22 (US$18) for children 6 to 16, under 6 free. Another cruising and whale-watching tour is with **Croisères Dufour** (© **800/463-5250** or 418/692-0222; www.groupedufour. com), which sails from Tadoussac on the Baie and spends 3 hours in the St-Lawrence looking for whales. Fares are C$52 (US$42) adults, C$47 (US$38) seniors and students, and C$22 (US$18) children 6 to 12. Available packages include a night at the Hotel Tadoussac, buffet dinner, and breakfast. You are most likely to spot whales during the summer.

WALKING TOURS

Points of departure for walking tours change, so to get up-to-date information on times and places of departure, check at the kiosk on Terrasse Dufferin near the Château Frontenac and beside the funicular entrance. Many tours leave from there. If you want to go at your own pace, an "audio-guide" CD player can be rented at the kiosk for C$10 (US$8). Its recorded narration leads past most of the major sites, taking anywhere from 1 to 3 hours.

The **Association des guides touristiques de Québec** (© 418/624-2851) can provide guides for any length of time, on foot or in your car or theirs. Walking tours of the villages of nearby Île d'Orléans (see chapter 19) are arranged by **Beau Temps, Mauvais Temps Tours** (© 418/828-2275).

5 Spectator Sports

Québec has not had a team in any of the major professional leagues since the NHL Nordiques left in 1995, but it is represented by the Capitales baseball club of the Northern League. Home games are played in the Municipal Stadium, 100 rue du Cardinal Maurice-Roy (© **418/521-2255**). Tickets cost from C$10 to C$18 (US$8–US$14).

Harness races take place at the **Hippodrome de Québec,** 250 bd. Wilfrid-Hamel ExpoCité (© **418/524-5283**). Races are held year-round Thursday to Tuesday at 1:30 or 7:30pm (times vary from season to season; call ahead). Admission is free. Le Cavallo clubhouse is open year-round.

6 Outdoor Activities

The waters and hills around Québec City provide countless opportunities for outdoor recreation, from swimming, rafting, and fishing, to skiing, snowmobiling, and sleigh rides. There are two centers in particular to keep in mind for most winter and summer activities, both within easy drives from the capital. Thirty minutes from Québec City, off Route 175 north, is the provincial **Parc de la Jacques-Cartier** (© **418/848-3169** or 418/528-8787). Closer by 10 minutes or so is **Parc Mont Ste-Anne** (© **418/827-4561**), only 40km (25 miles) northeast of the city. Both are mentioned repeatedly in the listings below. From mid-November to late March, taxis participate in a **winter shuttle** program, **HiverExpress,** picking up passengers at 16 hotels at 8:30am, taking them to Parc Mont Ste-Anne (p. 280), and Station Stoneham, about 27km (17 miles) from the city, and returning them to Québec City at about 4:30pm. Round-trip fare is C$23 (US$18). Call © **418/525-5191** to make a reservation or ask if your hotel participates when booking a room.

BIKING

Given the hilly topography of the Upper Town, biking isn't a particularly attractive option. But rented bicycles are available at a shop on a hill that descends to the flatter Lower Town. **Vélo Passe-Sport Plein Air,** at 22 Côte du Palais (© **418/692-3643;** www.velopasse-sport.com) rents bikes for C$14 (US$11) for 2 hours or C$30 (US$24) for 8 hours. It's open daily from 9am to 6pm in summer. A marked path for cyclists (and in-line skaters) follows much of the route described in the Lower Town Walking Tour 2 (p. 258). For more vigorous mountain biking, **Parc Mont Ste-Anne** (© **418/827-4561**) has 200km (124 miles) of trails.

CAMPING

There are almost 30 campgrounds in the greater Québec area, with as few as 20 individual campsites and as many as 368. All of them have showers and toilets available. One of the largest (they even accept credit cards) is in the **Parc Mont Ste-Anne** (p. 280). One of the smallest, but with a convenience store and snack bar, is **Camping La Loutre** (© **418/846-2201**) on Lac Jacques-Cartier in the park of the same name. It's north of the city, off Route 175. The booklet available at the tourist offices provides details about all the sites.

CANOEING

The several lakes and rivers of **Parc de la Jacques-Cartier** are fairly easy to reach, yet they seem to be in the midst of virtual wilderness. Canoes are available to rent in the park itself.

CROSS-COUNTRY SKIING

Greater Québec has 22 cross-country ski centers with 278 trails. In town, the **Parc des Champs-de-Bataille (Battlefields Park)** has 11km (6¾ miles) of groomed cross-country trails, a convenience for those who don't have cars or the time to get out of town. Cross-country skis can be rented in the city at **Vélo Passe-Sport Plein Air,** 22 Côte du Palais (☎ **418/692-3643**). Those who do have transportation should consider **Parc Mont Ste-Anne** (p. 280), which has more than 225km (140 miles) of cross-country trails at all levels of difficulty; equipment is available for rent.

DOG SLEDDING

Aventures Nord-Bec (☎ **418/889-8001**), at 665 rue Ste-Aimé in Saint-Lambert-de-Lauzon, about 30 minutes south of the city, offers dog sledding expeditions. While they aren't the equivalent of a 2-week mush across Alaska, there are choices of half-day to 5-day expeditions, and participants obtain a sense of what the experience is like. They get a four-dog sled meant for two passengers and take turns standing on the runners and sitting on the sled. (Shout "Yo" to go left, "Gee" to go right.) Out on the trail it's a hushed world of snow and evergreens. With the half-day trip costing C$75 (US$60) per adult, C$65 (US$52) for students, and C$25 (US$20) for children 12 and under, it's expensive for families, but the memory stays with you. Another firm providing similar experiences is **Aventure Québec** (☎ **418/827-2227**) at 3987 av. Royale at Mont Ste-Anne.

DOWNHILL SKIING

Foremost among the five area downhill centers is the one at **Parc Mont Ste-Anne,** containing the largest total skiing surface in eastern Canada, with 51 trails (many of them lit for night skiing) and 11 lifts. From November 15 to March 30, a daily Hiver-Express shuttle service operates between downtown hotels and alpine and cross-country ski centers. The cars or minivans are equipped to carry ski gear and cost about C$23 (US$18) round-trip per person. For information call ☎ **418/525-5191.**

FISHING

From May until early September, anglers can wet their lines in the river that flows through the **Parc de la Jacques-Cartier** and at the national wildlife reserve at **Cap-Tourmente** (☎ **418/827-3776**), on the St. Lawrence, not far from Mont Ste-Anne. Permits are available at many sporting-goods stores. The catches are mostly trout and salmon.

GOLF

Parc Mont Ste-Anne has two 18-hole courses, plus practice ranges and putting greens. Reservations are required, and fees are C$38 to C$80 (US$30–US$64), including golf cart. In all, there are two dozen courses in the area, most of them in the suburbs of Ste-Foy, Beauport, and Charlesbourg.

ICE SKATING

Outdoor rinks are located at place d'Youville, Terrasse Dufferin, and Parc de l'Esplanade inside the city walls, and at Parc des Champs-de-Bataille (Battlefields Park), where rock climbing, camping, canoeing, and mountain biking are also possible. Skates can be rented at **Vélo Passe-Sport Plein Air** (© **418/692-3643**), at 22 Côte du Palais in the old town.

SWIMMING

Those who want to swim during their visit should plan to stay at one of the handful of hotels with pools. **Fairmont Le Château Frontenac** has one, and the **Radisson** has a heated outdoor pool that can be entered from indoors. Other possibilities are the **Hilton, Manoir Victoria,** and **Loews le Concorde.** See chapter 13 for details.

   Village Vacances Valcartier, a two-season recreational center in St-Gabriel-de-Val-cartier (1860 bd. Valcartier; © **418/844-2200**), has an immense wave pool and water slides, as well as 38 trails for snow rafting in winter (it's kind of like sledding). The center is about 20 minutes west of the city.

TOBOGGANING

A toboggan run is created every winter down the stairs at the south end of the Terrasse Dufferin and all the way to the Château Frontenac. Tickets (only C$1/US80¢ per person) are sold at a temporary booth near the end of the run. The ticket includes the use of a toboggan.

Québec City Strolls

The many pleasures of walking in picturesque Québec are entirely comparable to walking in similar *quartiers* in northern European cities. Stone houses huddle close together; carriage wheels creak behind muscular horses; sunlight filters through leafy canopies, falling on drinkers and diners in sidewalk cafes; and childish shrieks of laughter echo down cobblestone streets. Not common to other cities, however, is the bewitching vista of river and mountains that the Dufferin promenade bestows. In winter, Old Québec takes on a Dickensian quality, with lamp glow flickering behind curtains of falling snow. A man who should know—Dickens himself—described the city as having "splendid views which burst upon the eye at every turn."

WALKING TOUR 1   **THE UPPER TOWN**

Start:	Terrasse Dufferin.
Finish:	Hôtel du Parlement.
Time:	2 hours.
Best Times:	Anytime.
Worst Times:	None.

Start the walk at the:
❶ Terrasse Dufferin
This boardwalk promenade, with its green-and-white–topped gazebos, looks much as it did 100 years ago, when ladies with parasols and gentlemen with top hats and canes strolled along it on sunny afternoons, with the Château Frontenac as a backdrop. The vistas of river, watercraft, and distant mountains will imprint themselves forever in your memory.

Stroll south on the Terrasse Dufferin, past the château. If possessed of sufficient energy and leg strength, some people may want to continue up the stairs at the end of the boardwalk and then walk south to:
❷ Promenade des Gouverneurs
This path skirts the sheer cliff wall and climbs up past Québec's Citadel, a 20-minute uphill walk away. Return to the Terrasse Dufferin, walking as far as the battery of ancient (but not original) cannons set up as they were in the old days.

Return to the middle of Terrasse Dufferin and climb the stairs to the:
❸ Jardin des Gouverneurs
This park, located just west of the Château Frontenac, is so named because it stands on the site of the mansion built to house the French governors of Québec. The house burned in 1834, and the ruins lie buried under the great bulk of the château. The obelisk monument at the lower end of the sloping park is dedicated to both generals in the momentous battle of September 13, 1759, when Wolfe

Walking Tour: The Upper Town

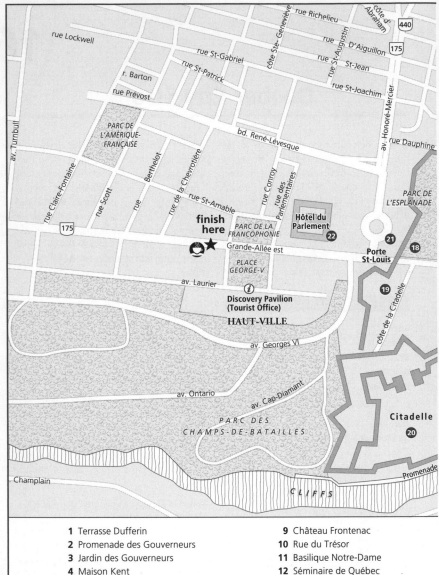

1 Terrasse Dufferin
2 Promenade des Gouverneurs
3 Jardin des Gouverneurs
4 Maison Kent
5 Maison Jacquet
6 Maison Maillou
7 Québec Ministry of Finance
8 Place d'Armes

9 Château Frontenac
10 Rue du Trésor
11 Basilique Notre-Dame
12 Séminaire de Québec
13 Hôtel-de-Ville (City Hall)
14 Anglican Cathedral of
    the Holy Trinity

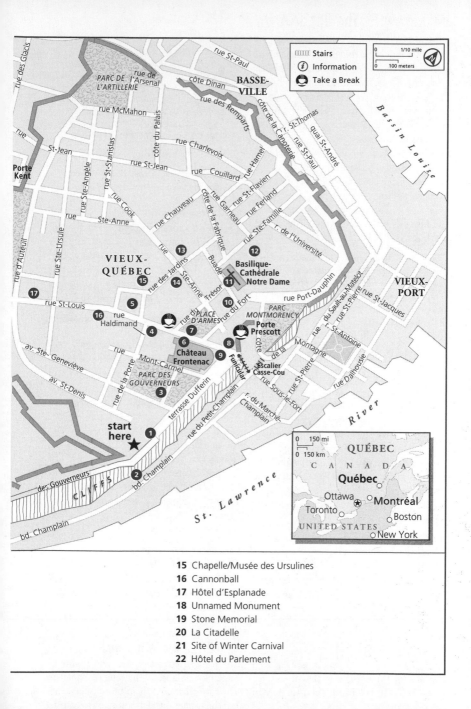

15 Chapelle/Musée des Ursulines
16 Cannonball
17 Hôtel d'Esplanade
18 Unnamed Monument
19 Stone Memorial
20 La Citadelle
21 Site of Winter Carnival
22 Hôtel du Parlement

(British) and Montcalm (French) fought for what would be the ultimate destiny of Québec and, quite possibly, all of North America. Wolfe, wounded in the fighting, lived only long enough to hear of England's victory. Montcalm died a few hours after Wolfe. Told that he was mortally wounded, Montcalm replied, "All the better. I will not see the English in Québec."

In summer, the park, also known as the Parc des Gouverneurs, is the scene of various shows and musical programs sponsored by the municipal government. The building near the southwest corner of the park is the American consulate.

Walk up rue Mont-Carmel, which runs between the park and the Château Frontenac, and turn right onto rue Haldimand. At the next corner, at rue St-Louis, stands a white house with blue trim called:

❹ Maison Kent

Built in 1648, this might be the oldest building in Québec. Although it's most famous for being the place in which France signed the capitulation to the British forces, its name comes from the duke of Kent. The duke, Queen Victoria's father, lived here for a few years at the end of the 18th century, just before he married Victoria's mother in an arranged liaison. His true love, it is said, had lived with him in Maison Kent. Today, the building houses the consulate general of France, as the tricolor over the door attests.

Diagonally across from Maison Kent, at rue St-Louis and rue des Jardins, is:

❺ Maison Jacquet

This small white dwelling with crimson roof and trim dates from 1677, and now houses a popular restaurant. Among the oldest houses in the province, it has sheltered some prominent Québecois, including Philippe Aubert de Gaspé, the author of *Aux Anciens Canadiens*, who lived here from 1815 to 1824. Gaspé's book recounts the history and folklore of Québec.

TAKE A BREAK
Try Québecois home cooking right here at the restaurant named for de Gaspé's book, **Aux Anciens Canadiens**, 34 rue St-Louis. Consider caribou in blueberry-wine sauce or duckling baked in maple syrup, but don't forget the sugar pie floating in cream.

Leaving the restaurant, walk downhill along attractive, if commercialized, rue St-Louis, to no. 17, the:

❻ Maison Maillou

This house's foundations date from 1736, though the house was enlarged in 1799 and restored in 1959. Note the metal shutters used to thwart weather and unfriendly fire. The building now houses the Québec Board of Trade and Industry.

The large building across the street from Maison Maillou is the impressive:

❼ Québec Ministry of Finance

This place started out in 1799 as a courthouse, was renovated between 1927 and 1934, and was restored again from 1983 to 1987. Since then it has been Québec's Ministry of Justice, the name on the facade notwithstanding. The architect of the exterior was Eugène-Etienne Taché, minister of public works at that time. The interior of the building is largely Art Deco. The street fronting the Ministry of Finance building is a popular parking spot for calèches, the horse-drawn carriages that tour the city.

Continue down rue St-Louis to arrive at:

❽ Place d'Armes

This plaza was once the military parade ground outside the governors' mansion (which no longer exists). In the small park at the center of the square is the Monument to the Faith, which recalls the arrival of the Recollet monks from France in 1615. The Recollet monks were granted a large plot of land by the king of France in 1681 for their church and monastery. Facing the square is the monument to Samuel de Champlain, who founded Québec in 1608. Created by French artists Paul Chevre and Paul le Cardonel, the statue has stood here since 1898. The statue's pedestal is made from stone that was also used in the Arc de Triomphe and Sacré-Coeur Basilica in Paris.

Near the Champlain statue is the diamond-shaped monument designating Québec City as a UNESCO World Heritage Site, the only city in North America with that distinction. Placed here in 1985, it is made of bronze, granite, and glass. A tourist information center is also at Place d'Armes, at 12 rue Ste-Anne.

Again, up to the right, is the:

⑨ Château Frontenac

This famous edifice defines the Québec City skyline. The first, lower part was built as a hotel from 1892 to 1893 by the Canadian Pacific Railway Company. The architect, Bruce Price of New York, raised his creation on the site of the governor's mansion and named it after Louis de Buade, Comte de Frontenac. Monsieur le Comte was the one who, in 1690, was faced with the threat of an English fleet under Sir William Phips during King William's War. Phips sent a messenger to demand Frontenac's surrender, but Frontenac replied, "Tell your lord that I will reply with the mouths of my cannons." Which he did. Phips sailed away.

TAKE A BREAK
This is a great part of town to sit and watch the world go by. Grab a sidewalk table and enjoy something to drink or a bite to eat at **Au Relais de la Place d'Armes**, a red-roofed building with a mock-Tudor facade at 16 rue Ste-Anne.

Leaving there, turn right, then right again into the narrow pedestrian lane called:

⑩ Rue du Trésor

Artists hang their prints and paintings of Québec scenes on both sides of the walkway. In decent weather, it's busy with browsers and sellers. Most prices are within the means of the average visitor. Several of the artists, positioned near adjacent sidewalk cafes, draw portraits or caricatures.

Follow rue du Trésor from rue Ste-Anne down to rue Buade and turn left. On the right, at the corner of rue Ste-Famille is the:

⑪ Basilique Notre-Dame (1647)

The basilica has suffered a tumultuous history of bombardment and repeated reconstruction. Its interior is ornate, the air rich with the scent of burning candles. Many artworks remain from the time of the French regime. The chancel lamp was a gift from Louis XIV, and the crypt is the final resting place for most of the bishops of Québec.

Downhill from the basilica on rue Ste-Famille, just past Côte de la Fabrique, is the historic:

⑫ Séminaire de Québec

Founded in 1663 by Bishop Laval, the first bishop in North America, the seminary had grown into Laval University by 1852, and for many years it occupied the expanded seminary campus. By the middle of the 20th century, however, a new university was constructed west of the city in Ste-Foy. The entire area is still known as the Latin Quarter—after the language that once dominated university life. An animated neighborhood at night, many visitors will want to return to rues Couillard, Garneau, and St-Jean after the sun goes down. During summer only, tours are given of the old seminary's grounds and some of its stone and wood buildings, revealing lavish decorations of stone, tile, brass, and gilt-framed oil paintings. Call ⓒ **418/694-1020** for tour details. The Musée de l'Amérique

Française, housed in the seminary, has an entrance at 9 rue de l'Université. It's open year-round.

From here, head back to the basilica. Take a right on rue de Buade and follow it to rue des Jardins to see the:

⑬ Hôtel-de-Ville (City Hall)

The building's lower level, with an entrance at 43 Côte de la Fabrique, houses the Centre d'Interprétation de la Vie Urbaine (Urban Life Interpretation Center), with a large-scale model of Québec City and its suburbs as they were in 1975. It helps strangers to get their bearings, and it might be surprising to see how spread out the city actually is. While the historic Upper and Lower Towns are compact, the city actually covers 92 sq. km (36 sq. miles).

The park next to the City Hall is often converted into an outdoor show area in summer, especially during the Festival d'Eté (Summer Festival), and concerts, dance recitals, and other programs are staged here.

Continue on rue des Jardins and cross rue Ste-Anne. On the left is the spire of the:

⑭ Anglican Cathedral of the Holy Trinity

Said to be modeled after St-Martin-in-the-Fields in London, the cathedral dates from 1804. The interior is simple but spacious, with pews of solid English oak from the Royal Windsor forest and a latticed ceiling in white with a gilded-chain motif. Visitors may happen upon an organ recital, or at least a rehearsal.

Farther along on rue des Jardins, at rue Donnacona, on the right side of the street, is the:

⑮ Chapelle/Musée des Ursulines

The museum displays the handiwork of the Ursuline nuns from the 17th, 18th, and 19th centuries. There are also Amerindian crafts and a cape that was made for Marie de l'Incarnation, the reverend mother and a founder of the convent, when she left for New France in 1639.

Be sure to peek into the restored chapel if it's open (May–Oct). It shelters the remains of General Montcalm, who was buried here after he fell in the battle that marked the end of French rule in Québec in 1759. Montcalm's tomb is actually under the chapel and not accessible to the public. His skull, on the other hand, is on display in the Ursuline Museum. The tomb of Marie de l'Incarnation, who died in 1672, is here. The altar, created by sculptor Pierre-Noël Levasseur between 1726 and 1736, is worth a look.

From the museum, turn right on rue Donnacona and walk to the entrance of the Ursuline Convent, built originally in 1642. The present complex is actually a succession of different buildings added and repaired at various times up to 1836, because frequent fires took their toll. A statue of founder Marie de l'Incarnation is outside. The convent is a private girls' school today and is not open to the public.

Continue left up the hill along what is now rue du Parloir to rue St-Louis. Cross the street and turn right. At the next block, rue du Corps-de-Garde, note the tree with a:

⑯ Cannonball

Lodged at the base of the trunk, it purportedly landed here during the War of 1759 and over the years became firmly embraced by the tree.

Continue along St-Louis another 1½ blocks to rue d'Auteuil. The house on the right corner is now the:

⑰ Hôtel d'Esplanade

Notice that many of the windows in the facade facing rue St-Louis are bricked up. This is because houses were once taxed by the number of windows they had, and the frugal homeowner found this way to get around the law, even though it cut down on his view.

Continue straight on rue St-Louis toward the Porte St-Louis, a gate in the walls. Next to it is the Esplanade powder magazine, part of the old fortifications. Just before the gate is an:

⑱ Unnamed monument

This monument commemorates the 1943 meeting in Québec of U.S. President Franklin D. Roosevelt and British Prime Minister Winston Churchill. It's a soft-pedaled reminder to French Québecois that it was English-speaking nations that rid France of the Nazis.

Cross over St-Louis and turn along Côte de la Citadelle. On the right are headquarters and barracks of a militia district, arranged around an inner court. Near its entrance is a:

⑲ Stone memorial

It marks the resting place of 13 soldiers of General Montgomery's American army, felled in the unsuccessful assault on Québec in 1775. Obviously, the conflicts that swirled around Québec for centuries didn't end with the fateful 1759 battle between the British and the French.

Continue up the hill to:

⑳ La Citadelle

The impressive star-shaped fortress keeps watch from a commanding position on a grassy plateau 108m (354 ft.) above the banks of the St. Lawrence. It took 30 years to complete, by which time it had become obsolete. Since 1920, the Citadel has been the home of the French-speaking Royal 22e Régiment, which fought in both world wars and in Korea. With good timing, it is possible to both visit the regimental museum and watch the changing of the guard or the ceremony called "beating the retreat," weather permitting (see p. 241 for times and days of the ceremonies).

Return to rue St-Louis and turn left through Porte St-Louis, which was built in 1873 on the site of a gate dating from 1692. Here the street broadens to become the Grande-Allée. To the right is a park that runs alongside the city walls. This is the:

㉑ Site of Winter Carnival

One of the most captivating events in the Canadian calendar, the 11-day celebration takes place every year from the first Thursday to the second Sunday of February. A palace of snow and ice, the centerpiece of the festivities, rises on this spot. Colorfully clad Québecois come to admire it, climb on it, and sample some maple-syrup candy at the nearby sugar shack set up for the occasion. On the other side of Grande-Allée, ice sculptures are created by 20 teams of artists from around the world participating in the International Snow Sculpture Competition. Each sculpture illustrates an aspect of the culture of the country it represents.

Fronting the park, on avenue Dufferin, stands Québec's stately:

㉒ Hôtel du Parlement

Constructed in 1884, it houses what Québecois are pleased to call their "National Assembly." Along the facade are 22 bronze statues of prominent figures in Québec's tumultuous history. The fountain in front of the door, the work of Philippe Hébert (1890), was dedicated to Québec's original Native Canadian, or Amerindian, inhabitants. There are tours of the sumptuous chambers inside, where symbols of the fleur-de-lis and the initials VR (for Victoria Regina) are reminders of Québec's dual heritage. If the crown on top is lit, Parliament is in session.

TAKE A BREAK
The Le Parlementaire restaurant in the Hôtel du Parlement is open to the public for breakfast and lunch Monday through Friday most of the year. If this is not the right day or time, continue along the Grande-Allée 2 more blocks. There are plenty of places to stop for a drink or a snack, at outdoor tables in summer. One good possibility is **Au Petit Coin Breton**, on the south side of the street, at 655 Grande-Allée est.

From the Grande-Allée, walk or take the no. 11 bus back to the old city. For a longer scenic hike, continue along Grande-Allée to visit the Musée du Québec, on the left at 1 av. Wolfe-Montcalm; then go into Parc des Champs-de-Bataille (Battlefields Park),

picking up the Promenade des Gouverneurs near La Citadelle and proceeding

down onto the Terrasse Dufferin and the
Château Frontenac.

WALKING TOUR 2　THE LOWER TOWN

Start:	On the Terrasse Dufferin.
Finish:	Place Royal.
Time:	1½ hours.
Best Times:	Anytime.
Worst Times:	Very late at night.

Descend to the Lower Town by the:

❶ Funicular (Option 1)

Its upper terminus is on Terrasse Dufferin near the Château Frontenac. As the
car descends the steep slope, its glass
front provides a broad view of the Basse-
Ville. The mammoth grain elevators
down by the harbor have a capacity of 8
million bushels. Beyond them is the
river, with its constant boat traffic, and
over to the left, the Laurentides Mountains rise in the distance.

**Or, if you prefer a more active (and free) means
of descent, use the stairs to the left of the funicular, the:**

❶ Escalier Casse-Cou (Option 2)

"Breakneck Stairs" is the self-explanatory
name given to this stairway. Stairs have
been in place here since the settlement
began. In fact, in 1698, the town council
forbade citizens from taking their animals
up or down the stairway.

**Both Breakneck Stairs and the funicular arrive
at the intersection of rues Petit-Champlain and
Sous-le-Fort. At the bottom of the stairs on the
left is the:**

❷ Verrerie la Mailloche

In the front room, craftsmen give glass-
blowing demonstrations—intriguing and
informative, especially for children who
haven't seen that ancient craft. The glass
is melted at 2,545°F (1,395°C) and is
worked at 2,000°F (1,092°C). There are
displays of the results and a small shop in
which to purchase them.

Exiting, walk straight ahead, passing:

❸ Maison Louis Jolliet

Built in 1683, this home belonged to the
Québec-born explorer who, with a priest,
Jacques Marquette, was the first person of
European parentage to explore the upper
reaches of the Mississippi River. Jolliet's
former house is now the lower terminus
for the funicular and full of tourist trin-
kets and gimcracks.

Continue down:

❹ Rue du Petit-Champlain

Allegedly the oldest street in North
America, it is usually swarming with
restaurant-goers, cafe sitters, strolling
couples, and gaggles of schoolchildren
ricocheting from one fetching store to
another along the way. (See chapter 17
for shopping suggestions.)

At the end of the street, turn left and
left again onto boulevard Champlain. A
lighthouse from the Gaspé Peninsula
used to stand across the street, but it has
been returned to its original home, leaving the anchor and three cannons that
surrounded it looking forlorn and misplaced.

**Following the curve of the street, pass more
shops and cafes, soon arriving at the crimson-
roofed:**

❺ Maison Chevalier

Dating from 1752, this was once the
home of merchant Jean-Baptiste Chevalier. Note the wealth of windows in the
house, more than 30 in the facade alone.
In 1763, the house was sold at auction to

Walking Tour: The Lower Town

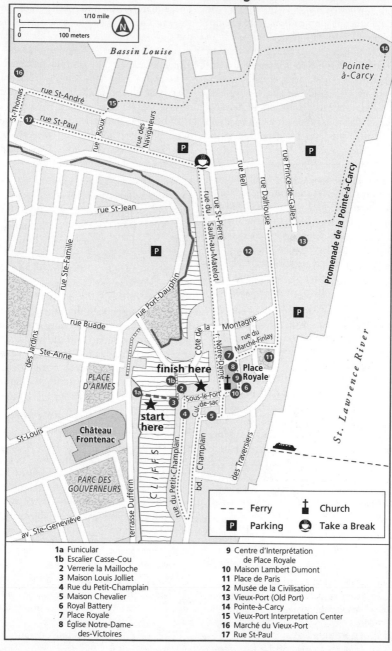

0 ———— 1/10 mile
0 ———— 100 meters

N

Bassin Louise

Pointe-à-Carcy

14

16

rue St-André

15

St-Thomas

17 rue St-Paul

rue Rioux

rue des Navigateurs

rue Bell

rue Dalhousie

rue Prince-de-Galles

P

P

rue St-Jean

rue Ste-Famille

P

rue du Sault-au-Matelot

rue St-Pierre

13

12

rue Port-Dauphin

rue Buade

des Jardins

Ste-Anne

Côte de la Montagne

rue Notre-Dame

rue du Marché-Finlay

P

Promenade de la Pointe-à-Carcy

finish here

1b

2

7

11

8 Place
9 Royale

10 **6**

PLACE
D'ARMES

1a

3 Sous-le-Fort

4 Cul-de-sac

5

St. Lawrence River

St-Louis

**start
here**

Château
Frontenac

rue du Petit-Champlain

Champlain

des Traversiers

bd Champlain

PARC DES
GOUVERNEURS

C L I F F S

terrasse Dufferin

av. Ste-Geneviève

- - - Ferry	✝ Church
P Parking	☕ Take a Break

1a Funicular	**9** Centre d'Interprétation
1b Escalier Casse-Cou	de Place Royale
2 Verrerie la Mailloche	**10** Maison Lambert Dumont
3 Maison Louis Jolliet	**11** Place de Paris
4 Rue du Petit-Champlain	**12** Musée de la Civilisation
5 Maison Chevalier	**13** Vieux-Port (Old Port)
6 Royal Battery	**14** Pointe-à-Carcy
7 Place Royale	**15** Vieux-Port Interpretation Center
8 Église Notre-Dame-	**16** Marché du Vieux-Port
des-Victoires	**17** Rue St-Paul

ship owner Jean-Louis Frémont, the grandfather of Virginia-born John Charles Frémont (1813–90). John Charles was an American explorer, soldier, and politician who mapped some 10 Western and Midwestern territories. This notable workaholic of French-Canadian heritage was also a governor of California and Arizona, a candidate for president of the United States in 1856, and a general during the Civil War.

The Chevalier House was sold in 1806 to an Englishman, who in turn rented it to a hotelier, who transformed it into an inn. From this time to the end of the century, it was known, under various owners, as the London Coffee House. In 1960, the Québec government restored the house, and it became a museum about 5 years later, overseen by the Musée de la Civilisation, which mounts temporary exhibitions here.

Turn left after exiting the house, walking up the short block of rue Notre-Dame to rue Sous-le-Fort. Turn right, and walk 1 more block to the:

6 Royal Battery

Fortifications were erected here in 1691 and the cannons were added in 1712 to defend the Lower Town. They got the chance in 1759, but the English victory silenced them; the exodus to the Upper Town left them to rust. Sunken foundations were all that remained of the Royal Battery by the turn of the 20th century, and when the time came to restore this area, it had to be rebuilt from the ground up.

From the Royal Battery, return to rue Sous-le-Fort. Here you'll find a good photo opportunity: Up the street, the Château Frontenac is framed between ancient houses.

Go up 1 block to rue Notre-Dame. Turn right. Half a block up the grade is the heart of Basse-Ville, the:

7 Place Royale

Occupying the center of the first permanent colony in New France, the enclosed square served as the town marketplace.

The square went into decline around 1860 and by 1950 had become a derelict, run-down part of town. Today it has been restored to very nearly recapture its historic appearance. The prominent bust is of Louis XIV, the Sun King, a gift from the city of Paris in 1928 that was installed here in 1931. The striking 17th- and 18th-century houses around the square once belonged to wealthy merchants. Note the ladders on some of the steep roofs used to fight snow and fire.

Facing directly onto the square is the small:

8 Eglise Notre-Dame-des-Victoires

Named for French naval victories over the British in 1690 and 1711, the oldest stone church in Québec was built in 1688. It was restored in 1763 after its partial destruction by the British in the 1759 siege. The white-and-gold interior has a few murky paintings and a large model boat suspended from the ceiling, a votive offering brought by early settlers to ensure safe voyages. On the walls, 14 small prints depict the stages of the Passion. The church is usually open to visitors daily from 10am to 4:30pm unless a wedding is underway.

Walk straight across the plaza, passing the new:

9 Centre d'Interprétation de Place-Royale

For decades, this was nothing but a propped-up facade with an empty lot behind it, but it has now been rebuilt to serve as an interpretation center with shows and exhibitions relating the history of this district.

At the corner on the right is the:

10 Maison Lambert Dumont

Its former function as a wine store is still recalled by the large wine cask spigot jutting from the wall. It's now Geomania, a store selling rocks and crystals.

Walk past the last building on your left about 15m (49 ft.) and turn around. The entire end of that building is a *trompe-l'oeil* mural of streets and houses and depictions of citizens from the earliest colonial days to the present, an amusing splash of fool-the-eye trickery.

Return to Place Royale and turn right (so that you're heading east) down rue du Marché-Finlay (in the far-right corner from the church), passing the:

⑪ Place de Paris

This plaza contains an undistinguished white sculpture that resembles a Rubik's Cube.

Continue ahead to rue Dalhousie and turn left. On the left is the:

⑫ Musée de la Civilisation

This museum, which opened in 1988, may be situated among the cobblestone streets in the historic Basse-Ville, but there is nothing traditional about it. Spacious and airy, with ingeniously arranged multidimensional exhibits, it is one of the most innovative museums in Canada, if not in all of North America. If there is no time now, put it at the top of the must-see list for a later visit.

Across the street from the museum is the:

⑬ Vieux-Port (Old Port)

In the 17th century, this 29-hectare (72-acre) riverfront area was the port of call for European ships bringing supplies and settlers to the new colony. With the decline of shipping and the shifting of economic power to Montréal by the early 20th century, the port fell into precipitous decline. But since the mid-1980s, it has experienced a rebirth, becoming the summer destination for international cruise ships.

Walk across the parking lot to the river and turn left at the water's edge on the port promenade, passing the Terminal de Croisières, the new cruise terminal. Then comes the Agora, a 6,000-seat outdoor theater with a clamshell-shaped stage, and behind it, the city's Customs House, built between 1830 and 1839.

Continue walking along the promenade, past the Agora, to the landscaped:

⑭ Pointe-à-Carcy

The bronze statue of a sailor here is a memorial to Canadian merchant seamen who lost their lives in World War II. From the point, look out across Louise Basin to the Bunge of Canada grain elevator, which stores wheat, barley, corn, and soybean crops that are produced in western Canada before they are shipped to Europe. The bridge to rural Île d'Orléans can also be seen. Île d'Orléans is the island that supplies Québec with much of its fresh fruits and vegetables (see chapter 19). The water below is the launch area for the boat race across the ice floes to Lévis during Winter Carnival.

Follow the walkway from Pointe-à-Carcy along the Louise Basin. On the left is the city's new Navy School. On the right are ticket offices and boarding docks for whale-watching and scenic river cruises.

Take a short jog left, then right along the water's edge. Up ahead, at 100 rue St-André and rue Rioux, is a modern three-story building with blue trim, the:

⑮ Vieux-Port Interpretation Center

This museum illustrates what the Port of Québec was like in the 19th century, during its heyday. Be sure to see the view of the port and the city from the top level of the Interpretation Center. Useful reference maps identify prominent landmarks. The Interpretation Center charges a small admission in summer, but at other times it's free. Texts are in English and French, and visitors are invited to touch most of the exhibits.

From the Vieux-Port Interpretation Center, go to rue St-André, turn right, and walk 1 block to the:

⑯ Marché du Vieux-Port

The market has jaunty green roofs and blue banners. From here look west to see the 1916 train station, designed by New York architect Bruce Price, who designed the Château Frontenac in 1893.

During season, the colorful farmers' market has rows of booths heaped with fresh fruits and vegetables, relishes, jams, handicrafts, flowers, and honey from local hives. Above each booth hangs a sign with the name and telephone number of the seller. A lot of them bear the initials I.O., meaning they come from Île d'Orléans, 16km (10 miles) outside the city. The market is enclosed, and the central part of it, with meats and cheeses for sale, is heated. There's a little cafe inside at which to order a cup of coffee or a meal, and there are also an ice-cream stand and a bakery.

Leaving the market, cross rue St-André at the light and walk ahead 1 short block to:

⑰ Rue St-Paul

Turn left onto this street, home to a burgeoning number of antiques shops and cafes. Most of the shops stretch from rue Rioux, opposite the Interpretation Center, to rue du Sault-au-Matelot. There's a real sense of neighborhood here.

TAKE A BREAK
The busy **Café de Saint-Malo,** at 75 rue St-Paul and rue du Sault-au-Matelot, has low ceilings, rough stone walls, and storefront windows that draw patrons inside. Come for a full meal or, on sunny days, a drink or coffee and dessert at a sidewalk table. From here, meander back toward Place Royale and the funicular along rue du Sault-au-Matelot or rue St-Pierre.

17

Québec City Shopping

The compact size of the Old Town, with its upper and lower sections, makes it especially convenient for browsing and shopping. Though similar from one place to the next, the merchandise is generally of high quality. There are several art galleries deserving of attention, including an outdoor version in the Upper Town. Antiques shops are proliferating along rue St-Paul in the Lower Town.

1 The Shopping Scene

In the Upper Town, wander along **rue St-Jean,** both within and outside the city walls, and on **rue Garneau** and **Côte de la Fabrique,** which branch off the east end of St-Jean. There's a shopping concourse on the lower level of the Château Frontenac. For T-shirts, postcards, and other souvenirs, myriad shops line **ruc St-Louis.**

The Lower Town, particularly the **Quartier du Petit-Champlain,** just off place Royale and encompassing rue du Petit-Champlain, boulevard Champlain, and rue Sous-le-Fort (opposite the funicular entrance), offers many possibilities—clothing, souvenirs, gifts, household items, collectibles—and is avoiding (so far) the trashiness that often afflicts heavily touristed areas.

Outside the walls, just beyond the strip of cafes that line Grande-Allée, **avenue Cartier** has shops and restaurants of some variety, from clothing and ceramics to housewares and gourmet foods. The 4 or 5 blocks attract crowds of generally youngish locals, and the hubbub revs up on summer nights and weekends. The area remains outside the tourist orbit.

Most stores are open Monday through Wednesday from 9 or 10am to 6pm, Thursday and/or Friday from 9am to 9pm, and Saturday from 9am to 5pm. Many stores are now also open on Sunday from noon to 5pm.

THE BEST BUYS

Indigenous crafts, handmade sweaters, and **Inuit art** are among the desirable items not seen everywhere else. An official igloo trademark identifies authentic Inuit (Eskimo) art, although the differences between the real thing and the manufactured variety become apparent with a little careful study. Inuit artworks, which usually means carvings in stone or bone, are "best buys" not because of low prices, but because of their high quality. Expect to pay hundreds of dollars for even a relatively small piece. Apart from a handful of boutiques, Québec City does not offer the high-profile designer clothing often showcased in Montréal.

SHOPPING COMPLEXES

In the Upper Town, there's a small complex filled with upscale shops called **Les Promenades du Vieux Québec,** at 43 rue Buade. You'll find a perfumery, a Christmas shop, shops selling Inuit carvings, cafes, a currency exchange, and clothing for men and

---

> **Tips** **Taxes & Refunds**
>
> Visitors can obtain refunds of taxes incurred for lodgings and shop purchases. See p. 68 for details.

---

women, including a Liz Claiborne factory outlet. Just outside the city walls at Porte Kent, **Place Québec** incorporates dozens of shops, a cinema, restaurants, a convention center, and the Hilton hotel, an easy-to-spot landmark. Place Québec is accessible from boulevard Réne-Lévesque and the Hilton. Shopping malls on a grander scale aren't found in or near the Old Town. For mall shopping, it's necessary to travel to the neighboring municipality of **Sainte-Foy.** The malls there differ little from their cousins throughout North America, in layout and available products. For sheer size, however, you can't beat **Place Fleur de Lys,** at 552 bd. Wilfrid-Hamel (© **418/529-8128**), with 250 retailers, and **Place Laurier,** at 2700 bd. Laurier (© **418/651-5000**), with 350 shops and 40 restaurants.

THE ANTIQUES DISTRICT

Dealers in antiques have gravitated to rue St-Paul in the Lower Town. To get there, follow rue St-Pierre from the Place Royale, and then head west on rue St-Paul. So far, there are more than 20 shops, with more likely to open, filled with brass beds, knick-knacks, Québec country furniture, candlesticks, old clocks, Victoriana, Art Deco and Art Moderne objects, and even the increasingly sought-after kitsch and housewares of the early post–World War II period.

2 Shopping from A to Z

ARTS & CRAFTS

Abaca The owners gather their own merchandise on trips abroad. Their inventory includes masks, jewelry, musical instruments, sculpture, and related pieces from Africa, India, Afghanistan, Japan, Korea, China, and a score of other places. Some jewelry and handcrafts by Québec artists are also sold here. The store takes its name from a tree that grows in the Philippines. Another store around the corner also carries the owners' finds: **Origines,** at 54 Côte de la Fabrique, is filled with jewelry and sculpture. 38 rue Garneau (near rue St-Jean). © **418/694-9761.**

Artisans Bas-Canada Crafts and cute hand-knits predominate, all a little on the expensive side. Duck decoys and burly sweaters for adults and kids are among the most engaging items, supplemented by lots of hats, gloves, mittens, headbands, moccasins, lumberjack coats, soapstone carvings, and Canada-themed books. They tell us they will give a 10% discount to patrons who present a copy of this book. 30 Côte de la Fabrique. © **418/692-2109.**

Aux Multiples Collections Inuit, vernacular, and modern Canadian art are on offer in this gallery. The most appealing items, and those given prominence in display, are the Native Canadian carvings in stone, bone, and tusk. The shop ships purchases. Prices are high, but competitive for merchandise of similar quality. Open 7 days. Check out its siblings, the new private museum called Galerie Brousseau et Brousseau at 35 rue St-Louis (© **418/694-1828**) and the Aux Multiples branch at 43 rue de Buade (© **418/692-4298**). 69 rue Ste-Anne (opposite the Hôtel-de-Ville). © **418/692-1230.**

Canadeau   Defying easy classification, this store purveys a wide range of Canadian crafts, ammolite jewelry, Inuit carvings, furs, watches, handmade knives, and sweaters in uncommon designs. 1124 rue St-Jean. ℭ **418/692-4850.**

Claude Berry, Inc   Here you'll find hand-painted porcelains from Limoges, jacquard replicas of medieval tapestries, and religious articles—a grab bag that might produce that elusive gift. 6 Côte de la Fabrique. ℭ **418/692-2628.**

Galerie d'Art du Petit-Champlain   This shop features the superbly detailed carvings of Roger Desjardins, who applies his skills to meticulous renderings of waterfowl. The inventory has been expanded to show lithographs, paintings, and some Inuit art. 88 rue du Petit-Champlain (near bd. Champlain). ℭ **418/692-5647.**

Galerie d'Art Trois Colombes   Quebecois and other Canadian artisans, including Inuits and Amerindians, produce these weavings, carvings, snowshoes, duck decoys, and soapstone sculptures. Upstairs are handmade hats, coats, sweaters, high-top boots, moccasins, and rag dolls. They ship worldwide. 46 rue St-Louis. ℭ **418/694-1114.**

Rue du Trésor Outdoor Gallery   Sooner or later, everyone passes this alley near the Place d'Armes. Artists gather along here much of the year to exhibit and sell their work, much like the artists on St-Amable Lane in Vieux-Montréal. Most of the prints on view are of Québec scenes, and one or two might make attractive souvenirs. The artists seem to enjoy chatting with interested passersby. Rue du Trésor (between rues Ste-Anne and Buade). No phone.

BOOKS, MAGAZINES & NEWSPAPERS

Librairie du Nouveau Monde   In the Lower Town, this store has a wide variety of books, mostly in French, including the *Historical Guide to Québec,* by Yves Tessier, a good read (available in English) about the city's past, filled with illustrations, photographs, and a foldout map. 103 rue St-Pierre (behind the Musée de la Civilisation). ℭ **418/694-9475.**

Librairie Ulysses   Specializing in travel, with guidebooks, travel accessories, and related items, it has smaller branches in the same building as the tourist information office at 12 rue Ste-Anne, opposite Place d'Armes, and at 2600 bd. Laurier in Ste-Foy (ℭ **418/654-9779**). 4 bd. René-Lévesque est (near av. Cartier). ℭ **418/529-5349.**

Maison de la Presse Internationale   As the name says, this large store in the midst of the St-Jean shopping and nightlife bustle stocks magazines, newspapers, and paperbacks from around the world, in many languages. It stays open daily 7am to 11pm or midnight, and it carries the *New York Times,* the *Wall Street Journal,* the *International Herald Tribune,* and many U.S. periodicals. There's another branch in the Place Québec, the mall between the Hilton and Radisson hotels. 1050 rue St-Jean (at the corner of rue Ste-Angèle). ℭ **418/694-1511.**

CLOTHING

Also see **Artisans Bas-Canada** and **Galerie d'Art Trois Colombes,** under "Arts & Crafts," above.

America   A link in a popular chain, this store offers dependably good quality and nice style in casual and dress clothes for men, with intriguing half-twists away from Gap and Banana Republic norms. 1147 rue St-Jean (near rue St-Stanislas). ℭ **418/692-5254.**

Excalibor   If you arrive in town during Québec's August Medieval Festival, here's the place to purchase doublets and shirts with big floppy sleeves. Fabrics are muslin and velvet and mock brocade. No armor, though. 1055 rue St-Jean. ℭ **418/692-5959.**

Fourrures du Vieux-Port   The fur trade underwrote the development and exploration of Québec and the vast lands west, and it continues to be highly important to this day. This merchant in the Basse-Ville has as good a selection as any, including knit furs and shearlings, along with designer coats by Christ, Louis Féraud, and Zuki, among others. 55 rue St-Pierre. ℂ **418/692–6686.**

La Maison Darlington   The popular emporium in this ancient house comes on strong with both tony and traditional clothing for men and women produced by such makers as Burberry's, Ballantyne, and Geiger Autrician. Better still are the hand-smocked dresses produced by Quebecois artisans for babies and little girls. 7 rue de Buade (near the Hôtel-de-Ville). ℂ **418/692–2268.**

La Maison du Hamac   Although this shop does indeed carry a wide selection of hammocks, as its name asserts, it also has clothing from Latin America—colorful hats, shirts, belts, vests, bags, and jewelry from Mexico, Nepal, Guatemala, Indonesia, and Brazil. Masks and kites, too. 91 rue Ste-Anne. ℂ **418/692–1109.**

Zazou   This little shop focuses primarily on casual and dressy fashions from Quebecois designers. 31 Petit-Champlain (near the funicular). ℂ **418/694–9990.**

A DEPARTMENT STORE
La Maison Simons   The only department store in the old city opened here in 1840. Small by modern standards, Simons has two floors for men's and women's clothing, emphasizing sportswear and household linens. Most of it is pretty basic. Tommy Hilfiger products are much in evidence. Their stores at Place Ste-Foy (2450 bd. Laurier) and Les Galeries de la Capitale (5401 bd. des Galeries) have a lot of floor space and carry far larger selections of fashions by such designers as Donna Karan and Hugo Boss. 20 Côte de la Fabrique (near the Hôtel-de-Ville). ℂ **418/692–3630.**

FOOD
La Petite Cabane à Sucre   Called the "little sugar shack," it sells ice cream, honey, maple syrup, maple candy, and related products, many in packaging suitable for gifts, including tin log cabins that pour syrup from their chimneys. 94 rue du Petit-Champlain (south end). ℂ **418/692–5875.**

LEATHER GOODS
Ibiza   Replacing a shop that sold toys and kids' things, this leather store sells coats, vests, hats, handbags and, oddly enough, knives. 57 Petit-Champlain (in mid-block). ℂ **418/692–2103.**

MUSIC
Archambault   This shop has two large floors of recorded music, mostly CDs with some cassettes, and the helpful staff goes to some lengths to find what you want. 1095 rue St-Jean. ℂ **418/694–2088.**

WINES
Société des Alcools de Québec   This is a virtual supermarket of wines and spirits, with thousands of bottles in stock. They recently expanded the selling area to incorporate a section featuring more than 120 kinds of imported beers. There are other SAQ outlets in the Château Frontenac and at 888 rue St-Jean (ℂ **418/643–4337**). 1059 av. Cartier (near rue Fraser). ℂ **418/643–4334.**

18

Québec City After Dark

Although Québec City can't pretend to match the volume of nighttime diversions of exuberant Montréal, there is more than enough after-dark activity to occupy your evenings during an average stay. Apart from theatrical productions, almost always in French, knowledge of the language is rarely necessary to enjoy nighttime entertainment.

Drop in at the tourism information office for a list of events, especially during the annual 11-day **Festival d'Eté (Summer Festival)** in July (© **888/992-5200** or 418/5239-5200; www.infofestival. com), when free concerts and shows are staged all over town in the evenings, and the upper portion of rue St-Jean is closed to cars and becomes a pedestrian promenade. Also check out events during the

Carnaval d'Hiver (Winter Carnival) in February (© **866/422-7628** or 418/626-3716; www.carnaval.qc.ca), when the city salutes the season with a grand ice palace, ice sculptures, and parades.

Concerts and theatrical performances usually begin at 8pm. Most bars and clubs stay open until 2 or 3am. A clear advantage of a night out in Québec City is that cover charges and drink minimums are rare in the bars and clubs that provide live entertainment. Mixed drinks aren't unusually expensive, but neither are they generously poured, which is the reason most people stick to beer, usually Canadian. Some popular brands brewed in Québec are Belle-Gueule, Saint-Ambroise, Boréale, and Maudite (with a winged Satan on the label).

1 The Performing Arts

CLASSICAL MUSIC, OPERA & DANCE

Many of the city's churches host sacred and secular music concerts, as well as special Christmas festivities. Among the possibilities are the Anglican Cathedral of the Holy Trinity (31 rue des Jardins), Eglise St-Jean-Baptiste (470 St. Jean), historic Chapelle Bon-Pasteur (1080 rue de la Chevrotière), and, on Île d'Orléans, the Eglise Ste-Pétronille. Outdoor performances in summer are staged beside City Hall in the Jardins de l'Hôtel-de-Ville, in the Pigeonnier at Parliament Hill, on the Grande-Allée, and at place d'Youville.

L'Orchestre Symphonique de Québec (© 418/643-8486; www.osq.org), Canada's oldest symphony, performs at the Grand Théâtre de Québec from September to May. The **Québec Opéra** (© 418/529-0688; www.operadequebec.qc.ca) mounts performances there in the spring and fall, as does, more occasionally, the **Danse-Partout** (© 418/649-4715) ballet company.

CONCERT HALLS & PERFORMANCE VENUES

Agora This 6,000-seat outdoor amphitheater at the Vieux-Port is the scene of rock and occasional classical concerts, and a variety of other shows in the summer. Iron

Maiden, Jethro Tull, Joe Cocker, and Johnny Winter have all appeared here. The city makes a dramatic backdrop. The box office, at 84 rue Dalhousie, is open daily 10am to 6pm in season. 120 rue Dalhousie (Vieux-Port). ℂ 418/692-4672.

Colisée Pepsi   Rock concerts by name acts on the order of Avril Lavigne and the Black Eyed Peas are often held in this arena, located in a park on the north side of the St-Charles River. The box office is open in summer Monday through Friday 9am to 4pm, in winter Monday through Friday 10am to 5pm. 250 bd. Wilfrid-Hamel (ExpoCité). ℂ 418/691-7110.

Grand Théâtre de Québec   Classical music concerts, opera, dance, jazz, blues, and theatrical productions are presented in two halls, one of them containing the largest stage in Canada. Visiting conductors, orchestras, and dance companies often perform here when resident organizations are away. The Trident Theatre troupe performs in French in the Salle Octave-Crémazie. L'Orchestre Symphonique de Québec performs here, as does the Québec Opéra. Québec's Conservatory of Music lies underneath the theater. The box office is open Monday through Saturday 10am to 6pm. 269 bd. René-Lévesque est (near av. Turnbull). ℂ 418/643-8131. www.grandtheatre.qc.ca.

Kiosque Edwin-Bélanger   The bandstand at the edge of Battlefields Park is home to a 10-week summer music season, from mid-June to late August. The outdoor performances are Wednesday through Sunday and range from operas, chorales, and classical recitals to jazz, pop, and blues. All concerts are free. 390 av. de Bernières (near the Musée de Québec). ℂ 418/648-4050. www.ccbn-nbc.qc.ca.

Le Capitole   Various shows are offered on an irregular schedule in this historic 1,262-seat theater. Dramatic productions and comedic performances are in French, but the theater also hosts rock groups and occasional classical recitals. An ongoing production, from June to October, is the "Elvis Story." 972 rue St-Jean (near Porte St-Jean). ℂ 800/261-9903 for tickets, or 418/694-4444 for information. www.lecapitole.com.

Palais Montcalm   The main performance space is the 1,100-seat Raoul-Jobin theater, which presents a mix of dance programs, classical music concerts, and plays. More intimate recitals and jazz groups are found in the much smaller Café-Spectacle. At press time, the venue was closed for renovations and scheduled to reopen in mid-March 2006. 995 place d'Youville (near Porte Saint-Jean). ℂ 418/691-2399 for tickets. www.surscene. qc.ca/montcalm.htm.

Tips **Finding Out What's On**

Check the "Culture and Entertainment" section of the *Greater Québec Area Tourist Guide* for suggestions. You can find the guide at any tourist office. A weekly information leaflet called *L'Info-Spectacles,* listing headline attractions and the venues in which they are appearing, is found at concierge desks and in many bars and restaurants, as is the tabloid-sized giveaway *Voir,* which provides greater detail. Also widely available is *Québec Scope,* a free monthly. The *Greater Québec Area Tourist Guide* has both French and English editions, while the rest of the guides are in French, but salient points (time, place, price) aren't difficult to decipher.

Moments Only in Québec City

The **Basilique Notre-Dame** schedules *son et lumière* (sound-and-light) shows projected upon the city's loveliest church eight times daily, May 1 to October 15. Tickets cost C$7.50 (US$6) for adults, C$5 (US$4) for seniors and students, free for children under 6.

An after-dinner stroll and a lounge on a bench on **Terrasse Dufferin**, the boardwalk above the Lower Town, may well be your most memorable night on the town. Ferries glide across the river burnished by moonglow, and the stars haven't seemed that close since childhood.

2 The Club & Music Scene

ROCK, FOLK, BLUES & JAZZ CLUBS

Most bars and clubs stay open until 2 or 3am, closing earlier if business doesn't warrant the extra hour or two. Cover charges and drink minimums are all but unknown in the bars and clubs that provide live entertainment. There are three principal streets to choose among for nightlife: the Grande-Allée, rue St-Jean, and the emerging avenue Cartier.

In addition to the listings below, also see the reviews under "Concert Halls & Performance Venues," above, and see **Le Pape-Georges** and **Saint Alexandre Pub** under "The Bar & Cafe Scene," below.

Chez Son Père   A musical institution in Québec since 1960, this is where French-Canadian folk singers (of both traditional and contemporary folk music) often get their start. The stage is on the second floor, with the usual brick walls and sparse decor. A young, friendly crowd can be found here. The club is a few steps uphill from bustling rue St-Jean. 24 rue St-Stanislas (near rue St-Jean). © **418/692-5308.**

D'Orsay   Visitors whose complexions have cleared up and who are well into their mortgages will want to keep this chummy pub-bistro in mind. Most of the clientele is on the far side of 35, and they strike up conversations easily—two active bars help. There's a small dance floor with a DJ, and in summer afternoons and evenings, entertainers sometime perch on a stool on the terrace out back. There is a full menu of conventional international dishes, from onion soup and fajitas to burgers and mussels. 65 rue de Buade (opposite Hôtel-de-Ville). © **418/694-1582.**

Kashmir   Upstairs, over the Pizzeria d'Youville, this bar puts on an eclectic variety of musical and artistic presentations, including rock, blues, and art exhibitions, with the added attraction of dancing to a DJ 3 or 4 nights a week. Scheduling is erratic. Thursday is ladies' night. Pass the time before the evening's performances at the pool tables or poker machines. 1018 rue St-Jean (near rue St-Stanislas). © **418/694-1648.** Cover depends upon performer, usually about C$3 (US$2.40).

L'Emprise   Live jazz, usually of the mainstream or fusion variety, is a long-standing tradition in this agreeable room. The bar, off the lobby of the venerable Hôtel Clarendon, has large windows and Art Deco touches. Seating is at tables, at the bar, and at the counter that surrounds the performance area. This place has a mellow atmosphere and attracts serious jazz fans who really listen. Music is presented nightly, from about 10pm. 57 rue Ste-Anne (at rue des Jardins). © **418/692-2480.**

Pub St-Patrick   This Irish pub just keeps getting on. Pints of Guinness are the steadiest pour, of course, and food is available, but the music of the Ould Sod is the big draw. For that, show up on Thursday through Sunday nights. 45 rue Couillard (near rue St-Jean). ℂ 418/694–0618.

Théâtre du Petit-Champlain   Québecois and French singers alternate with jazz groups in this roomy cafe-theater in the Lower Town. Have a drink on the patio before the show. The box office is open Monday through Friday 1 to 5pm, to 7pm the night of a show. Performances are usually Tuesday through Saturday. 68 rue du Petit-Champlain (near the funicular). ℂ 418/692–4744. www.theatrepetitchamplain.com. Ticket prices range C$15–C$30 (US$12–US$24) depending on the artist.

DANCE CLUBS

Boudoir Lounge   The hottest club (for the moment) in trendy St-Roch, it has two bars on the main floor and a disco downstairs. DJs work the fine sound systems in both rooms from 10pm to 3am, with live jazz on Sunday nights. The management dreams up a variety of events to get people in the door, including fashion shows and theme parties. The dramatic decor, including a fireplace in the front, is far more diverting than some of the dismal black holes popular elsewhere in town. 441 rue de l'Eglise (at bd. Charest est). ℂ 418/524–2777. www.boudoirlounge.com. No cover.

Chez Dagobert   Long one of the top discos in Québec City, this three-story club has an arena arrangement on the ground floor for live bands, with raised seating around the sides. Upper floors have a large dance floor, more bars, TV screens to keep track of sports events, and video games. The sound system, whether emitting live music (mostly cover or alternative bands) or recorded music, is just a decibel short of bedlam; more than a few habitués are seen donning earplugs. Things don't start jamming until well after 11pm. The crowd divides into students and their more fashionably attired older brothers and sisters. A whole lot of eyeballing and approaching goes on. 600 Grande-Allée (near av. Turnbull). ℂ 418/522–2645.

Le Bistro Plus   A bistro by day, things change at night when the three dance floors fill with grooving young bodies—very young, in many cases. During the week, the music is recorded. On the weekend, there are live Latin groups performing on the ground floor, and there is a disco on the second floor. This place gets frat-house raucous and messy, especially after the 4 to 7pm happy hour, but it's friendly, too, with darts, a pool table, and TVs tuned to sports to keep people entertained. 1063 rue St-Jean (near rue St-Stanislas). ℂ 418/694–9252.

Maurice   Successfully challenging Chez Dagobert (across the street and reviewed above) at the top rung of the nightlife ladder, this triple-tiered enterprise occupies a converted mansion at the thumping heart of the Grande-Allée scene. It includes a surprisingly good restaurant, a couple of bars, and a dance room that rotates live Latin and blues bands, filling the gaps with DJ music. Downstairs, the Charlotte Bar has a variety of live music most nights. Theme nights are frequent, and the balconies and bars overflow with up to 1,000 post-boomers. Happy hour means two-for-one drinks. 575 Grande-Allée est. ℂ 418/647–2000.

3 The Bar & Cafe Scene

In addition to the bars listed below, check out the strip of the **Grande-Allée** between place Montcalm and place George V, near the St-Louis Gate, where a beery collegiate atmosphere can sometimes rule as the evening wears on. The bars reviewed in this section are removed from the Grande-Allée melee.

Aviatic Club   A favorite for after-work drinks since 1945, this bar is located in the front of the city's restored train station. The theme is aviation (odd, given the venue), signaled by two miniature planes hanging from the ceiling. Food is served, ranging from sushi to Tex-Mex, along with local and imported beers. 450 de la Gare-du-Palais (near rue St-Paul, Lower Town). ℂ 418/522-3555.

L'Astral   Spinning slowly above a city that twinkles below like tangled necklaces, this restaurant and bar atop the Hôtel Loews le Concorde unveils a breathtaking 360-degree panorama. Many people come for dinner at the high-quality restaurant, but you can also just come for drinks and the view. 1225 place Montcalm (at the Grande-Allée). ℂ 418/647-2222.

Le Pape-Georges   This cozy stone-and-beamed wine bar features blues and *chanson* (a French cabaret singing style), along with other music styles, usually Thursday through Sunday at 10pm. Light fare—plates of mostly Québec cheeses, assorted cold meats, and smoked salmon—is served during the day. They play folk or blues weekends in winter, up to 5 nights in summer. Although it's in the middle of a tourist district, most of the patrons appear to be locals. 8 rue Cul-de-Sac (near bd. Champlain, Lower Town). ℂ 418/692-1320.

Saint Alexandre Pub   Roomy and sophisticated, this is one of the best-looking bars in town. It's done in British-pub style, with polished mahogany, exposed brick, and a working fireplace that's a particular comfort during the 8 cold months of the year. It serves 40 single-malt scotches and more than 200 beers, along with hearty victuals that complement the brews. (Stick to beer—the cocktails are skimpy.) Jazz duos and trios are irregularly presented, usually Friday and Saturday at 9pm, but don't plan your night around it. 1087 rue St-Jean (near St-Stanislas). ℂ 418/694-0015.

GAY BARS & CLUBS

The gay scene in Québec City is a small but vibrant one, centered in the Upper Town just outside the city walls, on **rue St-Jean** between **avenue Dufferin** and **rue St-Augustin,** and also along rue St-Augustin and nearby **rue d'Aiguillon,** which runs parallel to rue St-Jean. Recently, however, gays have constituted much of the chic crowd that has migrated in or near the St-Roch quarter downtown.

Chrome, at 99 St-Vallier est (ℂ 418/687-1331), fills its docket with music by DJs, drag shows, and good-looking people. Frankie's Cabaret, at 48 côte de la Fabrique (ℂ 418/692-2263), lately has trumpeted its monthly "Tupperware Nights" to liven a schedule that is primarily devoted to mingling and dancing to DJ selections. It's up the street from the east end of rue St-Jean.

Just off place d'Youville, is a two-zone club called **Le Drague** ("The Drag"), at 815 rue St-Augustin (ℂ 418/649-7212; www.ledrague.com), which has a basement disco, a bar with a pool table, patrons who wear leather, and—you guessed it—drag shows on Sunday. There are live performances of other kinds Thursday through Saturday. Lesbians form most of the clientele at **L'Amour Sorcier** at 789 côte Ste-Geneviève (ℂ 418/523-3395). There are a low-pressure bar inside the old building and a terrace out front. Gay men aren't turned away. It's about 3 blocks west of place d'Youville. The local gay, lesbian, bisexual, and transgender pride celebration, the **Fierté Québec Festival** (ℂ 418/523-2003), has had financial troubles in past years, but appears to be on firmer footing now. They've been held over Labor Day weekend, but check ahead. For information about current openings and happenings in the local gay community, look for *Être* magazine, often available at tourist offices.

19

Side Trips from Québec City

The first four excursions described below can be combined and completed in a day. Admittedly, it will be a breakfast-to-dark undertaking, especially if much time is taken to explore each destination, but the farthest of the four destinations is only 40km (25 miles) from Québec City.

The famous shrine of Ste-Anne-de-Beaupré and the Mont Ste-Anne ski area are only about half an hour from the city by car, while bucolic Île d'Orléans, with its maple groves, orchards, farms, and 18th- and 19th-century houses, is a mere 15 minutes away. With 2 or more days available, you can continue along the northern shore to Charlevoix, where inns and a gambling casino invite an overnight stay, and then take the ferry across the river and drive back toward Québec City, exploring the villages along the St. Lawrence's southern bank as you make your way.

Although it is preferable to drive in this region, tour buses go to Montmorency Falls and the shrine of Ste-Anne-de-Beaupré, and circle the Île d'Orléans.

For more information, log on to **www.quebecregion.com**.

1 Île d'Orléans

16km (10 miles) NE of Québec City

Until 1935, the only way to get to Île d'Orléans was by boat (in summer) or over the ice (in winter). The highway bridge that has since been built has allowed the fertile fields of the island to become Québec City's primary market-garden. During harvest periods, fruits and vegetables are picked fresh on the farms and trucked into the city daily. In mid-July, hand-painted signs posted by the main road on the island announce FRAISES: CUEILLIR VOUS-MEME (Strawberries: Pick 'em yourself). The same invitation is made during apple season, September through October. Farmers hand out baskets and quote the price, paid when the basket's full. Bring along a bag or box to carry away the bounty.

ESSENTIALS
GETTING THERE

BY BUS There are no local buses. For organized bus tours, contact **La Tournée du Québec Métro** (© **418/836-8687**), **Old Québec Tours** (© **418/664-0460**), or **Gray Line** (© **418/649-9226**).

BY CAR It's a short drive from Québec City to the island. Follow avenue Dufferin (in front of the Parliament building) to connect with Autoroute 440 east, in the direction of Ste-Anne-de-Beaupré. In about 15 minutes, the Île d'Orléans bridge is seen on the right. If you'd like a guide, **Maple Leaf Guide Services** (© **418/622-3677**) can provide one in your car or theirs.

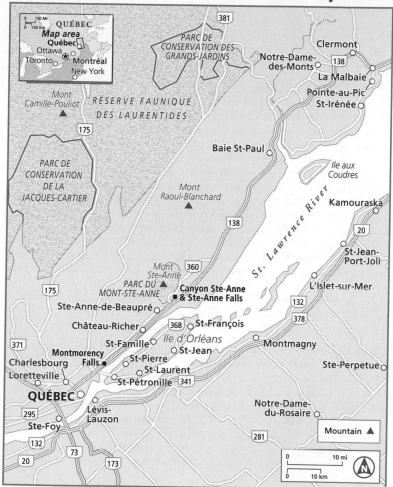

Québec City Environs

VISITOR INFORMATION

After arriving on the island, turn right on Route 368 East toward Ste-Pétronille. The **Bureau d'Accueil Touristique** (✆ **418/828-9411;** www.iledorleans.com) is in the house on the right corner, and it has a useful guidebook (C$1/US80¢) for the island. It's open late June to mid-October Sunday through Thursday 8:30am to 7:30pm, and Friday and Saturday 8:30am to 8pm; the rest of the year Monday through Friday 9am to 5pm, Saturday 10am to 5pm, and Sunday 10am to 4pm. A good substitute for the Île d'Orléans guide is the *Québec City and Area Guide,* available from Québec City tourism offices, which describes a short tour of Ile d'Orléans. A driving-tour cassette can be rented or purchased at the tourist office, and cycling maps are available there.

The lodgings recommended below for the Île d'Orléans are all of the *auberge* type, meaning they have six or more rooms and have full-service dining rooms open to both guests and nonguests. But there are also many bed-and-breakfast inns and *gîtes* (homes with a room or two available to travelers), which are cheaper and less elaborate than the auberges. You can see very brief details about many of these offerings on the tourist office's website, www.iledorleans.com. Many of the lodgings also provide leaflets and photos to the tourist office so that you can check them out there.

EXPLORING THE ISLAND

The island was long isolated from the mainland, as is evident in the three **stone churches** that date from the days of the French regime. There are only seven such churches left in all of Québec, so this is a point of pride for Île d'Orléans. A firm resistance to development has kept many of its old houses intact as well. Though this could easily have become just another sprawling bedroom community, it remains a largely rural farming area, and island residents work to keep it that way. They nourish hopes to bury their telephone lines and to put in a bicycle lane to cut down on car traffic.

A coast-hugging road circles the island, 39km (24 miles) long and 8km (5 miles) wide, and another couple of roads bisect it. Farms and picturesque houses dot the east side of the island, and abundant apple orchards enliven the west side.

There are six tiny villages on Île d'Orléans, each with a church as its focal point. It's possible to do a quick circuit of the island in half a day, but a full day may be justified if you eat in a couple of restaurants, visit a sugar shack, skip stones from the beach, and stay the night in one of the several waterside inns. If you're strapped for time, drive as far as St-Jean, then take Route du Mitan across the island, and return to the bridge, and Québec City, via Route 368 West.

STE-PETRONILLE

The first village reached on the recommended counterclockwise tour is Ste-Pétronille, only 3km (1¾ miles) from the bridge (take a right turn off the bridge). British general Wolfe had his headquarters here in 1759 before launching his successful attack on Québec City. With 1,050 inhabitants, the village is best known for its Victorian inn, **La Goéliche** (see below), and also claims the northernmost stand of **red oaks** in North America, dazzling in autumn. The houses were once the summer homes of wealthy English in the 1800s; the church dates from 1871. Even if you don't stay at the inn, drive down to the water's edge, where a small public area with benches is located. Strolling down the picturesque **rue Laflamme** is another pleasant way to while away an hour or two.

Where to Stay & Dine

La Goéliche ⊕   On a rocky point of land at the southern tip of the island stands this country inn and restaurant with a wraparound porch. This building is a virtual replica of the 1880 Victorian house that stood here until 1996. That one burned to the ground, leaving nothing but the staircase. This one was completed in record time and manages to retain the period flavor with tufted chairs, Tiffany-style lamps, and a few antiques. Only the two suites have TVs. The river slaps at the foundation of the glass-enclosed terrace dining room, which is a grand observation point for watching cruise ships and Great Lakes freighters steaming past.

22 chemin du Quai, Ste-Pétronille, PQ G0A 4C0. (℃) **888/511-2248** or 418/828-2248. Fax 418/828-2745. www.goeliche.ca. 18 units. C$199–C$239 (US$159–US$191) double. Rates include breakfast and dinner. AE, DC, DISC, MC, V. Free parking. **Amenities:** Restaurant (Contemporary French); bar; heated outdoor pool; golf and tennis nearby; massage; babysitting. *In room:* Minibar, coffeemaker, hair dryer.

ST-LAURENT

From Ste-Pétronille, continue on Route 368 East. After 6km (3¾ miles), you'll arrive at St-Laurent, founded in 1679, once a boat-building center turning out 400 craft per year. To learn more about the town's maritime history, visit **Le Parc Maritime de St-Laurent** (© **418/828-9672**), an active boatyard from 1908 to 1967. Before the bridge was built, islanders journeyed across the river to Québec City by boat from here. The Maritime Park incorporates the old Godbout Boatworks and offers demonstrations of the craft. It's open daily 10am to 5pm mid-June to Labor Day.

The town's church was erected in 1860, and there are a couple of picturesque roadside chapels as well. You'll find good views of farmland and the river from the St-Laurent golf course—follow signs from the main road.

Where to Stay & Dine

Auberge Champêtre/Le Canard Huppé   A roadside inn reminiscent of those found in the motherland, this tidy establishment takes considerable pride in its kitchen. Consider this one menu item: crimson raviolis stuffed with duck confit and smoked snails and drizzled with lobster butter. All meals are served; breakfast and lunch can be had in the bistro/bar or out on the terrace under the linden tree, while dinner is presented in the main dining room where the service meets professional standards. Rooms upstairs don't have TVs or phones, but they are attractively decorated, with firm mattresses.

The owners have a lodging annex 3km (1¾ miles) down the road called the **Villa de Grèves,** directly on the river. Five of its six rooms have electric fireplaces, three have whirlpool tubs, and all have TVs.

2198 chemin Royal, St-Laurent, PQ G0A 3Z0. © **800/838-2292** or 418/828-2292. Fax 418/828-2292. www.canard-huppe.com. 10 units in inn, 6 units in villa. Auberge Champêtre C$100–C$240 (US$80–US$192) double; Villa des Grèves C$150–C$210 (US$120–US$168) double. Rates include full breakfast. Packages available. AE, DC, MC, V. **Amenities:** Restaurant (French Contemporary); bar; small outdoor pool. *In room:* A/C, TVs in annex, no phone in inn.

Le Moulin de Saint-Laurent ⏦ COUNTRY FRENCH   This former flour mill, in operation from 1720 to 1928, has been transformed into one of the island's most romantic restaurants. Rubble-stone walls and hand-wrought beams form the interior, with candlelight glinting off hanging copper and brass pots. On a warm day, sit on the shaded terrace beside the waterfall, and be sure to wander upstairs to see the Quebecois antiques. Lunch can be light—maybe an omelet or a plate of assorted pâtés or cheeses. The light, dry cider made on the island is a refreshing alternative to wine. On weekends, a small combo plays in the evenings.

The owners also have cottages for rent at the shore. Rooms are from C$170 to C$260 (US$136–US$208) double, including breakfast, dinner. Rates are lower from November to April. Packages are available.

754 chemin Royal. © **888/629-3888** or 418/829-3888. Fax 418/829-3716. www.moulinstlaurent.qc.ca. Reservations recommended at dinner. Main courses lunch C$10–C$19 (US$8–US$15), dinner C$15–C$26 (US$12–US$21); table d'hôte add C$13 (US$10) to the price of the main course. AE, DC, MC, V. Daily 10:30am–2pm and 6–9pm. Closed mid-Oct to May 1.

ST-JEAN

St-Jean, 6km (3¾ miles) from St-Laurent, was home to sea captains. That might be why the houses in the village appear more luxurious than others on the island. The yellow bricks in the facades of several of the homes were ballast in boats that came over from Europe. The village church was built in 1732, and the walled cemetery is the final resting place of many fishermen and seafarers. On the way into town, look for **Le Tourne Pot,** 730 chemin Royal (ⓒ **418/829-3861**), if interested in locally produced ceramics in a distinctive speckled blue-and-white style.

On the left as you enter the village is one of the largest and best-preserved houses on the island: **Manoir Mauvide-Genest,** 1451 chemin Royale (ⓒ **418/829-2630**). Jean Mauvide was a seignior of this part of the island in the mid–18th century. His house was completed in 1752 and thoroughly restored in 2001, filled with authentic and reproduction furnishings of his time. A small chapel was added in 1930; Huron Indians made the altar. Guided tours are available, and afterward the docents invite visitors to view a 13-minute historical film on a wide-angle screen in the attic. The manor is open daily from 10am to 5pm May through October, by reservation only the rest of the year. Admission is C$5 (US$4) for adults, C$2 (US$1.60) for children under 12.

The manor also contains a **restaurant** serving light meals—soups and salads, assorted pâtés and cheeses, smoked trout, a quiche du jour, antipasto plates—as well as formal repasts of three to five courses. Table d'hôte lunches and dinners cost from C$14 to C$30 (US$11–US$24). It's open Tuesday through Sunday from 11:30am to well into the evening, depending on business. Call ⓒ **418/829-2630** for reservations.

If you're pressed for time, pick up **Route du Mitan,** which crosses Île d'Orléans from here to St-Famille on the west side of the island. Route du Mitan, not easy to spot, is on the left just past the church in St-Jean. If you have more time, a detour down the road is a diverting drive through farmland and forest. Return to St-Jean and proceed east on Route 368 to St-François.

ST-FRANÇOIS

The 9km (5⅔-mile) drive from St-Jean to St-François exposes vistas of the Laurentian Mountains off to the left on the western shore of the river. Just past the village center of St-Jean, **Mont Ste-Anne** can be seen, its slopes scored by ski trails. At St-François, home to about 500 people, the St. Lawrence, a constant and mighty presence, is 10 times wider than when it flows past Québec City. Regrettably, the town's original church (1734) burned in 1988. The 1992 replacement can be visited. At St-François, 24km (15 miles) from the bridge, the road becomes Route 368 West.

STE-FAMILLE

Founded in 1661 at the northern tip of the island, Ste-Famille is the oldest parish on the island. With 1,660 inhabitants, it is 8km (5 miles) from St-François and 19km (12 miles) from the bridge. Across the road from the triple-spired church (1743) is the convent of **Notre-Dame Congregation,** founded in 1685 by Marguerite Bourgeoys, one of Montréal's prominent early citizens. This area supports dairy and cattle farms and apple orchards.

Anglers might wish to swing by **Etang Richard Boily,** 4739 chemin Royal (ⓒ **418/ 829-2874**), where they can cast their lures for speckled or rainbow trout in a stocked pond, daily 9am to sunset. It isn't *entirely* like fishing in a rain barrel. Poles and bait are supplied—no permit is required—and customers pay only for what they catch, about C45¢ (US36¢) per inch; the fish run 9 to 12 inches. They'll clean, cut, and pack what you catch. Some island restaurants can even be persuaded to cook the fish for you. For more passive activity, buy a handful of fish pellets, toss them in the water, and watch the ravenous trout jump.

Farther along, you might wish to visit the **Sucrerie Blouin,** 2967 chemin Royal (© **418/829-2903**), a *cabane à sucre* (the traditional "sugar shack"), where maple syrup is made and casual meals are available. A family of bakers who have lived on the island for 300 years runs this place. See demonstrations of the syrup-making equipment and get debriefed on the process that turns the sap of a tree into syrup. Free tastes are offered and several types of products are for sale in a shop on the premises.

Also in town, at 3953 chemin Royal, you'll find a little shop called **Boutique Le Mitan** (© **418/829-3206**) that stocks local crafts and books about the island, and offers genealogical information about island residents.

ST-PIERRE

By Ile d'Orléans standards, St-Pierre is a big town, with a population of about 2,000. Its central attraction is the island's oldest church (1717). Services are no longer held there; it contains a large handicraft shop in the back, behind the altar, which is even older than the church (1695). The pottery, beeswax candles, dolls, scarves, woven rugs, and blankets aren't to every taste but are worth a look.

Thousands of migrating snow geese, ducks, and Canada geese stop by in the spring, a spectacular sight when they launch themselves into the air in flapping hordes so thick they almost blot out the sun.

2 Montmorency Falls

11km (7 miles) NE of Québec City

At 83m (272 ft.), the falls, named by Samuel de Champlain for his patron, the duke of Montmorency, are 30m (98 ft.) higher than Niagara—a boast no visitor is spared. They are, however, far narrower. The waterfall is surrounded by the provincial Parc de la Chute-Montmorency, where visitors can stop to take in the view and have a picnic. The park and falls are accessible year-round. In winter, the plunging waters contribute to a particularly impressive sight: The freezing spray sent up by the falls builds a mountain of white ice at the base called the *pain de sucre* (sugarloaf), which sometimes grows as high as 30m (98 ft.). On summer nights the falls are illuminated, and toward the end of July and into August, there is an international fireworks competition overhead, **Les Grands Feux Loto-Québec.** The yellow cast of the waterfall results from the high iron content of the riverbed.

ESSENTIALS
GETTING THERE

BY BUS   Schedules and programs are subject to frequent change, so check with **La Tournée du Québec Métro** (© **418/836-8687**), **Old Québec Tours** (© **418/664-0460**), or **Gray Line** (© **418/649-9226**) to see what's currently available.

BY CAR   Take Autoroute 40, which is north of Québec City, going east. At the end of the autoroute, where it intersects with Route 360 (av. Royale), the falls come into view.

VISITOR INFORMATION

A seasonal **tourist information** booth is located at 4300 bd. Sainte-Anne, just after the turnoff from the highway (© **418/663-3330;** www.sepaq.com/chutemontmorency). It's open from mid-June to the end of August daily from 9am to 5pm. Admission to the falls is free.

VIEWING THE FALLS

In 1759, General Wolfe and his army of 4,000 hauled 30 heavy cannons to the heights east of the cataract, aiming them at French troops deployed on the opposite side. The British lost the ensuing firefight but 6 weeks later won the decisive battle on the Plains of Abraham. One of the earthen strongholds they constructed survives.

There are a variety of platforms from which the falls can be viewed, including a footbridge that spans the river just where it flows over the cliff, stairs that descend one side from the top to near the bottom, and a cable car (not for the vertiginous) that runs from the parking lot to a terminal near a manor house that contains an interpretation center, a cafe-bar, and a restaurant. **Manoir Montmorency,** above the falls, was opened in 1994, replacing an earlier structure that burned down. Lunches and dinners of notably improved quality are served there daily, all year, except Monday and Tuesday January through March, when only lunches are served (© **418/663-3330** for meal reservations, which are suggested). The dining room and porch have a side view of the falls.

Round-trip fares on the cable car cost C$8 (US$6.40) for adults, C$4.75 (US$3.80) for ages 6 to 16. The cable car operates all day, every day from late April to late August, and on a more limited schedule the rest of the year.

3 Ste-Anne-de-Beaupré

35km (22 miles) NE of Québec City, 24km (15 miles) NE of Montmorency Falls

Legend has it that French mariners were sailing up the St. Lawrence River in the 1650s when they ran into a terrifying storm. They prayed to their patroness, St. Anne, to save them, and when they survived they dedicated a wooden chapel to her on the north shore of the St. Lawrence, near the site of their perils. Not long afterward, a laborer on the chapel was said to have been cured of lumbago, the first of many documented miracles. Since that time, pilgrims have made their way here—over a million a year—to pay their respects to St. Anne, the mother of the Virgin Mary and grandmother of Jesus.

ESSENTIALS
GETTING THERE

BY BUS   An intercity bus to Ste-Anne-de-Beaupré leaves the Québec City bus station three times a day, at around 9:15am, 3pm, and 6:15pm. Return trips are at 2:25pm and 6pm Monday through Saturday and 8pm Sunday. Always call ahead to confirm departure times (© **418/525-3000**). The round-trip fare is C$13 (US$10). Also check with **La Tournée du Québec Métro** (© **418/836-8687**), **Old Québec Tours** (© **416/664-0460**), or **Gray Line** (© **418/649-9226**).

BY CAR   From Montmorency Falls, it's a 20-minute drive along Route 138 east to the little town of Ste-Anne-de-Beaupré. The highway goes right past the basilica, with an easy entrance into the large parking lot. See the driving instructions in the "Montmorency Falls" section above for information on how to get to this area from Québec City.

VISITOR INFORMATION

An **information booth** at the southwestern side of the basilica, 10018 av. Royale (© **418/827-3781**), is open year-round, daily 8:30am to 4:30pm. The basilica itself is open year-round. Admission is free. Masses are held daily but hours vary.

EXPLORING THE BASILICA

The towering **basilica** is the most recent building raised on this spot in St. Anne's honor. After the sailors' first modest wooden chapel was swept away by a flood in the 1600s, another chapel was built on higher ground. Floods, fires, and the ravages of time dispatched later buildings, until a larger, presumably sturdier structure was erected in 1887. In 1926, it, too, lay in ruins, gutted by fire. As a result of a lesson finally learned, the present basilica is constructed in stone, following an essentially neo-Romanesque scheme.

Note that the church and the whole town of Ste-Anne-de-Beaupré are particularly busy on days of saintly significance: the first Sunday in May, mid- through late July, the fourth Sunday in August, and early September.

Other attractions in Ste-Anne-de-Beaupré include the **Way of the Cross,** lined with life-size bronze figures, on the hillside opposite the basilica; the **Scala Santa Chapel** (1891); and the **Memorial Chapel** (1878), with a bell tower and altar from the late 17th and early 18th centuries, respectively. More commercial than devotional are the Cyclorama, a 360-degree painting of Jerusalem, and the Musée Sainte-Anne, featuring art dedicated to Saint Anne. Admission to the Musée Sainte-Anne, open from May to October, is C$4 (US$3.20) for ages 12 and up, free for children under 12. Admission to the Cyclorama, open from May to October, is C$7 (US$5.60) adults, C$4 (US$3.20) children 6 to 15.

WHERE TO STAY & DINE

Auberge La Camarine 🦀   Why they named it after a bitter berry is uncertain, but this inn has a kitchen that is equaled by only a handful of restaurants in the region. The cuisine is of that variety of fusion cookery that joins French, Italian, and Asian techniques and ingredients. Rabbit stuffed with sweetbreads and spinach, and joined with two-mushroom risotto, is illustrative. The contrasting colors, flavors, and textures work well together. Presentation is of the edifice variety, too often employing upright groves of rosemary and thyme. The owners are justly proud of their wine cellar. Only dinner is served (overnight guests can get breakfast and a light lunch), daily from 6 to 8:30pm. The pace of a meal is leisurely. Reservations are required. The restaurant is open nightly for 10 months a year, and closed Sunday and Monday in November and May.

Guest rooms blend antique and contemporary notions, and some have fireplaces and/or Exercycles. The more expensive rooms have air-conditioning; two have Jacuzzis. The ski slopes of Mont Ste-Anne are a short drive away by car or regular shuttle.

10947 bd. Ste-Anne, Beaupré, PQ G0A 1E0. © **800/567-3939** or 418/827-5703. Fax 418/827-5430. www.camarine. com. 31 units. C$105–C$149 (US$84–C$119) double. Many packages available. AE, DC, MC, V. Go past the Promenades Ste-Anne outlet center, turning left off Rte. 138. **Amenities:** Restaurant (Fusion); bar; outdoor pool; golf nearby; access to nearby health club; babysitting; coin-op laundry. *In room:* A/C (some rooms), TV, coffeemaker.

4 Mont Ste-Anne

40km (25 miles) NE of Québec City, about 10km (6¼ miles) NE of Ste-Anne-de-Beaupré

Like Montréal, Québec City has its Laurentian hideaways. But there are differences: The Laurentians sweep down quite close to the St. Lawrence at this point, so Québecois need drive only about 30 minutes to be in the woods. And since Québec City is much smaller than Montréal, the Québec City area resorts are more modest in size and fewer in number, though their facilities and amenities are equal to those of resorts elsewhere in the Laurentian range.

Mont Ste-Anne is a four-season getaway offering the best skiing near Québec City as well as a plethora of outdoor activities during the summer, including golf, mountain biking, hiking, and paragliding.

ESSENTIALS
GETTING THERE
BY BUS   The **HiverExpress** (© **418/525-5191**) shuttle service from Québec City carries passengers to the slopes at Mont Ste-Anne, making it possible to stay in the city at night and ski the mountain by day. The round-trip fare is C$23 (US$18).

BY CAR   Continue along Route 138 from Ste-Anne-de-Beaupré, turning onto secondary Route 360 to the recreation area. See the driving instructions in the "Montmorency Falls" section above for information on how to get to this area from Québec City.

PARC MONT STE-ANNE
The park entrance is easy to spot from the highway. For information and rates for mountain bike or ski rentals, call © **418/827-4561** or 418/827-3121.

Parc Mont Ste-Anne, 49 sq. km (19 sq. miles) surrounding a 788m-high (2,585-ft.) peak, is an outdoor enthusiast's dream. In summer, there are camping, golfing, in-line skating, cycling, hiking, jogging, paragliding, and a 242km (150-mile) network of mountain biking trails (bikes can be rented at the park). An eight-passenger gondola to the top of the mountain operates every day between late June and early September, weather permitting, for the benefit of cyclists. Gondola ticket prices are C$13 (US$10) for adults, C$10 (US$8) for ages 14 to 20, C$11 (US$8.80) for seniors and children 7 to 13, and free for children under 7.

In winter, the park is Québec's largest and busiest ski area. Twelve lifts, including the gondola and three quad chair lifts, transport downhill skiers to the starting points of 50 trails and slopes. More than 210km (130 miles) of cross-country trails lace the park, dotted with eight heated rest huts. Full-day lift tickets are C$49 (US$39) adults, C$38 (US$30) for seniors and ages 14 to 22, and C$26 (US$21) for ages 7 to 13. Paragliding instruction is available in winter as well as summer.

The park is an easy commute from the city, which is what most people do. An additional nearby inn is Auberge La Camarine, described on p. 279.

WHERE TO STAY & DINE
Château Mont Sainte-Anne ✦   Settled in at the base of its namesake mountain, the resort, opened in 1979, continues to grow, adding more and more rooms as you read this. While the management is succeeding in its efforts to increase summer business, focusing on the resort's two golf courses, kids' day camp, and horseback and cycling trails, its real identity is as a ski center. (As a result, summer rates are significantly cheaper than winter rates.) It is well suited in its role as a ski lodge, with comprehensive facilities that include cable-car lifts, two summit chalets, downhill trails on both the north and south faces of the mountain, a fleet of 15 snowmobiles, ample snowmaking equipment, and related diversions—ice-skating and dog sledding among them. Many years they boast skiing into mid-May. The menu in the main dining room is unusually inventive for a mass feeding operation, and the two bars provide satisfying pub grub. A free shuttle van carries guests to and from Vieux-Québec.

500 bd. Beau-Pré, Beaupré, PQ G0A 1E0. © **888/824-2832** or 418/827-5211. Fax 418/827-3421. www.chateau montsainteanne.com. 240 units plus 185 condos and cottages. C$244–C$444 (US$195–US$355). Children under 17

stay free in parent's room. Many packages available. AE, DC, MC, V. **Amenities:** 2 restaurants (Eclectic, International); 2 bars; indoor and outdoor pools; golf on premises; health club and spa; children's programs; game room; activities desk; courtesy van; massage; babysitting; laundry service; dry cleaning. *In room:* A/C, TV, dataport, kitchenette, fridge, coffeemaker, hair dryer.

5 Canyon Ste-Anne & Ste-Anne Falls

40km (25 miles) NE of Québec City, about 60km (37 miles) NE of Ste-Anne-de-Beaupré

A short drive off Route 138 is the deep gorge and powerful waterfall created by the Ste-Anne-du-Nord River. Unseen from the main road, it's worth a detour and only takes about an hour to visit.

ESSENTIALS
GETTING THERE
BY CAR   Continue along Route 138 from Ste-Anne-de-Beaupré.

EXPLORING THE AREA

Driving north, the marked entrance is on the left. A dirt road leads through the trees to a parking lot. On the far side of the adjacent picnic grounds is a building containing a cafeteria and the ticket booth. Admission is C$9 (US$7.20) ages 13 and up, C$3.50 (US$2.80) ages 6 to 12. The site is open daily May to June 23 and the day after Labor Day through late October from 9am to 4:45pm; and June 24 to Labor Day daily 9am to 5:45pm. It's closed the rest of the year. To confirm these hours and fees, which are subject to change due to weather and season, call © **418/827-4057.**

An open-sided shuttle bus takes you to the first bridge, which crosses the river just above the thundering falls, 74m (243 ft.) high. At the turn of the 20th century, the river was used to float logs from lumbering operations, and part of the dramatic gorge was created by dynamiting around 1917. Trails descend both sides to a second bridge, 55m (180 ft.) above the yellowish iron-tinged water that crashes over massive rock walls. From there, a trail follows the northern rim to a third and final bridge, ending in an observation platform.

The woods that surround the gorge are privately owned, and weren't opened to the public until 1973. Management has wisely avoided commercial intrusions along the trails and the few descriptive signs are muted, letting the undeniable natural beauty of the site speak for itself. Visitors who have difficulty walking can get the effect of the falls without going too far from the bus, and those who suffer acrophobia can easily avoid the bridges.

6 The Charlevoix Region: Baie-St-Paul, La Malbaie & Tadoussac

Baie-St-Paul: 98km (61 miles) NE of Québec City; La Malbaie: 149km (92 miles) NE of Québec City; St-Siméon: 182km (113 miles) NE of Québec City

The Laurentians move closer to the shore of the St. Lawrence as they approach what used to be called Murray Bay at the mouth of the Malbaie River. While it can't be pretended that the entire length of Route 138 from Beaupré is fascinating, the Route 362 detour from Baie-St-Paul is scenic, with wooded hills interrupted by narrow riverbeds and billowing meadows, ending in harsh cliffs plunging down to the river. The air is scented by sea salt and rent by the shrieks of gulls.

Baie-St-Paul is an artists' colony, and there are several good-to-memorable inns between there and Cap à l'Aigle, a few miles beyond La Malbaie. St-Siméon is where travelers catch the ferry to the southern shore of the St. Lawrence. Farther along, Baie Ste-Catherine affords summer visitors numerous opportunities for whale-watching.

ESSENTIALS
GETTING THERE
BY CAR   Take Route 138 as far as Baie-St-Paul, then pick up Route 362 to La Malbaie, merging once again with Route 138 to reach the ferry at St-Siméon.

VISITOR INFORMATION
Baie-St-Paul has a year-round **tourist office** at 444 bd. Mgr-de Laval (© **418/435-4160**), open mid-June through Labor Day daily 8:30am to 7pm, and from the day after Labor Day to early June Monday to Friday 8:30am to 4:30pm and Saturday and Sunday 9am to 5pm. La Malbaie also has a tourist office, at 495 bd. de Comporté (© **418/665-4454**), with essentially the same hours. St-Siméon has seasonal tourist offices at 494 rue St-Laurent and at the ferry landing, open mid-June through Labor Day daily 9am to 7pm. Check out www.tourisme-charlevoix.com for more information.

EXPLORING THE AREA
In addition to the country inns dotting the region from Baie-St-Paul to Cap à l'Aigle to La Malbaie and beyond, nearby Pointe-au-Pic has a casino, a smaller offshoot of the one in Montréal. The northern end of the region is marked by the confluence of the Saguenay River and the St. Lawrence. These waters attract six species of whales, many of which can be seen from shore mid-June through late October. **Whale-watching cruises** are increasingly popular (p. 247). In 1988, Charlevoix was named a UNESCO World Biosphere Reserve. Though only 1 of 325 such regions in the world, it was the first one to include a human settlement.

BAIE-ST-PAUL
The first town of any size reached in Charlevoix via Route 138, this attractive community of more than 7,300 holds on to a reputation as an artists' retreat that began at the start of the 20th century. More than a dozen boutiques and galleries and a couple of small museums show the work of local painters and artisans. Given the setting, it isn't surprising that many of the artists are landscapists, but other styles and subjects are represented. Although some of their production is of the hobbyist level, much is highly professional. To see selections of the art, check the **Maison René-Richard,** at 58 rue St-Jean-Baptiste (© **418/435-5571**); the **Galerie d'Art Beauchamp,** 16 rue St-Jean-Baptiste (© **418/240-2244**); and **Le Centre d'Art,** 4 rue Ambroise-Fafard (© **418/435-3681**).

A Local Museum
Centre d'Exposition   Opened in 1992, this brick-and-glass museum has three floors of work primarily by regional artists, both past and present. Photography and Inuit sculptures are included, and temporary one-person and group shows are mounted throughout the year.

23 rue Ambroise-Fafard. © 418/435-3681. www.centredart-bsp.qc.ca. Admission C$3 (US$2.40).

Where to Stay & Dine
La Maison Otis   Slip into this rambling collection of connecting buildings as into a pair of favorite old jeans, the ones with the frayed cuffs and threadbare seat. Combinations of fireplaces, whirlpools, stereo systems, VCRs, four-poster beds, and suites that sleep four are all available. A long porch fronts the colorful main street, and a kidney-shaped indoor pool

and sauna are on the premises, as is a jovial piano bar. Meals are no sacrifice, served in a room with a stone fireplace and shaded candlesticks on pink tablecloths. Excellent clam chowder, salmon tartare, and pheasant have been notable in the past. Note that rates are Modified American Plan.

23 rue St-Jean-Baptiste, Baie-St-Paul, PQ G0A 1B0. (**©** 800/267-2254 or 418/435-2255. Fax 418/435-2464. www.maison otis.com. 30 units. C$106–C$163 (US$85–US$130) double. Rates include breakfast and dinner. AE, DC, MC, V. Pets accepted. **Amenities:** Restaurant (Regional); bar; indoor pool; golf nearby; exercise room; Jacuzzi; sauna; massage; babysitting. *In room:* A/C, TV, hair dryer.

ST-IRENEE

From Baie-St-Paul, take Route 362 toward La Malbaie. The route roller-coasters over bluffs above the river, and in 32km (about 20 miles) is this cliff-top hamlet of fewer than 800 year-round residents. Apart from the setting, the best reason for dawdling here is the lengthy music and dance festival held here every summer for over 25 years. **Domaine Forget,** 5 rang St-Antoine (**©** 888/336-7438 or 418/452-3535 for reservations; www.domaineforget.com), offers concerts from mid-June to late August on Wednesday, Saturday, and some Friday evenings, and Sunday from 11am to 2pm. Additional weekend concerts are spaced through autumn from September into December. This performing-arts festival was initiated in 1977, with the purchase of a large hillside property overlooking the river. Stables and barns were converted to use as studios and rehearsal halls, and the surrounding lawns were used to stage the concerts and recitals. Their success prompted the construction of a 600-seat hall, completed for the 1996 season. Although the program emphasizes classical music with solo instrumentalists and chamber groups, it is peppered with appearances by jazz combos and dance recitals. During the summer season, tickets are C$21 to C$34 (US$17–US$27) for adults (with 15% discount for seniors), C$16 (US$13) for students; children under 12 are admitted free.

POINTE-AU-PIC

From St-Irénée, the road starts to bend west after 10km (6¼ miles), as the mouth of the Malbaie River starts to form. Pointe-au-Pic is one of the trio of villages collectively known as La Malbaie (or "Murray Bay," as it was called by the wealthy Anglophones who made this their resort of choice from the Gilded Age through the 1950s). Although inhabitants of the region wax poetic about their hills and trees and wildlife "where the sea meets the sky," they now have something quite different to preen about: a casino.

A Casino & a Museum

Casino de Charlevoix   This is the second of Québec's gambling casinos (the first is in Montréal and the third opened in the Ottawa/Hull area in 1996). It is about as tasteful as such establishments get, at least this side of Monte Carlo. Cherrywood paneling and granite floors enclose the ranks of more than 800 slot machines, a keno lounge, and 22 tables, including blackjack, roulette, stud poker, and minibaccarat. Only soft drinks are allowed at the machines and tables, so players have to go to an adjacent bar to mourn their losses. Live entertainment is often scheduled there. And there is a dress code, forbidding, among other items, tank tops, bustiers, and "clothing associated with organizations known to be violent." Running shoes and "neat" blue jeans are allowed, although the management can get picky on weekends, when it gets very crowded. Parking is free.

183 av. Richelieu (Rte. 362). (**©** 800/665-2274 or 418/665-5300. www.casino-de-charlevoix.com. Free admission (persons 18 and over only allowed inside). Daily 10am–3am (but there are seasonal variations). Signs are frequent on Rte. 362 coming from the south, and on Rte. 138 from the north.

Musée de Charlevoix In existence since 1975, the museum moved to its present quarters in 1990. Folk art, sculptures, and paintings of variable quality by regional artists figure prominently in the permanent collection, supplemented by frequent temporary exhibitions with diverse themes.

1 chemin du Havre (at the intersection of Rte. 362/bd. Bellevue). (℗ **418/665-4411.** Admission C$5 (US$4) adults, C$4 (US$3.20) seniors and students, free for children under 12. June 24 to Labor Day daily 10am–6pm; day after Labor Day to late June Tues–Fri 10am–5pm, Sat–Sun 1–5pm.

Where to Stay & Dine

Fairmont Le Manoir Richelieu 🕸🕸 Since 1899, there has been a resort hotel here, first serving the swells who summered in this aristocratic haven. The opening of the casino just across the drive-up circle changed the makeup of visitors. To the mix of elderly people who have been coming here since they were youngsters, and families who have discovered they can be together and still have time for themselves, have been added those people who will go anywhere for the thrill of losing their money. When it became clear that facilities had become worn and service was falling short, the hotel was closed for 9 months for a massive renovation that even involved bulldozers *inside* the building. When it reopened, bright and shiny as a new loonie, there were marked improvements in every category. Rooms now brush up against deluxe standards, with all conveniences, including bathrobes, two or three phones, and easy modem connections. The Entrée Gold executive floor has 21 rooms with a lounge serving complimentary breakfasts and evening hors d'oeuvres. Buffet lovers are bound to be pleased with the dozens of platters and trays of food set out for all three meals of the day. The house band plays on past midnight for dancing.

181 rue Richelieu, La Malbaie, PQ G5A 1X7. (℗ **800/441-1414** or 418/665-3703. Fax 418/665-4566. www.fairmont.com. 405 units. Summer C$279–C$429 (US$223–US$343) double, from C$479 (US$383) suite; winter C$169–C$244 (US$135–US$195) double, from C$244 (US$195) suite. MAP and other packages available. AE, DC, MC, V. Valet parking C$24 (US$19). **Amenities:** 3 restaurants (International); 2 bars; indoor and outdoor pools; golf on premises; 3 tennis courts; health club and spa; watersports equipment rentals; children's center; concierge; car-rental desk; business center; shopping arcade; limited room service; massage; babysitting; laundry service; same-day dry cleaning; executive rooms. *In room:* A/C, TV w/pay movies, fax, dataport, minibar, coffeemaker, hair dryer, iron, safe.

CAP-A-L'AIGLE

Route 362 rejoins Route 138 in La Malbaie, the largest town in the area, with almost 4,000 inhabitants. It serves as a provisioning center, with supermarkets, hardware stores, and gas stations. There is a **tourist information office** at 495 bd. de Comporté (℗ **418/665-4454**), open mid-June through Labor Day daily 8:30am to 9pm, the rest of the year Monday to Friday 8:30am to 4:30pm, Saturday and Sunday 9am to 5pm. Continue through the town center and cross the bridge on the right, making a sharp right again on the other side. This is Route 138, with signs pointing to Cap-à-l'Aigle.

Where to Stay & Dine

La Pinsonnière 🕸🕸🕸 This was one of the first hostelries in Canada to be invited into the prestigious international Relais & Châteaux organization. Limited size, bedrooms that often border on princely luxury, and, most of all, an obsessive emphasis on excellent food and wine are characteristic. Rooms come in several categories, the priciest of which are equipped with Jacuzzis and gas fireplaces. Most of those facing the parking lot compensate with fireplaces and Jacuzzis. Romantic couples may want to request no. 315, which has a fireplace in both bedroom *and* bathroom, and a whirlpool for two. Packages include whale-watching cruises, dog-sled runs, and skiing at Mont Grand-Fonds.

You'll learn where the owners focus their laser-like attention when you're seated in the serene dining room beside the picture window, anticipating a dinner that will become the evening's entertainment. After an *amuse-bouche* and soup, the main event might be a succulent veal chop with a nest of shaved carrots, fiddleheads, and purple potatoes. Complete meals run from C$65 to C$125 (US$52–US$100); menus are changed every day. Wines are a particular point of pride here, evidenced by the impressive 12,000-bottle cellar.

124 rue St-Raphaël, La Malbaie (secteur Cap-à-l'Aigle), PQ G5A 1X9. ℂ 800/387-4431 or 418/665-4431. Fax 418/665-7156. www.lapinsonniere.com. 25 units. C$130–C$480 (US$104–US$384) double; from C$610 (US$488) suite. Meal plans and other packages available. Minimum 2-night stay on weekends, 3 nights on holiday weekends. AE, DISC, MC, V. **Amenities:** Restaurant (Creative French); bar; heated indoor pool; golf nearby; tennis court; access to nearby health club; spa; sauna; concierge; limited room service; massage; babysitting; dry cleaning. *In room:* A/C, TV, hair dryer.

ST-SIMEON

Rejoin Route 138 and continue 32km (20 miles) to St-Siméon. If you've decided to cross to Rivière-du-Loup on the other side of the St. Lawrence, returning to Québec City along the south shore, the ferry departs from here. With discretionary time left, I recommend continuing on to Baie-Ste-Catherine and Tadoussac, but if that isn't an option, it's only 150km (93 miles) back to the city the way you came on the north shore.

In St-Siméon, signs direct cars and trucks down to the ferry terminal. Boarding is on a first-come, first-served basis, and ferries leave on a carefully observed schedule, weather permitting, from April to early January. Departure times of the two to five daily sailings vary substantially from month to month, however, so get in touch with the company, **Clarke Transport Canada** (ℂ 418/638-2856), to obtain a copy of the schedule. For current fares, call ℂ 418/862-5094 or check the website at www.travrdlstsim. com. Always subject to change, one-way fares for passengers at press time are C$13 (US$10) ages 12 to 64 years, C$12 (US$9.50) seniors, C$8.60 (US$6.90) children 5 to 11. For cars, the one-way fare is C$34 (US$27). MasterCard and Visa are accepted. Arrive at least 30 minutes before departure, 1 hour ahead in summer. Voyages take 65 to 75 minutes.

From late June to September, passengers may enjoy a bonus on the ferry trip. Those are the months when the **whales** are most active. They are estimated at more than 500 in number when pelagic (migratory) species join the resident minke and beluga whales. They prefer the northern side of the estuary, roughly from La Malbaie to Baie-Ste-Catherine, at the mouth of the Saguenay River. Because that is the area the ferry steams through, sightings are an ever-present possibility, especially in summer.

BAIE STE-CATHERINE

To enhance your chances of seeing whales, continue northeast from St-Siméon on Route 138, arriving 32km (20 miles) later in Baie-Ste-Catherine, near the estuary of the Saguenay River. A half dozen companies offer cruises to see **whales** or the majestic Saguenay Fjord from here or from Tadoussac, on the opposite shore. The cruise companies use different sizes and types of watercraft, from powered inflatables called Zodiacs that carry 10 to 25 passengers up to stately catamarans and cruisers that carry up to 500. The Zodiacs don't provide food, drink, or narration, while the larger boats have snack bars and naturalists onboard to describe the action. The small boats, though, are more maneuverable, darting about at each sighting to get closer to the rolling and breaching behemoths.

Zodiac passengers are issued life jackets and waterproof overalls, but should expect to get wet anyway. It's cold out there, too, so layers and even gloves are a good idea. People on the large boats sit at tables inside or ride the observation bowsprit, high above the waves. Big boats are the wimp's choice for whale-watching. Mine, too.

Most cruises last 2 to 3 hours. One of the most active companies offering trips is **Croisières AML,** with offices in Québec City (© 800/563-4643 all year, 418/692-1159 in season; www.croisieresaml.com). From June to mid-October, they have up to three departures daily. Fares on the larger boats are C$52 (US$42) for adults, C$47 (US$38) for seniors and students, and C$22 (US$18) for children 3 to 12, while 2-hour Zodiac fares are C$50 (US$40) for adults, C$45 (US$36) for seniors and students, and C$35 (US$28) for children 6 to 16. Excursions of comparable duration and with similar fares are provided on the catamaran maintained by **Famille Dufour Croisières** (© 800/463-5250 or 418/692-0222; www.familledufour.com). Departures are from the Tadoussac and Baie-Ste-Catherine wharves.

From Baie Ste-Catherine, it's less than a half-hour drive back to St-Siméon and the ferry across to the opposite shore. Alternatively, continue north to the ferry, **Traverse Tadoussac** (© 418/235-4395), at the mouth of the dramatic Saguenay River. Palisades rise sharply from both shores, the reason this area is often referred to as a fjord. The ferry can board up to 400 passengers and 75 vehicles for the trip across to Tadoussac, which takes only 10 minutes. Departure times vary according to season and demand, of course, but in summer figure every hour from midnight to 6am, every 40 minutes from 6:20am to 8am, every 20 minutes from 8am to 8pm, and every 40 minutes from 8:20pm to midnight. The service is free.

TADOUSSAC

Known as "The Cradle of New France," the oldest permanent European settlement north of Florida was established in 1600 at the point where the Saguenay and St. Lawrence rivers meet. Missionaries followed and stayed until the middle of the 19th century. The hamlet might have vanished soon after, had a resort hotel not been built there in 1864. A steamship line brought vacationers downriver from Montréal and points farther west and deposited them here for stays that often lasted all summer. Apart from the hotel—the current building was erected in 1942—a few small support businesses, a post office, a marina, and more than a dozen small motels and B&Bs constitute the town. The sight of a beaver waddling up the hill along the road from the ferry terminal in daylight is met with only mild interest. Tadoussac's port is an important starting point for whale-watching and Saguenay cruises. It is the southernmost point of the tourist region designated as Manicouagan.

For 8 days in June, the town hosts a **Festival de la Chanson,** a festival of French song with more than a dozen concerts. Call © 866/861-4108 or 418/235-2002 or check www.tadoussac.com/newsite/tourismeeng/festival.htm.

Where to Stay & Dine
Hôtel Tadoussac   From the opposite shore, the bright-red mansard roof of this sprawling hotel dominates the point of land that slopes down to the river. (You might recognize it as the centerpiece in the film *Hotel New Hampshire.*) The lawn has a *pétanque* court, as well as groupings of chairs from which to watch the comings and goings of boats and Zodiacs. Inside, the public spaces and bedrooms have a shambling, country-cottage appearance—no pretense of luxe here. Maple furnishings and hand-woven rugs and bedspreads are all made in Québec. Meals in the large dining

room are better than might be expected, while falling well short of impressive. Reservations must be made for dinner, with the earlier seating drawing older guests and most of the families with children.

165 rue Bord de l'Eau, Tadoussac, PQ G0T 2A0. ⓒ **800/463-5250** or 418/235-4421. Fax 418/235-4607. www.familledufour.com. 149 units. C$165–C$220 (US$132–US$176) double. Rates include breakfast. Meal plan, golf, and whale-watching cruise packages available. AE, DC, DISC, MC, V. Closed mid-Oct to early May. **Amenities:** Restaurant (Regional); bar; heated outdoor pool; golf nearby; tennis court; babysitting; laundry service. *In room:* TV.

Appendix:
Montréal & Québec City in Depth

While decisions on where to eat, where to stay, what to see, and where to play occupy most hours of vacation time, seeking out and beginning to understand another culture and society comprise the most enriching experiences of travel.

1 A Look at French Canada: Now & Then

Québec is immense, the largest province in the second-largest country in the world (after Russia) and more than three times as large as France. It encompasses almost 1,544,000 sq. km (600,000 sq. miles)—two times the size of Texas—stretching from the northern borders of New York, Vermont, and New Hampshire almost to the Arctic Circle. To the east of it lie Maine and the province of New Brunswick; to the west, the province of Ontario and James and Hudson bays. (In fact, Québec would be even larger had Labrador not been awarded to Newfoundland in 1927.) Its substantial fund of natural resources includes 16% of the world's supply of fresh water. Most of the province's population lives in its lower regions—the St. Lawrence lowlands and parts of the Appalachians and the Laurentians. More than 80% of its almost seven million residents live within an area 322km (200 miles) long and 97km (60 miles) wide, one of the highest concentrations of people in sparsely populated Canada.

Montréal, home to a third of the province's population, occupies the island of Montréal, which is part of the Hochelaga Archipelago. The island is situated in the St. Lawrence River near where it joins the Ottawa River. At the city's center is a 229m (751-ft.) hill (which natives like to think of as a mountain) called Mont-Royal, from which the city takes its name. More mountains rise nearby: the Laurentides (the Laurentians), the oldest mountain range in the world and the playground of the Quebecois. The northern foothills of the Appalachian mountains separate Québec from the United States and add to the beauty of the Cantons-de-l'Est, the bucolic country on the opposite side of the St. Lawrence once known as the Eastern Townships, where many Montréalers have country homes. The capital city of Québec, 267km (166 miles) northeast of Montréal, commands a stunning location on the rim of a promontory overlooking the St. Lawrence River—the St-Laurent—which is at its narrowest point here, 591m (1,939 ft.) across.

THE EUROPEANS ARRIVE The Vikings landed in Canada more than 1,000 years ago, probably followed by Irish and Basque fishermen. English explorer John Cabot stepped ashore briefly on the east coast in 1497, but it was the French who managed the first meaningful European toehold in the wilderness. When **Jacques Cartier** sailed up the **St. Lawrence** in 1535, he recognized at once the tremendous strategic potential of **Cape Diamond**, "the Gibraltar of the North." But he was exploring, not empire building, and after stopping briefly on land he continued on his trip upriver.

Jacques Cartier sailed up the broad St. Lawrence River, past the spot that would become Québec City under Champlain, to what was then a large island with a fortified **Iroquois village** composed of 50 longhouses, called **Hochelaga**. Cartier, as usual, did not linger but pushed onward in his search for the sea route to China. His progress was halted by the fierce rapids just west of what is now the Island of Montréal. In a demonstration of mingled optimism and frustration, he dubbed the rapids **La Chine** on the assumption that China was just beyond them. He then decided to check out the Indian settlement after all, landing at a spot in what is now Old Montréal, and paid his respects to the native people before moving on. That was the extent of Cartier's contribution to the future city.

Samuel de Champlain arrived 73 years later, in 1608, determined to settle at Québec, a year after the Virginia Company founded its fledgling colony of Jamestown, hundreds of miles to the south. The British and French struggle for dominance in the new continent focused on their explorations, and there the French outdid the English. Their far-ranging fur trappers, navigators, soldiers, and missionaries opened up not only Canada but also most of what eventually became the United States, moving all the way south to the future New Orleans and claiming most of the territory to the west. This vast region

later comprised the **Louisiana Purchase.** At least 35 of the subsequent 50 states were discovered, mapped, or settled by Frenchmen, who left behind some 4,000 place names to prove it, among them Detroit, St. Louis, New Orleans, Duluth, and Des Moines.

Champlain's first settlement, or *habitation,* grew to become Québec City's **Basse-Ville,** or Lower Town, down on the flat riverbank beneath the cliffs of Cap Diamant—Cape Diamond. But almost from the beginning there were attacks, first by the Iroquois, then by the English, and later by the Americans. To better defend themselves, the Quebecois constructed a fortress on the cape, and gradually the center of urban life moved to the top of the cliffs.

THE FOUNDING OF MONTREAL
Paul de Chomedey, sieur de Maisonneuve, arrived in 1642 to establish a colony and to plant a crucifix atop the hill he called Mont-Royal. He and his band of settlers came ashore and founded **Ville-Marie,** dedicated to the Virgin Mary, at the spot now marked by Place Royale. They built a fort, a chapel, stores, and houses, and the energetic **Jeanne Mance** made her indelible mark by founding the hospital named Hotel-Dieu-de-Montréal, which still exists today.

Dateline

- **1534** Jacques Cartier sails up the St. Lawrence, claiming the territory for France and marking the first European discovery of Canada.
- **1608** Samuel de Champlain founds a settlement at Kebec, at the foot of Cape Diamond. It will become the city of Québec.
- **1642** Paul de Chomedey, sieur de Maisonneuve, estab-

lishes a colony called Ville-Marie that will become Montréal.
- **1668** Québec Seminary is founded in Québec City, later to become Laval University in 1852.
- **1759** British General Wolfe defeats French General Montcalm on the Plains of Abraham in Québec City.
- **1760** Montréal falls to the British.

- **1763** The king of France cedes all of Canada to the king of England in the Treaty of Paris.
- **1775** Montréal is occupied by American Revolutionary forces who withdraw after a few months, when an attempted siege of Québec City by Benedict Arnold fails.
- **1821** English-speaking McGill University is founded in Montréal.

continues

Life was not easy. Unlike the friendly Algonquins who lived in nearby regions, the Iroquois in Montréal had no intention of living in peace with the new settlers. Fierce battles raged for years, and the settlers were lucky that their numbers included such undauntable souls as la Salle, du Luth, de la Mothe Cadillac, and the brothers Lemoyne.

At **Place d'Armes** stands a statue of de Maisonneuve, marking the spot where the settlers defeated the Iroquois in bloody hand-to-hand fighting, with de Maisonneuve himself locked in mortal combat with the Iroquois chief. De Maisonneuve won.

From that time the settlement prospered, though in 1760 it fell to the British, the year after Wolfe defeated Montcalm on the Plains of Abraham in Québec. Until the 1800s the city was contained in the area known today as **Vieux-Montréal.** Its ancient walls no longer stand, but its long and colorful past is preserved in the streets, houses, and churches of the Old City.

ENGLAND CONQUERS NEW FRANCE In the 1750s the struggle between Britain and France had escalated, after a series of conflicts beginning in 1689 that had embroiled both Europe and the New World. The latest episode was known as the **French and Indian War** in North America, an extension of Europe's Seven Years' War. Strategic Québec became a valued prize. The French sent **Louis Joseph, marquis de Montcalm,** to command their forces in the town. The British sent an expedition of 4,500 men in a fleet under the command of a 32-year-old general, **James Wolfe.** The ensuing battle for Québec, fought on the **Plains of Abraham** southwest of the city on September 13, 1759, is one of the most famous battles in North American history, because it resulted in a continent that was under British influence for over a century.

Both generals perished as a result of the 20-minute battle on the Plains of Abraham. Wolfe lived just long enough to hear that he had won. Montcalm died a few hours later. Today a memorial to both men overlooks Terrasse Dufferin in Québec City, the only statue in the world commemorating both victor and vanquished of the same battle. The inscription, in neither French nor English but Latin, says, simply, COURAGE WAS FATAL TO THEM.

THE UNITED STATES INVADES The capture of Québec determined the course of the war, and the **Treaty of Paris** in 1763 ceded all of French Canada to England. In a sense, this victory led to Britain's worst defeat. If the French had

---

- **1867** The British North America Act creates the federation of the provinces of Québec, Ontario, Nova Scotia, and New Brunswick.

- **1883** "Je me souviens" becomes the official motto of Québec—an ominous "I remember."

- **1900–10** Three hundred twenty-five thousand French Canadians emigrate to the United States.

- **1922** Armand Bombardier invents the prototype for the Ski-Doo, the first snowmobile, which will make him famous and wealthy in the late 1950s.

- **1925** The Seagram Company is founded in Montréal.

- **1940** Women are granted the right to vote in provincial elections in Québec, having obtained that right in federal elections in 1917.

- **1948** The Québec flag, bearing four fleurs-de-lis, is adopted.

- **1962** Montréal's underground city is born, with the construction of Place Ville-Marie.

- **1967** Montréal hosts the successful Expo '67.

- **1968** The Parti Quebecois is founded by Reneé Lévesque, and the separatist movement begins in earnest. Quebecois Pierre Elliott Trudeau is

held Canada, the British government might have been more judicious in its treatment of the American colonists. As it was, the British decided to make the colonists pay the costs of the French and Indian War, on the principle that it was their homes being defended. They slapped so many taxes on all imports that the infuriated colonists openly rebelled against the Crown.

But if the British misjudged the temper of the colonists, the Americans were equally wrong about the mood of the Canadians. **George Washington** felt sure that French Canadians would want to join the revolution, or at least be supportive. He was mistaken on both counts. The Quebecois detested their British conquerors, but they were also staunch Royalists and devout Catholics, and saw their contentious neighbors as godless Republicans. Only a handful supported the Americans, as often as not to sell them supplies, and three of Washington's most competent commanders came to grief in attacks against Québec. Thirty-eight years later, in the **War of 1812,** another U.S. army marched up the banks of the Richelieu River where it flows from Lake Champlain to the St. Lawrence. And once again the French Canadians stuck by the British and drove back the invaders. The war ended essentially in a draw, but it had at least one encouraging result: Britain and the young United States agreed to demilitarize the Great Lakes and to extend their mutual border along the 49th parallel to the Rockies.

MONTREAL AND QUEBEC CITY TODAY The ancient walls that protected Québec City over the centuries are still in place today, the town within their embrace little changed, preserving for posterity the heart of New France. Montréal, though, has gone through a metamorphosis. It was "wet" when the United States was "dry" due to Prohibition. Bootleggers, hard drinkers, and prostitutes flocked to this large city situated so conveniently close to the American border and mixed with rowdy people from the port, much to the distress of Montréal's mainly upstanding citizenry. For half a century the city's image was decidedly racy, but in the 1950s a cleanup began, with a boom in high-rise construction and eventual restoration of much of the derelict Old Town. In **1967** Montréal welcomed the world to Expo. The great gleaming skyscrapers and towering hotels, the superb Métro system, and the highly practical underground city, so much a part of this modern city, date mostly from the past 40 years.

elected prime minister of Canada, and he holds that office for most of the following 18 years.
- **1976** The Parti Quebecois comes to power in Québec and remains in office until 1985, when the Liberal Party succeeds it. Montréal hosts the Olympics.
- **1984** Quebecois Brian Mulroney becomes prime minister of Canada.

- **1989** The North American Free-Trade Agreement goes into effect, gradually removing most tariffs on goods of national origin moving between the United States and Canada.
- **1990** The Meech Lake Accord, recognizing Québec as a "distinct society" within Canada, is voted down, and separatist agitation increases.
- **1992** Montréal celebrates its 350th birthday. The Charlotte-

town Accord, a reworking of Meech Lake, is defeated at the polls.
- **1993** Mulroney resigns with public approval ratings in the single digits. He is succeeded by Kim Campbell, the first female prime minister. She and the Tories are soundly defeated by Jean Chrétien and the Liberals in October.

continues

All this activity helped to fuel a phenomenon later labeled the **"Quiet Revolution."** It was to transform the largely rural, agricultural province into an urbanized, industrial entity with a pronounced secular outlook. French Canadians, long denied access to the upper echelons of desirable corporate careers, started to insist upon equal opportunity with the powerful Anglophone minority. Inevitably, a radical fringe movement of separatists emerged, signaling its intentions by bombing Anglophone businesses. The **FLQ (Québec Liberation Front),** as it was known, was behind most of the terrorist attacks, reaching its nadir with the kidnapping and murder of a cabinet minister, **Pierre Laporte.**

Most Quebecois separatists were not violent, and most Quebecois were not even separatists. **Pierre Trudeau,** a bilingual Quebecois, became prime minister in 1968. As flamboyant, eccentric, and brilliant as any Canadian who ever held the post, he necessarily devoted much of his time trying to placate voters on both sides of the issue. In 1969, the **Official Languages Act** mandated that all federal agencies provide services in both French and English. Yet by 1980, a provincial referendum on separation from the confederation was defeated by only 60% of the vote. Subsequent attempts to assuage the chafed sensibilities of French Quebecois failed again and again, as often at the hands of other provincial premiers as by the Quebecois, hounding at least three prime ministers from office.

In 1993, the governing Tories were defeated by the opposition Liberals. The new Prime Minister, **Jean Chrétien,** a federalist, was not aided in his task of national reconciliation by representation in the House of Commons of the militantly separatist **Bloc Quebecois,** which became the largest opposition party in the same election. And in Québec the following year, the **Parti Quebecois** won provincial elections to end 9 years of Liberal control. The new premier, **Jacques Parizeau,** vowed to hold an early referendum on sovereignty, which was held in late October 1995 and was narrowly defeated by a bare 1% of the total vote. Parizeau resigned the next day, after making intemperate remarks about the negative role of ethnic voters in the results. Recent polls suggest that pro-confederation sentiments have gained ground over separatism, but fluctuations have been the rule. Contention over the intractable issue isn't going to end anytime soon, but conversations with ordinary Quebecois suggest they are so weary of the seemingly endless sovereignty argument that they no longer care what happens as long as it is decided one way or the other.

- **1994** Québec's separatist Parti Quebecois wins provincial elections, ending 9 years of Liberal rule.
- **1995** Despite seemingly unstoppable momentum toward independence, a referendum on separation from the rest of Canada is narrowly defeated.
- **1996** Sharp cuts in federal contributions to Canada's cherished universal healthcare system provoke job actions by doctors. Accounts of unsanitary hospitals, outdated equipment, and ever-lengthening delays for treatment cause mounting unease in the face of governmental demands for even greater efficiencies and cost-cutting procedures.
- **1997** Prime Minister Jean Chrétien calls early elections in hopes of strengthening his party's hold on Parliament. Results are mixed. The separatist Bloc Quebecois loses its standing as the largest opposition party to the emerging western Reform Party. Chrétien's Liberals shrink from 174 seats to 155.
- **1998** The governing provincial Parti Quebecois wins reelection in November, beating off the resurgent Liberals, headed by Jean Charest. Still, the margin of victory is narrower than expected, and Premier Bouchard shelves

Chrétien resigned as Prime Minister and head of the Liberal Party in 2003 and was succeeded by Paul Martin. Martin inherited a corruption scandal involving payments to advertising companies in Québec. Over the following year-and-a-half, revelations grew ever more damaging and an investigative commission uncovered damning details. A vote of confidence was held in May 2005. The governing Liberals, who had held an overwhelming majority in the House of Commons, were arrayed against the Conservative Party and the Bloc Quebecois. A harrowing tie of 152 to 153 was broken by the Speaker of the House in favor of the Liberals.

2 The Politics of Language

The defining dialectic of Canadian life is language, the thorny issue that has long threatened to tear the country apart. Many Quebecois believe that a separate independent state is the only way to maintain their culture in the face of the Anglophone ocean that surrounds them. The role of Québec within the Canadian federation has long been the most debated and volatile issue in Canadian politics.

One attempt to smooth ruffled Francophone fur was made in 1969, when federal legislation stipulated that all services were henceforth to be offered in both English and French, in effect declaring the nation bilingual. That didn't long assuage militant Quebecois. Having made the two languages equal in the rest of the country, they undertook to guarantee the primacy of French in their own province. To prevent dilution by newcomers, the children of immigrants are required to enroll in French-language schools, even if English or a third language is spoken in the home. Bill 101 was passed in 1977, which all but banned the use of English on public signage. Stop signs now read ARRET, a word that actually refers to a stop on a bus or train route. (Even in France, the red signs read STOP, but then, Quebecois like to believe they speak a purer—by which they mean older—form of the language than is spoken in the mother country today.) The bill funded the establishment of enforcement units, virtual language police who let no nit go unpicked.

As a result of this backlash, which has resulted in the flight of an estimated 400,000 Anglophones to other parts of Canada, Canadian Prime Minister Brian Mulroney met with the 10 provincial premiers in April 1987 at a retreat at Québec's Meech Lake to cobble together plans for an early referendum on independence.

- **2000** Despite signs of Québec's emergence from a decade-long recession, by some measures surpassing the rest of Canada, support for Bouchard and separation falls below 40% of the electorate.
- **2001** Premier Bouchard resigns unexpectedly, throwing his separatist Parti Quebecois into disarray. Polls show increasing disaffection with the idea of Québec sovereignty. He is succeeded by Bernard Landry.
- **2002** The 28 towns and cities on Montréal Island are merged into one megacity with a population of 1.8 million inhabitants. Prime Minister Jean Chrétien, until then enjoying excellent approval ratings, runs afoul with an ethics scandal in midyear over favors exchanged for campaign donations. In August, he announces that he won't seek a fourth term.
- **2003** Landry and the Parti Québeois lose in a landslide to the Liberals and their leader, Jean Charest, an avowed federalist. Paul Martin takes over as Prime Minister in December.
- **2004** Martin calls for a new June election in the face of

continues

a collection of constitutional reforms. The Meech Lake Accord, as it came to be known, addressed a variety of issues, but most important to the Quebecois it recognized Québec as a "distinct society" within the federation. In the end, however, Manitoba and Newfoundland failed to ratify the accord by the June 23, 1990, deadline. As a result, support for the secessionist cause burgeoned in Québec, fueled by an election that firmly placed the separatist Parti Quebecois in control of the provincial government. A referendum held in 1995 was narrowly won by those Québec residents who favored staying within the union, but the vote settled nothing. The issue continues to divide families and dominate political discourse.

In the midst of the unshakable fray, Québec remains committed to ensuring, one way or another, the survival of the province's culture and language, its bedrock loyalty to its Gallic roots. France may have relinquished control of Québec in 1763, but its influence, after its century and a half of rule, remains powerful to this day. The Quebecois continue to look across the Atlantic for inspiration in fashion, food, and the arts. Culturally and linguistically, it is that tenacious French connection that gives the province its special character, which is a source of great regional pride and considerable national controversy.

There are reasons for the festering intransigence of the Quebecois, about 240 years' worth. After what they unfailingly call "The Conquest," their English rulers made a few concessions to French-Canadian pride, including allowing them a Gallic version of jurisprudence. But a kind of linguistic exclusionism prevailed, with wealthy Scottish and English bankers and merchants denying French-Canadians access to upper levels of business and government. The present strife, and the frequent foolishness and small-mindedness that attends it on both sides, is as much payback as it is pride in the French heritage.

None of this should deter potential visitors. The Quebecois are exceedingly gracious hosts. While Montréal may be the largest French-speaking city outside Paris, most Montréalers grow up speaking both French and English, switching effortlessly from one language to the other as the situation dictates. Telephone operators go from French to English the instant they hear an English word out of the other party, as do most store clerks, waiters, and hotel staff. This is less the case in country villages and in Québec City, but there is virtually no problem that can't be solved with a few French words, some expressive gestures, and a little goodwill.

---

another financial scandal. He wins, but there are substantial Liberal losses in Parliament. In Montréal, 15 of the boroughs vote to de-merge from the megacity imposed in 2002.

■ **2005** Continued revelations in the corruption scandal bring about a vote of confidence in the House of Commons in May. The Liberals win by only one vote. Follow-up polls suggest that

Quebecers are once again considering separation. Gay marriage is made legal in all of Canada's provinces and territories.

Index

ACCOMMODATIONS:
MONTRÉAL

ACCOMMODATIONS:
QUÉBEC CITY

ACCOMMODATIONS:
OTHER AREAS

RESTAURANTS:
MONTRÉAL

FROMMER'S® NATIONAL PARK GUIDES

Algonquin Provincial Park
Banff & Jasper
Family Vacations in the National
  Parks

Grand Canyon
National Parks of the American West
Rocky Mountain

Yellowstone & Grand Teton
Yosemite & Sequoia/Kings Canyon
Zion & Bryce Canyon

FROMMER'S® MEMORABLE WALKS

Chicago
London

New York
Paris

San Francisco

FROMMER'S® WITH KIDS GUIDES

Chicago
Hawaii
Las Vegas
New York City

Ottawa
San Francisco
Toronto

Vancouver
Walt Disney World® & Orlando
Washington, D.C.

SUZY GERSHMAN'S BORN TO SHOP GUIDES

Born to Shop: France
Born to Shop: Hong Kong, Shanghai
  & Beijing

Born to Shop: Italy
Born to Shop: London

Born to Shop: New York
Born to Shop: Paris

FROMMER'S® IRREVERENT GUIDES

Amsterdam
Boston
Chicago
Las Vegas
London

Los Angeles
Manhattan
New Orleans
Paris
Rome

San Francisco
Seattle & Portland
Vancouver
Walt Disney World®
Washington, D.C.

FROMMER'S® BEST-LOVED DRIVING TOURS

Austria
Britain
California
France

Germany
Ireland
Italy
New England

Northern Italy
Scotland
Spain
Tuscany & Umbria

THE UNOFFICIAL GUIDES®

Beyond Disney
California with Kids
Central Italy
Chicago
Cruises
Disneyland®
England
Florida
Florida with Kids
Inside Disney

Hawaii
Las Vegas
London
Maui
Mexico's Best Beach Resorts
Mini Las Vegas
Mini Mickey
New Orleans
New York City
Paris

San Francisco
Skiing & Snowboarding in the West
South Florida including Miami &
  the Keys
Walt Disney World®
Walt Disney World® for
  Grown-ups
Walt Disney World® with Kids
Washington, D.C.

SPECIAL-INTEREST TITLES

Athens Past & Present
Cities Ranked & Rated
Frommer's Best Day Trips from London
Frommer's Best RV & Tent Campgrounds
  in the U.S.A.
Frommer's Caribbean Hideaways
Frommer's China: The 50 Most Memorable Trips
Frommer's Exploring America by RV
Frommer's Gay & Lesbian Europe

Frommer's NYC Free & Dirt Cheap
Frommer's Road Atlas Europe
Frommer's Road Atlas France
Frommer's Road Atlas Ireland
Frommer's Wonderful Weekends from
  New York City
Retirement Places Rated
Rome Past & Present

THE NEW TRAVELOCITY GUARANTEE

EVERYTHING YOU BOOK WILL BE RIGHT, OR WE'LL WORK WITH OUR TRAVEL PARTNERS TO MAKE IT RIGHT, RIGHT AWAY.

To drive home the point, we're going to use the word "right" in every single sentence.

Let's get right to it. Right to the meat! Only Travelocity guarantees everything about your booking will be right, or we'll work with our travel partners to make it right, right away. Right on!

Here's a picture taken smack dab right in the middle of Antigua, where the guarantee also covers you.

The guarantee covers all but one of the items pictured to the right.

For example, what if the ocean view you booked actually looks out at a downright ugly parking lot? You'd be right to call – we're there for you. And no one in their right mind would be pleased to learn the rental car place has closed and left them stranded. Call Travelocity and we'll help get you back on the right track.

Now, you may be thinking, "Yeah, right, I'm so sure." That's OK; you have the right to remain skeptical. That is until we mention help is always right around the corner. Call us right off the bat, knowing that our customer service reps are there for you 24/7. Righting wrongs. Left and right.

Now if you're guessing there are some things we can't control, like the weather, well you're right. But we can help you with most things – to get all the details in righting,* visit **travelocity.com/guarantee.**

*Sorry, spelling things right is one of the few things not covered under the guarantee.

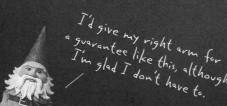

I'd give my right arm for a guarantee like this, although I'm glad I don't have to.

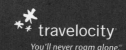

travelocity
You'll never roam alone.